Guide to the Software Engineering Body of Knowledge

Version 3.0

SWEBOK®

A Project of the IEEE Computer Society

Guide to the Software Engineering Body of Knowledge

Version 3.0

Editors

Pierre Bourque, École de technologie supérieure (ÉTS)
Richard E. (Dick) Fairley, Software and Systems Engineering Associates (S2EA)

 **IEEE**

IEEE **computer society**

Digital copies of *SWEBOK Guide* V3.0 may be downloaded free of charge for personal and academic use via www.swebok.org.

IEEE Computer Society Staff for This Publication
Angela Burgess, Executive Director
Anne Marie Kelly, Associate Executive Director, Director of Governance
Evan M. Butterfield, Director of Products and Services
John Keppler, Senior Manager, Professional Education
Kate Guillemette, Product Development Editor
Dorian McClenahan, Education Program Product Developer
Michelle Phon, Professional Education & Certification Program Coordinator
Jennie Zhu-Mai, Editorial Designer

IEEE Computer Society Products and Services. The world-renowned IEEE Computer Society publishes, promotes, and distributes a wide variety of authoritative computer science and engineering journals, magazines, conference proceedings, and professional education products. Visit the Computer Society at www.computer.org for more information.

TABLE OF CONTENTS

FOREWORD

Every profession is based on a body of knowledge, although that knowledge is not always defined in a concise manner. In cases where no formality exists, the body of knowledge is "generally recognized" by practitioners and may be codified in a variety of ways for a variety of different uses. But in many cases, a guide to a body of knowledge is formally documented, usually in a form that permits it to be used for such purposes as development and accreditation of academic and training programs, certification of specialists, or professional licensing. Generally, a professional society or similar body maintains stewardship of the formal definition of a body of knowledge.

During the past forty-five years, software engineering has evolved from a conference catchphrase into an engineering profession, characterized by 1) a professional society, 2) standards that specify generally accepted professional practices, 3) a code of ethics, 4) conference proceedings, 5) textbooks, 6) curriculum guidelines and curricula, 7) accreditation criteria and accredited degree programs, 8) certification and licensing, and 9) this Guide to the Body of Knowledge.

In this *Guide to the Software Engineering Body of Knowledge*, the IEEE Computer Society presents a revised and updated version of the body of knowledge formerly documented as SWEBOK 2004; this revised and updated version is denoted SWEBOK V3. This work is in partial fulfillment of the Society's responsibility to promote the advancement of both theory and practice for the profession of software engineering.

It should be noted that this *Guide* does not present the entire the body of knowledge for software engineering but rather serves as a guide to the body of knowledge that has been developed over more than four decades. The software engineering body of knowledge is constantly evolving. Nevertheless, this *Guide* constitutes a valuable characterization of the software engineering profession.

In 1958, John Tukey, the world-renowned statistician, coined the term *software*. The term software engineering was used in the title of a NATO conference held in Germany in 1968. The IEEE Computer Society first published its *Transactions on Software Engineering* in 1972, and a committee for developing software engineering standards was established within the IEEE Computer Society in 1976.

In 1990, planning was begun for an international standard to provide an overall view of software engineering. The standard was completed in 1995 with designation ISO/IEC 12207 and given the title of *Standard for Software Life Cycle Processes*. The IEEE version of 12207 was published in 1996 and provided a major foundation for the body of knowledge captured in SWEBOK 2004. The current version of 12207 is designated as ISO/IEC 12207:2008 and IEEE 12207-2008; it provides the basis for this SWEBOK V3.

This *Guide to the Software Engineering Body of Knowledge* is presented to you, the reader, as a mechanism for acquiring the knowledge you need in your lifelong career development as a software engineering professional.

Dick Fairley, Chair
Software and Systems Engineering Committee
IEEE Computer Society

Don Shafer, Vice President
Professional Activities Board
IEEE Computer Society

FOREWORD TO THE 2004 EDITION

In this *Guide*, the IEEE Computer Society establishes for the first time a baseline for the body of knowledge for the field of software engineering, and the work partially fulfills the Society's responsibility to promote the advancement of both theory and practice in this field. In so doing, the Society has been guided by the experience of disciplines with longer histories but was not bound either by their problems or their solutions.

It should be noted that the *Guide* does not purport to define the body of knowledge but rather to serve as a compendium and guide to the body of knowledge that has been developing and evolving over the past four decades. Furthermore, this body of knowledge is not static. The *Guide* must, necessarily, develop and evolve as software engineering matures. It nevertheless constitutes a valuable element of the software engineering infrastructure.

In 1958, John Tukey, the world-renowned statistician, coined the term *software*. The term *software engineering* was used in the title of a NATO conference held in Germany in 1968. The IEEE Computer Society first published its *Transactions on Software Engineering* in 1972. The committee established within the IEEE Computer Society for developing software engineering standards was founded in 1976.

The first holistic view of software engineering to emerge from the IEEE Computer Society resulted from an effort led by Fletcher Buckley to develop IEEE standard 730 for software quality assurance, which was completed in 1979. The purpose of IEEE Std. 730 was to provide uniform, minimum acceptable requirements for preparation and content of software quality assurance plans. This standard was influential in completing the developing standards in the following topics: configuration management, software testing, software requirements, software design, and software verification and validation.

During the period 1981–1985, the IEEE Computer Society held a series of workshops concerning the application of software engineering standards. These workshops involved practitioners sharing their experiences with existing standards. The workshops also held sessions on planning for future standards, including one involving measures and metrics for software engineering products and processes. The planning also resulted in IEEE Std. 1002, *Taxonomy of Software Engineering Standards* (1986), which provided a new, holistic view of software engineering. The standard describes the form and content of a software engineering standards taxonomy. It explains the various types of software engineering standards, their functional and external relationships, and the role of various functions participating in the software life cycle.

In 1990, planning for an international standard with an overall view was begun. The planning focused on reconciling the software process views from IEEE Std. 1074 and the revised US DoD standard 2167A. The revision was eventually published as DoD Std. 498. The international standard was completed in 1995 with designation, ISO/IEC 12207, and given the title of *Standard for Software Life Cycle Processes*. Std. ISO/IEC 12207 provided a major point of departure for the body of knowledge captured in this book.

It was the IEEE Computer Society Board of Governors' approval of the motion put forward in May 1993 by Fletcher Buckley which resulted in the writing of this book. The Association for Computing Machinery (ACM) Council approved a related motion in August 1993. The two motions led to a joint committee under the leadership of Mario Barbacci and Stuart Zweben who served as cochairs. The mission statement of the joint committee was "To establish the appropriate sets(s) of criteria and norms for professional practice of software engineering upon which industrial decisions, professional certification, and educational curricula can be based." The steering committee organized task forces in the following areas:

1. Define Required Body of Knowledge and Recommended Practices.

2. Define Ethics and Professional Standards.
3. Define Educational Curricula for undergraduate, graduate, and continuing education.

This book supplies the first component: required body of knowledge and recommend practices.

The code of ethics and professional practice for software engineering was completed in 1998 and approved by both the ACM Council and the IEEE Computer Society Board of Governors. It has been adopted by numerous corporations and other organizations and is included in several recent textbooks.

The educational curriculum for undergraduates is being completed by a joint effort of the IEEE Computer Society and the ACM and is expected to be completed in 2004.

Every profession is based on a body of knowledge and recommended practices, although they are not always defined in a precise manner. In many cases, these are formally documented, usually in a form that permits them to be used for such purposes as accreditation of academic programs, development of education and training programs, certification of specialists, or professional licensing. Generally, a professional society or related body maintains custody of such a formal definition. In cases where no such formality exists, the body of knowledge and recommended practices are "generally recognized" by practitioners and may be codified in a variety of ways for different uses.

It is hoped that readers will find this book useful in guiding them toward the knowledge and resources they need in their lifelong career development as software engineering professionals.

The book is dedicated to Fletcher Buckley in recognition of his commitment to promoting software engineering as a professional discipline and his excellence as a software engineering practitioner in radar applications.

Leonard L. Tripp, IEEE Fellow 2003
Chair, Professional Practices Committee, IEEE Computer Society (2001–2003)

Chair, Joint IEEE Computer Society and ACM Steering Committee for the Establishment of Software Engineering as a Profession (1998–1999)

Chair, Software Engineering Standards Committee, IEEE Computer Society (1992–1998)

EDITORS

Pierre Bourque, Department of Software and IT Engineering, École de technologie supérieure (ÉTS), Canada, pierre.bourque@etsmtl.ca

Richard E. (Dick) Fairley, Software and Systems Engineering Associates (S2EA), USA, dickfairley@gmail.com

COEDITORS

Alain Abran, Department of Software and IT Engineering, École de technologie supérieure (ÉTS), Canada, alain.abran@etsmtl.ca

Juan Garbajosa, Universidad Politecnica de Madrid (Technical University of Madrid, UPM), Spain, juan.garbajosa@upm.es

Gargi Keeni, Tata Consultancy Services, India, gargi@ieee.org

Beijun Shen, School of Software, Shanghai Jiao Tong University, China, bjshen@sjtu.edu.cn

CONTRIBUTING EDITORS

The following persons contributed to editing the *SWEBOK Guide* V3:
Don Shafer
Linda Shafer
Mary Jane Willshire
Kate Guillemette

CHANGE CONTROL BOARD

The following persons served on the *SWEBOK Guide* V3 Change Control Board:
Pierre Bourque
Richard E. (Dick) Fairley, Chair
Dennis Frailey
Michael Gayle
Thomas Hilburn
Paul Joannou
James W. Moore
Don Shafer
Steve Tockey

KNOWLEDGE AREA EDITORS

Software Requirements
Gerald Kotonya, School of Computing and Communications, Lancaster University, UK, gerald@comp.lancs.ac.uk
Peter Sawyer, School of Computing and Communications, Lancaster University, UK, sawyer@comp.lancs.ac.uk

Software Design
Yanchun Sun, School of Electronics Engineering and Computer Science, Peking University, China, sunyc@pku.edu.cn

Software Construction
Xin Peng, Software School, Fudan University, China, pengxin@fudan.edu.cn

Software Testing
Antonia Bertolino, ISTI-CNR, Italy, antonia.bertolino@isti.cnr.it
Eda Marchetti, ISTI-CNR, Italy, eda.marchetti@isti.cnr.it

Software Maintenance
Alain April, École de technologie supérieure (ÉTS), Canada, alain.april@etsmtl.ca
Mira Kajko-Mattsson, School of Information and Communication Technology, KTH Royal Institute of Technology, mekm2@kth.se

Software Configuration Management
Roger Champagne, École de technologie supérieure (ÉTS), Canada, roger.champagne@etsmtl.ca
Alain April, École de technologie supérieure (ÉTS), Canada, alain.april@etsmtl.ca

Software Engineering Management
James McDonald, Department of Computer Science and Software Engineering, Monmouth University, USA, jamesmc@monmouth.edu

Software Engineering Process
Annette Reilly, Lockheed Martin Information Systems & Global Solutions, USA, annette.reilly@computer.org
Richard E. Fairley, Software and Systems Engineering Associates (S2EA), USA, dickfairley@gmail.com

Software Engineering Models and Methods
Michael F. Siok, Lockheed Martin Aeronautics Company, USA, mike.f.siok@lmco.com

Software Quality
J. David Blaine, USA, jdavidblaine@gmail.com
Durba Biswas, Tata Consultancy Services, India, durba.biswas@tcs.com

Software Engineering Professional Practice

Aura Sheffield, USA, arsheff@acm.org

Hengming Zou, Shanghai Jiao Tong University, China, zou@sjtu.edu.cn

Software Engineering Economics

Christof Ebert, Vector Consulting Services, Germany, christof.ebert@vector.com

Computing Foundations

Hengming Zou, Shanghai Jiao Tong University, China, zou@sjtu.edu.cn

Mathematical Foundations

Nabendu Chaki, University of Calcutta, India, nabendu@ieee.org

Engineering Foundations

Amitava Bandyopadhayay, Indian Statistical Institute, India, bamitava@isical.ac.in

Mary Jane Willshire, Software and Systems Engineering Associates (S2EA), USA, mj.fairley@gmail.com

Appendix B: IEEE and ISO/IEC Standards Supporting SWEBOK

James W. Moore, USA, James.W.Moore@ieee.org

KNOWLEDGE AREA EDITORS OF PREVIOUS SWEBOK VERSIONS

The following persons served as Associate Editors for either the Trial version published in 2001 or for the 2004 version.

Software Requirements
Peter Sawyer, Computing Department, Lancaster University, UK
Gerald Kotonya, Computing Department, Lancaster University, UK

Software Design
Guy Tremblay, Département d'informatique, UQAM, Canada

Software Construction
Steve McConnell, Construx Software, USA
Terry Bollinger, the MITRE Corporation, USA
Philippe Gabrini, Département d'informatique, UQAM, Canada
Louis Martin, Département d'informatique, UQAM, Canada

Software Testing
Antonia Bertolino, ISTI-CNR, Italy
Eda Marchetti, ISTI-CNR, Italy

Software Maintenance
Thomas M. Pigoski, Techsoft Inc., USA
Alain April, École de technologie supérieure, Canada

Software Configuration Management
John A. Scott, Lawrence Livermore National Laboratory, USA
David Nisse, USA

Software Engineering Management
Dennis Frailey, Raytheon Company, USA
Stephen G. MacDonell, Auckland University of Technology, New Zealand
Andrew R. Gray, University of Otago, New Zealand

Software Engineering Process
Khaled El Emam, served while at the Canadian National Research Council, Canada

Software Engineering Tools and Methods
David Carrington, School of Information Technology and Electrical Engineering,
The University of Queensland, Australia

Software Quality

Alain April, École de technologie supérieure, Canada
Dolores Wallace, retired from the National Institute of Standards and Technology, USA
Larry Reeker, NIST, USA

References Editor

Marc Bouisset, Département d'informatique, UQAM

REVIEW TEAM

The people listed below participated in the public review process of *SWEBOK Guide* V3. Membership of the IEEE Computer Society was not a requirement to participate in this review process, and membership information was not requested from reviewers. Over 1500 individual comments were collected and duly adjudicated.

Carlos C. Amaro, USA
Mark Ardis, USA
Mora-Soto Arturo, Spain
Ohad Barzilay, Israel
Gianni Basaglia, Italy
Denis J. Bergquist, USA
Alexander Bogush, UK
Christopher Bohn, USA
Steve Bollweg, USA
Reto Bonderer, Switzerland
Alexei Botchkarev, Canada
Pieter Botman, Canada
Robert Bragner, USA
Kevin Brune, USA
Ogihara Bryan, USA
Luigi Buglione, Italy
Rick Cagle, USA
Barbara Canody, USA
Rogerio A. Carvalho, Brazil
Daniel Cerys, USA
Philippe Cohard, France
Ricardo Colomo-Palacios, Spain
Mauricio Coria, Argentina
Marek Cruz, UK
Stephen Danckert, USA
Bipul K. Das, Canada
James D. Davidson, USA
Jon Dehn, USA
Lincoln P. Djang, USA
Andreas Doblander, Austria
Yi-Ben Doo, USA
Scott J. Dougherty, UK
Regina DuBord, USA
Fedor Dzerzhinskiy, Russia
Ann M. Eblen, Australia
David M. Endres, USA
Marilyn Escue, USA
Varuna Eswer, India

Istvan Fay, Hungary
Jose L. Fernandez-Sanchez, Spain
Dennis J. Frailey, USA
Tihana Galinac Grbac, Croatia
Colin Garlick, New Zealand
Garth J.G. Glynn, UK
Jill Gostin, USA
Christiane Gresse von Wangenheim, Brazil
Thomas Gust, USA
H.N. Mok, Singapore
Jon D. Hagar, USA
Anees Ahmed Haidary, India
Duncan Hall, New Zealand
James Hart, USA
Jens H.J. Heidrich, Germany
Rich Hilliard, USA
Bob Hillier, Canada
Norman M. Hines, USA
Dave Hirst, USA
Theresa L. Hunt, USA
Kenneth Ingham, USA
Masahiko Ishikawa, Japan
Michael A. Jablonski, USA
G. Jagadeesh, India
Sebastian Justicia, Spain
Umut Kahramankaptan, Belgium
Pankaj Kamthan, Canada
Perry Kapadia, USA
Tarig A. Khalid, Sudan
Michael K.A. Klaes, Germany
Maged Koshty, Egypt
Claude C. Laporte, Canada
Dong Li, China
Ben Linders, Netherlands
Claire Lohr, USA
Vladimir Mandic, Serbia
Matt Mansell, New Zealand
John Marien, USA

ACKNOWLEDGEMENTS

Funding for the development of *SWEBOK Guide* V3 has been provided by the IEEE Computer Society. The editors and coeditors appreciate the important work performed by the KA editors and the contributing editors as well as by the the members of the Change Control Board. The editorial team must also acknowledge the indispensable contribution of reviewers.

The editorial team also wishes to thank the following people who contributed to the project in various ways: Pieter Botman, Evan Butterfield, Carine Chauny, Pierce Gibbs, Diane Girard, John Keppler, Dorian McClenahan, Kenza Meridji, Samuel Redwine, Annette Reilly, and Pam Thompson.

Finally, there are surely other people who have contributed to this *Guide*, either directly or indirectly, whose names we have inadvertently omitted. To those people, we offer our tacit appreciation and apologize for having omitted explicit recognition.

IEEE COMPUTER SOCIETY PRESIDENTS

Dejan Milojicic, 2014 President
David Alan Grier, 2013 President
Thomas Conte, 2015 President

PROFESSIONAL ACTIVITIES BOARD, 2013 MEMBERSHIP

Donald F. Shafer, Chair
Pieter Botman, CSDP
Pierre Bourque
Richard Fairley, CSDP
Dennis Frailey
S. Michael Gayle
Phillip Laplante, CSDP
Jim Moore, CSDP
Linda Shafer, CSDP
Steve Tockey, CSDP
Charlene "Chuck" Walrad

MOTIONS REGARDING THE APPROVAL OF SWEBOK GUIDE V3.0

The *SWEBOK Guide* V3.0 was submitted to ballot by verified IEEE Computer Society members in November 2013 with the following question: "Do you approve this manuscript of the *SWEBOK Guide* V3.0 to move forward to formatting and publication?"

The results of this ballot were 259 Yes votes and 5 No votes.

The following motion was unanimously adopted by the Professional Activities Board of the IEEE Computer Society in December 2013:

> *The Professional Activities Board of the IEEE Computer Society finds that the* Guide to the Software Engineering Body of Knowledge *Version 3.0 has been successfully completed; and endorses the* Guide to the Software Engineering Body of Knowledge *Version 3.0 and commends it to the IEEE Computer Society Board of Governors for their approval.*

The following motion was adopted by the IEEE Computer Society Board of Governors in December 2013:

> *MOVED, that the Board of Governors of the IEEE Computer Society approves Version 3.0 of the* Guide to the Software Engineering Body of Knowledge *and authorizes the Chair of the Professional Activities Board to proceed with printing.*

MOTIONS REGARDING THE APPROVAL OF SWEBOK GUIDE 2004 VERSION

The following motion was unanimously adopted by the Industrial Advisory Board of the *SWEBOK Guide* project in February 2004:

> *The Industrial Advisory Board finds that the Software Engineering Body of Knowledge project initiated in 1998 has been successfully completed; and endorses the 2004 Version of the* Guide to the SWEBOK *and commends it to the IEEE Computer Society Board of Governors for their approval.*

The following motion was adopted by the IEEE Computer Society Board of Governors in February 2004:

> *MOVED, that the Board of Governors of the IEEE Computer Society approves the 2004 Edition of the* Guide to the Software Engineering Body of Knowledge *and authorizes the Chair of the Professional Practices Committee to proceed with printing.*

Please also note that the 2004 edition of the *Guide to the Software Engineering Body of Knowledge* was submitted by the IEEE Computer Society to ISO/IEC without any change and was recognized as Technical Report ISO/IEC TR 19759:2005.

INTRODUCTION TO THE GUIDE

KA	Knowledge Area
SWEBOK	Software Engineering Body of Knowledge

Publication of the 2004 version of this *Guide to the Software Engineering Body of Knowledge* (SWEBOK 2004) was a major milestone in establishing software engineering as a recognized engineering discipline. The goal in developing this update to SWEBOK is to improve the currency, readability, consistency, and usability of the *Guide*.

All knowledge areas (KAs) have been updated to reflect changes in software engineering since publication of SWEBOK 2004. Four new foundation KAs and a Software Engineering Professional Practices KA have been added. The Software Engineering Tools and Methods KA has been revised as Software Engineering Models and Methods. Software engineering tools is now a topic in each of the KAs. Three appendices provide the specifications for the KA description, an annotated set of relevant standards for each KA, and a listing of the references cited in the *Guide*.

This *Guide*, written under the auspices of the Professional Activities Board of the IEEE Computer Society, represents a next step in the evolution of the software engineering profession.

WHAT IS SOFTWARE ENGINEERING?

ISO/IEC/IEEE Systems and Software Engineering Vocabulary (SEVOCAB) defines software engineering as "the application of a systematic, disciplined, quantifiable approach to the development, operation, and maintenance of software; that is, the application of engineering to software."[1]

WHAT ARE THE OBJECTIVES OF THE SWEBOK GUIDE?

The *Guide* should not be confused with the Body of Knowledge itself, which exists in the published literature. The purpose of the *Guide* is to describe the portion of the Body of Knowledge that is generally accepted, to organize that portion, and to provide topical access to it.

The *Guide to the Software Engineering Body of Knowledge* (*SWEBOK Guide*) was established with the following five objectives:

1. To promote a consistent view of software engineering worldwide
2. To specify the scope of, and clarify the place of software engineering with respect to other disciplines such as computer science, project management, computer engineering, and mathematics
3. To characterize the contents of the software engineering discipline
4. To provide a topical access to the Software Engineering Body of Knowledge
5. To provide a foundation for curriculum development and for individual certification and licensing material

The first of these objectives, a consistent worldwide view of software engineering, was supported by a development process which engaged approximately 150 reviewers from 33 countries. More information regarding the development process can be found on the website (www.swebok.org). Professional and learned societies and public agencies involved in software engineering were contacted, made aware of this project to update SWEBOK, and invited to participate in the review process. KA editors were recruited from North America, the Pacific Rim, and Europe. Presentations on the project were made at various international venues.

The second of the objectives, the desire to specify the scope of software engineering, motivates the fundamental organization of the Guide. The material that is recognized as being within this discipline is organized into the fifteen KAs listed in Table I.1. Each of these KAs is treated in a chapter in this *Guide*.

---

1 See www.computer.org/sevocab.

Table I.1. The 15 SWEBOK KAs
Software Requirements
Software Design
Software Construction
Software Testing
Software Maintenance
Software Configuration Management
Software Engineering Management
Software Engineering Process
Software Engineering Models and Methods
Software Quality
Software Engineering Professional Practice
Software Engineering Economics
Computing Foundations
Mathematical Foundations
Engineering Foundations

In specifying scope, it is also important to identify the disciplines that intersect with software engineering. To this end, SWEBOK V3 also recognizes seven related disciplines, listed in Table I.2. Software engineers should, of course, have knowledge of material from these disciplines (and the KA descriptions in this *Guide* may make reference to them). It is not, however, an objective of the *SWEBOK Guide* to characterize the knowledge of the related disciplines.

Table I.2. Related Disciplines
Computer Engineering
Computer Science
General Management
Mathematics
Project Management
Quality Management
Systems Engineering

The relevant elements of computer science and mathematics are presented in the Computing Foundations and Mathematical Foundations KAs of the *Guide* (Chapters 13 and 14).

HIERARCHICAL ORGANIZATION

The organization of the KA chapters supports the third of the project's objectives—a characterization of the contents of software engineering. The detailed specifications provided by the project's editorial team to the associate editors regarding the contents of the KA descriptions can be found in Appendix A.

The *Guide* uses a hierarchical organization to decompose each KA into a set of topics with recognizable labels. A two (sometime three) level breakdown provides a reasonable way to find topics of interest. The *Guide* treats the selected topics in a manner compatible with major schools of thought and with breakdowns generally found in industry and in software engineering literature and standards. The breakdowns of topics do not presume particular application domains, business uses, management philosophies, development methods, and so forth. The extent of each topic's description is only that needed to understand the generally accepted nature of the topics and for the reader to successfully find reference material; the Body of Knowledge is found in the reference materials themselves, not in the *Guide*.

REFERENCE MATERIAL AND MATRIX

To provide topical access to the knowledge—the fourth of the project's objectives—the *Guide* identifies authoritative reference material for each KA. Appendix C provides a Consolidated Reference List for the *Guide*. Each KA includes relevant references from the Consolidated Reference List and also includes a matrix relating the reference material to the included topics.

It should be noted that the *Guide* does not attempt to be comprehensive in its citations. Much material that is both suitable and excellent is not referenced. Material included in the Consolidated Reference List provides coverage of the topics described.

DEPTH OF TREATMENT

To achieve the SWEBOK fifth objective—providing a foundation for curriculum development, certification, and licensing, the criterion of *generally accepted* knowledge has been applied, to be distinguished from advanced and research knowledge (on the grounds of maturity) and from specialized knowledge (on the grounds of generality of application).

The equivalent term *generally recognized* comes from the Project Management Institute: "Generally recognized means the knowledge and practices described are applicable to most projects most of the time, and there is consensus about their value and usefulness."[2]

However, the terms "generally accepted" or "generally recognized" do not imply that the designated knowledge should be uniformly applied to all software engineering endeavors—each project's needs determine that—but it does imply that competent, capable software engineers should be equipped with this knowledge for potential application. More precisely, generally accepted knowledge should be included in the study material for the software engineering licensing examination that graduates would take after gaining four years of work experience. Although this criterion is specific to the US style of education and does not necessarily apply to other countries, we deem it useful.

STRUCTURE OF THE KA DESCRIPTIONS

The KA descriptions are structured as follows.

In the introduction, a brief definition of the KA and an overview of its scope and of its relationship with other KAs are presented.

---

2   *A Guide to the Project Management Body of Knowledge*, 5th ed., Project Management Institute, 2013; www.pmi.org.

The breakdown of topics in each KA constitutes the core the KA description, describing the decomposition of the KA into subareas, topics, and sub-topics. For each topic or subtopic, a short description is given, along with one or more references.

The reference material was chosen because it is considered to constitute the best presentation of the knowledge relative to the topic. A matrix links the topics to the reference material.

The last part of each KA description is the list of recommended references and (optionally) further readings. Relevant standards for each KA are presented in Appendix B of the *Guide*.

APPENDIX A. KA DESCRIPTION SPECIFICATIONS

Appendix A describes the specifications provided by the editorial team to the associate editors for the content, recommended references, format, and style of the KA descriptions.

APPENDIX B. ALLOCATION OF STANDARDS TO KAS

Appendix B is an annotated list of the relevant standards, mostly from the IEEE and the ISO, for each of the KAs of the *SWEBOK Guide*.

APPENDIX C. CONSOLIDATED REFERENCE LIST

Appendix C contains the consolidated list of recommended references cited in the KAs (these references are marked with an asterisk (*) in the text).

CHAPTER 1

SOFTWARE REQUIREMENTS

ACRONYMS

CIA	Confidentiality, Integrity, and Availability
DAG	Directed Acyclic Graph
FSM	Functional Size Measurement
INCOSE	International Council on Systems Engineering
UML	Unified Modeling Language
SysML	Systems Modeling Language

INTRODUCTION

The Software Requirements knowledge area (KA) is concerned with the elicitation, analysis, specification, and validation of software requirements as well as the management of requirements during the whole life cycle of the software product. It is widely acknowledged amongst researchers and industry practitioners that software projects are critically vulnerable when the requirements-related activities are poorly performed.

Software requirements express the needs and constraints placed on a software product that contribute to the solution of some real-world problem.

The term "requirements engineering" is widely used in the field to denote the systematic handling of requirements. For reasons of consistency, the term "engineering" will not be used in this KA other than for software engineering per se.

For the same reason, "requirements engineer," a term which appears in some of the literature, will not be used either. Instead, the term "software engineer" or, in some specific cases, "requirements specialist" will be used, the latter where the role in question is usually performed by an individual other than a software engineer. This does not imply, however, that a software engineer could not perform the function.

A risk inherent in the proposed breakdown is that a waterfall-like process may be inferred. To guard against this, topic 2, Requirements Process, is designed to provide a high-level overview of the requirements process by setting out the resources and constraints under which the process operates and which act to configure it.

An alternate decomposition could use a product-based structure (system requirements, software requirements, prototypes, use cases, and so on). The process-based breakdown reflects the fact that the requirements process, if it is to be successful, must be considered as a process involving complex, tightly coupled activities (both sequential and concurrent), rather than as a discrete, one-off activity performed at the outset of a software development project.

The Software Requirements KA is related closely to the Software Design, Software Testing, Software Maintenance, Software Configuration Management, Software Engineering Management, Software Engineering Process, Software Engineering Models and Methods, and Software Quality KAs.

BREAKDOWN OF TOPICS FOR SOFTWARE REQUIREMENTS

The breakdown of topics for the Software Requirements KA is shown in Figure 1.1.

1. Software Requirements Fundamentals
[1*, c4, c4s1, c10s1, c10s4] [2*, c1, c6, c12]

1.1. Definition of a Software Requirement

At its most basic, a software requirement is a property that must be exhibited by something in

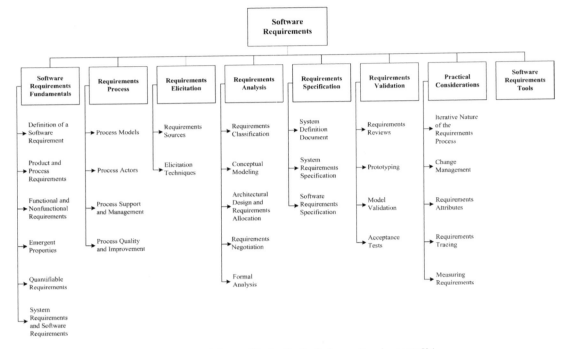

Figure 1.1. Breakdown of Topics for the Software Requirements KA

order to solve some problem in the real world. It may aim to automate part of a task for someone to support the business processes of an organization, to correct shortcomings of existing software, or to control a device—to name just a few of the many problems for which software solutions are possible. The ways in which users, business processes, and devices function are typically complex. By extension, therefore, the requirements on particular software are typically a complex combination from various people at different levels of an organization, and who are in one way or another involved or connected with this feature from the environment in which the software will operate.

An essential property of all software requirements is that they be verifiable as an individual feature as a functional requirement or at the system level as a nonfunctional requirement. It may be difficult or costly to verify certain software requirements. For example, verification of the throughput requirement on a call center may necessitate the development of simulation software. Software requirements, software testing, and quality personnel must ensure that the requirements can be verified within available resource constraints.

Requirements have other attributes in addition to behavioral properties. Common examples include a priority rating to enable tradeoffs in the face of finite resources and a status value to enable project progress to be monitored. Typically, software requirements are uniquely identified so that they can be subjected to software configuration management over the entire life cycle of the feature and of the software.

1.2. Product and Process Requirements

A product requirement is a need or constraint on the software to be developed (for example, "The software shall verify that a student meets all prerequisites before he or she registers for a course").

A process requirement is essentially a constraint on the development of the software (for example, "The software shall be developed using a RUP process").

Some software requirements generate implicit process requirements. The choice of verification technique is one example. Another might be the use of particularly rigorous analysis techniques (such as formal specification methods) to reduce faults that can lead to inadequate reliability. Process requirements may also be imposed directly by the development organization, their customer, or a third party such as a safety regulator.

1.3. Functional and Nonfunctional Requirements

Functional requirements describe the functions that the software is to execute; for example, formatting some text or modulating a signal. They are sometimes known as capabilities or features. A functional requirement can also be described as one for which a finite set of test steps can be written to validate its behavior.

Nonfunctional requirements are the ones that act to constrain the solution. Nonfunctional requirements are sometimes known as constraints or quality requirements. They can be further classified according to whether they are performance requirements, maintainability requirements, safety requirements, reliability requirements, security requirements, interoperability requirements or one of many other types of software requirements (see Models and Quality Characteristics in the Software Quality KA).

1.4. Emergent Properties

Some requirements represent emergent properties of software—that is, requirements that cannot be addressed by a single component but that depend on how all the software components interoperate. The throughput requirement for a call center would, for example, depend on how the telephone system, information system, and the operators all interacted under actual operating conditions. Emergent properties are crucially dependent on the system architecture.

1.5. Quantifiable Requirements

Software requirements should be stated as clearly and as unambiguously as possible, and, where appropriate, quantitatively. It is important to avoid vague and unverifiable requirements that depend for their interpretation on subjective judgment ("the software shall be reliable"; "the software shall be user-friendly"). This is particularly important for nonfunctional requirements. Two examples of quantified requirements are the following: a call center's software must increase the center's throughput by 20%; and a system shall have a probability of generating a fatal error during any hour of operation of less than $1 * 10^{-8}$. The throughput requirement is at a very high level and will need to be used to derive a number of detailed requirements. The reliability requirement will tightly constrain the system architecture.

1.6. System Requirements and Software Requirements

In this topic, "system" means

> an interacting combination of elements to accomplish a defined objective. These include hardware, software, firmware, people, information, techniques, facilities, services, and other support elements,

as defined by the International Council on Software and Systems Engineering (INCOSE) [3].

System requirements are the requirements for the system as a whole. In a system containing software components, *software* requirements are derived from system requirements.

This KA defines "user requirements" in a restricted way, as the requirements of the system's customers or end users. System requirements, by contrast, encompass user requirements, requirements of other stakeholders (such as regulatory authorities), and requirements without an identifiable human source.

2. Requirements Process
[1*, c4s4] [2*, c1–4, c6, c22, c23]

This section introduces the software requirements process, orienting the remaining five topics and showing how the requirements process dovetails with the overall software engineering process.

2.1. Process Models

The objective of this topic is to provide an understanding that the requirements process

- is not a discrete front-end activity of the software life cycle, but rather a process initiated at the beginning of a project that continues to be refined throughout the life cycle;
- identifies software requirements as configuration items and manages them using the same software configuration management practices as other products of the software life cycle processes;
- needs to be adapted to the organization and project context.

In particular, the topic is concerned with how the activities of elicitation, analysis, specification, and validation are configured for different types of projects and constraints. The topic also includes activities that provide input into the requirements process, such as marketing and feasibility studies.

2.2. Process Actors

This topic introduces the roles of the people who participate in the requirements process. This process is fundamentally interdisciplinary, and the requirements specialist needs to mediate between the domain of the stakeholder and that of software engineering. There are often many people involved besides the requirements specialist, each of whom has a stake in the software. The stakeholders will vary across projects, but will always include users/operators and customers (who need not be the same).

Typical examples of software stakeholders include (but are not restricted to) the following:

- Users: This group comprises those who will operate the software. It is often a heterogeneous group involving people with different roles and requirements.
- Customers: This group comprises those who have commissioned the software or who represent the software's target market.
- Market analysts: A mass-market product will not have a commissioning customer, so marketing people are often needed to establish what the market needs and to act as proxy customers.
- Regulators: Many application domains, such as banking and public transport, are regulated. Software in these domains must comply with the requirements of the regulatory authorities.
- Software engineers: These individuals have a legitimate interest in profiting from developing the software by, for example, reusing components in or from other products. If, in this scenario, a customer of a particular product has specific requirements that compromise the potential for component reuse, the software engineers must carefully weigh their own stake against those of the customer. Specific requirements, particularly constraints, may have major impact on project cost or delivery because they either fit well or poorly with the skill set of the engineers. Important tradeoffs among such requirements should be identified.

It will not be possible to perfectly satisfy the requirements of every stakeholder, and it is the software engineer's job to negotiate tradeoffs that are both acceptable to the principal stakeholders and within budgetary, technical, regulatory, and other constraints. A prerequisite for this is that all the stakeholders be identified, the nature of their "stake" analyzed, and their requirements elicited.

2.3. Process Support and Management

This section introduces the project management resources required and consumed by the requirements process. It establishes the context for the first topic (Initiation and Scope Definition) of the Software Engineering Management KA. Its principal purpose is to make the link between the process activities identified in 2.1 and the issues of cost, human resources, training, and tools.

2.4. Process Quality and Improvement

This topic is concerned with the assessment of the quality and improvement of the requirements process. Its purpose is to emphasize the key role the requirements process plays in terms of the cost and timeliness of a software product and of the customer's satisfaction with it. It will help to orient the requirements process with quality standards and process improvement models for software and systems. Process quality and improvement is closely related to both the Software Quality KA and Software Engineering Process KA, comprising

- requirements process coverage by process improvement standards and models;
- requirements process measures and benchmarking;
- improvement planning and implementation;
- security/CIA improvement/planning and implementation.

3. Requirements Elicitation

[1*, c4s5] [2*, c5, c6, c9]

Requirements elicitation is concerned with the origins of software requirements and how the software engineer can collect them. It is the first stage in building an understanding of the problem the software is required to solve. It is fundamentally a human activity and is where the stakeholders are identified and relationships established between the development team and the customer. It is variously termed "requirements capture," "requirements discovery," and "requirements acquisition."

One of the fundamental principles of a good requirements elicitation process is that of effective communication between the various stakeholders. This communication continues through the entire Software Development Life Cycle (SDLC) process with different stakeholders at different points in time. Before development begins, requirements specialists may form the conduit for this communication. They must mediate between the domain of the software users (and other stakeholders) and the technical world of the software engineer. A set of internally consistent models at different levels of abstraction facilitate communications between software users/stakeholders and software engineers.

A critical element of requirements elicitation is informing the project scope. This involves providing a description of the software being specified and its purpose and prioritizing the deliverables

to ensure the customer's most important business needs are satisfied first. This minimizes the risk of requirements specialists spending time eliciting requirements that are of low importance, or those that turn out to be no longer relevant when the software is delivered. On the other hand, the description must be scalable and extensible to accept further requirements not expressed in the first formal lists and compatible with the previous ones as contemplated in recursive methods.

3.1. Requirements Sources

Requirements have many sources in typical software, and it is essential that all potential sources be identified and evaluated. This topic is designed to promote awareness of the various sources of software requirements and of the frameworks for managing them. The main points covered are as follows:

- Goals. The term "goal" (sometimes called "business concern" or "critical success factor") refers to the overall, high-level objectives of the software. Goals provide the motivation for the software but are often vaguely formulated. Software engineers need to pay particular attention to assessing the value (relative to priority) and cost of goals. A feasibility study is a relatively low-cost way of doing this.
- Domain knowledge. The software engineer needs to acquire or have available knowledge about the application domain. Domain knowledge provides the background against which all elicited requirements knowledge must be set in order to understand it. It's a good practice to emulate an ontological approach in the knowledge domain. Relations between relevant concepts within the application domain should be identified.
- Stakeholders (see section 2.2, Process Actors). Much software has proved unsatisfactory because it has stressed the requirements of one group of stakeholders at the expense of others. Hence, the delivered software is difficult to use, or subverts the cultural or political structures of the customer organization. The software engineer needs to identify, represent, and manage

the "viewpoints" of many different types of stakeholders.

- Business rules. These are statements that define or constrain some aspect of the structure or the behavior of the business itself. "A student cannot register in next semester's courses if there remain some unpaid tuition fees" would be an example of a business rule that would be a requirement source for a university's course-registration software.
- The operational environment. Requirements will be derived from the environment in which the software will be executed. These may be, for example, timing constraints in real-time software or performance constraints in a business environment. These must be sought out actively because they can greatly affect software feasibility and cost as well as restrict design choices.
- The organizational environment. Software is often required to support a business process, the selection of which may be conditioned by the structure, culture, and internal politics of the organization. The software engineer needs to be sensitive to these since, in general, new software should not force unplanned change on the business process.

3.2. Elicitation Techniques

Once the requirements sources have been identified, the software engineer can start eliciting requirements information from them. Note that requirements are seldom elicited ready-made. Rather, the software engineer elicits information from which he or she formulates requirements. This topic concentrates on techniques for getting human stakeholders to articulate requirements-relevant information. It is a very difficult task and the software engineer needs to be sensitized to the fact that (for example) users may have difficulty describing their tasks, may leave important information unstated, or may be unwilling or unable to cooperate. It is particularly important to understand that elicitation is not a passive activity and that, even if cooperative and articulate stakeholders are available, the software engineer has to work hard to elicit the right information. Many business or technical requirements are tacit or in feedback that

has yet to be obtained from end users. The importance of planning, verification, and validation in requirements elicitation cannot be overstated. A number of techniques exist for requirements elicitation; the principal ones are these:

- Interviews. Interviewing stakeholders is a "traditional" means of eliciting requirements. It is important to understand the advantages and limitations of interviews and how they should be conducted.
- Scenarios. Scenarios provide a valuable means for providing context to the elicitation of user requirements. They allow the software engineer to provide a framework for questions about user tasks by permitting "what if" and "how is this done" questions to be asked. The most common type of scenario is the use case description. There is a link here to topic 4.2 (Conceptual Modeling) because scenario notations such as use case diagrams are common in modeling software.
- Prototypes. This technique is a valuable tool for clarifying ambiguous requirements. They can act in a similar way to scenarios by providing users with a context within which they can better understand what information they need to provide. There is a wide range of prototyping techniques—from paper mockups of screen designs to beta-test versions of software products—and a strong overlap of their separate uses for requirements elicitation and for requirements validation (see section 6.2, Prototyping). Low fidelity prototypes are often preferred to avoid stakeholder "anchoring" on minor, incidental characteristics of a higher quality prototype that can limit design flexibility in unintended ways.
- Facilitated meetings. The purpose of these meetings is to try to achieve a summative effect, whereby a group of people can bring more insight into their software requirements than by working individually. They can brainstorm and refine ideas that may be difficult to bring to the surface using interviews. Another advantage is that conflicting requirements surface early on in a way that lets the stakeholders recognize where these occur. When it works well, this technique

may result in a richer and more consistent set of requirements than might otherwise be achievable. However, meetings need to be handled carefully (hence the need for a facilitator) to prevent a situation in which the critical abilities of the team are eroded by group loyalty, or in which requirements reflecting the concerns of a few outspoken (and perhaps senior) people that are favored to the detriment of others.

- Observation. The importance of software context within the organizational environment has led to the adaptation of observational techniques such as ethnography for requirements elicitation. Software engineers learn about user tasks by immersing themselves in the environment and observing how users perform their tasks by interacting with each other and with software tools and other resources. These techniques are relatively expensive but also instructive because they illustrate that many user tasks and business processes are too subtle and complex for their actors to describe easily.
- User stories. This technique is commonly used in adaptive methods (see Agile Methods in the Software Engineering Models and Methods KA) and refers to short, high-level descriptions of required functionality expressed in customer terms. A typical user story has the form: *"As a <role>, I want <goal/desire> so that <benefit>."* A user story is intended to contain just enough information so that the developers can produce a reasonable estimate of the effort to implement it. The aim is to avoid some of the waste that often happens in projects where detailed requirements are gathered early but become invalid before the work begins. Before a user story is implemented, an appropriate acceptance procedure must be written by the customer to determine whether the goals of the user story have been fulfilled.
- Other techniques. A range of other techniques for supporting the elicitation of requirements information exist and range from analyzing competitors' products to applying data mining techniques to using sources of domain knowledge or customer request databases.

4. Requirements Analysis

[1*, c4s1, c4s5, c10s4, c12s5]
[2*, c7, c11, c12, c17]

This topic is concerned with the process of analyzing requirements to

- detect and resolve conflicts between requirements;
- discover the bounds of the software and how it must interact with its organizational and operational environment;
- elaborate system requirements to derive software requirements.

The traditional view of requirements analysis has been that it be reduced to conceptual modeling using one of a number of analysis methods, such as the structured analysis method. While conceptual modeling is important, we include the classification of requirements to help inform tradeoffs between requirements (requirements classification) and the process of establishing these tradeoffs (requirements negotiation).

Care must be taken to describe requirements precisely enough to enable the requirements to be validated, their implementation to be verified, and their costs to be estimated.

4.1. Requirements Classification

Requirements can be classified on a number of dimensions. Examples include the following:

- Whether the requirement is functional or nonfunctional (see section 1.3, Functional and Nonfunctional Requirements).
- Whether the requirement is derived from one or more high-level requirements or an emergent property (see section 1.4, Emergent Properties), or is being imposed directly on the software by a stakeholder or some other source.
- Whether the requirement is on the product or the process (see section 1.2, Product and Process Requirements). Requirements on the process can constrain the choice of contractor, the software engineering process to be adopted, or the standards to be adhered to.

- The requirement priority. The higher the priority, the more essential the requirement is for meeting the overall goals of the software. Often classified on a fixed-point scale such as mandatory, highly desirable, desirable, or optional, the priority often has to be balanced against the cost of development and implementation.
- The scope of the requirement. Scope refers to the extent to which a requirement affects the software and software components. Some requirements, particularly certain nonfunctional ones, have a global scope in that their satisfaction cannot be allocated to a discrete component. Hence, a requirement with global scope may strongly affect the software architecture and the design of many components, whereas one with a narrow scope may offer a number of design choices and have little impact on the satisfaction of other requirements.
- Volatility/stability. Some requirements will change during the life cycle of the software—and even during the development process itself. It is useful if some estimate of the likelihood that a requirement will change can be made. For example, in a banking application, requirements for functions to calculate and credit interest to customers' accounts are likely to be more stable than a requirement to support a particular kind of tax-free account. The former reflects a fundamental feature of the banking domain (that accounts can earn interest), while the latter may be rendered obsolete by a change to government legislation. Flagging potentially volatile requirements can help the software engineer establish a design that is more tolerant of change.

Other classifications may be appropriate, depending upon the organization's normal practice and the application itself.

There is a strong overlap between requirements classification and requirements attributes (see section 7.3, Requirements Attributes).

4.2. Conceptual Modeling

The development of models of a real-world problem is key to software requirements analysis. Their purpose is to aid in understanding the situation in which the problem occurs, as well as depicting a solution. Hence, conceptual models comprise models of entities from the problem domain, configured to reflect their real-world relationships and dependencies. This topic is closely related to the Software Engineering Models and Methods KA.

Several kinds of models can be developed. These include use case diagrams, data flow models, state models, goal-based models, user interactions, object models, data models, and many others. Many of these modeling notations are part of *the Unified Modeling Language (UML)*. Use case diagrams, for example, are routinely used to depict scenarios where the boundary separates the actors (users or systems in the external environment) from the internal behavior where each use case depicts a functionality of the system.

The factors that influence the choice of modeling notation include these:

- The nature of the problem. Some types of software demand that certain aspects be analyzed particularly rigorously. For example, state and parametric models, which are part of SysML [4], are likely to be more important for real-time software than for information systems, while it would usually be the opposite for object and activity models.
- The expertise of the software engineer. It is often more productive to adopt a modeling notation or method with which the software engineer has experience.
- The process requirements of the customer (see section 1.2, Product and Process Requirements). Customers may impose their favored notation or method or prohibit any with which they are unfamiliar. This factor can conflict with the previous factor.

Note that, in almost all cases, it is useful to start by building a model of the software context. The software context provides a connection between the intended software and its external environment.

This is crucial to understanding the software's context in its operational environment and to identifying its interfaces with the environment.

This subtopic does not seek to "teach" a particular modeling style or notation but rather provides guidance on the purpose and intent of modeling.

4.3. Architectural Design and Requirements Allocation

At some point, the solution architecture must be derived. Architectural design is the point at which the requirements process overlaps with software or systems design and illustrates how impossible it is to cleanly decouple the two tasks. This topic is closely related to Software Structure and Architecture in the Software Design KA. In many cases, the software engineer acts as software architect because the process of analyzing and elaborating the requirements demands that the architecture/design components that will be responsible for satisfying the requirements be identified. This is requirements allocation–the assignment to architecture components responsible for satisfying the requirements.

Allocation is important to permit detailed analysis of requirements. Hence, for example, once a set of requirements has been allocated to a component, the individual requirements can be further analyzed to discover further requirements on how the component needs to interact with other components in order to satisfy the allocated requirements. In large projects, allocation stimulates a new round of analysis for each subsystem. As an example, requirements for a particular braking performance for a car (braking distance, safety in poor driving conditions, smoothness of application, pedal pressure required, and so on) may be allocated to the braking hardware (mechanical and hydraulic assemblies) and an antilock braking system (ABS). Only when a requirement for an antilock braking system has been identified, and the requirements allocated to it, can the capabilities of the ABS, the braking hardware, and emergent properties (such as car weight) be used to identify the detailed ABS software requirements.

Architectural design is closely identified with conceptual modeling (see section 4.2, Conceptual Modeling).

4.4. Requirements Negotiation

Another term commonly used for this subtopic is "conflict resolution." This concerns resolving problems with requirements where conflicts occur between two stakeholders requiring mutually incompatible features, between requirements and resources, or between functional and nonfunctional requirements, for example. In most cases, it is unwise for the software engineer to make a unilateral decision, so it becomes necessary to consult with the stakeholder(s) to reach a consensus on an appropriate tradeoff. It is often important, for contractual reasons, that such decisions be traceable back to the customer. We have classified this as a software requirements analysis topic because problems emerge as the result of analysis. However, a strong case can also be made for considering it a requirements validation topic (see topic 6, Requirements Validation).

Requirements prioritization is necessary, not only as a means to filter important requirements, but also in order to resolve conflicts and plan for staged deliveries, which means making complex decisions that require detailed domain knowledge and good estimation skills. However, it is often difficult to get real information that can act as a basis for such decisions. In addition, requirements often depend on each other, and priorities are relative. In practice, software engineers perform requirements prioritization frequently without knowing about all the requirements. Requirements prioritization may follow a cost-value approach that involves an analysis from the stakeholders defining in a scale the benefits or the aggregated value that the implementation of the requirement brings them, versus the penalties of not having implemented a particular requirement. It also involves an analysis from the software engineers estimating in a scale the cost of implementing each requirement, relative to other requirements. Another requirements prioritization approach called the analytic hierarchy process involves comparing all unique pairs of requirements to determine which of the two is of higher priority, and to what extent.

4.5. *Formal Analysis*

Formal analysis concerns not only topic 4, but also sections 5.3 and 6.3. This topic is also related to Formal Methods in the Software Engineering Models and Methods Knowledge Area.

Formal analysis has made an impact on some application domains, particularly those of high-integrity systems. The formal expression of requirements requires a language with formally defined semantics. The use of a formal analysis for requirements expression has two benefits. First, it enables requirements expressed in the language to be specified precisely and unambiguously, thus (in principle) avoiding the potential for misinterpretation. Secondly, requirements can be reasoned over, permitting desired properties of the specified software to be proven. Formal reasoning requires tool support to be practicable for anything other than trivial systems, and tools generally fall into two types: theorem provers or model checkers. In neither case can proof be fully automated, and the level of competence in formal reasoning needed in order to use the tools restricts the wider application of formal analysis.

Most formal analysis is focused on relatively late stages of requirements analysis. It is generally counterproductive to apply formalization until the business goals and user requirements have come into sharp focus through means such as those described elsewhere in section 4. However, once the requirements have stabilized and have been elaborated to specify concrete properties of the software, it may be beneficial to formalize at least the critical requirements. This permits static validation that the software specified by the requirements does indeed have the properties (for example, absence of deadlock) that the customer, users, and software engineer expect it to have.

5. Requirements Specification
[1*, c4s2, c4s3, c12s2–5] [2*, c10]

For most engineering professions, the term "specification" refers to the assignment of numerical values or limits to a product's design goals. In software engineering, "software requirements specification" typically refers to the production of a document that can be systematically reviewed, evaluated, and approved. For complex systems, particularly those involving substantial nonsoftware components, as many as three different types of documents are produced: system definition, system requirements, and software requirements. For simple software products, only the third of these is required. All three documents are described here, with the understanding that they may be combined as appropriate. A description of systems engineering can be found in the Related Disciplines of Software Engineering chapter of this *Guide*.

5.1. *System Definition Document*

This document (sometimes known as the user requirements document or concept of operations document) records the system requirements. It defines the high-level system requirements from the domain perspective. Its readership includes representatives of the system users/customers (marketing may play these roles for market-driven software), so its content must be couched in terms of the domain. The document lists the system requirements along with background information about the overall objectives for the system, its target environment, and a statement of the constraints, assumptions, and nonfunctional requirements. It may include conceptual models designed to illustrate the system context, usage scenarios, and the principal domain entities, as well as workflows.

5.2. *System Requirements Specification*

Developers of systems with substantial software and nonsoftware components—a modern airliner, for example—often separate the description of system requirements from the description of software requirements. In this view, system requirements are specified, the software requirements are derived from the system requirements, and then the requirements for the software components are specified. Strictly speaking, system requirements specification is a systems engineering activity and falls outside the scope of this *Guide*.

5.3. Software Requirements Specification

Software requirements specification establishes the basis for agreement between customers and contractors or suppliers (in market-driven projects, these roles may be played by the marketing and development divisions) on what the software product is to do as well as what it is not expected to do.

Software requirements specification permits a rigorous assessment of requirements before design can begin and reduces later redesign. It should also provide a realistic basis for estimating product costs, risks, and schedules.

Organizations can also use a software requirements specification document as the basis for developing effective verification and validation plans.

Software requirements specification provides an informed basis for transferring a software product to new users or software platforms. Finally, it can provide a basis for software enhancement.

Software requirements are often written in natural language, but, in software requirements specification, this may be supplemented by formal or semiformal descriptions. Selection of appropriate notations permits particular requirements and aspects of the software architecture to be described more precisely and concisely than natural language. The general rule is that notations should be used that allow the requirements to be described as precisely as possible. This is particularly crucial for safety-critical, regulatory, and certain other types of dependable software. However, the choice of notation is often constrained by the training, skills, and preferences of the document's authors and readers.

A number of quality indicators have been developed that can be used to relate the quality of software requirements specification to other project variables such as cost, acceptance, performance, schedule, and reproducibility. Quality indicators for individual software requirements specification statements include imperatives, directives, weak phrases, options, and continuances. Indicators for the entire software requirements specification document include size, readability, specification, depth, and text structure.

6. Requirements Validation

[1*, c4s6] [2*, c13, c15]

The requirements documents may be subject to validation and verification procedures. The requirements may be validated to ensure that the software engineer has understood the requirements; it is also important to verify that a requirements document conforms to company standards and that it is understandable, consistent, and complete. In cases where documented company standards or terminology are inconsistent with widely accepted standards, a mapping between the two should be agreed on and appended to the document.

Formal notations offer the important advantage of permitting the last two properties to be proven (in a restricted sense, at least). Different stakeholders, including representatives of the customer and developer, should review the document(s). Requirements documents are subject to the same configuration management practices as the other deliverables of the software life cycle processes. When practical, the individual requirements are also subject to configuration management, generally using a requirements management tool (see topic 8, Software Requirements Tools).

It is normal to explicitly schedule one or more points in the requirements process where the requirements are validated. The aim is to pick up any problems before resources are committed to addressing the requirements. Requirements validation is concerned with the process of examining the requirements document to ensure that it defines the right software (that is, the software that the users expect).

6.1. Requirements Reviews

Perhaps the most common means of validation is by inspection or reviews of the requirements document(s). A group of reviewers is assigned a brief to look for errors, mistaken assumptions, lack of clarity, and deviation from standard practice. The composition of the group that conducts the review is important (at least one representative of the customer should be included for a customer-driven project, for example), and it may help to provide guidance on what to look for in the form of checklists.

Reviews may be constituted on completion of the system definition document, the system specification document, the software requirements specification document, the baseline specification for a new release, or at any other step in the process.

6.2. Prototyping

Prototyping is commonly a means for validating the software engineer's interpretation of the software requirements, as well as for eliciting new requirements. As with elicitation, there is a range of prototyping techniques and a number of points in the process where prototype validation may be appropriate. The advantage of prototypes is that they can make it easier to interpret the software engineer's assumptions and, where needed, give useful feedback on why they are wrong. For example, the dynamic behavior of a user interface can be better understood through an animated prototype than through textual description or graphical models. The volatility of a requirement that is defined after prototyping has been done is extremely low because there is agreement between the stakeholder and the software engineer—therefore, for safety-critical and crucial features prototyping would really help. There are also disadvantages, however. These include the danger of users' attention being distracted from the core underlying functionality by cosmetic issues or quality problems with the prototype. For this reason, some advocate prototypes that avoid software, such as flip-chart-based mockups. Prototypes may be costly to develop. However, if they avoid the wastage of resources caused by trying to satisfy erroneous requirements, their cost can be more easily justified. Early prototypes may contain aspects of the final solution. Prototypes may be evolutionary as opposed to throwaway.

6.3. Model Validation

It is typically necessary to validate the quality of the models developed during analysis. For example, in object models, it is useful to perform a static analysis to verify that communication paths exist between objects that, in the stakeholders'

domain, exchange data. If formal analysis notations are used, it is possible to use formal reasoning to prove specification properties. This topic is closely related to the Software Engineering Models and Methods KA.

6.4. Acceptance Tests

An essential property of a software requirement is that it should be possible to validate that the finished product satisfies it. Requirements that cannot be validated are really just "wishes." An important task is therefore planning how to verify each requirement. In most cases, designing acceptance tests does this for how end-users typically conduct business using the system.

Identifying and designing acceptance tests may be difficult for nonfunctional requirements (see section 1.3, Functional and Nonfunctional Requirements). To be validated, they must first be analyzed and decomposed to the point where they can be expressed quantitatively.

Additional information can be found in Acceptance/Qualification/Conformance Testing in the Software Testing KA.

7. Practical Considerations

[1*, c4s1, c4s4, c4s6, c4s7]
[2*, c3, c12, c14, c16, c18–21]

The first level of topic decomposition presented in this KA may seem to describe a linear sequence of activities. This is a simplified view of the process.

The requirements process spans the whole software life cycle. Change management and the maintenance of the requirements in a state that accurately mirrors the software to be built, or that has been built, are key to the success of the software engineering process.

Not every organization has a culture of documenting and managing requirements. It is common in dynamic start-up companies, driven by a strong "product vision" and limited resources, to view requirements documentation as unnecessary overhead. Most often, however, as these companies expand, as their customer base grows, and as their product starts to evolve, they discover that they need to recover the requirements that motivated product features in order to assess the impact of proposed changes. Hence, requirements documentation and change management are key to the success of any requirements process.

7.1. Iterative Nature of the Requirements Process

There is general pressure in the software industry for ever shorter development cycles, and this is particularly pronounced in highly competitive, market-driven sectors. Moreover, most projects are constrained in some way by their environment, and many are upgrades to, or revisions of, existing software where the architecture is a given. In practice, therefore, it is almost always impractical to implement the requirements process as a linear, deterministic process in which software requirements are elicited from the stakeholders, baselined, allocated, and handed over to the software development team. It is certainly a myth that the requirements for large software projects are ever perfectly understood or perfectly specified.

Instead, requirements typically iterate towards a level of quality and detail that is sufficient to permit design and procurement decisions to be made. In some projects, this may result in the requirements being baselined before all their properties are fully understood. This risks expensive rework if problems emerge late in the software engineering process. However, software engineers are necessarily constrained by project management plans and must therefore take steps to ensure that the "quality" of the requirements is as high as possible given the available resources. They should, for example, make explicit any assumptions that underpin the requirements as well as any known problems.

For software products that are developed iteratively, a project team may baseline only those requirements needed for the current iteration. The requirements specialist can continue to develop requirements for future iterations, while developers proceed with design and construction of the current iteration. This approach provides customers with business value quickly, while minimizing the cost of rework.

In almost all cases, requirements understanding continues to evolve as design and development proceeds. This often leads to the revision of requirements late in the life cycle. Perhaps the most crucial point in understanding software requirements is that a significant proportion of the requirements *will* change. This is sometimes due to errors in the analysis, but it is frequently an inevitable consequence of change in the "environment"—for example, the customer's operating or business environment, regulatory processes imposed by the authorities, or the market into which software must sell. Whatever the cause, it is important to recognize the inevitability of change and take steps to mitigate its effects. Change has to be managed by ensuring that proposed changes go through a defined review and approval process and by applying careful requirements tracing, impact analysis, and software configuration management (see the Software Configuration Management KA). Hence, the requirements process is not merely a front-end task in software development, but spans the whole software life cycle. In a typical project, the software requirements activities evolve over time from elicitation to change management. A combination of top-down analysis and design methods and bottom-up implementation and refactoring methods that meet in the middle could provide the best of both worlds. However, this is difficult to achieve in practice, as it depends heavily upon the maturity and expertise of the software engineers.

7.2. Change Management

Change management is central to the management of requirements. This topic describes the role of change management, the procedures that need to be in place, and the analysis that should be applied to proposed changes. It has strong links to the Software Configuration Management KA.

7.3. Requirements Attributes

Requirements should consist not only of a specification of what is required, but also of ancillary information, which helps manage and interpret the requirements. Requirements attributes must be defined, recorded, and updated as the software under development or maintenance evolves. This should include the various classification dimensions of the requirement (see section 4.1, Requirements Classification) and the verification method or relevant acceptance test plan section. It may also include additional information, such as a summary rationale for each requirement, the source of each requirement, and a change history. The most important requirements attribute, however, is an identifier that allows the requirements to be uniquely and unambiguously identified.

7.4. Requirements Tracing

Requirements tracing is concerned with recovering the source of requirements and predicting the effects of requirements. Tracing is fundamental to performing impact analysis when requirements change. A requirement should be traceable backward to the requirements and stakeholders that motivated it (from a software requirement back to the system requirement(s) that it helps satisfy, for example). Conversely, a requirement should be traceable forward into the requirements and design entities that satisfy it (for example, from a system requirement into the software requirements that have been elaborated from it, and on into the code modules that implement it, or the test cases related to that code and even a given section on the user manual which describes the actual functionality) and into the test case that verifies it.

The requirements tracing for a typical project will form a complex directed acyclic graph (DAG) (see Graphs in the Computing Foundations KA) of requirements. Maintaining an up-to-date graph or traceability matrix is an activity that must be considered during the whole life cycle of a product. If the traceability information is not updated as changes in the requirements continue to happen, the traceability information becomes unreliable for impact analysis.

7.5. Measuring Requirements

As a practical matter, it is typically useful to have some concept of the "volume" of the requirements for a particular software product. This number is useful in evaluating the "size" of a change in requirements, in estimating the cost of a development or maintenance task, or simply for use as the denominator in other measurements. Functional size measurement (FSM) is a technique for evaluating the size of a body of functional requirements.

Additional information on size measurement and standards will be found in the Software Engineering Process KA.

8. Software Requirements Tools

Tools for dealing with software requirements fall broadly into two categories: tools for modeling and tools for managing requirements.

Requirements management tools typically support a range of activities—including documentation, tracing, and change management—and have had a significant impact on practice. Indeed, tracing and change management are really only practicable if supported by a tool. Since requirements management is fundamental to good requirements practice, many organizations have invested in requirements management tools, although many more manage their requirements in more ad hoc and generally less satisfactory ways (e.g., using spreadsheets).

MATRIX OF TOPICS VS. REFERENCE MATERIAL

	Sommerville 2011 [1*]	Wiegers 2003 [2*]
1. Software Requirements Fundamentals		
1.1. Definition of a Software Requirement	c4	c1
1.2. Product and Process Requirements	c4s1	c1, c6
1.3. Functional and Nonfunctional Requirements	c4s1	c12
1.4. Emergent Properties	c10s1	
1.5. Quantifiable Requirements		c1
1.6. System Requirements and Software Requirements	c10s4	c1
2. Requirements Process		
2.1. Process Models	c4s4	c3
2.2. Process Actors		c1, c2, c4, c6
2.3. Process Support and Management		c3
2.4. Process Quality and Improvement		c22, c23
3. Requirements Elicitation		
3.1. Requirements Sources	c4s5	c5, c6,c9
3.2. Elicitation Techniques	c4s5	c6
4. Requirements Analysis		
4.1. Requirements Classification	c4s1	c12
4.2. Conceptual Modeling	c4s5	c11
4.3. Architectural Design and Requirements Allocation	c10s4	c17
4.4. Requirements Negotiation	c4s5	c7
4.5. Formal Analysis	c12s5	
5. Requirements Specification		
5.1. System Definition Document	c4s2	c10
5.2. System Requirements Specification	c4s2, c12s2, c12s3, c12s4, c12s5	c10
5.3. Software Requirements Specification	c4s3	c10
6. Requirements Validation		
6.1. Requirements Reviews	c4s6	c15
6.2. Prototyping	c4s6	c13
6.3. Model Validation	c4s6	c15
6.4. Acceptance Tests	c4s6	c15

	Sommerville 2011 [1*]	Wiegers 2003 [2*]
7. Practical Considerations		
7.1. Iterative Nature of the Requirements Process	c4s4	c3, c16
7.2. Change Management	c4s7	c18, c19
7.3. Requirements Attributes	c4s1	c12, c14
7.4. Requirements Tracing		c20
7.5. Measuring Requirements	c4s6	c18
8. Software Requirements Tools		c21

FURTHER READINGS

I. Alexander and L. Beus-Dukic, *Discovering Requirements* [5].

An easily digestible and practically oriented book on software requirements, this is perhaps the best of current textbooks on how the various elements of software requirements fit together. It is full of practical advice on (for example) how to identify the various system stakeholders and how to evaluate alternative solutions. Its coverage is exemplary and serves as a useful reference for key techniques such as use case modeling and requirements prioritization.

C. Potts, K. Takahashi, and A. Antón, "Inquiry-Based Requirements Analysis" [6].

This paper is an easily digested account of work that has proven to be very influential in the development of requirements handling. It describes how and why the elaboration of requirements cannot be a linear process by which the analyst simply transcribes and reformulates requirements elicited from the customer. The role of scenarios is described in a way that helps to define their use in discovering and describing requirements.

A. van Lamsweerde, *Requirements Engineering: From System Goals to UML Models to Software Specifications* [7].

Serves as a good introduction to requirements engineering but its unique value is as a reference book for the KAOS goal-oriented requirements modelling language. Explains why goal modelling is useful and shows how it can integrate with mainstream modelling techniques using UML.

O. Gotel and A. Finkelstein, "An Analysis of the Requirements Traceability Problem" [8].

This paper is a classic reference work on a key element of requirements management. Based on empirical studies, it sets out the reasons for and the barriers to the effective tracing of requirements. It is essential reading for an understanding of why requirements tracing is an essential element of an effective software process.

N. Maiden and C. Ncube, "Acquiring COTS Software Selection Requirements" [9].

This paper is significant because it recognises explicitly that software products often integrate third-party components. It offers insights into the problems of selecting off-the-shelf software to satisfy requirements: there is usually a mismatch. This challenges some of the assumptions underpinning much of traditional requirements handling, which tends to assume custom software.

REFERENCES

[1*] I. Sommerville, *Software Engineering*, 9th ed., Addison-Wesley, 2011.

[2*] K.E. Wiegers, *Software Requirements*, 2nd ed., Microsoft Press, 2003.

[3] INCOSE, *Systems Engineering Handbook: A Guide for System Life Cycle Processes and Activities*, version 3.2.2, International Council on Systems Engineering, 2012.

[4] S. Friedenthal, A. Moore, and R. Steiner, *A Practical Guide to SysML: The Systems Modeling Language*, 2nd ed., Morgan Kaufmann, 2012.

[5] I. Alexander and L. Beus-Deukic, *Discovering Requirements: How to Specify Products and Services*, Wiley, 2009.

[6] C. Potts, K. Takahashi, and A.I. Antón, "Inquiry-Based Requirements Analysis," *IEEE Software,* vol. 11, no. 2, Mar. 1994, pp. 21–32.

[7] A. van Lamsweerde, *Requirements Engineering: From System Goals to UML Models to Software Specifications*, Wiley, 2009.

[8] O. Gotel and C.W. Finkelstein, "An Analysis of the Requirements Traceability Problem," *Proc. 1st Int'l Conf. Requirements Eng.,* IEEE, 1994.

[9] N.A. Maiden and C. Ncube, "Acquiring COTS Software Selection Requirements," *IEEE Software,* vol. 15, no. 2, Mar.–Apr. 1998, pp. 46–56.

CHAPTER 2

SOFTWARE DESIGN

ACRONYMS

ADL	Architecture Description Language
CBD	Component-Based Design
CRC	Class Responsibility Collaborator
DFD	Data Flow Diagram
ERD	Entity Relationship Diagram
IDL	Interface Description Language
MVC	Model View Controller
OO	Object-Oriented
PDL	Program Design Language

INTRODUCTION

Design is defined as both "the process of defining the architecture, components, interfaces, and other characteristics of a system or component" and "the result of [that] process" [1]. Viewed as a process, software design is the software engineering life cycle activity in which software requirements are analyzed in order to produce a description of the software's internal structure that will serve as the basis for its construction. A software design (the result) describes the software architecture—that is, how software is decomposed and organized into components—and the interfaces between those components. It should also describe the components at a level of detail that enables their construction.

Software design plays an important role in developing software: during software design, software engineers produce various models that form a kind of blueprint of the solution to be implemented. We can analyze and evaluate these models to determine whether or not they will allow us to fulfill the various requirements.

We can also examine and evaluate alternative solutions and tradeoffs. Finally, we can use the resulting models to plan subsequent development activities, such as system verification and validation, in addition to using them as inputs and as the starting point of construction and testing.

In a standard list of software life cycle processes, such as that in ISO/IEC/IEEE Std. 12207, *Software Life Cycle Processes* [2], software design consists of two activities that fit between software requirements analysis and software construction:

- Software architectural design (sometimes called high-level design): develops top-level structure and organization of the software and identifies the various components.
- Software detailed design: specifies each component in sufficient detail to facilitate its construction.

This Software Design knowledge area (KA) does not discuss every topic that includes the word "design." In Tom DeMarco's terminology [3], the topics discussed in this KA deal mainly with D-design (decomposition design), the goal of which is to map software into component pieces. However, because of its importance in the field of software architecture, we will also address FP-design (family pattern design), the goal of which is to establish exploitable commonalities in a family of software products. This KA does not address I-design (invention design), which is usually performed during the software requirements process with the goal of conceptualizing and specifying software to satisfy discovered needs and requirements, since this topic is considered to be part of the requirements process (see the Software Requirements KA).

This Software Design KA is related specifically to the Software Requirements, Software

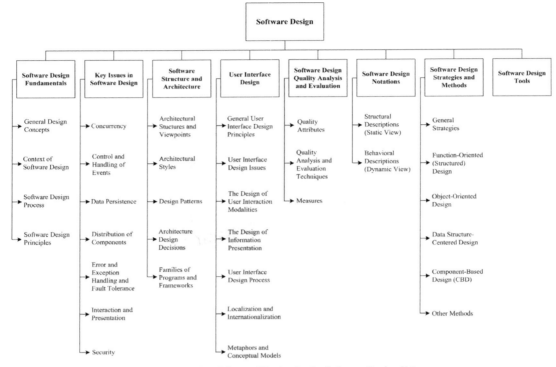

Figure 2.1. Breakdown of Topics for the Software Design KA

Construction, Software Engineering Management, Software Engineering Models and Methods, Software Quality, and Computing Foundations KAs.

BREAKDOWN OF TOPICS FOR SOFTWARE DESIGN

The breakdown of topics for the Software Design KA is shown in Figure 2.1.

1. Software Design Fundamentals

The concepts, notions, and terminology introduced here form an underlying basis for understanding the role and scope of software design.

1.1. General Design Concepts

[4*, c1]

In the general sense, design can be viewed as a form of problem solving. For example, the concept of a wicked problem—a problem with no definitive solution—is interesting in terms of

understanding the limits of design. A number of other notions and concepts are also of interest in understanding design in its general sense: goals, constraints, alternatives, representations, and solutions (see Problem Solving Techniques in the Computing Foundations KA).

1.2. Context of Software Design

[4*, c3]

Software design is an important part of the software development process. To understand the role of software design, we must see how it fits in the software development life cycle. Thus, it is important to understand the major characteristics of software requirements analysis, software design, software construction, software testing, and software maintenance.

1.3. Software Design Process

[4*, c2]

Software design is generally considered a two-step process:

- Architectural design (also referred to as high-level design and top-level design) describes how software is organized into components.
- Detailed design describes the desired behavior of these components.

The output of these two processes is a set of models and artifacts that record the major decisions that have been taken, along with an explanation of the rationale for each nontrivial decision. By recording the rationale, long-term maintainability of the software product is enhanced.

1.4. Software Design Principles
[4*] [5*, c6, c7, c21] [6*, c1, c8, c9]

A *principle* is "a comprehensive and fundamental law, doctrine, or assumption" [7]. Software design principles are key notions that provide the basis for many different software design approaches and concepts. Software design principles include abstraction; coupling and cohesion; decomposition and modularization; encapsulation/information hiding; separation of interface and implementation; sufficiency, completeness, and primitiveness; and separation of concerns.

- *Abstraction* is "a view of an object that focuses on the information relevant to a particular purpose and ignores the remainder of the information" [1] (see Abstraction in the Computing Foundations KA). In the context of software design, two key abstraction mechanisms are parameterization and specification. Abstraction by parameterization abstracts from the details of data representations by representing the data as named parameters. Abstraction by specification leads to three major kinds of abstraction: procedural abstraction, data abstraction, and control (iteration) abstraction.
- *Coupling and Cohesion.* Coupling is defined as "a measure of the interdependence among modules in a computer program," whereas cohesion is defined as "a measure of the strength of association of the elements within a module" [1].
- *Decomposition and modularization.* Decomposing and modularizing means that large

software is divided into a number of smaller named components having well-defined interfaces that describe component interactions. Usually the goal is to place different functionalities and responsibilities in different components.

- *Encapsulation and information hiding* means grouping and packaging the internal details of an abstraction and making those details inaccessible to external entities.
- *Separation of interface and implementation.* Separating interface and implementation involves defining a component by specifying a public interface (known to the clients) that is separate from the details of how the component is realized (see encapsulation and information hiding above).
- *Sufficiency, completeness, and primitiveness.* Achieving sufficiency and completeness means ensuring that a software component captures all the important characteristics of an abstraction and nothing more. Primitiveness means the design should be based on patterns that are easy to implement.
- *Separation of concerns.* A concern is an "area of interest with respect to a software design" [8]. A design concern is an area of design that is relevant to one or more of its stakeholders. Each architecture view frames one or more concerns. Separating concerns by views allows interested stakeholders to focus on a few things at a time and offers a means of managing complexity [9].

2. Key Issues in Software Design

A number of key issues must be dealt with when designing software. Some are quality concerns that all software must address—for example, performance, security, reliability, usability, etc. Another important issue is how to decompose, organize, and package software components. This is so fundamental that all design approaches address it in one way or another (see section 1.4, Software Design Principles, and topic 7, Software Design Strategies and Methods). In contrast, other issues "deal with some aspect of software's behavior that is not in the application domain, but which addresses some of the supporting domains" [10]. Such issues, which often crosscut the system's functionality, have been referred to as *aspects*, which "tend not to be units of software's functional decomposition, but rather to be properties that affect the performance or semantics of the components in systemic ways" [11]. A number of these key, crosscutting issues are discussed in the following sections (presented in alphabetical order).

2.1. Concurrency
[5*, c18]

Design for concurrency is concerned with decomposing software into processes, tasks, and threads and dealing with related issues of efficiency, atomicity, synchronization, and scheduling.

2.2. Control and Handling of Events
[5*, c21]

This design issue is concerned with how to organize data and control flow as well as how to handle reactive and temporal events through various mechanisms such as implicit invocation and call-backs.

2.3. Data Persistence
[12*, c9]

This design issue is concerned with how to handle long-lived data.

2.4. Distribution of Components
[5*, c18]

This design issue is concerned with how to distribute the software across the hardware (including computer hardware and network hardware), how the components communicate, and how middleware can be used to deal with heterogeneous software.

2.5. Error and Exception Handling and Fault Tolerance
[5*, c18]

This design issue is concerned with how to prevent, tolerate, and process errors and deal with exceptional conditions.

2.6. Interaction and Presentation
[5*, c16]

This design issue is concerned with how to structure and organize interactions with users as well as the presentation of information (for example, separation of presentation and business logic using the Model-View-Controller approach). Note that this topic does not specify user interface details, which is the task of user interface design (see topic 4, User Interface Design).

2.7. Security
[5*, c12, c18] [13*, c4]

Design for security is concerned with how to prevent unauthorized disclosure, creation, change, deletion, or denial of access to information and other resources. It is also concerned with how to tolerate security-related attacks or violations by limiting damage, continuing service, speeding repair and recovery, and failing and recovering securely. Access control is a fundamental concept of security, and one should also ensure the proper use of cryptology.

3. Software Structure and Architecture

In its strict sense, a software architecture is "the set of structures needed to reason about the system, which comprise software elements, relations among them, and properties of both" [14*]. During the mid-1990s, however, software architecture started to emerge as a broader discipline that involved the study of software structures and architectures in a more generic way. This gave rise to a number of interesting concepts about software design at different levels of abstraction. Some of these concepts can be useful during the architectural design (for example, architectural styles) as well as during the detailed design (for example, design patterns). These design concepts can also be used to design families of programs (also known as product lines). Interestingly, most of these concepts can be seen as attempts to describe, and thus reuse, design knowledge.

3.1. Architectural Structures and Viewpoints
[14*, c1]

Different high-level facets of a software design can be described and documented. These facets are often called views: "A view represents a partial aspect of a software architecture that shows specific properties of a software system" [14*]. Views pertain to distinct issues associated with software design—for example, the logical view (satisfying the functional requirements) vs. the process view (concurrency issues) vs. the physical view (distribution issues) vs. the development view (how the design is broken down into implementation units with explicit representation of the dependencies among the units). Various authors use different terminologies—like behavioral vs. functional vs. structural vs. data modeling views. In summary, a software design is a multifaceted artifact produced by the design process and generally composed of relatively independent and orthogonal views.

3.2. Architectural Styles
[14*, c1, c2, c3, c4, c5]

An architectural style is "a specialization of element and relation types, together with a set of constraints on how they can be used" [14*]. An architectural style can thus be seen as providing the software's high-level organization. Various authors have identified a number of major architectural styles:

- General structures (for example, layers, pipes and filters, blackboard)
- Distributed systems (for example, client-server, three-tiers, broker)
- Interactive systems (for example, Model-View-Controller, Presentation-Abstraction-Control)
- Adaptable systems (for example, microkernel, reflection)
- Others (for example, batch, interpreters, process control, rule-based).

3.3. Design Patterns
[15*, c3, c4, c5]

Succinctly described, a pattern is "a common solution to a common problem in a given context" [16]. While architectural styles can be viewed as patterns describing the high-level organization of software, other design patterns can be used to describe details at a lower level. These lower level design patterns include the following:

- Creational patterns (for example, builder, factory, prototype, singleton)
- Structural patterns (for example, adapter, bridge, composite, decorator, façade, flyweight, proxy)
- Behavioral patterns (for example, command, interpreter, iterator, mediator, memento, observer, state, strategy, template, visitor).

3.4. Architecture Design Decisions
[5*, c6]

Architectural design is a creative process. During the design process, software designers have to make a number of fundamental decisions that profoundly affect the software and the development process. It is useful to think of the architectural design process from a decision-making perspective rather than from an activity perspective. Often, the impact on quality attributes and tradeoffs among competing quality attributes are the basis for design decisions.

3.5. Families of Programs and Frameworks
[5*, c6, c7, c16]

One approach to providing for reuse of software designs and components is to design families of programs, also known as software product lines. This can be done by identifying the commonalities among members of such families and by designing reusable and customizable components to account for the variability among family members.

In object-oriented (OO) programming, a key related notion is that of a framework: a partially completed software system that can be extended by appropriately instantiating specific extensions (such as plug-ins).

4. User Interface Design

User interface design is an essential part of the software design process. User interface design should ensure that interaction between the human and the machine provides for effective operation and control of the machine. For software to achieve its full potential, the user interface should be designed to match the skills, experience, and expectations of its anticipated users.

4.1. General User Interface Design Principles
[5*, c29-web] [17*, c2][1]

- *Learnability.* The software should be easy to learn so that the user can rapidly start working with the software.
- *User familiarity.* The interface should use terms and concepts drawn from the experiences of the people who will use the software.
- *Consistency.* The interface should be consistent so that comparable operations are activated in the same way.
- *Minimal surprise.* The behavior of software should not surprise users.
- *Recoverability.* The interface should provide mechanisms allowing users to recover from errors.
- *User guidance.* The interface should give meaningful feedback when errors occur and provide context-related help to users.
- *User diversity.* The interface should provide appropriate interaction mechanisms for diverse types of users and for users with different capabilities (blind, poor eyesight, deaf, colorblind, etc.).

4.2. User Interface Design Issues
[5*, c29-web] [17*, c2]

User interface design should solve two key issues:

- How should the user interact with the software?
- How should information from the software be presented to the user?

User interface design must integrate user interaction and information presentation. User interface design should consider a compromise between the most appropriate styles of interaction

and presentation for the software, the background and experience of the software users, and the available devices.

4.3. The Design of User Interaction Modalities
[5*, c29-web] [17*, c2]

User interaction involves issuing commands and providing associated data to the software. User interaction styles can be classified into the following primary styles:

- *Question-answer.* The interaction is essentially restricted to a single question-answer exchange between the user and the software. The user issues a question to the software, and the software returns the answer to the question.
- *Direct manipulation.* Users interact with objects on the computer screen. Direct manipulation often includes a pointing device (such as a mouse, trackball, or a finger on touch screens) that manipulates an object and invokes actions that specify what is to be done with that object.
- *Menu selection.* The user selects a command from a menu list of commands.
- *Form fill-in.* The user fills in the fields of a form. Sometimes fields include menus, in which case the form has action buttons for the user to initiate action.
- *Command language.* The user issues a command and provides related parameters to direct the software what to do.
- *Natural language.* The user issues a command in natural language. That is, the natural language is a front end to a command language and is parsed and translated into software commands.

4.4. The Design of Information Presentation
[5*, c29-web] [17*, c2]

Information presentation may be textual or graphical in nature. A good design keeps the information presentation separate from the information itself. The MVC (Model-View-Controller) approach is an effective way to keep information presentation separating from the information being presented.

---

1 Chapter 29 is a web-based chapter available at http://ifs.host.cs.st-andrews.ac.uk/Books/SE9/WebChapters/.

Software engineers also consider software response time and feedback in the design of information presentation. Response time is generally measured from the point at which a user executes a certain control action until the software responds with a response. An indication of progress is desirable while the software is preparing the response. Feedback can be provided by restating the user's input while processing is being completed.

Abstract visualizations can be used when large amounts of information are to be presented.

According to the style of information presentation, designers can also use color to enhance the interface. There are several important guidelines:

- Limit the number of colors used.
- Use color change to show the change of software status.
- Use color-coding to support the user's task.
- Use color-coding in a thoughtful and consistent way.
- Use colors to facilitate access for people with color blindness or color deficiency (e.g., use the change of color saturation and color brightness, try to avoid blue and red combinations).
- Don't depend on color alone to convey important information to users with different capabilities (blindness, poor eyesight, color-blindness, etc.).

4.5. User Interface Design Process
[5*, c29-web] [17*, c2]

User interface design is an iterative process; interface prototypes are often used to determine the features, organization, and look of the software user interface. This process includes three core activities:

- *User analysis.* In this phase, the designer analyzes the users' tasks, the working environment, other software, and how users interact with other people.
- *Software prototyping.* Developing prototype software help users to guide the evolution of the interface.
- *Interface evaluation.* Designers can observe users' experiences with the evolving interface.

4.6. Localization and Internationalization
[17*, c8, c9]

User interface design often needs to consider internationalization and localization, which are means of adapting software to the different languages, regional differences, and the technical requirements of a target market. Internationalization is the process of designing a software application so that it can be adapted to various languages and regions without major engineering changes. Localization is the process of adapting internationalized software for a specific region or language by adding locale-specific components and translating the text. Localization and internationalization should consider factors such as symbols, numbers, currency, time, and measurement units.

4.7. Metaphors and Conceptual Models
[17*, c5]

User interface designers can use metaphors and conceptual models to set up mappings between the software and some reference system known to the users in the real world, which can help the users to more readily learn and use the interface. For example, the operation "delete file" can be made into a metaphor using the icon of a trash can.

When designing a user interface, software engineers should be careful to not use more than one metaphor for each concept. Metaphors also present potential problems with respect to internationalization, since not all metaphors are meaningful or are applied in the same way within all cultures.

5. Software Design Quality Analysis and Evaluation

This section includes a number of quality analysis and evaluation topics that are specifically related to software design. (See also the Software Quality KA.)

5.1. Quality Attributes
[4*, c4]

Various attributes contribute to the quality of a software design, including various "-ilities" (maintainability, portability, testability, usability) and "-nesses" (correctness, robustness). There is an interesting distinction between quality attributes discernible at runtime (for example, performance, security, availability, functionality, usability), those not discernible at runtime (for example, modifiability, portability, reusability, testability), and those related to the architecture's intrinsic qualities (for example, conceptual integrity, correctness, completeness). (See also the Software Quality KA.)

5.2. *Quality Analysis and Evaluation Techniques*
[4*, c4] [5*, c24]

Various tools and techniques can help in analyzing and evaluating software design quality.

- Software design reviews: informal and formalized techniques to determine the quality of design artifacts (for example, architecture reviews, design reviews, and inspections; scenario-based techniques; requirements tracing). Software design reviews can also evaluate security. Aids for installation, operation, and usage (for example, manuals and help files) can be reviewed.
- Static analysis: formal or semiformal static (nonexecutable) analysis that can be used to evaluate a design (for example, fault-tree analysis or automated cross-checking). Design vulnerability analysis (for example, static analysis for security weaknesses) can be performed if security is a concern. Formal design analysis uses mathematical models that allow designers to predicate the behavior and validate the performance of the software instead of having to rely entirely on testing. Formal design analysis can be used to detect residual specification and design errors (perhaps caused by imprecision, ambiguity, and sometimes other kinds of mistakes). (See also the Software Engineering Models and Methods KA.)
- Simulation and prototyping: dynamic techniques to evaluate a design (for example, performance simulation or feasibility prototypes).

5.3. *Measures*
[4*, c4] [5*, c24]

Measures can be used to assess or to quantitatively estimate various aspects of a software design; for example, size, structure, or quality. Most measures that have been proposed depend on the approach used for producing the design. These measures are classified in two broad categories:

- Function-based (structured) design measures: measures obtained by analyzing functional decomposition; generally represented using a structure chart (sometimes called a hierarchical diagram) on which various measures can be computed.
- Object-oriented design measures: the design structure is typically represented as a class diagram, on which various measures can be computed. Measures on the properties of the internal content of each class can also be computed.

6. Software Design Notations

Many notations exist to represent software design artifacts. Some are used to describe the structural organization of a design, others to represent software behavior. Certain notations are used mostly during architectural design and others mainly during detailed design, although some notations can be used for both purposes. In addition, some notations are used mostly in the context of specific design methods (see topic 7, Software Design Strategies and Methods). Please note that software design is often accomplished using multiple notations. Here, they are categorized into notations for describing the structural (static) view vs. the behavioral (dynamic) view.

6.1. *Structural Descriptions (Static View)*
[4*, c7] [5*, c6, c7] [6*, c4, c5, c6, c7]
[12*, c7] [14*, c7]

The following notations, mostly but not always graphical, describe and represent the structural aspects of a software design—that is, they are used to describe the major components and how they are interconnected (static view):

- Architecture description languages (ADLs): textual, often formal, languages used to describe software architecture in terms of components and connectors.
- Class and object diagrams: used to represent a set of classes (and objects) and their interrelationships.
- Component diagrams: used to represent a set of components ("physical and replaceable part[s] of a system that [conform] to and [provide] the realization of a set of interfaces" [18]) and their interrelationships.
- Class responsibility collaborator cards (CRCs): used to denote the names of components (class), their responsibilities, and their collaborating components' names.
- Deployment diagrams: used to represent a set of (physical) nodes and their interrelationships, and, thus, to model the physical aspects of software.
- Entity-relationship diagrams (ERDs): used to represent conceptual models of data stored in information repositories.
- Interface description languages (IDLs): programming-like languages used to define the interfaces (names and types of exported operations) of software components.
- Structure charts: used to describe the calling structure of programs (which modules call, and are called by, which other modules).

6.2. Behavioral Descriptions (Dynamic View)
[4*, c7, c13] [5*, c6, c7] [6*, c4, c5, c6, c7] [14*, c8]

The following notations and languages, some graphical and some textual, are used to describe the dynamic behavior of software systems and components. Many of these notations are useful mostly, but not exclusively, during detailed design. Moreover, behavioral descriptions can include a rationale for design decision such as how a design will meet security requirements.

- Activity diagrams: used to show control flow from activity to activity. Can be used to represent concurrent activities.
- Communication diagrams: used to show the interactions that occur among a group of objects; emphasis is on the objects, their links, and the messages they exchange on those links.
- Data flow diagrams (DFDs): used to show data flow among elements. A data flow diagram provides "a description based on modeling the flow of information around a network of operational elements, with each element making use of or modifying the information flowing into that element" [4*]. Data flows (and therefore data flow diagrams) can be used for security analysis, as they offer identification of possible paths for attack and disclosure of confidential information.
- Decision tables and diagrams: used to represent complex combinations of conditions and actions.
- Flowcharts: used to represent the flow of control and the associated actions to be performed.
- Sequence diagrams: used to show the interactions among a group of objects, with emphasis on the time ordering of messages passed between objects.
- State transition and state chart diagrams: used to show the control flow from state to state and how the behavior of a component changes based on its current state in a state machine.
- Formal specification languages: textual languages that use basic notions from mathematics (for example, logic, set, sequence) to rigorously and abstractly define software component interfaces and behavior, often in terms of pre- and postconditions. (See also the Software Engineering Models and Methods KA.)
- Pseudo code and program design languages (PDLs): structured programming-like languages used to describe, generally at the detailed design stage, the behavior of a procedure or method.

7. Software Design Strategies and Methods

There exist various general strategies to help guide the design process. In contrast with general strategies, methods are more specific in that they generally provide a set of notations to be used with the method, a description of the process to be used when following the method, and a set of guidelines for using the method. Such methods are useful as a common framework for teams of software engineers. (See also the Software Engineering Models and Methods KA).

7.1. General Strategies
[4*, c8, c9, c10] [12*, c7]

Some often-cited examples of general strategies useful in the design process include the divide-and-conquer and stepwise refinement strategies, top-down vs. bottom-up strategies, and strategies making use of heuristics, use of patterns and pattern languages, and use of an iterative and incremental approach.

7.2. Function-Oriented (Structured) Design
[4*, c13]

This is one of the classical methods of software design, where decomposition centers on identifying the major software functions and then elaborating and refining them in a hierarchical top-down manner. Structured design is generally used after structured analysis, thus producing (among other things) data flow diagrams and associated process descriptions. Researchers have proposed various strategies (for example, transformation analysis, transaction analysis) and heuristics (for example, fan-in/fan-out, scope of effect vs. scope of control) to transform a DFD into a software architecture generally represented as a structure chart.

7.3. Object-Oriented Design
[4*, c16]

Numerous software design methods based on objects have been proposed. The field has evolved from the early object-oriented (OO) design of the mid-1980s (noun = object; verb = method; adjective = attribute), where inheritance and polymorphism play a key role, to the field of component-based design, where metainformation can be defined and accessed (through reflection, for example). Although OO design's roots stem from the concept of data abstraction, responsibility-driven design has been proposed as an alternative approach to OO design.

7.4. Data Structure-Centered Design
[4*, c14, c15]

Data structure-centered design starts from the data structures a program manipulates rather than from the function it performs. The software engineer first describes the input and output data structures and then develops the program's control structure based on these data structure diagrams. Various heuristics have been proposed to deal with special cases—for example, when there is a mismatch between the input and output structures.

7.5. Component-Based Design (CBD)
[4*, c17]

A software component is an independent unit, having well-defined interfaces and dependencies that can be composed and deployed independently. Component-based design addresses issues related to providing, developing, and integrating such components in order to improve reuse. Reused and off-the-shelf software components should meet the same security requirements as new software. Trust management is a design concern; components treated as having a certain degree of trustworthiness should not depend on less trustworthy components or services.

7.6. Other Methods
[5*, c19, c21]

Other interesting approaches also exist (see the Software Engineering Models and Methods KA). Iterative and adaptive methods implement software increments and reduce emphasis on rigorous software requirement and design.

Aspect-oriented design is a method by which software is constructed using aspects to implement the crosscutting concerns and extensions that are identified during the software requirements process. Service-oriented architecture is a way to build distributed software using web services executed on distributed computers. Software systems are often constructed by using services from different providers because standard protocols (such as HTTP, HTTPS, SOAP) have been designed to support service communication and service information exchange.

8. Software Design Tools

[14*, c10, Appendix A]

Software design tools can be used to support the creation of the software design artifacts during the software development process. They can support part or whole of the following activities:

- to translate the requirements model into a design representation;
- to provide support for representing functional components and their interface(s);
- to implement heuristics refinement and partitioning;
- to provide guidelines for quality assessment.

MATRIX OF TOPICS VS. REFERENCE MATERIAL

	Budgen 2003 [4*]	Sommerville 2011 [5*]	Page-Jones 1999 [6*]	Brookshear 2008 [12*]	Allen 2008 [13*]	Clements et al. 2010 [14*]	Gamma et al. 1994 [15*]	Nielsen 1993 [17*]
1. Software Design Fundamentals								
1.1. General Design Concepts	c1							
1.2. The Context of Software Design	c3							
1.3. The Software Design Process	c2							
1.4. Software Design Principles	c1	c6, c7, c21	c1, c8, c9					
2. Key Issues in Software Design								
2.1. Concurrency		c18						
2.2. Control and Handling of Events		c21						
2.3. Data Persistence				c9				
2.4. Distribution of Components		c18						
2.5. Error and Exception Handling and Fault Tolerance		c18						
2.6. Interaction and Presentation		c16						
2.7. Security		c12, c18			c4			
3. Software Structure and Architecture								
3.1. Architectural Structures and Viewpoints						c1		
3.2. Architectural Styles						c1, c2, c3, c4, c5		
3.3. Design Patterns							c3, c4, c5	

	Budgen 2003 [4*]	Sommerville 2011 [5*]	Page-Jones 1999 [6*]	Brookshear 2008 [12*]	Allen 2008 [13*]	Clements et al. 2010 [14*]	Gamma et al. 1994 [15*]	Nielsen 1993 [17*]
3.4. Architecture Design Decisions		c6						
3.5. Families of Programs and Frameworks		c6, c7, c16						
4. User Interface Design								
4.1. General User Interface Design Principle		c29-web						c2
4.2. User Interface Design Issues		c29-web						
4.3. The Design of User Interaction Modalities		c29-web						
4.4. The Design of Information Presentation		c29-web						
4.5. User Interface Design Process		c29-web						
4.6. Localization and Internationalization								c8, c9
4.7. Metaphors and Conceptual Models								c5
5. Software Design Quality Analysis and Evaluation								
5.1. Quality Attributes	c4							
5.2. Quality Analysis and Evaluation Techniques	c4	c24						
5.3. Measures	c4	c24						

	Budgen 2003 [4*]	Sommerville 2011 [5*]	Page-Jones 1999 [6*]	Brookshear 2008 [12*]	Allen 2008 [13*]	Clements et al. 2010 [14*]	Gamma et al. 1994 [15*]	Nielsen 1993 [17*]
6. Software Design Notations								
6.1. Structural Descriptions (Static View)	c7	c6, c7	c4, c5, c6, c7	c7			c7	
6.2. Behavioral Descriptions (Dynamic View)	c7, c13, c18	c6, c7	c4, c5, c6, c7				c8	
7. Software Design Strategies and Methods								
7.1. General Strategies	c8, c9, c10			c7				
7.2. Function-Oriented (Structured) Design	c13							
7.3. Object-Oriented Design	c16							
7.4. Data Structure-Centered Design	c14, c15							
7.5. Component-Based Design (CBD)	c17							
7.6. Other Methods		c19, c21						
8. Software Design Tools						c10, App. A		

FURTHER READINGS

Roger Pressman, *Software Engineering: A Practitioner's Approach (Seventh Edition)* [19].

For roughly three decades, Roger Pressman's *Software Engineering: A Practitioner's Approach* has been one of the world's leading textbooks in software engineering. Notably, this complementary textbook to [5*] comprehensively presents software design—including design concepts, architectural design, component-level design, user interface design, pattern-based design, and web application design.

"The 4+1 View Model of Architecture" [20].

The seminal paper "The 4+1 View Model" organizes a description of a software architecture using five concurrent views. The four views of the model are the logical view, the development view, the process view, and the physical view. In addition, selected use cases or scenarios are utilized to illustrate the architecture. Hence, the model contains 4+1 views. The views are used to describe the software as envisioned by different stakeholders—such as end-users, developers, and project managers.

Len Bass, Paul Clements, and Rick Kazman, *Software Architecture in Practice* [21].

This book introduces the concepts and best practices of software architecture, meaning how software is structured and how the software's components interact. Drawing on their own experience, the authors cover the essential technical topics for designing, specifying, and validating software architectures. They also emphasize the importance of the business context in which large software is designed. Their aim is to present software architecture in a real-world setting, reflecting both the opportunities and constraints that organizations encounter. This is one of the best books currently available on software architecture.

REFERENCES

[1] *ISO/IEC/IEEE 24765:2010 Systems and Software Engineering—Vocabulary*, ISO/IEC/IEEE, 2010.

[2] *IEEE Std. 12207-2008 (a.k.a. ISO/IEC 12207:2008) Standard for Systems and Software Engineering—Software Life Cycle Processes*, IEEE, 2008.

[3] T. DeMarco, "The Paradox of Software Architecture and Design," Stevens Prize Lecture, 1999.

[4*] D. Budgen, *Software Design*, 2nd ed., Addison-Wesley, 2003.

[5*] I. Sommerville, *Software Engineering*, 9th ed., Addison-Wesley, 2011.

[6*] M. Page-Jones, *Fundamentals of Object-Oriented Design in UML*, 1st ed., Addison-Wesley, 1999.

[7] *Merriam-Webster's Collegiate Dictionary*, 11th ed., 2003.

[8] *IEEE Std. 1069-2009 Standard for Information Technology—Systems Design—Software Design Descriptions*, IEEE, 2009.

[9] *ISO/IEC 42010:2011 Systems and Software Engineering—Recommended Practice for Architectural Description of Software-Intensive Systems*, ISO/IEC, 2011.

[10] J. Bosch, *Design and Use of Software Architectures: Adopting and Evolving a Product-Line Approach*, ACM Press, 2000.

[11] G. Kiczales et al., "Aspect-Oriented Programming," *Proc. 11th European Conf. Object-Oriented Programming* (ECOOP 97), Springer, 1997.

[12*] J.G. Brookshear, *Computer Science: An Overview*, 10th ed., Addison-Wesley, 2008.

[13*] J.H. Allen et al., *Software Security Engineering: A Guide for Project Managers*, Addison-Wesley, 2008.

[14*] P. Clements et al., *Documenting Software Architectures: Views and Beyond*, 2nd ed., Pearson Education, 2010.

[15*] E. Gamma et al., *Design Patterns: Elements of Reusable Object-Oriented Software*, 1st ed., Addison-Wesley Professional, 1994.

[16] I. Jacobson, G. Booch, and J. Rumbaugh, *The Unified Software Development Process*, Addison-Wesley Professional, 1999.

[17*] J. Nielsen, *Usability Engineering*, Morgan Kaufmann, 1993.

[18] G. Booch, J. Rumbaugh, and I. Jacobson, The Unified Modeling Language User Guide, Addison-Wesley, 1999.

[19] R.S. Pressman, *Software Engineering: A Practitioner's Approach*, 7th ed., McGraw-Hill, 2010.

[20] P.B. Kruchten, "The 4+1 View Model of Architecture," *IEEE Software,* vol. 12, no. 6, 1995, pp. 42–55.

[21] L. Bass, P. Clements, and R. Kazman, *Software Architecture in Practice*, 3rd ed., Addison-Wesley Professional, 2013.

CHAPTER 3

SOFTWARE CONSTRUCTION

ACRONYMS

API	Application Programming Interface
COTS	Commercial Off-the-Shelf
GUI	Graphical User Interface
IDE	Integrated Development Environment
OMG	Object Management Group
POSIX	Portable Operating System Interface
TDD	Test-Driven Development
UML	Unified Modeling Language

INTRODUCTION

The term software construction refers to the detailed creation of working software through a combination of coding, verification, unit testing, integration testing, and debugging.

The Software Construction knowledge area (KA) is linked to all the other KAs, but it is most strongly linked to Software Design and Software Testing because the software construction process involves significant software design and testing. The process uses the design output and provides an input to testing ("design" and "testing" in this case referring to the activities, not the KAs). Boundaries between design, construction, and testing (if any) will vary depending on the software life cycle processes that are used in a project.

Although some detailed design may be performed prior to construction, much design work is performed during the construction activity. Thus, the Software Construction KA is closely linked to the Software Design KA.

Throughout construction, software engineers both unit test and integration test their work.

Thus, the Software Construction KA is closely linked to the Software Testing KA as well.

Software construction typically produces the highest number of configuration items that need to be managed in a software project (source files, documentation, test cases, and so on). Thus, the Software Construction KA is also closely linked to the Software Configuration Management KA.

While software quality is important in all the KAs, code is the ultimate deliverable of a software project, and thus the Software Quality KA is closely linked to the Software Construction KA.

Since software construction requires knowledge of algorithms and of coding practices, it is closely related to the Computing Foundations KA, which is concerned with the computer science foundations that support the design and construction of software products. It is also related to project management, insofar as the management of construction can present considerable challenges.

BREAKDOWN OF TOPICS FOR SOFTWARE CONSTRUCTION

Figure 3.1 gives a graphical representation of the top-level decomposition of the breakdown for the Software Construction KA.

1. Software Construction Fundamentals

Software construction fundamentals include

- minimizing complexity
- anticipating change
- constructing for verification
- reuse
- standards in construction.

The first four concepts apply to design as well as to construction. The following sections define

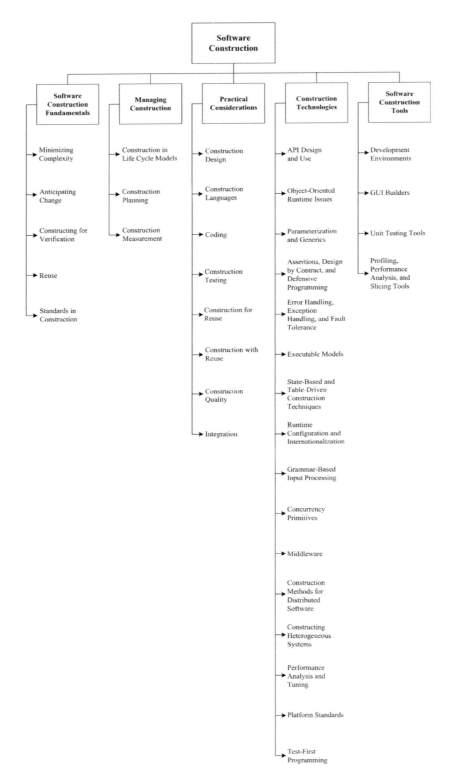

Figure 3.1. Breakdown of Topics for the Software Construction KA

these concepts and describe how they apply to construction.

1.1. Minimizing Complexity

[1*]

Most people are limited in their ability to hold complex structures and information in their working memories, especially over long periods of time. This proves to be a major factor influencing how people convey intent to computers and leads to one of the strongest drives in software construction: *minimizing* complexity. The need to reduce complexity applies to essentially every aspect of software construction and is particularly critical to testing of software constructions.

In software construction, reduced complexity is achieved through emphasizing code creation that is simple and readable rather than clever. It is accomplished through making use of standards (see section 1.5, Standards in Construction), modular design (see section 3.1, Construction Design), and numerous other specific techniques (see section 3.3, Coding). It is also supported by construction-focused quality techniques (see section 3.7, Construction Quality).

1.2. Anticipating Change

[1*]

Most software will change over time, and the anticipation of *change* drives many aspects of software construction; changes in the environments in which software operates also affect software in diverse ways.

Anticipating change helps software engineers build extensible software, which means they can enhance a software product without disrupting the underlying structure.

Anticipating change is supported by many specific techniques (see section 3.3, Coding).

1.3. Constructing for Verification

[1*]

Constructing for verification means building software in such a way that faults can be readily found by the software engineers writing the software as well as by the testers and users during independent testing and operational activities. Specific techniques that support constructing for verification include following coding standards to support code reviews and unit testing, organizing code to support automated testing, and restricting the use of complex or hard-to-understand language structures, among others.

1.4. Reuse

[2*]

Reuse refers to using existing assets in solving different problems. In software construction, typical assets that are reused include libraries, modules, components, source code, and commercial off-the-shelf (COTS) assets. Reuse is best practiced systematically, according to a well-defined, repeatable process. Systematic reuse can enable significant software productivity, quality, and cost improvements.

Reuse has two closely related facets: "construction for reuse" and "construction with reuse." The former means to create reusable software assets, while the latter means to reuse software assets in the construction of a new solution. Reuse often transcends the boundary of projects, which means reused assets can be constructed in other projects or organizations.

1.5. Standards in Construction

[1*]

Applying external or internal development standards during construction helps achieve a project's objectives for efficiency, quality, and cost. Specifically, the choices of allowable programming language subsets and usage standards are important aids in achieving higher security.

Standards that directly affect construction issues include

- communication methods (for example, standards for document formats and contents)
- programming languages (for example, language standards for languages like Java and C++)
- coding standards (for example, standards for naming conventions, layout, and indentation)
- platforms (for example, interface standards for operating system calls)

- tools (for example, diagrammatic standards for notations like UML (Unified Modeling Language)).

Use of external standards. Construction depends on the use of external standards for construction languages, construction tools, technical interfaces, and interactions between the Software Construction KA and other KAs. Standards come from numerous sources, including hardware and software interface specifications (such as the Object Management Group (OMG)) and international organizations (such as the IEEE or ISO).

Use of internal standards. Standards may also be created on an organizational basis at the corporate level or for use on specific projects. These standards support coordination of group activities, minimizing complexity, anticipating change, and constructing for verification.

2. Managing Construction

2.1. Construction in Life Cycle Models
[1*]

Numerous models have been created to develop software; some emphasize construction more than others.

Some models are more linear from the construction point of view—such as the waterfall and staged-delivery life cycle models. These models treat construction as an activity that occurs only after significant prerequisite work has been completed—including detailed requirements work, extensive design work, and detailed planning. The more linear approaches tend to emphasize the activities that precede construction (requirements and design) and to create more distinct separations between activities. In these models, the main emphasis of construction may be coding.

Other models are more iterative—such as evolutionary prototyping and agile development. These approaches tend to treat construction as an activity that occurs concurrently with other software development activities (including requirements, design, and planning) or that overlaps them. These approaches tend to mix design, coding, and testing activities, and they often treat the combination of activities as construction (see the Software Management and Software Process KAs).

Consequently, what is considered to be "construction" depends to some degree on the life cycle model used. In general, software construction is mostly coding and debugging, but it also involves construction planning, detailed design, unit testing, integration testing, and other activities.

2.2. Construction Planning
[1*]

The choice of construction method is a key aspect of the construction-planning activity. The choice of construction method affects the extent to which construction prerequisites are performed, the order in which they are performed, and the degree to which they should be completed before construction work begins.

The approach to construction affects the project team's ability to reduce complexity, anticipate change, and construct for verification. Each of these objectives may also be addressed at the process, requirements, and design levels—but they will be influenced by the choice of construction method.

Construction planning also defines the order in which components are created and integrated, the integration strategy (for example, phased or incremental integration), the software quality management processes, the allocation of task assignments to specific software engineers, and other tasks, according to the chosen method.

2.3. Construction Measurement
[1*]

Numerous construction activities and artifacts can be measured—including code developed, code modified, code reused, code destroyed, code complexity, code inspection statistics, fault-fix and fault-find rates, effort, and scheduling. These measurements can be useful for purposes of managing construction, ensuring quality during construction, and improving the construction process, among other uses (see the Software Engineering Process KA for more on measurement).

3. Practical Considerations

Construction is an activity in which the software engineer has to deal with sometimes chaotic and changing real-world constraints, and he or she must do so precisely. Due to the influence of real-world constraints, construction is more driven by practical considerations than some other KAs, and software engineering is perhaps most craft-like in the construction activities.

3.1. Construction Design

[1*]

Some projects allocate considerable design activity to construction, while others allocate design to a phase explicitly focused on design. Regardless of the exact allocation, some detailed design work will occur at the construction level, and that design work tends to be dictated by constraints imposed by the real-world problem that is being addressed by the software.

Just as construction workers building a physical structure must make small-scale modifications to account for unanticipated gaps in the builder's plans, software construction workers must make modifications on a smaller or larger scale to flesh out details of the software design during construction.

The details of the design activity at the construction level are essentially the same as described in the Software Design KA, but they are applied on a smaller scale of algorithms, data structures, and interfaces.

3.2. Construction Languages

[1*]

Construction languages include all forms of communication by which a human can specify an executable problem solution to a problem. Construction languages and their implementations (for example, compilers) can affect software quality attributes of performance, reliability, portability, and so forth. They can be serious contributors to security vulnerabilities.

The simplest type of construction language is a *configuration language,* in which software engineers choose from a limited set of predefined options to create new or custom software

installations. The text-based configuration files used in both the Windows and Unix operating systems are examples of this, and the menu-style selection lists of some program generators constitute another example of a configuration language.

Toolkit languages are used to build applications out of elements in toolkits (integrated sets of application-specific reusable parts); they are more complex than configuration languages. Toolkit languages may be explicitly defined as application programming languages, or the applications may simply be implied by a toolkit's set of interfaces.

Scripting languages are commonly used kinds of application programming languages. In some scripting languages, scripts are called batch files or macros.

Programming languages are the most flexible type of construction languages. They also contain the least amount of information about specific application areas and development processes—therefore, they require the most training and skill to use effectively. The choice of programming language can have a large effect on the likelihood of vulnerabilities being introduced during coding—for example, uncritical usage of C and C++ are questionable choices from a security viewpoint.

There are three general kinds of notation used for programming languages, namely

- linguistic (e.g., C/C++, Java)
- formal (e.g., Event-B)
- visual (e.g., MatLab).

Linguistic notations are distinguished in particular by the use of textual strings to represent complex software constructions. The combination of textual strings into patterns may have a sentence-like syntax. Properly used, each such string should have a strong semantic connotation providing an immediate intuitive understanding of what will happen when the software construction is executed.

Formal notations rely less on intuitive, everyday meanings of words and text strings and more on definitions backed up by precise, unambiguous, and formal (or mathematical) definitions. Formal construction notations and formal methods are at the semantic base of most forms of system programming notations, where accuracy, time behavior, and testability are more important than ease of mapping into natural language. Formal constructions also use precisely defined ways of combining symbols that avoid the ambiguity of many natural language constructions.

Visual notations rely much less on the textual notations of linguistic and formal construction and instead rely on direct visual interpretation and placement of visual entities that represent the underlying software. Visual construction tends to be somewhat limited by the difficulty of making "complex" statements using only the arrangement of icons on a display. However, these icons can be powerful tools in cases where the primary programming task is simply to build and "adjust" a visual interface to a program, the detailed behavior of which has an underlying definition.

3.3. Coding
[1*]

The following considerations apply to the software construction coding activity:

- Techniques for creating understandable source code, including naming conventions and source code layout;
- Use of classes, enumerated types, variables, named constants, and other similar entities;
- Use of control structures;
- Handling of error conditions—both anticipated and exceptional (input of bad data, for example);
- Prevention of code-level security breaches (buffer overflows or array index bounds, for example);
- Resource usage via use of exclusion mechanisms and discipline in accessing serially reusable resources (including threads and database locks);
- Source code organization (into statements, routines, classes, packages, or other structures);
- Code documentation;
- Code tuning,

3.4. Construction Testing
[1*]

Construction involves two forms of testing, which are often performed by the software engineer who wrote the code:

- Unit testing
- Integration testing.

The purpose of construction testing is to reduce the gap between the time when faults are inserted into the code and the time when those faults are detected, thereby reducing the cost incurred to fix them. In some instances, test cases are written after code has been written. In other instances, test cases may be created before code is written.

Construction testing typically involves a subset of the various types of testing, which are described in the Software Testing KA. For instance, construction testing does not typically include system testing, alpha testing, beta testing, stress testing, configuration testing, usability testing, or other more specialized kinds of testing.

Two standards have been published on the topic of construction testing: IEEE Standard 829-1998, *IEEE Standard for Software Test Documentation,* and IEEE Standard 1008-1987, *IEEE Standard for Software Unit Testing.*

(See sections 2.1.1., Unit Testing, and 2.1.2., Integration Testing, in the Software Testing KA for more specialized reference material.)

3.5. Construction for Reuse
[2*]

Construction for reuse creates software that has the potential to be reused in the future for the present project or other projects taking a broad-based, multisystem perspective. Construction for reuse is usually based on variability analysis and design. To avoid the problem of code clones, it is desired to encapsulate reusable code fragments into well-structured libraries or components.

The tasks related to software construction for reuse during coding and testing are as follows:

- Variability implementation with mechanisms such as parameterization, conditional compilation, design patterns, and so forth.
- Variability encapsulation to make the software assets easy to configure and customize.
- Testing the variability provided by the reusable software assets.
- Description and publication of reusable software assets.

3.6. Construction with Reuse

[2*]

Construction with reuse means to create new software with the reuse of existing software assets. The most popular method of reuse is to reuse code from the libraries provided by the language, platform, tools being used, or an organizational repository. Asides from these, the applications developed today widely make use of many open-source libraries. Reused and off-the-shelf software often have the same—or better—quality requirements as newly developed software (for example, security level).

The tasks related to software construction with reuse during coding and testing are as follows:

- The selection of the reusable units, databases, test procedures, or test data.
- The evaluation of code or test reusability.
- The integration of reusable software assets into the current software.
- The reporting of reuse information on new code, test procedures, or test data.

3.7. Construction Quality

[1*]

In addition to faults resulting from requirements and design, faults introduced during construction can result in serious quality problems—for example, security vulnerabilities. This includes not only faults in security functionality but also faults elsewhere that allow bypassing of this functionality and other security weaknesses or violations.

Numerous techniques exist to ensure the quality of code as it is constructed. The primary techniques used for construction quality include

- unit testing and integration testing (see section 3.4, Construction Testing)
- test-first development (see section 2.2 in the Software Testing KA)
- use of assertions and defensive programming
- debugging
- inspections
- technical reviews, including security-oriented reviews (see section 2.3.2 in the Software Quality KA)
- static analysis (see section 2.3 of the Software Quality KA)

The specific technique or techniques selected depend on the nature of the software being constructed as well as on the skillset of the software engineers performing the construction activities. Programmers should know good practices and common vulnerabilities—for example, from widely recognized lists about common vulnerabilities. Automated static analysis of code for security weaknesses is available for several common programming languages and can be used in security-critical projects.

Construction quality activities are differentiated from other quality activities by their focus. Construction quality activities focus on code and artifacts that are closely related to code—such as detailed design—as opposed to other artifacts that are less directly connected to the code, such as requirements, high-level designs, and plans.

3.8. Integration

[1*]

A key activity during construction is the integration of individually constructed routines, classes, components, and subsystems into a single system. In addition, a particular software system may need to be integrated with other software or hardware systems.

Concerns related to construction integration include planning the sequence in which components will be integrated, identifying what hardware is needed, creating scaffolding to support interim versions of the software, determining the degree of testing and quality work performed on components before they are integrated, and determining points in the project at which interim versions of the software are tested.

Programs can be integrated by means of either the phased or the incremental approach. Phased integration, also called "big bang" integration, entails delaying the integration of component software parts until all parts intended for release in a version are complete. Incremental integration is thought to offer many advantages over the traditional phased integration—for example, easier error location, improved progress monitoring, earlier product delivery, and improved customer relations. In incremental integration, the developers write and test a program in small pieces and then combine the pieces one at a time. Additional test infrastructure, such as stubs, drivers, and mock objects, are usually needed to enable incremental integration. By building and integrating one unit at a time (for example, a class or component), the construction process can provide early feedback to developers and customers. Other advantages of incremental integration include easier error location, improved progress monitoring, more fully tested units, and so forth.

4. Construction Technologies

4.1. API Design and Use

[3*]

An application programming interface (API) is the set of signatures that are exported and available to the users of a library or a framework to write their applications. Besides signatures, an API should always include statements about the program's effects and/or behaviors (i.e., its semantics).

API design should try to make the API easy to learn and memorize, lead to readable code, be hard to misuse, be easy to extend, be complete, and maintain backward compatibility. As the APIs usually outlast their implementations for a widely used library or framework, it is desired that the API be straightforward and kept stable to facilitate the development and maintenance of the client applications.

API use involves the processes of selecting, learning, testing, integrating, and possibly extending APIs provided by a library or framework (see section 3.6, Construction with Reuse).

4.2. Object-Oriented Runtime Issues

[1*]

Object-oriented languages support a series of runtime mechanisms including polymorphism and reflection. These runtime mechanisms increase the flexibility and adaptability of object-oriented programs. Polymorphism is the ability of a language to support general operations without knowing until runtime what kind of concrete objects the software will include. Because the program does not know the exact types of the objects in advance, the exact behaviour is determined at runtime (called dynamic binding).

Reflection is the ability of a program to observe and modify its own structure and behavior at runtime. Reflection allows inspection of classes, interfaces, fields, and methods at runtime without knowing their names at compile time. It also allows instantiation at runtime of new objects and invocation of methods using parameterized class and method names.

4.3. Parameterization and Generics

[4*]

Parameterized types, also known as generics (Ada, Eiffel) and templates (C++), enable the definition of a type or class without specifying all the other types it uses. The unspecified types are supplied as parameters at the point of use. Parameterized types provide a third way (in addition to class inheritance and object composition) to compose behaviors in object-oriented software.

4.4. Assertions, Design by Contract, and Defensive Programming

[1*]

An assertion is an executable predicate that's placed in a program—usually a routine or macro—that allows runtime checks of the program. Assertions are especially useful in high-reliability programs. They enable programmers to more quickly flush out mismatched interface assumptions, errors that creep in when code is modified, and so on. Assertions are normally compiled into the code at development time and are later compiled out of the code so that they don't degrade the performance.

Design by contract is a development approach in which preconditions and postconditions are included for each routine. When preconditions and postconditions are used, each routine or class is said to form a contract with the rest of the program. Furthermore, a contract provides a precise specification of the semantics of a routine, and thus helps the understanding of its behavior. Design by contract is thought to improve the quality of software construction.

Defensive programming means to protect a routine from being broken by invalid inputs. Common ways to handle invalid inputs include checking the values of all the input parameters and deciding how to handle bad inputs. Assertions are often used in defensive programming to check input values.

4.5. Error Handling, Exception Handling, and Fault Tolerance

[1*]

The way that errors are handled affects software's ability to meet requirements related to correctness, robustness, and other nonfunctional attributes. Assertions are sometimes used to check for errors. Other error handling techniques—such as returning a neutral value, substituting the next piece of valid data, logging a warning message, returning an error code, or shutting down the software—are also used.

Exceptions are used to detect and process errors or exceptional events. The basic structure of an exception is that a routine uses *throw* to throw a detected exception and an exception handling block will *catch* the exception in a *try-catch* block. The try-catch block may process the erroneous condition in the routine or it may return control to the calling routine. Exception handling policies should be carefully designed following common principles such as including in the exception message all information that led to the exception, avoiding empty catch blocks, knowing the exceptions the library code throws, perhaps building a centralized exception reporter, and standardizing the program's use of exceptions.

Fault tolerance is a collection of techniques that increase software reliability by detecting errors and then recovering from them if possible or containing their effects if recovery is not possible. The most common fault tolerance strategies include backing up and retrying, using auxiliary code, using voting algorithms, and replacing an erroneous value with a phony value that will have a benign effect.

4.6. Executable Models

[5*]

Executable models abstract away the details of specific programming languages and decisions about the organization of the software. Different from traditional software models, a specification built in an executable modeling language like xUML (executable UML) can be deployed in various software environments without change. An executable-model compiler (transformer) can turn an executable model into an implementation using a set of decisions about the target hardware and software environment. Thus, constructing executable models can be regarded as a way of constructing executable software.

Executable models are one foundation supporting the Model-Driven Architecture (MDA) initiative of the Object Management Group (OMG). An executable model is a way to completely specify a Platform Independent Model (PIM); a PIM is a model of a solution to a problem that does not rely on any implementation technologies. Then a Platform Specific Model (PSM), which is a model that contains the details of the implementation, can be produced by weaving together the PIM and the platform on which it relies.

4.7. State-Based and Table-Driven Construction Techniques

[1*]

State-based programming, or automata-based programming, is a programming technology using finite state machines to describe program behaviours. The transition graphs of a state machine are used in all stages of software development (specification, implementation, debugging, and documentation). The main idea is to construct computer programs the same way the automation of technological processes is done. State-based programming is usually combined with object-oriented programming, forming a new composite approach called *state-based, object-oriented programming.*

A table-driven method is a schema that uses tables to look up information rather than using logic statements (such as *if* and *case*). Used in appropriate circumstances, table-driven code is simpler than complicated logic and easier to modify. When using table-driven methods, the programmer addresses two issues: what information to store in the table or tables, and how to efficiently access information in the table.

4.8. Runtime Configuration and Internationalization

[1*]

To achieve more flexibility, a program is often constructed to support late binding time of its variables. Runtime configuration is a technique that binds variable values and program settings when the program is running, usually by updating and reading configuration files in a just-in-time mode.

Internationalization is the technical activity of preparing a program, usually interactive software, to support multiple locales. The corresponding activity, *localization,* is the activity of modifying a program to support a specific local language. Interactive software may contain dozens or hundreds of prompts, status displays, help messages, error messages, and so on. The design and construction processes should accommodate string and character-set issues including which character set is to be used, what kinds of strings are used, how to maintain the strings without changing the code, and translating the strings into different languages with minimal impact on the processing code and the user interface.

4.9. Grammar-Based Input Processing

[1*] [6*]

Grammar-based input processing involves syntax analysis, or *parsing*, of the input token stream. It involves the creation of a data structure (called a *parse tree* or *syntax tree*) representing the input data. The inorder traversal of the parse tree usually gives the expression just parsed. The parser checks the symbol table for the presence of programmer-defined variables that populate the tree. After building the parse tree, the program uses it as input to the computational processes.

4.10. Concurrency Primitives

[7*]

A synchronization primitive is a programming abstraction provided by a programming language or the operating system that facilitates concurrency and synchronization. Well-known concurrency primitives include semaphores, monitors, and mutexes.

A semaphore is a protected variable or abstract data type that provides a simple but useful abstraction for controlling access to a common resource by multiple processes or threads in a concurrent programming environment.

A monitor is an abstract data type that presents a set of programmer-defined operations that are executed with mutual exclusion. A monitor contains the declaration of shared variables and procedures or functions that operate on those variables. The monitor construct ensures that only one process at a time is active within the monitor.

A mutex (mutual exclusion) is a synchronization primitive that grants exclusive access to a shared resource by only one process or thread at a time.

4.11. Middleware

[3*] [6*]

Middleware is a broad classification for software that provides services above the operating system layer yet below the application program layer. Middleware can provide runtime containers for software components to provide message passing, persistence, and a transparent location across a network. Middleware can be viewed as a connector between the components that use the middleware. Modern message-oriented middleware usually provides an Enterprise Service Bus (ESB), which supports service-oriented interaction and communication between multiple software applications.

4.12. Construction Methods for Distributed Software

[7*]

A distributed system is a collection of physically separate, possibly heterogeneous computer systems that are networked to provide the users with access to the various resources that the system maintains. Construction of distributed software is distinguished from traditional software construction by issues such as parallelism, communication, and fault tolerance.

Distributed programming typically falls into one of several basic architectural categories: client-server, 3-tier architecture, n-tier architecture, distributed objects, loose coupling, or tight coupling (see section 14.3 of the Computing Foundations KA and section 3.2 of the Software Design KA).

4.13. Constructing Heterogeneous Systems

[6*]

Heterogeneous systems consist of a variety of specialized computational units of different types, such as Digital Signal Processors (DSPs), microcontrollers, and peripheral processors. These computational units are independently controlled and communicate with one another. Embedded systems are typically heterogeneous systems.

The design of heterogeneous systems may require the combination of several specification languages in order to design different parts of the system—in other words, hardware/software codesign. The key issues include multilanguage validation, cosimulation, and interfacing.

During the hardware/software codesign, software development and virtual hardware development proceed concurrently through stepwise decomposition. The hardware part is usually simulated in field programmable gate arrays (FPGAs) or application-specific integrated circuits (ASICs). The software part is translated into a low-level programming language.

4.14. Performance Analysis and Tuning

[1*]

Code efficiency—determined by architecture, detailed design decisions, and data-structure and algorithm selection—influences an execution speed and size. Performance analysis is the investigation of a program's behavior using information gathered as the program executes, with the goal of identifying possible hot spots in the program to be improved.

Code tuning, which improves performance at the code level, is the practice of modifying correct code in ways that make it run more efficiently. Code tuning usually involves only small-scale changes that affect a single class, a single routine, or, more commonly, a few lines of code. A rich set of code tuning techniques is available, including those for tuning logic expressions, loops, data transformations, expressions, and routines. Using a low-level language is another common technique for improving some hot spots in a program.

4.15. Platform Standards

[6*] [7*]

Platform standards enable programmers to develop portable applications that can be executed in compatible environments without changes. Platform standards usually involve a set of standard services and APIs that compatible platform implementations must implement. Typical examples of platform standards are Java 2 Platform Enterprise Edition (J2EE) and the POSIX standard for operating systems (Portable Operating System Interface), which represents a set of standards implemented primarily for UNIX-based operating systems.

4.16. Test-First Programming

[1*]

Test-first programming (also known as Test-Driven Development—TDD) is a popular development style in which test cases are written prior to writing any code. Test-first programming can usually detect defects earlier and correct them more easily than traditional programming styles. Furthermore, writing test cases first forces programmers to think about requirements and design before coding, thus exposing requirements and design problems sooner.

5. Software Construction Tools

5.1. Development Environments

[1*]

A development environment, or integrated development environment (IDE), provides comprehensive facilities to programmers for software construction by integrating a set of development tools. The choices of development environments can affect the efficiency and quality of software construction.

In additional to basic code editing functions, modern IDEs often offer other features like compilation and error detection from within the editor, integration with source code control, build/test/debugging tools, compressed or outline views of programs, automated code transforms, and support for refactoring.

5.2. GUI Builders

[1*]

A GUI (Graphical User Interface) builder is a software development tool that enables the developer to create and maintain GUIs in a WYSIWYG (what you see is what you get) mode. A GUI builder usually includes a visual editor for the developer to design forms and windows and manage the layout of the widgets by dragging, dropping, and parameter setting. Some GUI builders can automatically generate the source code corresponding to the visual GUI design.

Because current GUI applications usually follow the event-driven style (in which the flow of the program is determined by events and event handling), GUI builder tools usually provide code generation assistants, which automate the most repetitive tasks required for event handling. The supporting code connects widgets with the outgoing and incoming events that trigger the functions providing the application logic.

Some modern IDEs provide integrated GUI builders or GUI builder plug-ins. There are also many standalone GUI builders.

5.3. Unit Testing Tools

[1*] [2*]

Unit testing verifies the functioning of software modules in isolation from other software elements that are separately testable (for example, classes, routines, components). Unit testing is often automated. Developers can use unit testing tools and frameworks to extend and create automated testing environment. With unit testing tools and frameworks, the developer can code criteria into the test to verify the unit's correctness under various data sets. Each individual test is implemented as an object, and a test runner runs all of the tests. During the test execution, those failed test cases will be automatically flagged and reported.

5.4. Profiling, Performance Analysis, and Slicing Tools

[1*]

Performance analysis tools are usually used to support code tuning. The most common performance analysis tools are profiling tools. An execution profiling tool monitors the code while it runs and records how many times each statement is executed or how much time the program spends on each statement or execution path. Profiling the code while it is running gives insight into how the program works, where the hot spots are, and where the developers should focus the code tuning efforts.

Program slicing involves computation of the set of program statements (i.e., the program slice) that may affect the values of specified variables at some point of interest, which is referred to as a slicing criterion. Program slicing can be used for locating the source of errors, program understanding, and optimization analysis. Program slicing tools compute program slices for various programming languages using static or dynamic analysis methods.

MATRIX OF TOPICS VS. REFERENCE MATERIAL

	McConnell 2004 [1*]	Sommerville 2011 [2*]	Clements et al. 2010 [3*]	Gamma et al. 1994 [4*]	Mellor and Balcer 2002 [5*]	Null and Lobur 2006 [6*]	Silberschatz et al. 2008 [7*]
1. Software Construction Fundamentals							
1.1. Minimizing Complexity	c2, c3, c7-c9, c24, c27, c28, c31, c32, c34						
1.2. Anticipating Change	c3–c5, c24, c31, c32, c34						
1.3. Constructing for Verification	c8, c20–c23, c31, c34						
1.4. Reuse		c16					
1.5. Standards in Construction	c4						
2. Managing Construction							
2.1. Construction in Life Cycle Models	c2, c3, c27, c29						
2.2. Construction Planning	c3, c4, c21, c27–c29						
2.3. Construction Measurement	c25, c28						
3. Practical Considerations							
3.1. Construction Design	c3, c5, c24						
3.2. Construction Languages	c4						
3.3. Coding	c5–c19, c25–c26						

	McConnell 2004 [1*]	Sommerville 2011 [2*]	Clements et al. 2010 [3*]	Gamma et al. 1994 [4*]	Mellor and Balcer 2002 [5*]	Null and Lobur 2006 [6*]	Silberschatz et al. 2008 [7*]
3.4. Construction Testing	c22, c23						
3.5. Construction for Reuse		c16					
3.6. Construction with Reuse		c16					
3.7. Construction Quality	c8, c20–c25						
3.8. Integration	c29						
4. Construction Technologies							
4.1. API Design and Use			c7				
4.2. Object-Oriented Runtime Issues	c6, c7						
4.3. Parameterization and Generics				c1			
4.4. Assertions, Design by Contract, and Defensive Programming	c8, c9						
4.5. Error Handling, Exception Handling, and Fault Tolerance	c3, c8						
4.6. Executable Models					c1		
4.7. State-Based and Table-Driven Construction Techniques	c18						
4.8. Runtime Configuration and Internationalization	c3, c10						
4.9. Grammar-Based Input Processing	c5					c8	

	McConnell 2004 [1*]	Sommerville 2011 [2*]	Clements et al. 2010 [3*]	Gamma et al. 1994 [4*]	Mellor and Balcer 2002 [5*]	Null and Lobur 2006 [6*]	Silberschatz et al. 2008 [7*]
4.10. Concurrency Primitives							c6
4.11. Middleware			c1			c8	
4.12. Construction Methods for Distributed Software							c2
4.13. Constructing Heterogeneous Systems						c9	
4.14. Performance Analysis and Tuning	c25, c26						
4.15. Platform Standards						c10	c1
4.16. Test-First Programming	c22						
5. Construction Tools							
5.1. Development Environments	c30						
5.2. GUI Builders	c30						
5.3. Unit Testing Tools	c22	c8					
5.4. Profiling, Performance Analysis, and Slicing Tools	c25, c26						

FURTHER READINGS

IEEE Std. 1517-2010 Standard for Information Technology—System and Software Life Cycle Processes—Reuse Processes, IEEE, 2010 [8].

This standard specifies the processes, activities, and tasks to be applied during each phase of the software life cycle to enable a software product to be constructed from reusable assets. It covers the concept of reuse-based development and the processes of construction for reuse and construction with reuse.

IEEE Std. 12207-2008 (a.k.a. ISO/IEC 12207:2008) Standard for Systems and Software Engineering—Software Life Cycle Processes, IEEE, 2008 [9].

This standard defines a series of software development processes, including software construction process, software integration process, and software reuse process.

REFERENCES

[1*] S. McConnell, *Code Complete*, 2nd ed., Microsoft Press, 2004.

[2*] I. Sommerville, *Software Engineering*, 9th ed., Addison-Wesley, 2011.

[3*] P. Clements et al., *Documenting Software Architectures: Views and Beyond*, 2nd ed., Pearson Education, 2010.

[4*] E. Gamma et al., *Design Patterns: Elements of Reusable Object-Oriented Software*, 1st ed., Addison-Wesley Professional, 1994.

[5*] S.J. Mellor and M.J. Balcer, *Executable UML: A Foundation for Model-Driven Architecture*, 1st ed., Addison-Wesley, 2002.

[6*] L. Null and J. Lobur, *The Essentials of Computer Organization and Architecture*, 2nd ed., Jones and Bartlett Publishers, 2006.

[7*] A. Silberschatz, P.B. Galvin, and G. Gagne, *Operating System Concepts*, 8th ed., Wiley, 2008.

[8] *IEEE Std. 1517-2010 Standard for Information Technology—System and Software Life Cycle Processes—Reuse Processes*, IEEE, 2010.

[9] *IEEE Std. 12207-2008 (a.k.a. ISO/IEC 12207:2008) Standard for Systems and Software Engineering—Software Life Cycle Processes*, IEEE, 2008.

CHAPTER 4

SOFTWARE TESTING

ACRONYMS

API	Application Program Interface
TDD	Test-Driven Development
TTCN3	Testing and Test Control Notation Version 3
XP	Extreme Programming

INTRODUCTION

Software testing consists of the *dynamic* verification that a program provides *expected* behaviors on a *finite* set of test cases, suitably *selected* from the usually infinite execution domain.

In the above definition, italicized words correspond to key issues in describing the Software Testing knowledge area (KA):

- *Dynamic:* This term means that testing always implies executing the program on selected inputs. To be precise, the input value alone is not always sufficient to specify a test, since a complex, nondeterministic system might react to the same input with different behaviors, depending on the system state. In this KA, however, the term "input" will be maintained, with the implied convention that its meaning also includes a specified input state in those cases for which it is important. Static techniques are different from and complementary to dynamic testing. Static techniques are covered in the Software Quality KA. It is worth noting that terminology is not uniform among different communities and some use the term "testing" also in reference to static techniques.
- *Finite:* Even in simple programs, so many test cases are theoretically possible that exhaustive testing could require months or years to execute. This is why, in practice, a complete set of tests can generally be considered infinite, and testing is conducted on a subset of all possible tests, which is determined by risk and prioritization criteria. Testing always implies a tradeoff between limited resources and schedules on the one hand and inherently unlimited test requirements on the other.
- *Selected:* The many proposed test techniques differ essentially in how the test set is selected, and software engineers must be aware that different selection criteria may yield vastly different degrees of effectiveness. How to identify the most suitable selection criterion under given conditions is a complex problem; in practice, risk analysis techniques and software engineering expertise are applied.
- *Expected:* It must be possible, although not always easy, to decide whether the observed outcomes of program testing are acceptable or not; otherwise, the testing effort is useless. The observed behavior may be checked against user needs (commonly referred to as testing for validation), against a specification (testing for verification), or, perhaps, against the anticipated behavior from implicit requirements or expectations (see Acceptance Tests in the Software Requirements KA).

In recent years, the view of software testing has matured into a constructive one. Testing is no longer seen as an activity that starts only after the coding phase is complete with the limited purpose of detecting failures. Software testing is, or should be, pervasive throughout the entire development and maintenance life cycle. Indeed, planning for software testing should start with the early stages of the software requirements process,

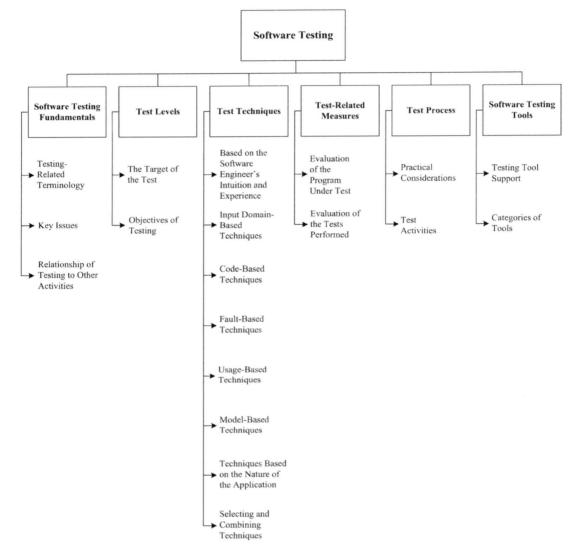

Figure 4.1. Breakdown of Topics for the Software Testing KA

and test plans and procedures should be systematically and continuously developed—and possibly refined—as software development proceeds. These test planning and test designing activities provide useful input for software designers and help to highlight potential weaknesses, such as design oversights/contradictions, or omissions/ambiguities in the documentation.

For many organizations, the approach to software quality is one of prevention: it is obviously much better to prevent problems than to correct them. Testing can be seen, then, as a means for providing information about the functionality

and quality attributes of the software and also for identifying faults in those cases where error prevention has not been effective. It is perhaps obvious but worth recognizing that software can still contain faults, even after completion of an extensive testing activity. Software failures experienced after delivery are addressed by corrective maintenance. Software maintenance topics are covered in the Software Maintenance KA.

In the Software Quality KA (see Software Quality Management Techniques), software quality management techniques are notably categorized into static techniques (no code execution) and dynamic techniques (code execution). Both categories are useful. This KA focuses on dynamic techniques.

Software testing is also related to software construction (see Construction Testing in the Software Construction KA). In particular, unit and integration testing are intimately related to software construction, if not part of it.

BREAKDOWN OF TOPICS FOR SOFTWARE TESTING

The breakdown of topics for the Software Testing KA is shown in Figure 4.1. A more detailed breakdown is provided in the Matrix of Topics vs. Reference Material at the end of this KA.

The first topic describes Software Testing Fundamentals. It covers the basic definitions in the field of software testing, the basic terminology and key issues, and software testing's relationship with other activities.

The second topic, Test Levels, consists of two (orthogonal) subtopics: the first subtopic lists the levels in which the testing of large software is traditionally subdivided, and the second subtopic considers testing for specific conditions or properties and is referred to as Objectives of Testing. Not all types of testing apply to every software product, nor has every possible type been listed.

The test target and test objective together determine how the test set is identified, both with regard to its consistency—*how much testing is enough for achieving the stated objective*—and to its composition—*which test cases should be selected for achieving the stated objective* (although usually "for achieving the stated objective" remains implicit and only the first part of the two italicized questions above is posed). Criteria for addressing the first question are referred to as *test adequacy criteria*, while those addressing the second question are the test *selection criteria*.

Several Test Techniques have been developed in the past few decades, and new ones are still being proposed. Generally accepted techniques are covered in the third topic.

Test-Related Measures are dealt with in the fourth topic, while the issues relative to Test Process are covered in the fifth. Finally, Software Testing Tools are presented in topic six.

1. Software Testing Fundamentals

1.1. Testing-Related Terminology

1.1.1. Definitions of Testing and Related Terminology
[1*, c1, c2] [2*, c8]

Definitions of testing and testing-related terminology are provided in the cited references and summarized as follows.

1.1.2. Faults vs. Failures
[1*, c1s5] [2*, c11]

Many terms are used in the software engineering literature to describe a malfunction: notably *fault*, *failure*, and *error*, among others. This terminology is precisely defined in [3, c2]. It is essential to clearly distinguish between the *cause* of a malfunction (for which the term fault will be used here) and an undesired effect observed in the system's delivered service (which will be called a failure). Indeed there may well be faults in the software that never manifest themselves as failures (see Theoretical and Practical Limitations of Testing in section 1.2, Key Issues). Thus testing can reveal failures, but it is the faults that can and must be removed [3]. The more generic term *defect* can be used to refer to either a fault or a failure, when the distinction is not important [3].

However, it should be recognized that the cause of a failure cannot always be unequivocally identified. No theoretical criteria exist to definitively determine, in general, the fault that caused an observed failure. It might be said that it was the fault that had to be modified to remove the failure, but other modifications might have worked just as well. To avoid ambiguity, one could refer to *failure-causing inputs* instead of faults—that is, those sets of inputs that cause a failure to appear.

1.2. Key Issues

1.2.1. Test Selection Criteria / Test Adequacy Criteria (Stopping Rules)
[1*, c1s14, c6s6, c12s7]

A test selection criterion is a means of selecting test cases or determining that a set of test cases is sufficient for a specified purpose. Test adequacy criteria can be used to decide when sufficient testing will be, or has been accomplished [4] (see Termination in section 5.1, Practical Considerations).

1.2.2. Testing Effectiveness / Objectives for Testing
[1*, c11s4, c13s11]

Testing effectiveness is determined by analyzing a set of program executions. Selection of tests to be executed can be guided by different objectives: it is only in light of the objective pursued that the effectiveness of the test set can be evaluated.

1.2.3. Testing for Defect Discovery
[1*, c1s14]

In testing for defect discovery, a successful test is one that causes the system to fail. This is quite different from testing to demonstrate that the software meets its specifications or other desired properties, in which case testing is successful if no failures are observed under realistic test cases and test environments.

1.2.4. The Oracle Problem
[1*, c1s9, c9s7]

An oracle is any human or mechanical agent that decides whether a program behaved correctly in a given test and accordingly results in a verdict of "pass" or "fail." There exist many different kinds of oracles; for example, unambiguous requirements specifications, behavioral models, and code annotations. Automation of mechanized oracles can be difficult and expensive.

1.2.5. Theoretical and Practical Limitations of Testing
[1*, c2s7]

Testing theory warns against ascribing an unjustified level of confidence to a series of successful tests. Unfortunately, most established results of testing theory are negative ones, in that they state what testing can never achieve as opposed to what is actually achieved. The most famous quotation in this regard is the Dijkstra aphorism that "program testing can be used to show the presence of bugs, but never to show their absence" [5]. The obvious reason for this is that complete testing is not feasible in realistic software. Because of this, testing must be driven based on risk [6, part 1] and can be seen as a risk management strategy.

1.2.6. The Problem of Infeasible Paths
[1*, c4s7]

Infeasible paths are control flow paths that cannot be exercised by any input data. They are a significant problem in path-based testing, particularly in automated derivation of test inputs to exercise control flow paths.

1.2.7. Testability
[1*, c17s2]

The term "software testability" has two related but different meanings: on the one hand, it refers to the ease with which a given test coverage criterion can be satisfied; on the other hand, it is defined as the likelihood, possibly measured statistically, that a set of test cases will expose a failure *if* the software is faulty. Both meanings are important.

1.3. Relationship of Testing to Other Activities

Software testing is related to, but different from, static software quality management techniques, proofs of correctness, debugging, and program construction. However, it is informative to consider testing from the point of view of software quality analysts and of certifiers.

- Testing vs. Static Software Quality Management Techniques (see Software Quality Management Techniques in the Software Quality KA [1*, c12]).
- Testing vs. Correctness Proofs and Formal Verification (see the Software Engineering Models and Methods KA [1*, c17s2]).
- Testing vs. Debugging (see Construction Testing in the Software Construction KA and Debugging Tools and Techniques in the Computing Foundations KA [1*, c3s6]).

• Testing vs. Program Construction (see Construction Testing in the Software Construction KA [1*, c3s2]).

2. Test Levels

Software testing is usually performed at different *levels* throughout the development and maintenance processes. Levels can be distinguished based on the object of testing, which is called the *target*, or on the purpose, which is called the *objective* (of the test level).

2.1. The Target of the Test

[1*, c1s13] [2*, c8s1]

The target of the test can vary: a single module, a group of such modules (related by purpose, use, behavior, or structure), or an entire system. Three test stages can be distinguished: unit, integration, and system. These three test stages do not imply any process model, nor is any one of them assumed to be more important than the other two.

2.1.1. Unit Testing

[1*, c3] [2*, c8]

Unit testing verifies the functioning in isolation of software elements that are separately testable. Depending on the context, these could be the individual subprograms or a larger component made of highly cohesive units. Typically, unit testing occurs with access to the code being tested and with the support of debugging tools. The programmers who wrote the code typically, but not always, conduct unit testing.

2.1.2. Integration Testing

[1*, c7] [2*, c8]

Integration testing is the process of verifying the interactions among software components. Classical integration testing strategies, such as top-down and bottom-up, are often used with hierarchically structured software.

Modern, systematic integration strategies are typically architecture-driven, which involves incrementally integrating the software components or subsystems based on identified functional threads. Integration testing is often an ongoing activity at each stage of development during which software engineers abstract away lower-level perspectives and concentrate on the perspectives of the level at which they are integrating. For other than small, simple software, incremental integration testing strategies are usually preferred to putting all of the components together at once—which is often called "big bang" testing.

2.1.3. System Testing

[1*, c8] [2*, c8]

System testing is concerned with testing the behavior of an entire system. Effective unit and integration testing will have identified many of the software defects. System testing is usually considered appropriate for assessing the non-functional system requirements—such as security, speed, accuracy, and reliability (see Functional and Non-Functional Requirements in the Software Requirements KA and Software Quality Requirements in the Software Quality KA). External interfaces to other applications, utilities, hardware devices, or the operating environments are also usually evaluated at this level.

2.2. Objectives of Testing

[1*, c1s7]

Testing is conducted in view of specific objectives, which are stated more or less explicitly and with varying degrees of precision. Stating the objectives of testing in precise, quantitative terms supports measurement and control of the test process.

Testing can be aimed at verifying different properties. Test cases can be designed to check that the functional specifications are correctly implemented, which is variously referred to in the literature as conformance testing, correctness testing, or functional testing. However, several other nonfunctional properties may be tested as well—including performance, reliability, and usability, among many others (see Models and Quality Characteristics in the Software Quality KA).

Other important objectives for testing include but are not limited to reliability measurement, identification of security vulnerabilities, usability evaluation, and software acceptance, for which different approaches would be taken. Note that, in general, the test objectives vary with the test target; different purposes are addressed at different levels of testing.

The subtopics listed below are those most often cited in the literature. Note that some kinds of testing are more appropriate for custom-made software packages—installation testing, for example—and others for consumer products, like beta testing.

2.2.1. Acceptance / Qualification Testing
[1*, c1s7] [2*, c8s4]

Acceptance / qualification testing determines whether a system satisfies its acceptance criteria, usually by checking desired system behaviors against the customer's requirements. The customer or a customer's representative thus specifies or directly undertakes activities to check that their requirements have been met, or in the case of a consumer product, that the organization has satisfied the stated requirements for the target market. This testing activity may or may not involve the developers of the system.

2.2.2. Installation Testing
[1*, c12s2]

Often, after completion of system and acceptance testing, the software is verified upon installation in the target environment. Installation testing can be viewed as system testing conducted in the operational environment of hardware configurations and other operational constraints. Installation procedures may also be verified.

2.2.3. Alpha and Beta Testing
[1*, c13s7, c16s6] [2*, c8s4]

Before software is released, it is sometimes given to a small, selected group of potential users for trial use (*alpha* testing) and/or to a larger set of representative users (*beta* testing). These users report problems with the product. Alpha and beta testing are often uncontrolled and are not always referred to in a test plan.

2.2.4. Reliability Achievement and Evaluation
[1*, c15] [2*, c15s2]

Testing improves reliability by identifying and correcting faults. In addition, statistical measures of reliability can be derived by randomly generating test cases according to the operational profile of the software (see Operational Profile in section 3.5, Usage-Based Techniques). The latter approach is called *operational testing*. Using reliability growth models, both objectives can be pursued together [3] (see *Life* Test, Reliability Evaluation in section 4.1, Evaluation of the Program under Test).

2.2.5. Regression Testing
[1*, c8s11, c13s3]

According to [7], regression testing is the "selective retesting of a system or component to verify that modifications have not caused unintended effects and that the system or component still complies with its specified requirements." In practice, the approach is to show that software still passes previously passed tests in a test suite (in fact, it is also sometimes referred to as nonregression testing). For incremental development, the purpose of regression testing is to show that software behavior is unchanged by incremental changes to the software, except insofar as it should. In some cases, a tradeoff must be made between the assurance given by regression testing every time a change is made and the resources required to perform the regression tests, which can be quite time consuming due to the large number of tests that may be executed. Regression testing involves selecting, minimizing, and/or prioritizing a subset of the test cases in an existing test suite [8]. Regression testing can be conducted at each of the test levels described in section 2.1, The Target of the Test, and may apply to functional and nonfunctional testing.

2.2.6. Performance Testing
[1*, c8s6]

Performance testing verifies that the software meets the specified performance requirements and assesses performance characteristics—for instance, capacity and response time.

2.2.7. Security Testing

[1*, c8s3] [2*, c11s4]

Security testing is focused on the verification that the software is protected from external attacks. In particular, security testing verifies the confidentiality, integrity, and availability of the systems and its data. Usually, security testing includes verification against misuse and abuse of the software or system (negative testing).

2.2.8. Stress Testing

[1*, c8s8]

Stress testing exercises software at the maximum design load, as well as beyond it, with the goal of determining the behavioral limits, and to test defense mechanisms in critical systems.

2.2.9. Back-to-Back Testing

[7]

IEEE/ISO/IEC Standard 24765 defines back-to-back testing as "testing in which two or more variants of a program are executed with the same inputs, the outputs are compared, and errors are analyzed in case of discrepancies."

2.2.10. Recovery Testing

[1*, c14s2]

Recovery testing is aimed at verifying software restart capabilities after a system crash or other "disaster."

2.2.11. Interface Testing

[2*, c8s1.3] [9*, c4s4.5]

Interface defects are common in complex systems. Interface testing aims at verifying whether the components interface correctly to provide the correct exchange of data and control information. Usually the test cases are generated from the interface specification. A specific objective of interface testing is to simulate the use of APIs by end-user applications. This involves the generation of parameters of the API calls, the setting of external environment conditions, and the definition of internal data that affect the API.

2.2.12. Configuration Testing

[1*, c8s5]

In cases where software is built to serve different users, configuration testing verifies the software under different specified configurations.

2.2.13. Usability and Human Computer Interaction Testing

[10*, c6]

The main task of usability and human computer interaction testing is to evaluate how easy it is for end users to learn and to use the software. In general, it may involve testing the software functions that supports user tasks, documentation that aids users, and the ability of the system to recover from user errors (see User Interface Design in the Software Design KA).

3. Test Techniques

One of the aims of testing is to detect as many failures as possible. Many techniques have been developed to do this [6, part 4]. These techniques attempt to "break" a program by being as systematic as possible in identifying inputs that will produce representative program behaviors; for instance, by considering subclasses of the input domain, scenarios, states, and data flows.

The classification of testing techniques presented here is based on how tests are generated: from the software engineer's intuition and experience, the specifications, the code structure, the real or imagined faults to be discovered, predicted usage, models, or the nature of the application. One category deals with the combined use of two or more techniques.

Sometimes these techniques are classified as *white-box* (also called *glass-box*), if the tests are based on information about how the software has been designed or coded, or as *black-box* if the test cases rely only on the input/output behavior of the software. The following list includes those testing techniques that are commonly used, but some practitioners rely on some of the techniques more than others.

3.1. Based on the Software Engineer's Intuition and Experience

3.1.1. Ad Hoc

Perhaps the most widely practiced technique is ad hoc testing: tests are derived relying on the software engineer's skill, intuition, and experience with similar programs. Ad hoc testing can be useful for identifying tests cases that not easily generated by more formalized techniques.

3.1.2. Exploratory Testing

Exploratory testing is defined as simultaneous learning, test design, and test execution [6, part 1]; that is, the tests are not defined in advance in an established test plan, but are dynamically designed, executed, and modified. The effectiveness of exploratory testing relies on the software engineer's knowledge, which can be derived from various sources: observed product behavior during testing, familiarity with the application, the platform, the failure process, the type of possible faults and failures, the risk associated with a particular product, and so on.

3.2. Input Domain-Based Techniques

3.2.1. Equivalence Partitioning
[1*, c9s4]

Equivalence partitioning involves partitioning the input domain into a collection of subsets (or equivalent classes) based on a specified criterion or relation. This criterion or relation may be different computational results, a relation based on control flow or data flow, or a distinction made between valid inputs that are accepted and processed by the system and invalid inputs, such as out of range values, that are not accepted and should generate an error message or initiate error processing. A representative set of tests (sometimes only one) is usually taken from each equivalency class.

3.2.2. Pairwise Testing
[1*, c9s3]

Test cases are derived by combining interesting values for every pair of a set of input variables instead of considering all possible combinations. Pairwise testing belongs to combinatorial testing, which in general also includes higher-level combinations than pairs: these techniques are referred to as *t-wise*, whereby every possible combination of *t* input variables is considered.

3.2.3. Boundary-Value Analysis
[1*, c9s5]

Test cases are chosen on or near the boundaries of the input domain of variables, with the underlying rationale that many faults tend to concentrate near the extreme values of inputs. An extension of this technique is robustness testing, wherein test cases are also chosen outside the input domain of variables to test program robustness in processing unexpected or erroneous inputs.

3.2.4. Random Testing
[1*, c9s7]

Tests are generated purely at random (not to be confused with statistical testing from the operational profile, as described in Operational Profile in section 3.5). This form of testing falls under the heading of input domain testing since the input domain must be known in order to be able to pick random points within it. Random testing provides a relatively simple approach for test automation; recently, enhanced forms of random testing have been proposed in which the random input sampling is directed by other input selection criteria [11]. Fuzz testing or fuzzing is a special form of random testing aimed at breaking the software; it is most often used for security testing.

3.3. Code-Based Techniques

3.3.1. Control Flow-Based Criteria
[1*, c4]

Control flow-based coverage criteria are aimed at covering all the statements, blocks of statements, or specified combinations of statements in a program. The strongest of the control flow-based criteria is path testing, which aims to execute all entry-to-exit control flow paths in a program's control flow graph. Since exhaustive path testing is generally not feasible because of loops, other less stringent criteria focus on coverage of paths that limit loop iterations such as statement coverage, branch coverage, and condition/decision testing. The adequacy of such tests is measured in percentages; for example, when all branches have been executed at least once by the tests, 100% branch coverage has been achieved.

3.3.2. Data Flow-Based Criteria

[1*, c5]

In data flow-based testing, the control flow graph is annotated with information about how the program variables are defined, used, and killed (undefined). The strongest criterion, all definition-use paths, requires that, for each variable, every control flow path segment from a definition of that variable to a use of that definition is executed. In order to reduce the number of paths required, weaker strategies such as all-definitions and all-uses are employed.

3.3.3. Reference Models for Code-Based Testing

[1*, c4]

Although not a technique in itself, the control structure of a program can be graphically represented using a flow graph to visualize code-based testing techniques. A flow graph is a directed graph, the nodes and arcs of which correspond to program elements (see Graphs and Trees in the Mathematical Foundations KA). For instance, nodes may represent statements or uninterrupted sequences of statements, and arcs may represent the transfer of control between nodes.

3.4. Fault-Based Techniques

[1*, c1s14]

With different degrees of formalization, fault-based testing techniques devise test cases specifically aimed at revealing categories of likely or predefined faults. To better focus the test case generation or selection, a *fault model* can be introduced that classifies the different types of faults.

3.4.1. Error Guessing

[1*, c9s8]

In error guessing, test cases are specifically designed by software engineers who try to anticipate the most plausible faults in a given program. A good source of information is the history of faults discovered in earlier projects, as well as the software engineer's expertise.

3.4.2. Mutation Testing

[1*, c3s5]

A mutant is a slightly modified version of the program under test, differing from it by a small syntactic change. Every test case exercises both the original program and all generated mutants: if a test case is successful in identifying the difference between the program and a mutant, the latter is said to be "killed." Originally conceived as a technique to evaluate test sets (see section 4.2. Evaluation of the Tests Performed), mutation testing is also a testing criterion in itself: either tests are randomly generated until enough mutants have been killed, or tests are specifically designed to kill surviving mutants. In the latter case, mutation testing can also be categorized as a code-based technique. The underlying assumption of mutation testing, the coupling effect, is that by looking for simple syntactic faults, more complex but real faults will be found. For the technique to be effective, a large number of mutants must be automatically generated and executed in a systematic way [12].

3.5. Usage-Based Techniques

3.5.1. Operational Profile

[1*, c15s5]

In testing for reliability evaluation (also called operational testing), the test environment reproduces the operational environment of the software, or the *operational profile*, as closely as possible. The goal is to infer from the observed test results the future reliability of the software when in actual use. To do this, inputs are assigned probabilities, or profiles, according to their frequency of occurrence in actual operation. Operational profiles can be used during system testing to guide derivation of test cases that will assess the achievement of reliability objectives and exercise relative usage and criticality of different functions similar to what will be encountered in the operational environment [3].

3.5.2. User Observation Heuristics
[10*, c5, c7]

Usability principles can provide guidelines for discovering problems in the design of the user interface [10*, c1s4] (see User Interface Design in the Software Design KA). Specialized heuristics, also called usability inspection methods, are applied for the systematic observation of system usage under controlled conditions in order to determine how well people can use the system and its interfaces. Usability heuristics include cognitive walkthroughs, claims analysis, field observations, thinking aloud, and even indirect approaches such as user questionnaires and interviews.

3.6. Model-Based Testing Techniques

A model in this context is an abstract (formal) representation of the software under test or of its software requirements (see Modeling in the Software Engineering Models and Methods KA). Model-based testing is used to validate requirements, check their consistency, and generate test cases focused on the behavioral aspects of the software. The key components of model-based testing are [13]: the notation used to represent the model of the software or its requirements; workflow models or similar models; the test strategy or algorithm used for test case generation; the supporting infrastructure for the test execution; and the evaluation of test results compared to expected results. Due to the complexity of the techniques, model-based testing approaches are often used in conjunction with test automation harnesses. Model-based testing techniques include the following.

3.6.1. Decision Tables
[1*, c9s6]

Decision tables represent logical relationships between conditions (roughly, inputs) and actions (roughly, outputs). Test cases are systematically derived by considering every possible combination of conditions and their corresponding resultant actions. A related technique is *cause-effect graphing* [1*, c13s6].

3.6.2. Finite-State Machines
[1*, c10]

By modeling a program as a finite state machine, tests can be selected in order to cover the states and transitions.

3.6.3. Formal Specifications
[1*, c10s11] [2*, c15]

Stating the specifications in a formal language (see Formal Methods in the Software Engineering Models and Methods KA) permits automatic derivation of functional test cases, and, at the same time, provides an oracle for checking test results.

TTCN3 (Testing and Test Control Notation version 3) is a language developed for writing test cases. The notation was conceived for the specific needs of testing telecommunication systems, so it is particularly suitable for testing complex communication protocols.

3.6.4. Workflow Models
[2*, c8s3.2, c19s3.1]

Workflow models specify a sequence of activities performed by humans and/or software applications, usually represented through graphical notations. Each sequence of actions constitutes one workflow (also called a scenario). Both typical and alternate workflows should be tested [6, part 4]. A special focus on the roles in a workflow specification is targeted in business process testing.

3.7. Techniques Based on the Nature of the Application

The above techniques apply to all kinds of software. Additional techniques for test derivation and execution are based on the nature of the software being tested; for example,

- object-oriented software
- component-based software
- web-based software
- concurrent programs
- protocol-based software
- real-time systems
- safety-critical systems
- service-oriented software
- open-source software
- embedded software

3.8. Selecting and Combining Techniques

3.8.1. Combining Functional and Structural
[1*, c9]

Model-based and code-based test techniques are often contrasted as functional vs. structural testing. These two approaches to test selection are not to be seen as alternatives but rather as complements; in fact, they use different sources of information and have been shown to highlight different kinds of problems. They could be used in combination, depending on budgetary considerations.

3.8.2. Deterministic vs. Random
[1*, c9s6]

Test cases can be selected in a deterministic way, according to one of many techniques, or randomly drawn from some distribution of inputs, such as is usually done in reliability testing. Several analytical and empirical comparisons have been conducted to analyze the conditions that make one approach more effective than the other.

4. Test-Related Measures

Sometimes testing techniques are confused with testing objectives. Testing techniques can be viewed as aids that help to ensure the achievement of test objectives [6, part 4]. For instance, branch coverage is a popular testing technique. Achieving a specified branch coverage measure (e.g., 95% branch coverage) should not be the objective of testing per se: it is a way of improving the chances of finding failures by attempting to systematically exercise every program branch

at every decision point. To avoid such misunderstandings, a clear distinction should be made between test-related measures that provide an evaluation of the program under test, based on the observed test outputs, and the measures that evaluate the thoroughness of the test set. (See Software Engineering Measurement in the Software Engineering Management KA for information on measurement programs. See Software Process and Product Measurement in the Software Engineering Process KA for information on measures.)

Measurement is usually considered fundamental to quality analysis. Measurement may also be used to optimize the planning and execution of the tests. Test management can use several different process measures to monitor progress. (See section 5.1, Practical Considerations, for a discussion of measures of the testing process useful for management purposes.)

4.1. Evaluation of the Program Under Test

4.1.1. Program Measurements That Aid in Planning and Designing Tests
[9*, c11]

Measures based on software size (for example, source lines of code or functional size; see Measuring Requirements in the Software Requirements KA) or on program structure can be used to guide testing. Structural measures also include measurements that determine the frequency with which modules call one another.

4.1.2. Fault Types, Classification, and Statistics
[9*, c4]

The testing literature is rich in classifications and taxonomies of faults. To make testing more effective, it is important to know which types of faults may be found in the software under test and the relative frequency with which these faults have occurred in the past. This information can be useful in making quality predictions as well as in process improvement (see Defect Characterization in the Software Quality KA).

4.1.3. Fault Density

[1*, c13s4] [9*, c4]

A program under test can be evaluated by counting discovered faults as the ratio between the number of faults found and the size of the program.

4.1.4. Life Test, Reliability Evaluation

[1*, c15] [9*, c3]

A statistical estimate of software reliability, which can be obtained by observing reliability achieved, can be used to evaluate a software product and decide whether or not testing can be stopped (see section 2.2, Reliability Achievement and Evaluation).

4.1.5. Reliability Growth Models

[1*, c15] [9*, c8]

Reliability growth models provide a prediction of reliability based on failures. They assume, in general, that when the faults that caused the observed failures have been fixed (although some models also accept imperfect fixes), the estimated product's reliability exhibits, on average, an increasing trend. There are many published reliability growth models. Notably, these models are divided into *failure-count* and *time-between-failure* models.

4.2. Evaluation of the Tests Performed

4.2.1. Coverage / Thoroughness Measures

[9*, c11]

Several test adequacy criteria require that the test cases systematically exercise a set of elements identified in the program or in the specifications (see topic 3, Test Techniques). To evaluate the thoroughness of the executed tests, software engineers can monitor the elements covered so that they can dynamically measure the ratio between covered elements and the total number. For example, it is possible to measure the percentage of branches covered in the program flow graph or the percentage of functional requirements exercised among those listed in the specifications document. Code-based adequacy criteria require appropriate instrumentation of the program under test.

4.2.2. Fault Seeding

[1*, c2s5] [9*, c6]

In fault seeding, some faults are artificially introduced into a program before testing. When the tests are executed, some of these seeded faults will be revealed as well as, possibly, some faults that were already there. In theory, depending on which and how many of the artificial faults are discovered, testing effectiveness can be evaluated and the remaining number of genuine faults can be estimated. In practice, statisticians question the distribution and representativeness of seeded faults relative to genuine faults and the small sample size on which any extrapolations are based. Some also argue that this technique should be used with great care since inserting faults into software involves the obvious risk of leaving them there.

4.2.3. Mutation Score

[1*, c3s5]

In mutation testing (see Mutation Testing in section 3.4, Fault-Based Techniques), the ratio of killed mutants to the total number of generated mutants can be a measure of the effectiveness of the executed test set.

4.2.4. Comparison and Relative Effectiveness of Different Techniques

Several studies have been conducted to compare the relative effectiveness of different testing techniques. It is important to be precise as to the property against which the techniques are being assessed; what, for instance, is the exact meaning given to the term "effectiveness"? Possible interpretations include the number of tests needed to find the first failure, the ratio of the number of faults found through testing to all the faults found during and after testing, and how much reliability was improved. Analytical and empirical comparisons between different techniques have been conducted according to each of the notions of effectiveness specified above.

5. Test Process

Testing concepts, strategies, techniques, and measures need to be integrated into a defined and controlled process. The test process supports testing activities and provides guidance to testers and testing teams, from test planning to test output evaluation, in such a way as to provide assurance that the test objectives will be met in a cost-effective way.

5.1. Practical Considerations

5.1.1. Attitudes / Egoless Programming
[1*c16] [9*, c15]

An important element of successful testing is a collaborative attitude towards testing and quality assurance activities. Managers have a key role in fostering a generally favorable reception towards failure discovery and correction during software development and maintenance; for instance, by overcoming the mindset of individual code ownership among programmers and by promoting a collaborative environment with team responsibility for anomalies in the code.

5.1.2. Test Guides
[1*, c12s1] [9*, c15s1]

The testing phases can be guided by various aims—for example, risk-based testing uses the product risks to prioritize and focus the test strategy, and scenario-based testing defines test cases based on specified software scenarios.

5.1.3. Test Process Management
[1*, c12] [9*, c15]

Test activities conducted at different levels (see topic 2, Test Levels) must be organized—together with people, tools, policies, and measures—into a well-defined process that is an integral part of the life cycle.

5.1.4. Test Documentation and Work Products
[1*, c8s12] [9*, c4s5]

Documentation is an integral part of the formalization of the test process [6, part 3]. Test documents may include, among others, the test plan, test design specification, test procedure specification, test case specification, test log, and test incident report. The software under test is documented as the test item. Test documentation should be produced and continually updated to the same level of quality as other types of documentation in software engineering. Test documentation should also be under the control of software configuration management (see the Software Configuration Management KA). Moreover, test documentation includes work products that can provide material for user manuals and user training.

5.1.5. Test-Driven Development
[1*, c1s16]

Test-driven development (TDD) originated as one of the core XP (extreme programming) practices and consists of writing unit tests prior to writing the code to be tested (see Agile Methods in the Software Engineering Models and Method KA). In this way, TDD develops the test cases as a surrogate for a software requirements specification document rather than as an independent check that the software has correctly implemented the requirements. Rather than a testing strategy, TDD is a practice that requires software developers to define and maintain unit tests; it thus can also have a positive impact on elaborating user needs and software requirements specifications.

5.1.6. Internal vs. Independent Test Team
[1*, c16]

Formalizing the testing process may also involve formalizing the organization of the testing team. The testing team can be composed of internal members (that is, on the project team, involved or not in software construction), of external members (in the hope of bringing an unbiased, independent perspective), or of both internal and external members. Considerations of cost, schedule, maturity levels of the involved organizations, and criticality of the application can guide the decision.

5.1.7. Cost/Effort Estimation and Test Process Measures
[1*, c18s3] [9*, c5s7]

Several measures related to the resources spent on testing, as well as to the relative fault-finding effectiveness of the various test phases, are used by managers to control and improve the testing process. These test measures may cover such aspects as number of test cases specified, number of test cases executed, number of test cases passed, and number of test cases failed, among others.

Evaluation of test phase reports can be combined with root-cause analysis to evaluate test-process effectiveness in finding faults as early as possible. Such an evaluation can be associated with the analysis of risks. Moreover, the resources that are worth spending on testing should be commensurate with the use/criticality of the application: different techniques have different costs and yield different levels of confidence in product reliability.

5.1.8. Termination

[9*, c10s4]

A decision must be made as to how much testing is enough and when a test stage can be terminated. Thoroughness measures, such as achieved code coverage or functional coverage, as well as estimates of fault density or of operational reliability, provide useful support but are not sufficient in themselves. The decision also involves considerations about the costs and risks incurred by possible remaining failures, as opposed to the costs incurred by continuing to test (see Test Selection Criteria / Test Adequacy Criteria in section 1.2, Key Issues).

5.1.9. Test Reuse and Test Patterns

[9*, c2s5]

To carry out testing or maintenance in an organized and cost-effective way, the means used to test each part of the software should be reused systematically. A repository of test materials should be under the control of software configuration management so that changes to software requirements or design can be reflected in changes to the tests conducted.

The test solutions adopted for testing some application types under certain circumstances, with the motivations behind the decisions taken, form a test pattern that can itself be documented for later reuse in similar projects.

5.2. Test Activities

As shown in the following description, successful management of test activities strongly depends on the software configuration management process (see the Software Configuration Management KA).

5.2.1. Planning

[1*, c12s1, c12s8]

Like all other aspects of project management, testing activities must be planned. Key aspects of test planning include coordination of personnel, availability of test facilities and equipment, creation and maintenance of all test-related documentation, and planning for possible undesirable outcomes. If more than one baseline of the software is being maintained, then a major planning consideration is the time and effort needed to ensure that the test environment is set to the proper configuration.

5.2.2. Test-Case Generation

[1*, c12s1, c12s3]

Generation of test cases is based on the level of testing to be performed and the particular testing techniques. Test cases should be under the control of software configuration management and include the expected results for each test.

5.2.3. Test Environment Development

[1*, c12s6]

The environment used for testing should be compatible with the other adopted software engineering tools. It should facilitate development and control of test cases, as well as logging and recovery of expected results, scripts, and other testing materials.

5.2.4. Execution

[1*, c12s7]

Execution of tests should embody a basic principle of scientific experimentation: everything done during testing should be performed and documented clearly enough that another person could replicate the results. Hence, testing should be performed in accordance with documented procedures using a clearly defined version of the software under test.

5.2.5. Test Results Evaluation

[9*, c15]

The results of testing should be evaluated to determine whether or not the testing has been successful. In most cases, "successful" means that the software performed as expected and did not have any major unexpected outcomes. Not all unexpected outcomes are necessarily faults but are sometime determined to be simply noise. Before a fault can be removed, an analysis and debugging effort is needed to isolate, identify, and describe it. When test results are particularly important, a formal review board may be convened to evaluate them.

5.2.6. Problem Reporting / Test Log

[1*, c13s9]

Testing activities can be entered into a testing log to identify when a test was conducted, who performed the test, what software configuration was used, and other relevant identification information. Unexpected or incorrect test results can be recorded in a problem reporting system, the data for which forms the basis for later debugging and fixing the problems that were observed as failures during testing. Also, anomalies not classified as faults could be documented in case they later turn out to be more serious than first thought. Test reports are also inputs to the change management request process (see Software Configuration Control in the Software Configuration Management KA).

5.2.7. Defect Tracking

[9*, c9]

Defects can be tracked and analyzed to determine when they were introduced into the software, why they were created (for example, poorly defined requirements, incorrect variable declaration, memory leak, programming syntax error), and when they could have been first observed in the software. Defect tracking information is used to determine what aspects of software testing and other processes need improvement and how effective previous approaches have been.

6. Software Testing Tools

6.1. Testing Tool Support

[1*, c12s11] [9*, c5]

Testing requires many labor-intensive tasks, running numerous program executions, and handling a great amount of information. Appropriate tools can alleviate the burden of clerical, tedious operations and make them less error-prone. Sophisticated tools can support test design and test case generation, making it more effective.

6.1.1. Selecting Tools

[1*, c12s11]

Guidance to managers and testers on how to select testing tools that will be most useful to their organization and processes is a very important topic, as tool selection greatly affects testing efficiency and effectiveness. Tool selection depends on diverse evidence, such as development choices, evaluation objectives, execution facilities, and so on. In general, there may not be a unique tool that will satisfy particular needs, so a suite of tools could be an appropriate choice.

6.2. Categories of Tools

We categorize the available tools according to their functionality:

- *Test harnesses* (drivers, stubs) [1*, c3s9] provide a controlled environment in which tests can be launched and the test outputs can be logged. In order to execute parts of a program, drivers and stubs are provided to simulate calling and called modules, respectively.
- *Test generators* [1*, c12s11] provide assistance in the generation test cases. The generation can be random, path-based, model-based, or a mix thereof.
- *Capture/replay tools* [1*, c12s11] automatically reexecute, or replay, previously

executed tests which have recorded inputs and outputs (e.g., screens).

- *Oracle/file comparators/assertion checking tools* [1*, c9s7] assist in deciding whether a test outcome is successful or not.
- *Coverage analyzers and instrumenters* [1*, c4] work together. Coverage analyzers assess which and how many entities of the program flow graph have been exercised amongst all those required by the selected test coverage criterion. The analysis can be done thanks to program instrumenters that insert recording probes into the code.
- *Tracers* [1*, c1s7] record the history of a program's execution paths.
- *Regression testing tools* [1*, c12s16] support the reexecution of a test suite after a section of software has been modified. They can also help to select a test subset according to the change made.
- *Reliability evaluation tools* [9*, c8] support test results analysis and graphical visualization in order to assess reliability-related measures according to selected models.

MATRIX OF TOPICS VS. REFERENCE MATERIAL

	Naik and Tripathy 2008 [1*]	Sommerville 2011 [2*]	Kan 2003 [9*]	Nielsen 1993 [10*]
1. Software Testing Fundamentals				
1.1. Testing-Related Terminology				
1.1.1. Definitions of Testing and Related Terminology	c1,c2	c8		
1.1.2. Faults vs. Failures	c1s5	c11		
1.2. Key Issues				
1.2.1. Test Selection Criteria / Test Adequacy Criteria (Stopping Rules)	c1s14, c6s6, c12s7			
1.2.2. Testing Effectiveness / Objectives for Testing	c13s11, c11s4			
1.2.3. Testing for Defect Identification	c1s14			
1.2.4. The Oracle Problem	c1s9, c9s7			
1.2.5. Theoretical and Practical Limitations of Testing	c2s7			
1.2.6. The Problem of Infeasible Paths	c4s7			
1.2.7. Testability	c17s2			
1.3. Relationship of Testing to Other Activities				
1.3.1. Testing vs. Static Software Quality Management Techniques	c12			
1.3.2. Testing vs. Correctness Proofs and Formal Verification	c17s2			
1.3.3. Testing vs. Debugging	c3s6			
1.3.4. Testing vs. Programming	c3s2			
2. Test Levels				
2.1. The Target of the Test	c1s13	c8s1		
2.1.1. Unit Testing	c3	c8		
2.1.2. Integration Testing	c7	c8		
2.1.3. System Testing	c8	c8		

	Naik and Tripathy 2008 [1*]	Sommerville 2011 [2*]	Kan 2003 [9*]	Nielsen 1993 [10*]
2.2. Objectives of Testing	c1s7			
2.2.1. Acceptance / Qualification	c1s7	c8s4		
2.2.2. Installation Testing	c12s2			
2.2.3. Alpha and Beta Testing	c13s7, c16s6	c8s4		
2.2.4. Reliability Achievement and Evaluation	c15	c15s2		
2.2.5. Regression Testing	c8s11, c13s3			
2.2.6. Performance Testing	c8s6			
2.2.7. Security Testing	c8s3	c11s4		
2.2.8. Stress Testing	c8s8			
2.2.9. Back-to-Back Testing				
2.2.10. Recovery Testing	c14s2			
2.2.11. Interface Testing		c8s1.3	c4s4.5	
2.2.12. Configuration Testing	c8s5			
2.2.13. Usability and Human Computer Interaction Testing				c6
3. Test Techniques				
3.1. Based on the Software Engineer's Intuition and Experience				
3.1.1. Ad Hoc				
3.1.2. Exploratory Testing				
3.2. Input Domain-Based Techniques				
3.2.1. Equivalence Partitioning	c9s4			
3.2.2. Pairwise Testing	c9s3			
3.2.3. Boundary-Value Analysis	c9s5			
3.2.4. Random Testing	c9s7			
3.3. Code-Based Techniques				
3.3.1. Control Flow-Based Criteria	c4			

	Naik and Tripathy 2008 [1*]	Sommerville 2011 [2*]	Kan 2003 [9*]	Nielsen 1993 [10*]
3.3.2. Data Flow-Based Criteria	c5			
3.3.3. Reference Models for Code-Based Testing	c4			
3.4. Fault-Based Techniques	c1s14			
3.4.1. Error Guessing	c9s8			
3.4.2. Mutation Testing	c3s5			
3.5. Usage-Based Techniques				
3.5.1. Operational Profile	c15s5			
3.5.2. User Observation Heuristics				c5, c7
3.6. Model-Based Testing Techniques				
3.6.1. Decision Table	c9s6			
3.6.2. Finite-State Machines	c10			
3.6.3. Testing from Formal Specifications	c10s11	c15		
3.7. Techniques Based on the Nature of the Application				
3.8. Selecting and Combining Techniques				
3.8.1. Functional and Structural	c9			
3.8.2. Deterministic vs. Random	c9s6			
4. Test-Related Measures				
4.1. Evaluation of the Program Under Test				
4.1.1. Program Measurements That Aid in Planning and Designing Testing			c11	
4.1.2. Fault Types, Classification, and Statistics			c4	
4.1.3. Fault Density	c13s4		c4	
4.1.4. Life Test, Reliability Evaluation	c15		c3	
4.1.5. Reliability Growth Models	c15		c8	

	Naik and Tripathy 2008 [1*]	Sommerville 2011 [2*]	Kan 2003 [9*]	Nielsen 1993 [10*]
4.2. Evaluation of the Tests Performed				
4.2.1. Coverage / Thoroughness Measures			c11	
4.2.2. Fault Seeding	c2s5		c6	
4.2.3. Mutation Score	c3s5			
4.2.4. Comparison and Relative Effectiveness of Different Techniques				
5. Test Process				
5.1. Practical Considerations				
5.1.1. Attitudes / Egoless Programming	c16		c15	
5.1.2. Test Guides	c12s1		c15s1	
5.1.3. Test Process Management	c12		c15	
5.1.4. Test Documentation and Work Products	c8s12		c4s5	
5.1.5. Test-Driven Development	c1s16			
5.1.6. Internal vs. Independent Test Team	c16			
5.1.7. Cost/Effort Estimation and Other Process Measures	c18s3		c5s7	
5.1.8. Termination			c10s4	
5.1.9. Test Reuse and Patterns			c2s5	
5.2. Test Activities				
5.2.1. Planning	c12s1 c12s8			
5.2.2. Test-Case Generation	c12s1 c12s3			
5.2.3. Test Environment Development	c12s6			
5.2.4. Execution	c12s7			
5.2.5. Test Results Evaluation			c15	

	Naik and Tripathy 2008 [1*]	Sommerville 2011 [2*]	Kan 2003 [9*]	Nielsen 1993 [10*]
5.2.6. Problem Reporting / Test Log	c13s9			
5.2.7. Defect Tracking			c9	
6. Software Testing Tools				
6.1. Testing Tool Support	c12s11		c5	
6.1.1. Selecting Tools	c12s11			
6.2. Categories of Tools	c1s7, c3s9, c4, c9s7, c12s11, c12s16		c8	

REFERENCES

[1*] S. Naik and P. Tripathy, *Software Testing and Quality Assurance: Theory and Practice*, Wiley-Spektrum, 2008.

[2*] I. Sommerville, *Software Engineering*, 9th ed., Addison-Wesley, 2011.

[3] M.R. Lyu, ed., *Handbook of Software Reliability Engineering*, McGraw-Hill and IEEE Computer Society Press, 1996.

[4] H. Zhu, P.A.V. Hall, and J.H.R. May, "Software Unit Test Coverage and Adequacy," *ACM Computing Surveys,* vol. 29, no. 4, Dec. 1997, pp. 366–427.

[5] E.W. Dijkstra, "Notes on Structured Programming," T.H.-Report 70-WSE-03, Technological University, Eindhoven, 1970; http://www.cs.utexas.edu/users/EWD/ewd02xx/EWD249.PDF.

[6] *ISO/IEC/IEEE P29119-1/DIS Draft Standard for Software and Systems Engineering—Software Testing—Part 1: Concepts and Definitions*, ISO/IEC/IEEE, 2012.

[7] *ISO/IEC/IEEE 24765:2010 Systems and Software Engineering—Vocabulary*, ISO/IEC/IEEE, 2010.

[8] S. Yoo and M. Harman, "Regression Testing Minimization, Selection and Prioritization: A Survey," *Software Testing Verification and Reliability,* vol. 22, no. 2, Mar. 2012, pp. 67–120.

[9*] S.H. Kan, *Metrics and Models in Software Quality Engineering*, 2nd ed., Addison-Wesley, 2002.

[10*] J. Nielsen, *Usability Engineering*, Morgan Kaufmann, 1993.

[11] T.Y. Chen et al., "Adaptive Random Testing: The ART of Test Case Diversity," *Journal of Systems and Software,* vol. 83, no. 1, Jan. 2010, pp. 60–66.

[12] Y. Jia and M. Harman, "An Analysis and Survey of the Development of Mutation Testing," *IEEE Trans. Software Engineering,* vol. 37, no. 5, Sep.–Oct. 2011, pp. 649–678.

[13] M. Utting and B. Legeard, *Practical Model-Based Testing: A Tools Approach*, Morgan Kaufmann, 2007.

CHAPTER 5

SOFTWARE MAINTENANCE

ACRONYMS

MR	Modification Request
PR	Problem Report
SCM	Software Configuration Management
SLA	Service-Level Agreement
SQA	Software Quality Assurance
V&V	Verification and Validation

INTRODUCTION

Software development efforts result in the delivery of a software product that satisfies user requirements. Accordingly, the software product must change or evolve. Once in operation, defects are uncovered, operating environments change, and new user requirements surface. The maintenance phase of the life cycle begins following a warranty period or postimplementation support delivery, but maintenance activities occur much earlier.

Software maintenance is an integral part of a software life cycle. However, it has not received the same degree of attention that the other phases have. Historically, software development has had a much higher profile than software maintenance in most organizations. This is now changing, as organizations strive to squeeze the most out of their software development investment by keeping software operating as long as possible. The open source paradigm has brought further attention to the issue of maintaining software artifacts developed by others.

In this *Guide*, software maintenance is defined as the totality of activities required to provide cost-effective support to software. Activities are performed during the predelivery stage as well as during the postdelivery stage. Predelivery activities include planning for postdelivery operations, maintainability, and logistics determination for transition activities [1*, c6s9]. Postdelivery activities include software modification, training, and operating or interfacing to a help desk.

The Software Maintenance knowledge area (KA) is related to all other aspects of software engineering. Therefore, this KA description is linked to all other software engineering KAs of the *Guide*.

BREAKDOWN OF TOPICS FOR SOFTWARE MAINTENANCE

The breakdown of topics for the Software Maintenance KA is shown in Figure 5.1.

1. Software Maintenance Fundamentals

This first section introduces the concepts and terminology that form an underlying basis to understanding the role and scope of software maintenance. The topics provide definitions and emphasize why there is a need for maintenance. Categories of software maintenance are critical to understanding its underlying meaning.

1.1. Definitions and Terminology
[1*, c3] [2*, c1s2, c2s2]

The purpose of software maintenance is defined in the international standard for software maintenance: ISO/IEC/IEEE 14764 [1*].[1] In the context of software engineering, software maintenance is essentially one of the many technical processes.

---

1   For the purpose of conciseness and ease of reading, this standard is referred to simply as IEEE 14764 in the subsequent text of this KA.

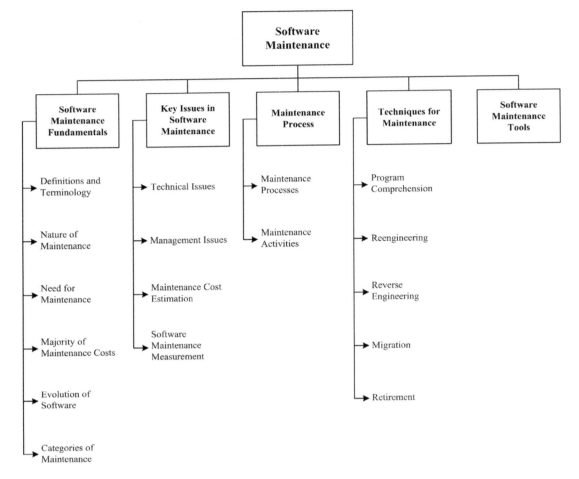

Figure 5.1. Breakdown of Topics for the Software Maintenance KA

The objective of software maintenance is to modify existing software while preserving its integrity. The international standard also states the importance of having some maintenance activities prior to the final delivery of software (predelivery activities). Notably, IEEE 14764 emphasizes the importance of the predelivery aspects of maintenance—planning, for example.

1.2. Nature of Maintenance

[2*, c1s3]

Software maintenance sustains the software product throughout its life cycle (from development to operations). Modification requests are logged and tracked, the impact of proposed changes is determined, code and other software artifacts are modified, testing is conducted, and a new version of the software product is released. Also, training and daily support are provided to users. The term *maintainer* is defined as an organization that performs maintenance activities. In this KA, the term will sometimes refer to individuals who perform those activities, contrasting them with the developers.

IEEE 14764 identifies the primary activities of software maintenance as process implementation, problem and modification analysis, modification implementation, maintenance review/acceptance, migration, and retirement. These activities are discussed in section 3.2, Maintenance Activities.

Maintainers can learn from the developers' knowledge of the software. Contact with the developers and early involvement by the maintainer helps reduce the overall maintenance effort. In some instances, the initial developer cannot be reached or has moved on to other tasks, which creates an additional challenge for maintainers. Maintenance must take software artifacts from development (for example, code or documentation) and support them immediately, then progressively evolve/maintain them over a software life cycle.

1.3. Need for Maintenance
[2*, c1s5]

Maintenance is needed to ensure that the software continues to satisfy user requirements. Maintenance is applicable to software that is developed using any software life cycle model (for example, spiral or linear). Software products change due to corrective and noncorrective software actions. Maintenance must be performed in order to

- correct faults;
- improve the design;
- implement enhancements;
- interface with other software;
- adapt programs so that different hardware, software, system features, and telecommunications facilities can be used;
- migrate legacy software; and
- retire software.

Five key characteristics comprise the maintainer's activities:

- maintaining control over the software's day-to-day functions;
- maintaining control over software modification;
- perfecting existing functions;
- identifying security threats and fixing security vulnerabilities; and
- preventing software performance from degrading to unacceptable levels.

1.4. Majority of Maintenance Costs
[2*, c4s3, c5s5.2]

Maintenance consumes a major share of the financial resources in a software life cycle. A common perception of software maintenance is that it merely fixes faults. However, studies and surveys over the years have indicated that the majority, over 80 percent, of software maintenance is used for noncorrective actions [2*, figure 4.1]. Grouping enhancements and corrections together in management reports contributes to some misconceptions regarding the high cost of corrections. Understanding the categories of software maintenance helps to understand the structure of software maintenance costs. Also, understanding the factors that influence the maintainability of software can help to contain costs. Some environmental factors and their relationship to software maintenance costs include the following:

- Operating environment refers to hardware and software.
- Organizational environment refers to policies, competition, process, product, and personnel.

1.5. Evolution of Software
[2*, c3s5]

Software maintenance in terms of evolution was first addressed in the late 1960s. Over a period of twenty years, research led to the formulation of eight "Laws of Evolution." Key findings include a proposal that maintenance is evolutionary development and that maintenance decisions are aided by understanding what happens to software over time. Some state that maintenance is continued development, except that there is an extra input (or constraint)–in other words, existing large software is never complete and continues to evolve; as it evolves, it grows more complex unless some action is taken to reduce this complexity.

1.6. Categories of Maintenance
[1*, c3, c6s2] [2*, c3s3.1]

Three categories (types) of maintenance have been defined: corrective, adaptive, and perfective [2*, c4s3]. IEEE 14764 includes a fourth category–preventative.

- Corrective maintenance: reactive modification (or repairs) of a software product performed after delivery to correct discovered problems. Included in this category is emergency maintenance, which is an unscheduled modification performed to temporarily keep a software product operational pending corrective maintenance.

- Adaptive maintenance: modification of a software product performed after delivery to keep a software product usable in a changed or changing environment. For example, the operating system might be upgraded and some changes to the software may be necessary.
- Perfective maintenance: modification of a software product after delivery to provide enhancements for users, improvement of program documentation, and recoding to improve software performance, maintainability, or other software attributes.
- Preventive maintenance: modification of a software product after delivery to detect and correct latent faults in the software product before they become operational faults.

IEEE 14764 classifies adaptive and perfective maintenance as maintenance enhancements. It also groups together the corrective and preventive maintenance categories into a correction category, as shown in Table 5.1.

Table 5.1. Software Maintenance Categories

	Correction	Enhancement
Proactive	Preventive	Perfective
Reactive	Corrective	Adaptive

2. Key Issues in Software Maintenance

A number of key issues must be dealt with to ensure the effective maintenance of software. Software maintenance provides unique technical and management challenges for software engineers—for example, trying to find a fault in software containing a large number of lines of code that another software engineer developed. Similarly, competing with software developers for resources is a constant battle. Planning for a future release, which often includes coding the

next release while sending out emergency patches for the current release, also creates a challenge. The following section presents some of the technical and management issues related to software maintenance. They have been grouped under the following topic headings:

- technical issues,
- management issues,
- cost estimation, and
- measurement.

2.1. Technical Issues

2.1.1. Limited Understanding

[2*, c6]

Limited understanding refers to how quickly a software engineer can understand where to make a change or correction in software that he or she did not develop. Research indicates that about half of the total maintenance effort is devoted to understanding the software to be modified. Thus, the topic of software comprehension is of great interest to software engineers. Comprehension is more difficult in text-oriented representation—in source code, for example—where it is often difficult to trace the evolution of software through its releases/versions if changes are not documented and if the developers are not available to explain it, which is often the case. Thus, software engineers may initially have a limited understanding of the software; much has to be done to remedy this.

2.1.2. Testing

[1*, c6s2.2.2] [2*, c9]

The cost of repeating full testing on a major piece of software is significant in terms of time and money. In order to ensure that the requested problem reports are valid, the maintainer should replicate or verify problems by running the appropriate tests. Regression testing (the selective retesting of software or a component to verify that the modifications have not caused unintended effects) is an important testing concept in maintenance. Additionally, finding time to test is often difficult. Coordinating tests when different members of the maintenance team are working on different problems at the same time remains a challenge. When software performs critical functions, it may be difficult to bring it offline to test. Tests cannot be executed in the most meaningful place–the production system. The Software Testing KA provides additional information and references on this matter in its subtopic on regression testing.

2.1.3. Impact Analysis
[1*, c5s2.5] [2*, c13s3]

Impact analysis describes how to conduct, cost-effectively, a complete analysis of the impact of a change in existing software. Maintainers must possess an intimate knowledge of the software's structure and content. They use that knowledge to perform impact analysis, which identifies all systems and software products affected by a software change request and develops an estimate of the resources needed to accomplish the change. Additionally, the risk of making the change is determined. The change request, sometimes called a modification request (MR) and often called a problem report (PR), must first be analyzed and translated into software terms. Impact analysis is performed after a change request enters the software configuration management process. IEEE 14764 states the impact analysis tasks:

- analyze MRs/PRs;
- replicate or verify the problem;
- develop options for implementing the modification;
- document the MR/PR, the results, and the execution options;
- obtain approval for the selected modification option.

The severity of a problem is often used to decide how and when it will be fixed. The software engineer then identifies the affected components. Several potential solutions are provided, followed by a recommendation as to the best course of action.

Software designed with maintainability in mind greatly facilitates impact analysis. More information can be found in the Software Configuration Management KA.

2.1.4. Maintainability
[1*, c6s8] [2*, c12s5.5]

IEEE 14764 [1*, c3s4] defines maintainability as the capability of the software product to be modified. Modifications may include corrections, improvements, or adaptation of the software to changes in environment as well as changes in requirements and functional specifications.

As a primary software quality characteristic, maintainability should be specified, reviewed, and controlled during software development activities in order to reduce maintenance costs. When done successfully, the software's maintainability will improve. Maintainability is often difficult to achieve because the subcharacteristics are often not an important focus during the process of software development. The developers are, typically, more preoccupied with many other activities and frequently prone to disregard the maintainer's requirements. This in turn can, and often does, result in a lack of software documentation and test environments, which is a leading cause of difficulties in program comprehension and subsequent impact analysis. The presence of systematic and mature processes, techniques, and tools helps to enhance the maintainability of software.

2.2. Management Issues

2.2.1. Alignment with Organizational Objectives
[2*, c4]

Organizational objectives describe how to demonstrate the return on investment of software maintenance activities. Initial software development is usually project-based, with a defined time scale and budget. The main emphasis is to deliver a product that meets user needs on time and within budget. In contrast, software maintenance often has the objective of extending the life of software for as long as possible. In addition, it may be driven by the need to meet user demand for software updates and enhancements. In both cases, the return on investment is much less clear, so that the view at the senior management level is often that of a major activity consuming significant resources with no clear quantifiable benefit for the organization.

2.2.2. Staffing

[2*, c4s5, c10s4]

Staffing refers to how to attract and keep software maintenance staff. Maintenance is not often viewed as glamorous work. As a result, software maintenance personnel are frequently viewed as "second-class citizens," and morale therefore suffers.

2.2.3. Process

[1*, c5] [2*, c5]

The software life cycle process is a set of activities, methods, practices, and transformations that people use to develop and maintain software and its associated products. At the process level, software maintenance activities share much in common with software development (for example, software configuration management is a crucial activity in both). Maintenance also requires several activities that are not found in software development (see section 3.2 on unique activities for details). These activities present challenges to management.

2.2.4. Organizational Aspects of Maintenance
[1*, c7s2.3] [2*, c10]

Organizational aspects describe how to identify which organization and/or function will be responsible for the maintenance of software. The team that develops the software is not necessarily assigned to maintain the software once it is operational.

In deciding where the software maintenance function will be located, software engineering organizations may, for example, stay with the original developer or go to a permanent maintenance-specific team (or maintainer). Having a permanent maintenance team has many benefits:

- allows for specialization;
- creates communication channels;
- promotes an egoless, collegiate atmosphere;
- reduces dependency on individuals;
- allows for periodic audit checks.

Since there are many pros and cons to each option, the decision should be made on a case-by-case basis. What is important is the delegation or assignment of the maintenance responsibility to a single group or person, regardless of the organization's structure.

2.2.5. Outsourcing

[3*]

Outsourcing and offshoring software maintenance has become a major industry. Organizations are outsourcing entire portfolios of software, including software maintenance. More often, the outsourcing option is selected for less mission-critical software, as organizations are unwilling to lose control of the software used in their core business. One of the major challenges for outsourcers is to determine the scope of the maintenance services required, the terms of a service-level agreement, and the contractual details. Outsourcers will need to invest in a maintenance infrastructure, and the help desk at the remote site should be staffed with native-language speakers. Outsourcing requires a significant initial investment and the setup of a maintenance process that will require automation.

2.3. Maintenance Cost Estimation

Software engineers must understand the different categories of software maintenance, discussed above, in order to address the question of estimating the cost of software maintenance. For planning purposes, cost estimation is an important aspect of planning for software maintenance.

2.3.1. Cost Estimation

[2*, c7s2.4]

Section 2.1.3 describes how impact analysis identifies all systems and software products affected by a software change request and develops an estimate of the resources needed to accomplish that change.

Maintenance cost estimates are affected by many technical and nontechnical factors. IEEE 14764 states that "the two most popular approaches to estimating resources for software maintenance are the use of parametric models and the use of experience" [1*, c7s4.1]. A combination of these two can also be used.

2.3.2. Parametric Models
[2*, c12s5.6]

Parametric cost modeling (mathematical models) has been applied to software maintenance. Of significance is that historical data from past maintenance are needed in order to use and calibrate the mathematical models. Cost driver attributes affect the estimates.

2.3.3. Experience
[2*, c12s5.5]

Experience, in the form of expert judgment, is often used to estimate maintenance effort. Clearly, the best approach to maintenance estimation is to combine historical data and experience. The cost to conduct a modification (in terms of number of people and amount of time) is then derived. Maintenance estimation historical data should be provided as a result of a measurement program.

2.4. Software Maintenance Measurement
[1*, c6s5] [2*, c12]

Entities related to software maintenance, whose attributes can be subjected to measurement, include process, resource, and product [2*, c12s3.1].

There are several software measures that can be derived from the attributes of the software, the maintenance process, and personnel, including size, complexity, quality, understandability, maintainability, and effort. Complexity measures of software can also be obtained using available commercial tools. These measures constitute a good starting point for the maintainer's measurement program. Discussion of software process and product measurement is also presented in the Software Engineering Process KA. The topic of a software measurement program is described in the Software Engineering Management KA.

2.4.1. Specific Measures
[2*, c12]

The maintainer must determine which measures are appropriate for a specific organization based on that organization's own context. The software quality model suggests measures that are specific for software maintenance. Measures for subcharacterists of maintainability include the following [4*, p. 60]:

- Analyzability: measures of the maintainer's effort or resources expended in trying either to diagnose deficiencies or causes of failure or to identify parts to be modified.
- Changeability: measures of the maintainer's effort associated with implementing a specified modification.
- Stability: measures of the unexpected behavior of software, including that encountered during testing.
- Testability: measures of the maintainer's and users' effort in trying to test the modified software.
- Other measures that maintainers use include
- size of the software,
- complexity of the software ,
- understandability, and
- maintainability.

Providing software maintenance effort, by categories, for different applications provides business information to users and their organizations. It can also enable the comparison of software maintenance profiles internally within an organization.

3. Maintenance Process

In addition to standard software engineering processes and activities described in IEEE 14764, there are a number of activities that are unique to maintainers.

3.1. Maintenance Processes
[1*, c5] [2*, c5] [5, s5.5]

Maintenance processes provide needed activities and detailed inputs/outputs to those activities as described in IEEE 14764. The maintenance process activities of IEEE 14764 are shown in Figure 5.2. Software maintenance activities include

- process implementation,
- problem and modification analysis,
- modification implementation,

- maintenance review/acceptance,
- migration, and
- software retirement.

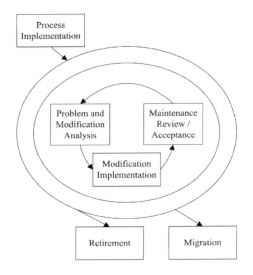

Figure 5.2. Software Maintenance Process

Other maintenance process models include:

- quick fix,
- spiral,
- Osborne's,
- iterative enhancement, and
- reuse-oriented.

Recently, agile methodologies, which promote light processes, have been also adapted to maintenance. This requirement emerges from the ever-increasing demand for fast turnaround of maintenance services. Improvement to the software maintenance process is supported by specialized software maintenance capability maturity models (see [6] and [7], which are briefly annotated in the Further Readings section).

3.2. Maintenance Activities
[1*, c5, c6s8.2, c7s3.3]

The maintenance process contains the activities and tasks necessary to modify an existing software product while preserving its integrity. These activities and tasks are the responsibility of the maintainer. As already noted, many maintenance activities are similar to those of software development. Maintainers perform analysis, design, coding, testing, and documentation. They must track requirements in their activities—just as is done in development—and update documentation as baselines change. IEEE 14764 recommends that when a maintainer uses a development process, it must be tailored to meet specific needs [1*, c5s3.2.2]. However, for software maintenance, some activities involve processes unique to software maintenance.

3.2.1. Unique Activities
[1*, c3s10, c6s9, c7s2, c7s3] [2*, c6, c7]

There are a number of processes, activities, and practices that are unique to software maintenance:

- Program understanding: activities needed to obtain a general knowledge of what a software product does and how the parts work together.
- Transition: a controlled and coordinated sequence of activities during which software is transferred progressively from the developer to the maintainer.
- Modification request acceptance/rejection: modifications requesting work beyond a certain size/effort/complexity may be rejected by maintainers and rerouted to a developer.
- Maintenance help desk: an end-user and maintenance coordinated support function that triggers the assessment, prioritization, and costing of modification requests.
- Impact analysis: a technique to identify areas impacted by a potential change;
- Maintenance Service-Level Agreements (SLAs) and maintenance licenses and contracts: contractual agreements that describe the services and quality objectives.

3.2.2. Supporting Activities
[1*, c4s1, c5, c6s7] [2*, c9]

Maintainers may also perform support activities, such as documentation, software configuration management, verification and validation, problem resolution, software quality assurance, reviews, and audits. Another important support activity consists of training the maintainers and users.

3.2.3. Maintenance Planning Activities
[1*, c7s3]

An important activity for software maintenance is planning, and maintainers must address the issues associated with a number of planning perspectives, including

* business planning (organizational level),
* maintenance planning (transition level),
* release/version planning (software level), and
* individual software change request planning (request level).

At the individual request level, planning is carried out during the impact analysis (see section 2.1.3, Impact Analysis). The release/version planning activity requires that the maintainer:

* collect the dates of availability of individual requests,
* agree with users on the content of subsequent releases/versions,
* identify potential conflicts and develop alternatives,
* assess the risk of a given release and develop a back-out plan in case problems should arise, and
* inform all the stakeholders.

Whereas software development projects can typically last from some months to a few years, the maintenance phase usually lasts for many years. Making estimates of resources is a key element of maintenance planning. Software maintenance planning should begin with the decision to develop a new software product and should consider quality objectives. A concept document should be developed, followed by a maintenance plan. The maintenance concept for each software product needs to be documented in the plan [1*, c7s2] and should address the

* scope of the software maintenance,
* adaptation of the software maintenance process,

* identification of the software maintenance organization, and
* estimate of software maintenance costs.

The next step is to develop a corresponding software maintenance plan. This plan should be prepared during software development and should specify how users will request software modifications or report problems. Software maintenance planning is addressed in IEEE 14764. It provides guidelines for a maintenance plan. Finally, at the highest level, the maintenance organization will have to conduct business planning activities (budgetary, financial, and human resources) just like all the other divisions of the organization. Management is discussed in the chapter Related Disciplines of Software Engineering.

3.2.4. Software Configuration Management
[1*, c5s1.2.3] [2*, c11]

IEEE 14764 describes software configuration management as a critical element of the maintenance process. Software configuration management procedures should provide for the verification, validation, and audit of each step required to identify, authorize, implement, and release the software product.

It is not sufficient to simply track modification requests or problem reports. The software product and any changes made to it must be controlled. This control is established by implementing and enforcing an approved software configuration management (SCM) process. The Software Configuration Management KA provides details of SCM and discusses the process by which software change requests are submitted, evaluated, and approved. SCM for software maintenance is different from SCM for software development in the number of small changes that must be controlled on operational software. The SCM process is implemented by developing and following a software configuration management plan and operating procedures. Maintainers participate in Configuration Control Boards to determine the content of the next release/version.

3.2.5. Software Quality
[1*, c6s5, c6s7, c6s8] [2*, c12s5.3]

It is not sufficient to simply hope that increased quality will result from the maintenance of software. Maintainers should have a software quality program. It must be planned and processes must be implemented to support the maintenance process. The activities and techniques for Software Quality Assurance (SQA), V&V, reviews, and audits must be selected in concert with all the other processes to achieve the desired level of quality. It is also recommended that the maintainer adapt the software development processes, techniques and deliverables (for instance, testing documentation), and test results. More details can be found in the Software Quality KA.

4. Techniques for Maintenance

This topic introduces some of the generally accepted techniques used in software maintenance.

4.1. Program Comprehension
[2*, c6, c14s5]

Programmers spend considerable time reading and understanding programs in order to implement changes. Code browsers are key tools for program comprehension and are used to organize and present source code. Clear and concise documentation can also aid in program comprehension.

4.2. Reengineering
[2*, c7]

Reengineering is defined as the examination and alteration of software to reconstitute it in a new form, and includes the subsequent implementation of the new form. It is often not undertaken to improve maintainability but to replace aging legacy software. Refactoring is a reengineering technique that aims at reorganizing a program without changing its behavior. It seeks to improve a program structure and its maintainability. Refactoring techniques can be used during minor changes.

4.3. Reverse Engineering
[1*, c6s2] [2*, c7, c14s5]

Reverse engineering is the process of analyzing software to identify the software's components and their inter-relationships and to create representations of the software in another form or at higher levels of abstraction. Reverse engineering is passive; it does not change the software or result in new software. Reverse engineering efforts produce call graphs and control flow graphs from source code. One type of reverse engineering is redocumentation. Another type is design recovery. Finally, data reverse engineering, where logical schemas are recovered from physical databases, has grown in importance over the last few years. Tools are key for reverse engineering and related tasks such as redocumentation and design recovery.

4.4. Migration
[1*, c5s5]

During software's life, it may have to be modified to run in different environments. In order to migrate it to a new environment, the maintainer needs to determine the actions needed to accomplish the migration, and then develop and document the steps required to effect the migration in a migration plan that covers migration requirements, migration tools, conversion of product and data, execution, verification, and support. Migrating software can also entail a number of additional activities such as

- notification of intent: a statement of why the old environment is no longer to be supported, followed by a description of the new environment and its date of availability;
- parallel operations: make available the old and new environments so that the user experiences a smooth transition to the new environment;
- notification of completion: when the scheduled migration is completed, a notification is sent to all concerned;

- postoperation review: an assessment of parallel operation and the impact of changing to the new environment;
- data archival: storing the old software data.

4.5. Retirement

[1*, c5s6]

Once software has reached the end of its useful life, it must be retired. An analysis should be performed to assist in making the retirement decision. This analysis should be included in the retirement plan, which covers retirement requirements, impact, replacement, schedule, and effort. Accessibility of archive copies of data may also be included. Retiring software entails a number of activities similar to migration.

5. Software Maintenance Tools

[1*, c6s4] [2*, c14]

This topic encompasses tools that are particularly important in software maintenance where existing software is being modified. Examples regarding program comprehension include

- program slicers, which select only parts of a program affected by a change;
- static analyzers, which allow general viewing and summaries of a program content;
- dynamic analyzers, which allow the maintainer to trace the execution path of a program;
- data flow analyzers, which allow the maintainer to track all possible data flows of a program;
- cross-referencers, which generate indices of program components; and
- dependency analyzers, which help maintainers analyze and understand the interrelationships between components of a program.

Reverse engineering tools assist the process by working backwards from an existing product to create artifacts such as specification and design descriptions, which can then be transformed to generate a new product from an old one. Maintainers also use software test, software configuration management, software documentation, and software measurement tools.

MATRIX OF TOPICS VS. REFERENCE MATERIAL

	IEEE/ISO/IEC 14764 2006 [1*]	Grubb and Takang 2003 [2*]	Sneed 2008 [3*]
1. Software Maintenance Fundamentals			
1.1. Definitions and Terminology	c3	c1s2, c2s2	
1.2. Nature of Maintenance		c1s3	
1.3. Need for Maintenance		c1s5	
1.4. Majority of Maintenance Costs		c4s3, c5s5.2	
1.5. Evolution of Software		c3s5	
1.6. Categories of Maintenance	c3, c6s2	c3s3.1, c4s3	
2. Key Issues in Software Maintenance			
2.1. Technical Issues			
2.1.1. Limited Understanding		c6	
2.1.2. Testing	c6s2.2.2	c9	
2.1.3. Impact Analysis	c5s2.5	c13s3	
2.1.4. Maintainability	c6s8, c3s4	c12s5.5	
2.2. Management Issues			
2.2.1. Alignment with Organizational objectives		c4	
2.2.2. Staffing		c4s5, c10s4	
2.2.3. Process	c5	c5	
2.2.4. Organizational Aspects of Maintenance	c7s.2.3	c10	
2.2.5. Outsourcing/Offshoring			all
2.3. Maintenance Cost Estimation			
2.3.1. Cost Estimation	c7s4.1	c7s2.4	

	IEEE/ISO/IEC 14764 2006 [1*]	Grubb and Takang 2003 [2*]	Sneed 2008 [3*]
2.3.2. Parametric Models		c12s5.6	
2.3.3. Experience		c12s5.5	
2.4. Software Maintenance Measurement	c6s5	c12, c12s3.1	
2.4.1. Specific Measures		c12	
3. Maintenance Process			
3.1. Maintenance Processes	c5	c5	
3.2. Maintenance Activities	c5, c5s3.2.2, c6s8.2, c7s3.3		
3.2.1. Unique Activities	c3s10, c6s9, c7s2, c7s3	c6,c7	
3.2.2. Supporting Activities	c4s1, c5, c6s7	c9	
3.2.3. Maintenance Planning Activities	c7s2, c7s.3		
3.2.4. Software Configuration Management	c5s1.2.3	c11	
3.2.5. Software Quality	c6s5, c6s7, c6s8	c12s5.3	
4. Techniques for Maintenance			
4.1. Program Comprehension		c6,c14s5	
4.2. Reengineering		c7	
4.3. Reverse Engineering	c6s2	c7, c14s5	
4.4. Migration	c5s5		
4.5. Retirement	c5s6		
5. Software Maintenance Tools	c6s4	c14	

FURTHER READINGS

A. April and A. Abran, *Software Maintenance Management: Evaluation and Continuous Improvement* [6].

This book explores the domain of small software maintenance processes (S3M). It provides roadmaps for improving software maintenance processes in organizations. It describes a software maintenance specific maturity model organized by levels which allow for benchmarking and continuous improvement. Goals for each key practice area are provided, and the process model presented is fully aligned with the architecture and framework of international standards ISO12207, ISO14764 and ISO15504 and popular maturity models like ITIL, CoBIT, CMMI and CM3.

M. Kajko-Mattsson, "Towards a Business Maintenance Model," IEEE Int'l Conf. Software Maintenance [7].

This paper presents an overview of the Corrective Maintenance Maturity Model (CM3). In contrast to other process models, CM3 is a specialized model, entirely dedicated to corrective maintenance of software. It views maintenance in terms of the activities to be performed and their order, in terms of the information used by these activities, goals, rules and motivations for their execution, and organizational levels and roles involved at various stages of a typical corrective maintenance process.

REFERENCES

[1*] *IEEE Std. 14764-2006 (a.k.a. ISO/IEC 14764:2006) Standard for Software Engineering—Software Life Cycle Processes—Maintenance*, IEEE, 2006.

[2*] P. Grubb and A.A. Takang, *Software Maintenance: Concepts and Practice*, 2nd ed., World Scientific Publishing, 2003.

[3*] H.M. Sneed, "Offering Software Maintenance as an Offshore Service," *Proc. IEEE Int'l Conf. Software Maintenance* (ICSM 08), IEEE, 2008, pp. 1–5.

[4*] J.W. Moore, *The Road Map to Software Engineering: A Standards-Based Guide*, Wiley-IEEE Computer Society Press, 2006.

[5] *ISO/IEC/IEEE 24765:2010 Systems and Software Engineering—Vocabulary*, ISO/IEC/IEEE, 2010.

[6] A. April and A. Abran, *Software Maintenance Management: Evaluation and Continuous Improvement*, Wiley-IEEE Computer Society Press, 2008.

[7] M. Kajko-Mattsson, "Towards a Business Maintenance Model," *Proc. Int'l Conf. Software Maintenance*, IEEE, 2001, pp. 500–509.

CHAPTER 6

SOFTWARE CONFIGURATION MANAGEMENT

ACRONYMS

CCB	Configuration Control Board
CM	Configuration Management
FCA	Functional Configuration Audit
PCA	Physical Configuration Audit
SCCB	Software Configuration Control Board
SCI	Software Configuration Item
SCM	Software Configuration Management
SCMP	Software Configuration Management Plan
SCR	Software Change Request
SCSA	Software Configuration Status Accounting
SDD	Software Design Document
SEI/ CMMI	Software Engineering Institute's Capability Maturity Model Integration
SQA	Software Quality Assurance
SRS	Software Requirement Specification

INTRODUCTION

A system can be defined as the combination of interacting elements organized to achieve one or more stated purposes [1]. The configuration of a system is the functional and physical characteristics of hardware or software as set forth in technical documentation or achieved in a product [1]; it can also be thought of as a collection of specific versions of hardware, firmware, or software items combined according to specific build procedures to serve a particular purpose. Configuration management (CM), then, is the discipline of identifying the configuration of a system at distinct points in time for the purpose of systematically controlling changes to the configuration and maintaining the integrity and traceability of the configuration throughout the system life cycle. It is formally defined as

> A discipline applying technical and administrative direction and surveillance to: identify and document the functional and physical characteristics of a configuration item, control changes to those characteristics, record and report change processing and implementation status, and verify compliance with specified requirements. [1]

Software configuration management (SCM) is a supporting-software life cycle process that benefits project management, development and maintenance activities, quality assurance activities, as well as the customers and users of the end product.

The concepts of configuration management apply to all items to be controlled, although there are some differences in implementation between hardware CM and software CM.

SCM is closely related to the software quality assurance (SQA) activity. As defined in the Software Quality knowledge area (KA), SQA processes provide assurance that the software products and processes in the project life cycle conform to their specified requirements by planning, enacting, and performing a set of activities to provide adequate confidence that quality is being built into the software. SCM activities help in accomplishing these SQA goals. In some project contexts, specific SQA requirements prescribe certain SCM activities.

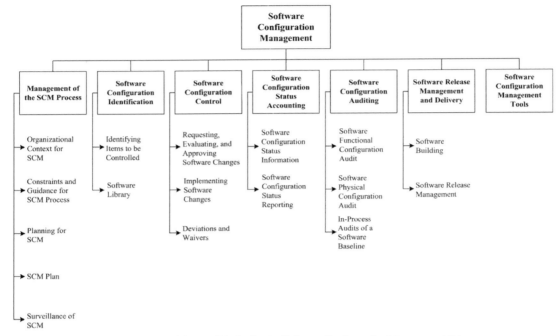

Figure 6.1. Breakdown of Topics for the Software Configuration Management KA

The SCM activities are management and planning of the SCM process, software configuration identification, software configuration control, software configuration status accounting, software configuration auditing, and software release management and delivery.

The Software Configuration Management KA is related to all the other KAs, since the object of configuration management is the artifact produced and used throughout the software engineering process.

BREAKDOWN OF TOPICS FOR SOFTWARE CONFIGURATION MANAGEMENT

The breakdown of topics for the Software Configuration Management KA is shown in Figure 6.1.

1. Management of the SCM Process

SCM controls the evolution and integrity of a product by identifying its elements; managing and controlling change; and verifying, recording, and reporting on configuration information. From the software engineer's perspective, SCM facilitates

development and change implementation activities. A successful SCM implementation requires careful planning and management. This, in turn, requires an understanding of the organizational context for, and the constraints placed on, the design and implementation of the SCM process.

1.1. Organizational Context for SCM
[2*, c6, ann. D] [3*, introduction] [4*, c29]

To plan an SCM process for a project, it is necessary to understand the organizational context and the relationships among organizational elements. SCM interacts with several other activities or organizational elements.

The organizational elements responsible for the software engineering supporting processes may be structured in various ways. Although the responsibility for performing certain SCM tasks might be assigned to other parts of the organization (such as the development organization), the overall responsibility for SCM often rests with a distinct organizational element or designated individual.

Software is frequently developed as part of a larger system containing hardware and firmware elements. In this case, SCM activities take place in parallel with hardware and firmware CM activities and must be consistent with system-level CM. Note that firmware contains hardware and software; therefore, both hardware and software CM concepts are applicable.

SCM might interface with an organization's quality assurance activity on issues such as records management and nonconforming items. Regarding the former, some items under SCM control might also be project records subject to provisions of the organization's quality assurance program. Managing nonconforming items is usually the responsibility of the quality assurance activity; however, SCM might assist with tracking and reporting on software configuration items falling into this category.

Perhaps the closest relationship is with the software development and maintenance organizations. It is within this context that many of the software configuration control tasks are conducted. Frequently, the same tools support development, maintenance, and SCM purposes.

1.2. Constraints and Guidance for the SCM Process

> [2*, c6, ann. D, ann. E] [3*, c2, c5]
> [5*, c19s2.2]

Constraints affecting, and guidance for, the SCM process come from a number of sources. Policies and procedures set forth at corporate or other organizational levels might influence or prescribe the design and implementation of the SCM process for a given project. In addition, the contract between the acquirer and the supplier might contain provisions affecting the SCM process. For example, certain configuration audits might be required, or it might be specified that certain items be placed under CM. When software products to be developed have the potential to affect public safety, external regulatory bodies may impose constraints. Finally, the particular software life cycle process chosen for a software project and the level of formalism selected to implement the software affect the design and implementation of the SCM process.

Guidance for designing and implementing an SCM process can also be obtained from "best practice," as reflected in the standards on software

engineering issued by the various standards organizations (see Appendix B on standards).

1.3. Planning for SCM

> [2*, c6, ann. D, ann. E] [3*, c23] [4*, c29]

The planning of an SCM process for a given project should be consistent with the organizational context, applicable constraints, commonly accepted guidance, and the nature of the project (for example, size, safety criticality, and security). The major activities covered are software configuration identification, software configuration control, software configuration status accounting, software configuration auditing, and software release management and delivery. In addition, issues such as organization and responsibilities, resources and schedules, tool selection and implementation, vendor and subcontractor control, and interface control are typically considered. The results of the planning activity are recorded in an SCM Plan (SCMP), which is typically subject to SQA review and audit.

Branching and merging strategies should be carefully planned and communicated, since they impact many SCM activities. From an SCM standpoint, a branch is defined as a set of evolving source file versions [1]. Merging consists in combining different changes to the same file [1]. This typically occurs when more than one person changes a configuration item. There are many branching and merging strategies in common use (see the Further Readings section for additional discussion).

The software development life cycle model (see Software Life Cycle Models in the Software Engineering Process KA) also impacts SCM activities, and SCM planning should take this into account. For instance, continuous integration is a common practice in many software development approaches. It is typically characterized by frequent build-test-deploy cycles. SCM activities must be planned accordingly.

1.3.1. SCM Organization and Responsibilities

> [2*, ann. Ds5, ann. Ds6] [3*, c10-11]
> [4*, introduction, c29]

To prevent confusion about who will perform given SCM activities or tasks, organizational roles to be involved in the SCM process need to be clearly identified. Specific responsibilities for given SCM activities or tasks also need to be assigned to organizational entities, either by title or by organizational element. The overall authority and reporting channels for SCM should also be identified, although this might be accomplished at the project management or quality assurance planning stage.

1.3.2. SCM Resources and Schedules
[2*, ann. Ds8] [3*, c23]

Planning for SCM identifies the staff and tools involved in carrying out SCM activities and tasks. It addresses scheduling questions by establishing necessary sequences of SCM tasks and identifying their relationships to the project schedules and milestones established at the project management planning stage. Any training requirements necessary for implementing the plans and training new staff members are also specified.

1.3.3. Tool Selection and Implementation
[3*, c26s2, c26s6] [4*, c29s5]

As for any area of software engineering, the selection and implementation of SCM tools should be carefully planned. The following questions should be considered:

- Organization: what motivates tool acquisition from an organizational perspective?
- Tools: can we use commercial tools or develop them ourselves?
- Environment: what are the constraints imposed by the organization and its technical context?
- Legacy: how will projects use (or not) the new tools?
- Financing: who will pay for the tools' acquisition, maintenance, training, and customization?
- Scope: how will the new tools be deployed—for instance, through the entire organization or only on specific projects?
- Ownership: who is responsible for the introduction of new tools?

- Future: what is the plan for the tools' use in the future?
- Change: how adaptable are the tools?
- Branching and merging: are the tools' capabilities compatible with the planned branching and merging strategies?
- Integration: do the various SCM tools integrate among themselves? With other tools in use in the organization?
- Migration: can the repository maintained by the version control tool be ported to another version control tool while maintaining complete history of the configuration items it contains?

SCM typically requires a set of tools, as opposed to a single tool. Such tool sets are sometimes referred to as workbenches. In such a context, another important consideration in planning for tool selection is determining if the SCM workbench will be *open* (in other words, tools from different suppliers will be used in different activities of the SCM process) or *integrated* (where elements of the workbench are designed to work together).

The size of the organization and the type of projects involved may also impact tool selection (see topic 7, Software Configuration Management Tools).

1.3.4. Vendor/Subcontractor Control
[2*, c13] [3*, c13s9, c14s2]

A software project might acquire or make use of purchased software products, such as compilers or other tools. SCM planning considers if and how these items will be taken under configuration control (for example, integrated into the project libraries) and how changes or updates will be evaluated and managed.

Similar considerations apply to subcontracted software. When using subcontracted software, both the SCM requirements to be imposed on the subcontractor's SCM process as part of the subcontract and the means for monitoring compliance need to be established. The latter includes consideration of what SCM information must be available for effective compliance monitoring.

1.3.5. Interface Control
[2*, c12] [3*, c24s4]

When a software item will interface with another software or hardware item, a change to either item can affect the other. Planning for the SCM process considers how the interfacing items will be identified and how changes to the items will be managed and communicated. The SCM role may be part of a larger, system-level process for interface specification and control; it may involve interface specifications, interface control plans, and interface control documents. In this case, SCM planning for interface control takes place within the context of the system-level process.

1.4. SCM Plan
[2*, ann. D] [3*, c23] [4*, c29s1]

The results of SCM planning for a given project are recorded in a software configuration management plan (SCMP), a "living document" which serves as a reference for the SCM process. It is maintained (that is, updated and approved) as necessary during the software life cycle. In implementing the SCMP, it is typically necessary to develop a number of more detailed, subordinate procedures defining how specific requirements will be carried out during day-to-day activities—for example, which branching strategies will be used and how frequently builds occur and automated tests of all kinds are run.

Guidance on the creation and maintenance of an SCMP, based on the information produced by the planning activity, is available from a number of sources, such as [2*]. This reference provides requirements for the information to be contained in an SCMP; it also defines and describes six categories of SCM information to be included in an SCMP:

- Introduction (purpose, scope, terms used)
- SCM Management (organization, responsibilities, authorities, applicable policies, directives, and procedures)
- SCM Activities (configuration identification, configuration control, and so on)

- SCM Schedules (coordination with other project activities)
- SCM Resources (tools, physical resources, and human resources)
- SCMP Maintenance.

1.5. Surveillance of Software Configuration Management
[3*, c11s3]

After the SCM process has been implemented, some degree of surveillance may be necessary to ensure that the provisions of the SCMP are properly carried out. There are likely to be specific SQA requirements for ensuring compliance with specified SCM processes and procedures. The person responsible for SCM ensures that those with the assigned responsibility perform the defined SCM tasks correctly. The software quality assurance authority, as part of a compliance auditing activity, might also perform this surveillance.

The use of integrated SCM tools with process control capability can make the surveillance task easier. Some tools facilitate process compliance while providing flexibility for the software engineer to adapt procedures. Other tools enforce process, leaving the software engineer with less flexibility. Surveillance requirements and the level of flexibility to be provided to the software engineer are important considerations in tool selection.

1.5.1. SCM Measures and Measurement
[3*, c9s2, c25s2–s3]

SCM measures can be designed to provide specific information on the evolving product or to provide insight into the functioning of the SCM process. A related goal of monitoring the SCM process is to discover opportunities for process improvement. Measurements of SCM processes provide a good means for monitoring the effectiveness of SCM activities on an ongoing basis. These measurements are useful in characterizing the current state of the process as well as in providing a basis for making comparisons over time. Analysis of the measurements may produce insights leading to process changes and corresponding updates to the SCMP.

Software libraries and the various SCM tool capabilities provide sources for extracting information about the characteristics of the SCM process (as well as providing project and management information). For example, information about the time required to accomplish various types of changes would be useful in an evaluation of the criteria for determining what levels of authority are optimal for authorizing certain types of changes and for estimating future changes.

Care must be taken to keep the focus of the surveillance on the insights that can be gained from the measurements, not on the measurements themselves. Discussion of software process and product measurement is presented in the Software Engineering Process KA. Software measurement programs are described in the Software Engineering Management KA.

1.5.2. In-Process Audits of SCM
[3*, c1s1]

Audits can be carried out during the software engineering process to investigate the current status of specific elements of the configuration or to assess the implementation of the SCM process. In-process auditing of SCM provides a more formal mechanism for monitoring selected aspects of the process and may be coordinated with the SQA function (see topic 5, Software Configuration Auditing).

2. Software Configuration Identification
[2*, c8] [4*, c29s1.1]

Software configuration identification identifies items to be controlled, establishes identification schemes for the items and their versions, and establishes the tools and techniques to be used in acquiring and managing controlled items. These activities provide the basis for the other SCM activities.

2.1. Identifying Items to Be Controlled
[2*, c8s2.2] [4*, c29s1.1]

One of the first steps in controlling change is identifying the software items to be controlled.

This involves understanding the software configuration within the context of the system configuration, selecting software configuration items, developing a strategy for labeling software items and describing their relationships, and identifying both the baselines to be used and the procedure for a baseline's acquisition of the items.

2.1.1. Software Configuration
[1, c3]

Software configuration is the functional and physical characteristics of hardware or software as set forth in technical documentation or achieved in a product. It can be viewed as part of an overall system configuration.

2.1.2. Software Configuration Item
[4*, c29s1.1]

A configuration item (CI) is an item or aggregation of hardware or software or both that is designed to be managed as a single entity. A software configuration item (SCI) is a software entity that has been established as a configuration item [1]. The SCM typically controls a variety of items in addition to the code itself. Software items with potential to become SCIs include plans, specifications and design documentation, testing materials, software tools, source and executable code, code libraries, data and data dictionaries, and documentation for installation, maintenance, operations, and software use.

Selecting SCIs is an important process in which a balance must be achieved between providing adequate visibility for project control purposes and providing a manageable number of controlled items.

2.1.3. Software Configuration Item Relationships
[3*, c7s4]

Structural relationships among the selected SCIs, and their constituent parts, affect other SCM activities or tasks, such as software building or analyzing the impact of proposed changes. Proper tracking of these relationships is also important for supporting traceability. The design of the identification scheme for SCIs

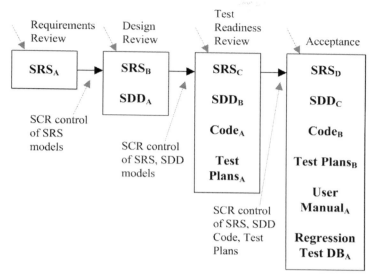

Figure 6.2. Acquisition of Items

should consider the need to map identified items to the software structure, as well as the need to support the evolution of the software items and their relationships.

2.1.4. Software Version
[1, c3] [4*, c29s3]

Software items evolve as a software project proceeds. A version of a software item is an identified instance of an item. It can be thought of as a state of an evolving item. A variant is a version of a program resulting from the application of software diversity.

2.1.5. Baseline
[1, c3]

A software baseline is a formally approved version of a configuration item (regardless of media) that is formally designated and fixed at a specific time during the configuration item's life cycle. The term is also used to refer to a particular version of a software configuration item that has been agreed on. In either case, the baseline can only be changed through formal change control procedures. A baseline, together with all approved changes to the baseline, represents the current approved configuration.

Commonly used baselines include functional, allocated, developmental, and product

baselines. The functional baseline corresponds to the reviewed system requirements. The allocated baseline corresponds to the reviewed software requirements specification and software interface requirements specification. The developmental baseline represents the evolving software configuration at selected times during the software life cycle. Change authority for this baseline typically rests primarily with the development organization but may be shared with other organizations (for example, SCM or Test). The product baseline corresponds to the completed software product delivered for system integration. The baselines to be used for a given project, along with the associated levels of authority needed for change approval, are typically identified in the SCMP.

2.1.6. Acquiring Software Configuration Items
[3*, c18]

Software configuration items are placed under SCM control at different times; that is, they are incorporated into a particular baseline at a particular point in the software life cycle. The triggering event is the completion of some form of formal acceptance task, such as a formal review. Figure 6.2 characterizes the growth of baselined items as the life cycle proceeds. This figure is based on the waterfall model for purposes of illustration only; the subscripts used in the figure indicate versions of the evolving items. The software change request (SCR) is described in section 3.1.

In acquiring an SCI, its origin and initial integrity must be established. Following the acquisition of an SCI, changes to the item must be formally approved as appropriate for the SCI and the baseline involved, as defined in the SCMP. Following approval, the item is incorporated into the software baseline according to the appropriate procedure.

2.2. Software Library

[3*, c1s3] [4*, c29s1.2]

A software library is a controlled collection of software and related documentation designed to aid in software development, use, or maintenance [1]. It is also instrumental in software release management and delivery activities. Several types of libraries might be used, each corresponding to the software item's particular level of maturity. For example, a working library could support coding and a project support library could support testing, while a master library could be used for finished products. An appropriate level of SCM control (associated baseline and level of authority for change) is associated with each library. Security, in terms of access control and the backup facilities, is a key aspect of library management.

The tool(s) used for each library must support the SCM control needs for that library—both in terms of controlling SCIs and controlling access to the library. At the working library level, this is a code management capability serving developers, maintainers, and SCM. It is focused on managing the versions of software items while supporting the activities of multiple developers. At higher levels of control, access is more restricted and SCM is the primary user.

These libraries are also an important source of information for measurements of work and progress.

3. Software Configuration Control

[2*, c9] [4*, c29s2]

Software configuration control is concerned with managing changes during the software life cycle. It covers the process for determining what changes to make, the authority for approving certain changes, support for the implementation of those changes, and the concept of formal deviations from project requirements as well as waivers of them. Information derived from these activities is useful in measuring change traffic and breakage as well as aspects of rework.

3.1. Requesting, Evaluating, and Approving Software Changes

[2*, c9s2.4] [4*, c29s2]

The first step in managing changes to controlled items is determining what changes to make. The software change request process (see a typical flow of a change request process in Figure 6.3) provides formal procedures for submitting and recording change requests, evaluating the potential cost and impact of a proposed change, and accepting, modifying, deferring, or rejecting the proposed change. A change request (CR) is a request to expand or reduce the project scope; modify policies, processes, plans, or procedures; modify costs or budgets; or revise schedules [1]. Requests for changes to software configuration items may be originated by anyone at any point in the software life cycle and may include a suggested solution and requested priority. One source of a CR is the initiation of corrective action in response to problem reports. Regardless of the source, the type of change (for example, defect or enhancement) is usually recorded on the Software CR (SCR).

This provides an opportunity for tracking defects and collecting change activity measurements by change type. Once an SCR is received, a technical evaluation (also known as an impact analysis) is performed to determine the extent of the modifications that would be necessary should the change request be accepted. A good understanding of the relationships among software (and, possibly, hardware) items is important for this task. Finally, an established authority—commensurate with the affected baseline, the SCI involved, and the nature of the change—will evaluate the technical and managerial aspects of the change request and either accept, modify, reject, or defer the proposed change.

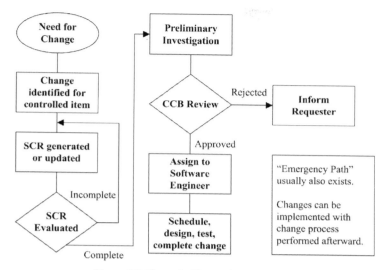

Figure 6.3. Flow of a Change Control Process

3.1.1. Software Configuration Control Board
[2*, c9s2.2] [3*, c11s1] [4*, c29s2]

The authority for accepting or rejecting proposed changes rests with an entity typically known as a Configuration Control Board (CCB). In smaller projects, this authority may actually reside with the leader or an assigned individual rather than a multiperson board. There can be multiple levels of change authority depending on a variety of criteria—such as the criticality of the item involved, the nature of the change (for example, impact on budget and schedule), or the project's current point in the life cycle. The composition of the CCBs used for a given system varies depending on these criteria (an SCM representative would always be present). All stakeholders, appropriate to the level of the CCB, are represented. When the scope of authority of a CCB is strictly software, it is known as a Software Configuration Control Board (SCCB). The activities of the CCB are typically subject to software quality audit or review.

3.1.2. Software Change Request Process
[3*, c1s4, c8s4]

An effective software change request (SCR) process requires the use of supporting tools and procedures for originating change requests, enforcing the flow of the change process, capturing

CCB decisions, and reporting change process information. A link between this tool capability and the problem-reporting system can facilitate the tracking of solutions for reported problems.

3.2. Implementing Software Changes
[4*, c29]

Approved SCRs are implemented using the defined software procedures in accordance with the applicable schedule requirements. Since a number of approved SCRs might be implemented simultaneously, it is necessary to provide a means for tracking which SCRs are incorporated into particular software versions and baselines. As part of the closure of the change process, completed changes may undergo configuration audits and software quality verification—this includes ensuring that only approved changes have been made. The software change request process described above will typically document the SCM (and other) approval information for the change.

Changes may be supported by source code version control tools. These tools allow a team of software engineers, or a single software engineer, to track and document changes to the source code. These tools provide a single repository for storing the source code, can prevent more than one software engineer from editing the same module at the same time, and record all changes made to the source code. Software engineers check modules out of the repository, make changes, document the changes, and then save the edited modules in the repository. If needed, changes can also be discarded, restoring a previous baseline. More powerful tools can support parallel development and geographically distributed environments. These tools may be manifested as separate, specialized applications under the control of an independent SCM group. They may also appear as an integrated part of the software engineering environment. Finally, they may be as elementary as a rudimentary change control system provided with an operating system.

3.3. Deviations and Waivers
[1, c3]

The constraints imposed on a software engineering effort or the specifications produced during the development activities might contain provisions that cannot be satisfied at the designated point in the life cycle. A deviation is a written authorization, granted prior to the manufacture of an item, to depart from a particular performance or design requirement for a specific number of units or a specific period of time. A waiver is a written authorization to accept a configuration item or other designated item that is found, during production or after having been submitted for inspection, to depart from specified requirements but is nevertheless considered suitable for use as-is or after rework by an approved method. In these cases, a formal process is used for gaining approval for deviations from, or waivers of, the provisions.

4. Software Configuration Status Accounting
[2*, c10]

Software configuration status accounting (SCSA) is an element of configuration management consisting of the recording and reporting of information needed to manage a configuration effectively.

4.1. Software Configuration Status Information
[2*, c10s2.1]

The SCSA activity designs and operates a system for the capture and reporting of necessary information as the life cycle proceeds. As in any

information system, the configuration status information to be managed for the evolving configurations must be identified, collected, and maintained. Various information and measurements are needed to support the SCM process and to meet the configuration status reporting needs of management, software engineering, and other related activities. The types of information available include the approved configuration identification as well as the identification and current implementation status of changes, deviations, and waivers.

Some form of automated tool support is necessary to accomplish the SCSA data collection and reporting tasks; this could be a database capability, a stand-alone tool, or a capability of a larger, integrated tool environment.

4.2. Software Configuration Status Reporting
[2*, c10s2.4] [3*, c1s5, c9s1, c17]

Reported information can be used by various organizational and project elements—including the development team, the maintenance team, project management, and software quality activities. Reporting can take the form of ad hoc queries to answer specific questions or the periodic production of predesigned reports. Some information produced by the status accounting activity during the course of the life cycle might become quality assurance records.

In addition to reporting the current status of the configuration, the information obtained by the SCSA can serve as a basis of various measurements. Examples include the number of change requests per SCI and the average time needed to implement a change request.

5. Software Configuration Auditing
[2*, c11]

A software audit is an independent examination of a work product or set of work products to assess compliance with specifications, standards, contractual agreements, or other criteria [1]. Audits are conducted according to a well-defined process consisting of various auditor roles and responsibilities. Consequently, each audit must be carefully planned. An audit can require a number of individuals to perform a variety of tasks over a fairly short period of time. Tools to support the planning and conduct of an audit can greatly facilitate the process.

Software configuration auditing determines the extent to which an item satisfies the required functional and physical characteristics. Informal audits of this type can be conducted at key points in the life cycle. Two types of formal audits might be required by the governing contract (for example, in contracts covering critical software): the Functional Configuration Audit (FCA) and the Physical Configuration Audit (PCA). Successful completion of these audits can be a prerequisite for the establishment of the product baseline.

5.1. Software Functional Configuration Audit
[2*, c11s2.1]

The purpose of the software FCA is to ensure that the audited software item is consistent with its governing specifications. The output of the software verification and validation activities (see Verification and Validation in the Software Quality KA) is a key input to this audit.

5.2. Software Physical Configuration Audit
[2*, c11s2.2]

The purpose of the software physical configuration audit (PCA) is to ensure that the design and reference documentation is consistent with the as-built software product.

5.3. In-Process Audits of a Software Baseline
[2*, c11s2.3]

As mentioned above, audits can be carried out during the development process to investigate the current status of specific elements of the configuration. In this case, an audit could be applied to sampled baseline items to ensure that performance is consistent with specifications or to ensure that evolving documentation continues to be consistent with the developing baseline item.

6. Software Release Management and Delivery
[2*, c14] [3*, c8s2]

In this context, *release* refers to the distribution of a software configuration item outside the development activity; this includes internal releases as well as distribution to customers. When different versions of a software item are available for delivery (such as versions for different platforms or versions with varying capabilities), it is frequently necessary to recreate specific versions and package the correct materials for delivery of the version. The software library is a key element in accomplishing release and delivery tasks.

6.1. Software Building
[4*, c29s4]

Software building is the activity of combining the correct versions of software configuration items, using the appropriate configuration data, into an executable program for delivery to a customer or other recipient, such as the testing activity. For systems with hardware or firmware, the executable program is delivered to the system-building activity. Build instructions ensure that the proper build steps are taken in the correct sequence. In addition to building software for new releases, it is usually also necessary for SCM to have the capability to reproduce previous releases for recovery, testing, maintenance, or additional release purposes.

Software is built using particular versions of supporting tools, such as compilers (see Compiler Basics in the Computing Foundations KA). It might be necessary to rebuild an exact copy of a previously built software configuration item. In this case, supporting tools and associated build instructions need to be under SCM control to ensure availability of the correct versions of the tools.

A tool capability is useful for selecting the correct versions of software items for a given target environment and for automating the process of building the software from the selected versions and appropriate configuration data. For projects with parallel or distributed development environments, this tool capability is necessary. Most software engineering environments provide this capability. These tools vary in complexity from requiring the software engineer to learn a specialized scripting language to graphics-oriented approaches that hide much of the complexity of an "intelligent" build facility.

The build process and products are often subject to software quality verification. Outputs of the build process might be needed for future reference and may become quality assurance records.

6.2. *Software Release Management*
[4*, c29s3.2]

Software release management encompasses the identification, packaging, and delivery of the elements of a product—for example, an executable program, documentation, release notes, and configuration data. Given that product changes can occur on a continuing basis, one concern for release management is determining when to issue a release. The severity of the problems addressed by the release and measurements of the fault densities of prior releases affect this decision. The packaging task must identify which product items are to be delivered and then select the correct variants of those items, given the intended application of the product. The information documenting the physical contents of a release is known as a version description document. The release notes typically describe new capabilities, known problems, and platform requirements necessary for proper product operation. The package to be released also contains installation or upgrading instructions. The latter can be complicated by the fact that some current users might have versions that are several releases old. In some cases, release management might be required in order to track distribution of the product to various customers or target systems—for example, in a case where the supplier was required to notify a customer of newly reported problems. Finally, a mechanism to ensure the integrity of the released item can be implemented—for example by releasing a digital signature with it.

A tool capability is needed for supporting these release management functions. It is useful to have a connection with the tool capability supporting the change request process in order to map release contents to the SCRs that have been received. This tool capability might also maintain information on various target platforms and on various customer environments.

7. Software Configuration Management Tools
[3*, c26s1] [4*, c8s2]

When discussing software configuration management tools, it is helpful to classify them. SCM tools can be divided into three classes in terms of the scope at which they provide support: individual support, project-related support, and companywide-process support.

Individual support tools are appropriate and typically sufficient for small organizations or development groups without variants of their software products or other complex SCM requirements. They include:

- Version control tools: track, document, and store individual configuration items such as source code and external documentation.
- Build handling tools: in their simplest form, such tools compile and link an executable version of the software. More advanced building tools extract the latest version from the version control software, perform quality checks, run regression tests, and produce various forms of reports, among other tasks.
- Change control tools: mainly support the control of change requests and events notification (for example, change request status changes, milestones reached).

Project-related support tools mainly support workspace management for development teams and integrators; they are typically able to support distributed development environments. Such tools are appropriate for medium to large organizations with variants of their software products and parallel development but no certification requirements.

Companywide-process support tools can typically automate portions of a companywide process, providing support for workflow managements, roles, and responsibilities. They are able to handle many items, data, and life cycles. Such tools add to project-related support by supporting a more formal development process, including certification requirements.

MATRIX OF TOPICS VS. REFERENCE MATERIAL

	IEEE 828-2012 [2*]	Hass 2003 [3*]	Moore 2006 [5*]	Sommerville 2011 [4*]
1. Management of the SCM Process				
1.1. Organizational Context for SCM	c6, ann.D	introduction		c29
1.2. Constraints and Guidance for the SCM Process	c6, ann.D, ann.E	c2	c19s2.2	c29 intro
1.3. Planning for SCM	c6, ann.D, ann.E	c23		c29
1.3.1. SCM Organization and Responsibilities	ann.Ds5–6	c10–11		c29 intro
1.3.2. SCM Resources and Schedules	ann.Ds8	c23		
1.3.3. Tool Selection and Implementation		c26s2; s6		c29s5
1.3.4. Vendor/Subcontractor Control	c13	c13s9–c14s2		
1.3.5. Interface Control	c12	c24s4		
1.4. SCM Plan	ann.D	c23		c29s1
1.5. Surveillance of Software Configuration Management		c11s3		
1.5.1. SCM Measures and Measurement		c9s2; c25s2–s3		
1.5.2. In-Process Audits of SCM		c1s1		
2. Software Configuration Identification				c29s1.1
2.1. Identifying Items to Be Controlled	c8s2.2			c29s1.1
2.1.1. Software Configuration				
2.1.2. Software Configuration Item				c29s1.1
2.1.3. Software Configuration Item Relationships		c7s4		
2.1.4. Software Version				c29s3

	IEEE 828-2012 [2*]	Hass 2003 [3*]	Moore 2006 [5*]	Sommerville 2011 [4*]
2.1.5. Baseline				
2.1.6. Acquiring Software Configuration Items		c18		
2.2. Software Library		c1s3		c29s1.2
3. Software Configuration Control	c9			c29s2
3.1. Requesting, Evaluating, and Approving Software Changes	c9s2.4			c29s2
3.1.1. Software Configuration Control Board	c9s2.2	c11s1		c29s2
3.1.2. Software Change Request Process		c1s4, c8s4		
3.2. Implementing Software Changes				c29
3.3. Deviations and Waivers				
4. Software Configuration Status Accounting	c10			
4.1. Software Configuration Status Information	c10s2.1			
4.2. Software Configuration Status Reporting	c10s2.4	c1s5, c9s1, c17		
5. Software Configuration Auditing	c11			
5.1. Software Functional Configuration Audit	c11s2.1			
5.2. Software Physical Configuration Audit	c11s2.2			
5.3. In-Process Audits of a Software Baseline	c11s2.3			
6. Software Release Management and Delivery	c14	c8s2		c29s3
6.1. Software Building				c29s4
6.2. Software Release Management				c29s3.2
7. Software Configuration Management Tools		c26s1		

FURTHER READINGS

Stephen P. Berczuk and Brad Appleton, *Software Configuration Management Patterns: Effective Teamwork, Practical Integration* [6].

This book expresses useful SCM practices and strategies as patterns. The patterns can be implemented using various tools, but they are expressed in a tool-agnostic fashion.

"CMMI for Development," Version 1.3, pp. 137–147 [7].

This model presents a collection of best practices to help software development organizations improve their processes. At maturity level 2, it suggests configuration management activities.

REFERENCES

[1] *ISO/IEC/IEEE 24765:2010 Systems and Software Engineering—Vocabulary*, ISO/IEC/IEEE, 2010.

[2*] *IEEE Std. 828-2012, Standard for Configuration Management in Systems and Software Engineering*, IEEE, 2012.

[3*] A.M.J. Hass, *Configuration Management Principles and Practices*, 1st ed., Addison-Wesley, 2003.

[4*] I. Sommerville, *Software Engineering*, 9th ed., Addison-Wesley, 2011.

[5*] J.W. Moore, *The Road Map to Software Engineering: A Standards-Based Guide*, Wiley-IEEE Computer Society Press, 2006.

[6] S.P. Berczuk and B. Appleton, *Software Configuration Management Patterns: Effective Teamwork, Practical Integration*, Addison-Wesley Professional, 2003.

[7] CMMI Product Team, "CMMI for Development, Version 1.3," Software Engineering Institute, 2010; http://resources.sei.cmu.edu/library/asset-view.cfm?assetID=9661.

CHAPTER 7

SOFTWARE ENGINEERING MANAGEMENT

ACRONYMS

PMBOK® Guide	Guide to the Project Management Body of Knowledge
SDLC	Software Development Life Cycle
SEM	Software Engineering Management
SQA	Software Quality Assurance
SWX	Software Extension to the PMBOK® Guide
WBS	Work Breakdown Structure

INTRODUCTION

Software engineering management can be defined as the application of management activities—planning, coordinating, measuring, monitoring, controlling, and reporting[1]—to ensure that software products and software engineering services are delivered efficiently, effectively, and to the benefit of stakeholders. The related discipline of management is an important element of all the knowledge areas (KAs), but it is of course more relevant to this KA than to other KAs. Measurement is also an important aspect of all KAs; the topic of measurement programs is presented in this KA.

In one sense, it should be possible to manage a software engineering project in the same way other complex endeavors are managed. However, there are aspects specific to software projects and software life cycle processes that complicate effective management, including these:

- Clients often don't know what is needed or what is feasible.
- Clients often lack appreciation for the complexities inherent in software engineering, particularly regarding the impact of changing requirements.
- It is likely that increased understanding and changing conditions will generate new or changed software requirements.
- As a result of changing requirements, software is often built using an iterative process rather than as a sequence of closed tasks.
- Software engineering necessarily incorporates creativity and discipline. Maintaining an appropriate balance between the two is sometimes difficult.
- The degree of novelty and complexity is often high.
- There is often a rapid rate of change in the underlying technology.

Software engineering management activities occur at three levels: organizational and infrastructure management, project management, and management of the measurement program. The last two are covered in detail in this KA description. However, this is not to diminish the importance of organizational and infrastructure management issues. It is generally agreed that software organizational engineering managers should be conversant with the project management and software measurement knowledge described in this KA. They should also possess some target domain knowledge. Likewise, it is also helpful if managers of complex projects and programs in which software is a component of the system architecture are aware of the differences that software processes introduce into project management and project measurement.

---

1 The terms Initiating, Planning, Executing, Monitoring and Controlling, and Closing are used to describe process groups in the *PMBOK® Guide* and *SWX*.

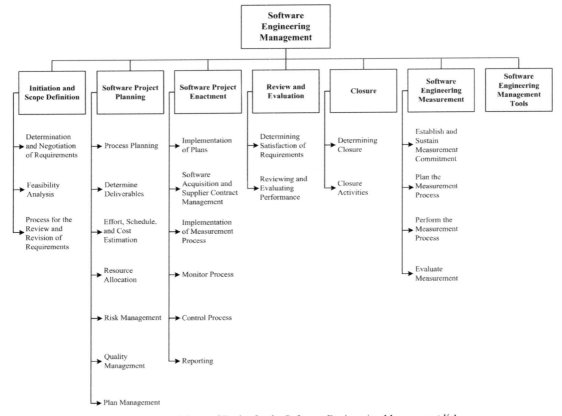

Figure 7.1. Breakdown of Topics for the Software Engineering Management KA

Other aspects of organizational management exert an impact on software engineering (for example, organizational policies and procedures that provide the framework in which software engineering projects are undertaken). These policies and procedures may need to be adjusted by the requirements for effective software development and maintenance. In addition, a number of policies specific to software engineering may need to be in place or established for effective management of software engineering at the organizational level. For example, policies are usually necessary to establish specific organization-wide processes or procedures for software engineering tasks such as software design, software construction, estimating, monitoring, and reporting. Such policies are important for effective long-term management of software engineering projects across an organization (for example, establishing a consistent basis by which to analyze past project performance and implement improvements).

Another important aspect of organizational management is personnel management policies and procedures for hiring, training, and mentoring personnel for career development, not only at the project level, but also to the longer-term success of an organization. Software engineering personnel may present unique training or personnel management challenges (for example, maintaining currency in a context where the underlying technology undergoes rapid and continuous change).

Communication management is also often mentioned as an overlooked but important aspect of the performance of individuals in a field where precise understanding of user needs, software requirements, and software designs is necessary. Furthermore, portfolio management, which provides an overall view, not only of software currently under development in various projects and programs (integrated projects), but also of software planned and currently in use in an organization, is desirable. Also, software reuse is a key factor in maintaining and improving productivity and competitiveness. Effective reuse requires a strategic vision that reflects the advantages and disadvantages of reuse.

In addition to understanding the aspects of management that are uniquely influenced by software projects, software engineers should have some knowledge of the more general aspects of management that are discussed in this KA (even in the first few years after graduation).

Attributes of organizational culture and behavior, plus management of other functional areas of the enterprise, have an influence, albeit indirectly, on an organization's software engineering processes.

Extensive information concerning software project management can be found in the *Guide to the Project Management Body of Knowledge (PMBOK® Guide)* and the *Software Extension to the PMBOK® Guide (SWX)* [1] [2]. Each of these guides includes ten project management KAs: project integration management, project scope management, project time management, project cost management, project quality management, project human resource management, project communications management, project risk management, project procurement management, and project stakeholder management. Each KA has direct relevance to this Software Engineering Management KA.

Additional information is also provided in the other references and further readings for this KA.

This Software Engineering Management KA consists of the software project management processes in the first five topics in Figure 7.1 (Initiation and Scope Definition, Software Project Planning, Software Project Enactment, Review and Evaluation, Closure), plus Software Engineering Measurement in the sixth topic and Software Engineering Management Tools in the seventh topic. While project management and measurement management are often regarded as being separate, and indeed each does possess many unique attributes, the close relationship has led to combined treatment in this KA.

Unfortunately, a common perception of the software industry is that software products are delivered late, over budget, of poor quality, and with incomplete functionality. Measurement-informed management—a basic principle of any true engineering discipline (see Measurement in the Engineering Foundations KA)—can help improve the perception and the reality. In essence, management without measurement (qualitative and quantitative) suggests a lack of discipline, and measurement without management suggests a lack of purpose or context. Effective management requires a combination of both measurement and experience.

The following working definitions are adopted here:

- *Management* is a system of processes and controls required to achieve the strategic objectives set by the organization.
- *Measurement* refers to the assignment of values and labels to software engineering work products, processes, and resources plus the models that are derived from them, whether these models are developed using statistical or other techniques [3* , c7, c8].

The software engineering project management sections in this KA make extensive use of the software engineering measurement section.

This KA is closely related to others in the *SWEBOK Guide*, and reading the following KA descriptions in conjunction with this one will be particularly helpful:

- The Engineering Foundations KA describes some general concepts of measurement that are directly applicable to the Software Engineering Measurement section of this KA. In addition, the concepts and techniques presented in the Statistical Analysis section of the Engineering Foundations KA apply directly to many topics in this KA.
- The Software Requirements KA describes some of the activities that should be performed during the Initiation and Scope definition phase of the project.
- The Software Configuration Management KA deals with identification, control, status accounting, and auditing of software configurations along with software release management and delivery and software configuration management tools.

- The Software Engineering Process KA describes software life cycle models and the relationships between processes and work products.
- The Software Quality KA emphasizes quality as a goal of management and as an aim of many software engineering activities.
- The Software Engineering Economics KA discusses how to make software-related decisions in a business context.

BREAKDOWN OF TOPICS FOR SOFTWARE ENGINEERING MANAGEMENT

Because most software development life cycle models require similar activities that may be executed in different ways, the breakdown of topics is activity-based. That breakdown is shown in Figure 7.1. The elements of the top-level breakdown shown in that figure are the activities that are usually performed when a software development project is being managed, independent of the software development life cycle model (see Software Life Cycle Models in the Software Engineering Process KA) that has been chosen for a specific project. There is no intent in this breakdown to recommend a specific life cycle model. The breakdown implies only what happens and does not imply when, how, or how many times each activity occurs. The seven topics are:

- Initiation and Scope Definition, which deal with the decision to embark on a software engineering project;
- Software Project Planning, which addresses the activities undertaken to prepare for a successful software engineering project from the management perspective;
- Software Project Enactment, which deals with generally accepted software engineering management activities that occur during the execution of a software engineering project;
- Review and Evaluation, which deal with ensuring that technical, schedule, cost, and quality engineering activities are satisfactory;
- Closure, which addresses the activities accomplished to complete a project;
- Software Engineering Measurement, which deals with the effective development and

implementation of measurement programs in software engineering organizations;
- Software Engineering Management Tools, which describes the selection and use of tools for managing a software engineering project.

1. Initiation and Scope Definition

The focus of these activities is on effective determination of software requirements using various elicitation methods and the assessment of project feasibility from a variety of standpoints. Once project feasibility has been established, the remaining tasks within this section are the specification of requirements and selection of the processes for revision and review of requirements.

1.1. Determination and Negotiation of Requirements
[3*, c3]

Determining and negotiating requirements set the visible boundaries for the set of tasks being undertaken (see the Software Requirements KA). Activities include requirements elicitation, analysis, specification, and validation. Methods and techniques should be selected and applied, taking into account the various stakeholder perspectives. This leads to the determination of project scope in order to meet objectives and satisfy constraints.

1.2. Feasibility Analysis
[4*, c4]

The purpose of feasibility analysis is to develop a clear description of project objectives and evaluate alternative approaches in order to determine whether the proposed project is the best alternative given the constraints of technology, resources, finances, and social/political considerations. An initial project and product scope statement, project deliverables, project duration constraints, and an estimate of resources needed should be prepared.

Resources include a sufficient number of people who have the needed skills, facilities, infrastructure, and support (either internally or externally). Feasibility analysis often requires approximate estimations of effort and cost based on appropriate methods (see section 2.3, Effort, Schedule, and Cost Estimation).

1.3. Process for the Review and Revision of Requirements

[3*, c3]

Given the inevitability of change, stakeholders should agree on the means by which requirements and scope are to be reviewed and revised (for example, change management procedures, iterative cycle retrospectives). This clearly implies that scope and requirements will not be "set in stone" but can and should be revisited at predetermined points as the project unfolds (for example, at the time when backlog priorities are created or at milestone reviews). If changes are accepted, then some form of traceability analysis and risk analysis should be used to ascertain the impact of those changes (see section 2.5, Risk Management, and Software Configuration Control in the Software Configuration Management KA).

A managed-change approach can also form the basis for evaluation of success during closure of an incremental cycle or an entire project, based on changes that have occurred along the way (see topic 5, Closure).

2. Software Project Planning

The first step in software project planning should be selection of an appropriate software development life cycle model and perhaps tailoring it based on project scope, software requirements, and a risk assessment. Other factors to be considered include the nature of the application domain, functional and technical complexity, and software quality requirements (see Software Quality Requirements in the Software Quality KA).

In all SDLCs, risk assessment should be an element of initial project planning, and the "risk profile" of the project should be discussed and accepted by all relevant stakeholders. Software quality management processes (see Software Quality Management Processes in the Software Quality KA) should be determined as part of the planning process and result in procedures and responsibilities for software quality assurance, verification and validation, reviews, and audits (see the Software Quality KA). Processes and responsibilities for ongoing review and revision of the project plan and related plans should also be clearly stated and agreed upon.

2.1. Process Planning

[3*, c3, c4, c5] [5*, c1]

Software development life cycle (SDLC) models span a continuum from predictive to adaptive (see Software Life Cycle Models in the Software Engineering Process KA). Predictive SDLCs are characterized by development of detailed software requirements, detailed project planning, and minimal planning for iteration among development phases. Adaptive SDLCs are designed to accommodate emergent software requirements and iterative adjustment of plans. A highly predictive SDLC executes the first five processes listed in Figure 7.1 in a linear sequence with revisions to earlier phases only as necessary. Adaptive SDLCs are characterized by iterative development cycles. SDLCs in the mid-range of the SDLC continuum produce increments of functionality on either a preplanned schedule (on the predictive side of the continuum) or as the products of frequently updated development cycles (on the adaptive side of the continuum).

Well-known SDLCs include the waterfall, incremental, and spiral models plus various forms of agile software development [2] [3*, c2].

Relevant methods (see the Software Engineering Models and Methods KA) and tools should be selected as part of planning. Automated tools that will be used throughout the project should also be planned for and acquired. Tools may include tools for project scheduling, software requirements, software design, software construction, software maintenance, software configuration management, software engineering process, software quality, and others. While many of these tools should be selected based primarily on the technical considerations discussed in other KAs, some of them are closely related to the management considerations discussed in this chapter.

2.2. Determine Deliverables

[3*, c4, c5, c6]

The work product(s) of each project activity (for example, software architecture design documents, inspection reports, tested software) should be identified and characterized. Opportunities to reuse software components from previous projects or to utilize off-the-shelf software products should be evaluated. Procurement of software and use of third parties to develop deliverables should be planned and suppliers selected (see section 3.2, Software Acquisition and Supplier Contract Management).

2.3. Effort, Schedule, and Cost Estimation
[3*, c6]

The estimated range of effort required for a project, or parts of a project, can be determined using a calibrated estimation model based on historical size and effort data (when available) and other relevant methods such as expert judgment and analogy. Task dependencies can be established and potential opportunities for completing tasks concurrently and sequentially can be identified and documented using a Gantt chart, for example. For predictive SDLC projects, the expected schedule of tasks with projected start times, durations, and end times is typically produced during planning. For adaptive SDLC projects, an overall estimate of effort and schedule is typically developed from the initial understanding of the requirements, or, alternatively, constraints on overall effort and schedule may be specified and used to determine an initial estimate of the number of iterative cycles and estimates of effort and other resources allocated to each cycle.

Resource requirements (for example, people and tools) can be translated into cost estimates. Initial estimation of effort, schedule, and cost is an iterative activity that should be negotiated and revised among affected stakeholders until consensus is reached on resources and time available for project completion.

2.4. Resource Allocation
[3*, c5, c10, c11]

Equipment, facilities, and people should be allocated to the identified tasks, including the allocation of responsibilities for completion of various elements of a project and the overall project. A matrix that shows who is responsible for, accountable for, consulted about, and informed about each of the tasks can be used. Resource allocation is based on, and constrained by, the availability of resources and their optimal use, as

well as by issues relating to personnel (for example, productivity of individuals and teams, team dynamics, and team structures).

2.5. Risk Management
[3*, c9] [5*, c5]

Risk and uncertainty are related but distinct concepts. Uncertainty results from lack of information. Risk is characterized by the probability of an event that will result in a negative impact plus a characterization of the negative impact on a project. Risk is often the result of uncertainty. The converse of risk is opportunity, which is characterized by the probability that an event having a positive outcome might occur.

Risk management entails identification of risk factors and analysis of the probability and potential impact of each risk factor, prioritization of risk factors, and development of risk mitigation strategies to reduce the probability and minimize the negative impact if a risk factor becomes a problem. Risk assessment methods (for example, expert judgment, historical data, decision trees, and process simulations) can sometimes be used in order to identify and evaluate risk factors.

Project abandonment conditions can also be determined at this point in discussion with all relevant stakeholders. Software-unique aspects of risk, such as software engineers' tendency to add unneeded features, or the risks related to software's intangible nature, can influence risk management of a software project. Particular attention should be paid to the management of risks related to software quality requirements such as safety or security (see the Software Quality KA). Risk management should be done not only at the beginning of a project, but also at periodic intervals throughout the project life cycle.

2.6. Quality Management
[3*, c4] [4*, c24]

Software quality requirements should be identified, perhaps in both quantitative and qualitative terms, for a software project and the associated work products. Thresholds for acceptable quality measurements should be set for each software quality requirement based on stakeholder needs and expectations. Procedures concerned with ongoing Software Quality Assurance (SQA) and quality improvement throughout the development process, and for verification and validation of the deliverable software product, should also be specified during quality planning (for example, technical reviews and inspections or demonstrations of completed functionality; see the Software Quality KA).

2.7. Plan Management

[3*, c4]

For software projects, where change is an expectation, plans should be managed. Managing the project plan should thus be planned. Plans and processes selected for software development should be systematically monitored, reviewed, reported, and, when appropriate, revised. Plans associated with supporting processes (for example, documentation, software configuration management, and problem resolution) also should be managed. Reporting, monitoring, and controlling a project should fit within the selected SDLC and the realities of the project; plans should account for the various artifacts that will be used to manage the project.

3. Software Project Enactment

During software project enactment (also known as project execution) plans are implemented and the processes embodied in the plans are enacted. Throughout, there should be a focus on adherence to the selected SDLC processes, with an overriding expectation that adherence will lead to the successful satisfaction of stakeholder requirements and achievement of the project's objectives. Fundamental to enactment are the ongoing management activities of monitoring, controlling, and reporting.

3.1. Implementation of Plans

[4*, c2]

Project activities should be undertaken in accordance with the project plan and supporting plans. Resources (for example, personnel, technology, and funding) are utilized and work products (for example, software design, software code, and software test cases) are generated.

3.2. Software Acquisition and Supplier Contract Management

[3*, c3, c4]

Software acquisition and supplier contract management is concerned with issues involved in contracting with customers of the software development organization who acquire the deliverable work products and with suppliers who supply products or services to the software engineering organization.

This may involve selection of appropriate kinds of contracts, such as fixed price, time and materials, cost plus fixed fee, or cost plus incentive fee. Agreements with customers and suppliers typically specify the scope of work and the deliverables and include clauses such as penalties for late delivery or nondelivery and intellectual property agreements that specify what the supplier or suppliers are providing and what the acquirer is paying for, plus what will be delivered to and owned by the acquirer. For software being developed by suppliers (both internal to or external to the software development organization), agreements commonly indicate software quality requirements for acceptance of the delivered software.

After the agreement has been put in place, execution of the project in compliance with the terms of the agreement should be managed (see chapter 12 of SWX, Software Procurement Management, for more information on this topic [2]).

3.3. Implementation of Measurement Process

[3*, c7]

The measurement process should be enacted during the software project to ensure that relevant and useful data are collected (see sections 6.2, Plan the Measurement Process, and 6.3, Perform the Measurement Process).

3.4. Monitor Process

[3*, c8]

Adherence to the project plan and related plans should be assessed continually and at predetermined intervals. Also, outputs and completion criteria for each task should be assessed. Deliverables should be evaluated in terms of their required characteristics (for example, via inspections or by demonstrating working functionality). Effort expenditure, schedule adherence, and costs to date should be analyzed, and resource usage examined. The project risk profile (see section 2.5, Risk Management) should be revisited, and adherence to software quality requirements evaluated (see Software Quality Requirements in the Software Quality KA).

Measurement data should be analyzed (see Statistical Analysis in the Engineering Foundations KA). Variance analysis based on the deviation of actual from expected outcomes and values should be determined. This may include cost overruns, schedule slippage, or other similar measures. Outlier identification and analysis of quality and other measurement data should be performed (for example, defect analysis; see Software Quality Measurement in the Software Quality KA). Risk exposures should be recalculated (see section 2.5, Risk Management). These activities can enable problem detection and exception identification based on thresholds that have been exceeded. Outcomes should be reported when thresholds have been exceeded, or as necessary.

3.5. Control Process

[3*, c7, c8]

The outcomes of project monitoring activities provide the basis on which decisions can be made. Where appropriate, and when the probability and impact of risk factors are understood, changes can be made to the project. This may take the form of corrective action (for example, retesting certain software components); it may involve incorporating additional actions (for example, deciding to use prototyping to assist in software requirements validation; see Prototyping in the Software Requirements KA); and/or it may entail revision of the project plan and other project documents (for example, the software requirements specification) to accommodate unanticipated events and their implications.

In some instances, the control process may lead to abandonment of the project. In all cases,

software configuration control and software configuration management procedures should be adhered to (see the Software Configuration Management KA), decisions should be documented and communicated to all relevant parties, plans should be revisited and revised when necessary, and relevant data recorded (see section 6.3, Perform the Measurement Process).

3.6. Reporting

[3*, c11]

At specified and agreed-upon times, progress to date should be reported—both within the organization (for example, to a project steering committee) and to external stakeholders (for example, clients or users). Reports should focus on the information needs of the target audience as opposed to the detailed status reporting within the project team.

4. Review and Evaluation

At prespecified times and as needed, overall progress towards achievement of the stated objectives and satisfaction of stakeholder (user and customer) requirements should be evaluated. Similarly, assessments of the effectiveness of the software process, the personnel involved, and the tools and methods employed should also be undertaken regularly and as determined by circumstances.

4.1. Determining Satisfaction of Requirements

[4*, c8]

Because achieving stakeholder satisfaction is a principal goal of the software engineering manager, progress towards this goal should be assessed periodically. Progress should be assessed on achievement of major project milestones (for example, completion of software design architecture or completion of a software technical review), or upon completion of an iterative development cycle that results in a product increment. Variances from software requirements should be identified and appropriate actions should be taken.

As in the control process activity above (see section 3.5, Control Process), software configuration control and software configuration management procedures should be followed (see the Software Configuration Management KA), decisions documented and communicated to all relevant parties, plans revisited and revised where necessary, and relevant data recorded (see section 6.3, Perform the Measurement Process).

4.2. Reviewing and Evaluating Performance
[3*, c8, c10]

Periodic performance reviews for project personnel can provide insights as to the likelihood of adherence to plans and processes as well as possible areas of difficulty (for example, team member conflicts). The various methods, tools, and techniques employed should be evaluated for their effectiveness and appropriateness, and the process being used by the project should also be systematically and periodically assessed for relevance, utility, and efficacy in the project context. Where appropriate, changes should be made and managed.

5. Closure

An entire project, a major phase of a project, or an iterative development cycle reaches closure when all the plans and processes have been enacted and completed. The criteria for project, phase, or iteration success should be evaluated. Once closure is established, archival, retrospective, and process improvement activities can be performed.

5.1. Determining Closure
[1, s3.7, s4.6]

Closure occurs when the specified tasks for a project, a phase, or an iteration have been completed and satisfactory achievement of the completion criteria has been confirmed. Software requirements can be confirmed as satisfied or not, and the degree of achieving the objectives can be determined. Closure processes should involve relevant stakeholders and result in documentation of relevant stakeholders' acceptance; any known problems should be documented.

5.2. Closure Activities
[2, s3.7, s4.8]

After closure has been confirmed, archiving of project materials should be accomplished in accordance with stakeholder agreed-upon methods, location, and duration—possibly including destruction of sensitive information, software, and the medium on which copies are resident. The organization's measurement database should be updated with relevant project data. A project, phase, or iteration retrospective analysis should be undertaken so that issues, problems, risks, and opportunities encountered can be analyzed (see topic 4, Review and Evaluation). Lessons learned should be drawn from the project and fed into organizational learning and improvement endeavors.

6. Software Engineering Measurement

The importance of measurement and its role in better management and engineering practices is widely acknowledged (see Measurement in the Engineering Foundations KA). Effective measurement has become one of the cornerstones of organizational maturity. Measurement can be applied to organizations, projects, processes, and work products. In this section the focus is on the application of measurement at the levels of projects, processes, and work products.

This section follows the IEEE 15939:2008 standard [6], which describes a process to define the activities and tasks necessary to implement a software measurement process. The standard also includes a measurement information model.

6.1. Establish and Sustain Measurement Commitment
[7*, c1, c2][2]

- Requirements for measurement. Each measurement endeavor should be guided by organizational objectives and driven by a set of measurement requirements established by

---

2   Please note that these two chapters can be downloaded free of charge from www.psmsc.com/PSMBook.asp.

the organization and the project (for example, an organizational objective might be "first-to-market with new products").

- Scope of measurement. The organizational unit to which each measurement requirement is to be applied should be established. This may consist of a functional area, a single project, a single site, or an entire enterprise. The temporal scope of the measurement effort should also be considered because time series of some measurements may be required; for example, to calibrate estimation models (see section 2.3, Effort, Schedule, and Cost Estimation).
- Team commitment to measurement. The commitment should be formally established, communicated, and supported by resources (see next item).
- Resources for measurement. An organization's commitment to measurement is an essential factor for success, as evidenced by the assignment of resources for implementing the measurement process. Assigning resources includes allocation of responsibility for the various tasks of the measurement process (such as analyst and librarian). Adequate funding, training, tools, and support to conduct the process should also be allocated.

6.2. Plan the Measurement Process
[7*, c1, c2]

- Characterize the organizational unit. The organizational unit provides the context for measurement, so the organizational context should be made explicit, including the constraints that the organization imposes on the measurement process. The characterization can be stated in terms of organizational processes, application domains, technology, organizational interfaces, and organizational structure.
- Identify information needs. Information needs are based on the goals, constraints, risks, and problems of the organizational unit. They may be derived from business, organizational, regulatory, and/or product objectives. They should be identified and

prioritized. Then a subset of objectives to be addressed can be selected, documented, communicated, and reviewed by stakeholders.

- Select measures. Candidate measures should be selected, with clear links to the information needs. Measures should be selected based on the priorities of the information needs and other criteria such as cost of collection, degree of process disruption during collection, ease of obtaining accurate, consistent data, and ease of analysis and reporting. Because internal quality characteristics (see Models and Quality Characteristics in the Software Quality KA) are often not contained in the contractually binding software requirements, it is important to consider measuring the internal quality of the software to provide an early indicator of potential issues that may impact external stakeholders.
- Define data collection, analysis, and reporting procedures. This encompasses collection procedures and schedules, storage, verification, analysis, reporting, and configuration management of data.
- Select criteria for evaluating the information products. Criteria for evaluation are influenced by the technical and business objectives of the organizational unit. Information products include those associated with the product being produced, as well as those associated with the processes being used to manage and measure the project.
- Provide resources for measurement tasks. The measurement plan should be reviewed and approved by the appropriate stakeholders to include all data collection procedures; storage, analysis, and reporting procedures; evaluation criteria; schedules; and responsibilities. Criteria for reviewing these artifacts should have been established at the organizational-unit level or higher and should be used as the basis for these reviews. Such criteria should take into consideration previous experience, availability of resources, and potential disruptions to projects when changes from current practices are proposed. Approval demonstrates commitment to the measurement process.
- Identify resources to be made available for implementing the planned and approved

measurement tasks. Resource availability may be staged in cases where changes are to be piloted before widespread deployment. Consideration should be paid to the resources necessary for successful deployment of new procedures or measures.

- Acquire and deploy supporting technologies. This includes evaluation of available supporting technologies, selection of the most appropriate technologies, acquisition of those technologies, and deployment of those technologies.

6.3. Perform the Measurement Process
[7*, c1, c2]

- Integrate measurement procedures with relevant software processes. The measurement procedures, such as data collection, should be integrated into the software processes they are measuring. This may involve changing current software processes to accommodate data collection or generation activities. It may also involve analysis of current software processes to minimize additional effort and evaluation of the effect on employees to ensure that the measurement procedures will be accepted. Morale issues and other human factors should be considered. In addition, the measurement procedures should be communicated to those providing the data. Training and support may also need to be provided. Data analysis and reporting procedures are typically integrated into organizational and/or project processes in a similar manner.

- Collect data. Data should be collected, verified, and stored. Collection can sometimes be automated by using software engineering management tools (see topic 7, Software Engineering Management Tools) to analyze data and develop reports. Data may be aggregated, transformed, or recoded as part of the analysis process, using a degree of rigor appropriate to the nature of the data and the information needs. The results of this analysis are typically indicators such as graphs, numbers, or other indications that will be interpreted, resulting in conclusions and recommendations to be presented to stakeholders (see Statistical Analysis in the Engineering Foundations KA). The results and conclusions are usually reviewed, using a process defined by the organization (which may be formal or informal). Data providers and measurement users should participate in reviewing the data to ensure that they are meaningful and accurate and that they can result in reasonable actions.

- Communicate results. Information products should be documented and communicated to users and stakeholders.

6.4. Evaluate Measurement
[7*, c1, c2]

- Evaluate information products and the measurement process against specified evaluation criteria and determine strengths and weaknesses of the information products or process, respectively. Evaluation may be performed by an internal process or an external audit; it should include feedback from measurement users. Lessons learned should be recorded in an appropriate database.

- Identify potential improvements. Such improvements may be changes in the format of indicators, changes in units measured, or reclassification of measurement categories. The costs and benefits of potential improvements should be determined and appropriate improvement actions should be reported.

- Communicate proposed improvements to the measurement process owner and stakeholders for review and approval. Also, lack of potential improvements should be communicated if the analysis fails to identify any improvements.

7. Software Engineering Management Tools
[3*, c5, c6, c7]

Software engineering management tools are often used to provide visibility and control of software engineering management processes. Some tools are automated while others are manually implemented. There has been a recent trend towards the use of integrated suites of software engineering tools that are used throughout a project to plan, collect and record, monitor and control, and report project and product information. Tools can be divided into the following categories:

Project Planning and Tracking Tools. Project planning and tracking tools can be used to estimate project effort and cost and to prepare project schedules. Some projects use automated estimation tools that accept as input the estimated size and other characteristics of a software product and produce estimates of the required total effort, schedule, and cost. Planning tools also include automated scheduling tools that analyze the tasks within a work breakdown structure, their estimated durations, their precedence relationships, and the resources assigned to each task to produce a schedule in the form of a Gantt chart.

Tracking tools can be used to track project milestones, regularly scheduled project status meetings, scheduled iteration cycles, product demonstrations, and/or action items.

Risk Management Tools. Risk management tools (see section 2.5, Risk Management) can be used to track risk identification, estimation, and monitoring. These tools include the use of approaches such as simulation or decision trees to analyze the effect of costs versus payoffs and subjective estimates of the probabilities of risk events. Monte Carlo simulation tools can be used to produce probability distributions of effort, schedule, and risk by combining multiple input probability distributions in an algorithmic manner.

Communications Tools. Communication tools can assist in providing timely and consistent information to relevant stakeholders involved in a project. These tools can include things like email notifications and broadcasts to team members and stakeholders. They also include communication of minutes from regularly scheduled project meetings, daily stand-up meetings, plus charts showing progress, backlogs, and maintenance request resolutions.

Measurement Tools. Measurement tools support activities related to the software measurement program (see topic 6, Software Engineering Measurement). There are few completely automated tools in this category. Measurement tools used to gather, analyze, and report project measurement data may be based on spreadsheets developed by project team members or organizational employees.

MATRIX OF TOPICS VS. REFERENCE MATERIAL

	Fairley 2009 [3*]	Sommerville 2011 [4*]	Boehm and Turner 2003 [5*]	McGarry et al. 2001 [7*]
1. Initiation and Scope Definition				
1.1. Determination and Negotiation of Requirements	c3			
1.2. Feasibility Analysis		c4		
1.3. Process for the Review and Revision of Requirements	c3			
2. Software Project Planning				
2.1. Process Planning	c2, c3, c4, c5		c1	
2.2. Determine Deliverables	c4, c5, c6			
2.3. Effort, Schedule, and Cost Estimation	c6			
2.4. Resource Allocation	c5, c10, c11			
2.5. Risk Management	c9		c5	
2.6. Quality Management	c4	c24		
2.7. Plan Management	c4			
3. Software Project Enactment				
3.1. Implementation of Plans		c2		
3.2. Software Acquisition and Supplier Contract Management	c3, c4			
3.3. Implementation of Measurement Process	c7			
3.4. Monitor Process	c8			
3.5. Control Process	c7, c8			
3.6. Reporting	c11			
4. Review and Evaluation				
4.1. Determining Satisfaction of Requirements				
4.2. Reviewing and Evaluating Performance	c8, c10			

	Fairley 2009 [3*]	Sommerville 2011 [4*]	Boehm and Turner 2003 [5*]	McGarry et al. 2001 [7*]
5. Closure				
5.1. Determining Closure				
5.2. Closure Activities				
6. Software Engineering Measurement				
6.1. Establish and Sustain Measurement Commitment				c1, c2
6.2. Plan the Measurement Process				c1, c2
6.3. Perform the Measurement Process				c1, c2
6.4. Evaluate Measurement				c1, c2
7. Software Engineering Management Tools	c5, c6, c7			

FURTHER READINGS

A Guide to the Project Management Body of Knowledge (PMBOK® Guide) [1].

The *PMBOK® Guide* provides guidelines for managing individual projects and defines project management-related concepts. It also describes the project management life cycle and its related processes, as well as the project life cycle. It is a globally recognized guide for the project management profession.

Software Extension to the Guide to the Project Management Body of Knowledge (PMBOK® Guide) [2].

SWX provides adaptations and extensions to the generic practices of project management documented in the *PMBOK® Guide* for managing software projects. The primary contribution of this extension to the *PMBOK® Guide* is a description of processes that are applicable for managing adaptive life cycle software projects.

IEEE Standard Adoption of ISO/IEC 15939 [6].

This international standard identifies a process that supports defining a suitable set of measures to address specific information needs. It identifies the activities and tasks that are necessary to successfully identify, define, select, apply, and improve measurement within an overall project or organizational measurement structure.

J. McDonald, *Managing the Development of Software Intensive Systems*, Wiley, 2010 [8].

This textbook provides an introduction to project management for beginning software and hardware developers plus unique advanced material for experienced project managers. Case studies are included for planning and managing verification and validation for large software projects, complex software, and hardware systems, as well as inspection results and testing metrics to monitor project status.

REFERENCES

[1] Project Management Institute, *A Guide to the Project Management Body of Knowledge (PMBOK(R) Guide)*, 5th ed., Project Management Institute, 2013.

[2] Project Management Institute and IEEE Computer Society, *Software Extension to the PMBOK® Guide Fifth Edition*, Project Management Institute, 2013.

[3*] R.E. Fairley, *Managing and Leading Software Projects*, Wiley-IEEE Computer Society Press, 2009.

[4*] I. Sommerville, *Software Engineering*, 9th ed., Addison-Wesley, 2011.

[5*] B. Boehm and R. Turner, *Balancing Agility and Discipline: A Guide for the Perplexed*, Addison-Wesley, 2003.

[6] *IEEE Std. 15939-2008 Standard Adoption of ISO/IEC 15939:2007 Systems and Software Engineering—Measurement Process*, IEEE, 2008.

[7*] J. McGarry et al., *Practical Software Measurement: Objective Information for Decision Makers*, Addison-Wesley Professional, 2001.

[8] J. McDonald, *Managing the Development of Software Intensive Systems*, John Wiley and Sons, Inc., 2010.

CHAPTER 8

SOFTWARE ENGINEERING PROCESS

ACRONYMS

BPMN	Business Process Modeling Notation
CASE	Computer-Assisted Software Engineering
CM	Configuration Management
CMMI	Capability Maturity Model Integration
GQM	Goal-Question-Metric
IDEF0	Integration Definition
LOE	Level of Effort
ODC	Orthogonal Defect Classification
SDLC	Software Development Life Cycle
SPLC	Software Product Life Cycle
UML	Unified Modeling Language

INTRODUCTION

An engineering process consists of a set of inter-related activities that transform one or more inputs into outputs while consuming resources to accomplish the transformation. Many of the processes of traditional engineering disciplines (e.g., electrical, mechanical, civil, chemical) are concerned with transforming energy and physical entities from one form into another, as in a hydroelectric dam that transforms potential energy into electrical energy or a petroleum refinery that uses chemical processes to transform crude oil into gasoline.

In this knowledge area (KA), software engineering processes are concerned with work activities accomplished by software engineers to develop, maintain, and operate software, such as requirements, design, construction, testing, configuration management, and other software engineering processes. For readability, "software engineering process" will be referred to as "software process" in this KA. In addition, please note that "software process" denotes work activities—not the execution process for implemented software.

Software processes are specified for a number of reasons: to facilitate human understanding, communication, and coordination; to aid management of software projects; to measure and improve the quality of software products in an efficient manner; to support process improvement; and to provide a basis for automated support of process execution.

SWEBOK KAs closely related to this Software Engineering Process KA include Software Engineering Management, Software Engineering Models and Methods, and Software Quality; the Measurement and Root Cause Analysis topic found in the Engineering Foundations KA is also closely related. Software Engineering Management is concerned with tailoring, adapting, and implementing software processes for a specific software project (see Process Planning in the Software Engineering Management KA). Models and methods support a systematic approach to software development and modification.

The Software Quality KA is concerned with the planning, assurance, and control processes for project and product quality. Measurement and measurement results in the Engineering Foundations KA are essential for evaluating and controlling software processes.

BREAKDOWN OF TOPICS FOR SOFTWARE ENGINEERING PROCESS

As illustrated in Figure 8.1, this KA is concerned with software process definition, software life cycles, software process assessment and improvement, software measurement, and software engineering process tools.

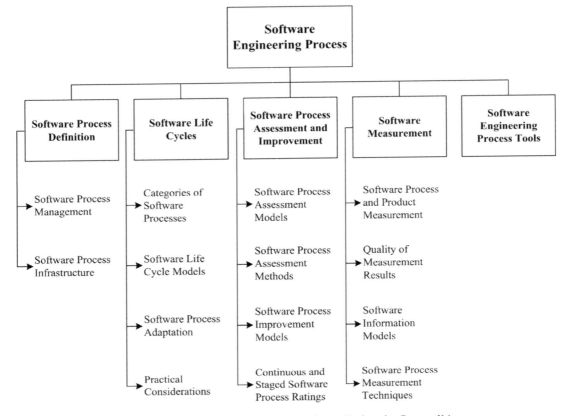

Figure 8.1. Breakdown of Topics for the Software Engineering Process KA

1. Software Process Definition
[1*, p177] [2*, p295] [3*, p28–29, p36, c5]

This topic is concerned with a definition of software process, software process management, and software process infrastructure.

As stated above, a software process is a set of interrelated activities and tasks that transform input work products into output work products. At minimum, the description of a software process includes required inputs, transforming work activities, and outputs generated. As illustrated in Figure 8.2, a software process may also include its entry and exit criteria and decomposition of the work activities into tasks, which are the smallest units of work subject to management accountability. A process input may be a triggering event or the output of another process. Entry criteria should be satisfied before a process can commence. All specified conditions should be satisfied before a process can be successfully concluded, including the acceptance criteria for the output work product or work products.

A software process may include subprocesses. For example, software requirements validation is a process used to determine whether the requirements will provide an adequate basis for software development; it is a subprocess of the software requirements process. Inputs for requirements validation are typically a software requirements specification and the resources needed to perform validation (personnel, validation tools, sufficient time). The tasks of the requirements validation activity might include requirements reviews, prototyping, and model validation. These tasks involve work assignments for individuals and teams. The output of requirements validation is typically a validated software requirements specification that provides inputs to the software design and software testing processes. Requirements validation and other subprocesses of the software requirements process are often interleaved and iterated in various ways;

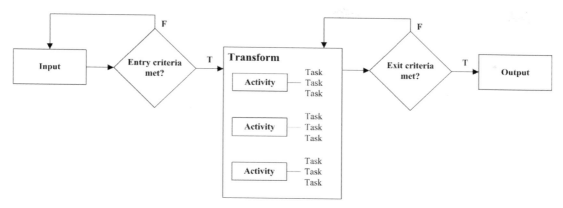

Figure 8.2. Elements of a Software Process

the software requirements process and its subprocesses may be entered and exited multiple times during software development or modification.

Complete definition of a software process may also include the roles and competencies, IT support, software engineering techniques and tools, and work environment needed to perform the process, as well as the approaches and measures (Key Performance Indicators) used to determine the efficiency and effectiveness of performing the process.

In addition, a software process may include interleaved technical, collaborative, and administrative activities.

Notations for defining software processes include textual lists of constituent activities and tasks described in natural language; data-flow diagrams; state charts; BPMN; IDEF0; Petri nets; and UML activity diagrams. The transforming tasks within a process may be defined as procedures; a procedure may be specified as an ordered set of steps or, alternatively, as a checklist of the work to be accomplished in performing a task.

It must be emphasized that there is no best software process or set of software processes. Software processes must be selected, adapted, and applied as appropriate for each project and each organizational context. No ideal process, or set of processes, exists.

1.1. Software Process Management
[3*, s26.1] [4*, p453–454]

Two objectives of software process management are to realize the efficiency and effectiveness that result from a systematic approach to accomplishing software processes and producing work products—be it at the individual, project, or organizational level—and to introduce new or improved processes.

Processes are changed with the expectation that a new or modified process will improve the efficiency and/or effectiveness of the process and the quality of the resulting work products. Changing to a new process, improving an existing process, organizational change, and infrastructure change (technology insertion or changes in tools) are closely related, as all are usually initiated with the goal of improving the cost, development schedule, or quality of the software products. Process change has impacts not only for the software product; they often lead to organizational change. Changing a process or introducing a new process can have ripple effects throughout an organization. For example, changes in IT infrastructure tools and technology often require process changes.

Existing processes may be modified when other new processes are deployed for the first time (for example, introducing an inspection activity within a software development project will likely impact the software testing process—see Reviews and Audits in the Software Quality KA and in the Software Testing KA). These situations can also be termed "process evolution." If the modifications are extensive, then changes in the organizational culture and business model will likely be necessary to accommodate the process changes.

1.2. Software Process Infrastructure
[2*, p183, p186] [4*, p437–438]

Establishing, implementing, and managing software processes and software life cycle models often occurs at the level of individual software projects. However, systematic application of software processes and software life cycle models across an organization can provide benefits to all software work within the organization, although it requires commitment at the organizational level. A software process infrastructure can provide process definitions, policies for interpreting and applying the processes, and descriptions of the procedures to be used to implement the processes. Additionally, a software process infrastructure may provide funding, tools, training, and staff members who have been assigned responsibilities for establishing and maintaining the software process infrastructure.

Software process infrastructure varies, depending on the size and complexity of the organization and the projects undertaken within the organization. Small, simple organizations and projects have small, simple infrastructure needs. Large, complex organizations and projects, by necessity, have larger and more complex software process infrastructures. In the latter case, various organizational units may be established (such as a software engineering process group or a steering committee) to oversee implementation and improvement of the software processes.

A common misperception is that establishing a software process infrastructure and implementing repeatable software processes will add time and cost to software development and maintenance. There is a cost associated with introducing or improving a software process; however, experience has shown that implementing systematic improvement of software processes tends to result in lower cost through improved efficiency, avoidance of rework, and more reliable and affordable software. Process performance thus influences software product quality.

2. Software Life Cycles

[1*, c2] [2*, p190]

This topic addresses categories of software processes, software life cycle models, software process adaptation, and practical considerations. A software development life cycle (SDLC) includes the software processes used to specify and transform software requirements into a deliverable software product. A software product life cycle (SPLC) includes a software development life cycle plus additional software processes that provide for deployment, maintenance, support, evolution, retirement, and all other inception-to-retirement processes for a software product, including the software configuration management and software quality assurance processes that are applied throughout a software product life cycle. A software product life cycle may include multiple software development life cycles for evolving and enhancing the software.

Individual software processes have no temporal ordering among them. The temporal relationships among software processes are provided by a software life cycle model: either an SDLC or SPLC. Life cycle models typically emphasize the key software processes within the model and their temporal and logical interdependencies and relationships. Detailed definitions of the software processes in a life cycle model may be provided directly or by reference to other documents.

In addition to conveying the temporal and logical relationships among software processes, the software development life cycle model (or models used within an organization) includes the control mechanisms for applying entry and exit criteria (e.g., project reviews, customer approvals, software testing, quality thresholds, demonstrations, team consensus). The output of one software process often provides the input for others (e.g., software requirements provide input for a software architectural design process and the software construction and software testing processes). Concurrent execution of several software process activities may produce a shared output (e.g., the interface specifications for interfaces among multiple software components developed by different teams). Some software processes may be regarded as less effective unless other software processes are being performed at the same time (e.g., software test planning during software requirements analysis can improve the software requirements).

2.1. Categories of Software Processes
[1*, Preface] [2* , p294–295] [3*, c22–c24]

Many distinct software processes have been defined for use in the various parts of the software development and software maintenance life cycles. These processes can be categorized as follows:

1. *Primary processes* include software processes for development, operation, and maintenance of software.
2. *Supporting processes* are applied intermittently or continuously throughout a software product life cycle to support primary processes; they include software processes such as configuration management, quality assurance, and verification and validation.
3. *Organizational processes* provide support for software engineering; they include training, process measurement analysis, infrastructure management, portfolio and reuse management, organizational process improvement, and management of software life cycle models.
4. *Cross-project processes,* such as reuse, software product line, and domain engineering; they involve more than a single software project in an organization.

Software processes in addition to those listed above include the following.

Project management processes include processes for planning and estimating, resource management, measuring and controlling, leading, managing risk, managing stakeholders, and coordinating the primary, supporting, organizational, and cross-project processes of software development and maintenance projects.

Software processes are also developed for particular needs, such as process activities that address software quality characteristics (see the Software Quality KA). For example, security concerns during software development may necessitate one or more software processes to protect the security of the development environment and reduce the risk of malicious acts. Software processes may also be developed to provide adequate grounds for establishing confidence in the integrity of the software.

2.2. Software Life Cycle Models
[1*, c2] [2*, s3.2] [3*, s2.1] [5]

The intangible and malleable nature of software permits a wide variety of software development life cycle models, ranging from linear models in which the phases of software development are accomplished sequentially with feedback and iteration as needed followed by integration, testing, and delivery of a single product; to iterative models in which software is developed in increments of increasing functionality on iterative cycles; to agile models that typically involve frequent demonstrations of working software to a customer or user representative who directs development of the software in short iterative cycles that produce small increments of working, deliverable software. Incremental, iterative, and agile models can deliver early subsets of working software into the user environment, if desired.

Linear SDLC models are sometimes referred to as predictive software development life cycle models, while iterative and agile SDLCs are referred to as adaptive software development life cycle models. It should be noted that various maintenance activities during an SPLC can be conducted using different SDLC models, as appropriate to the maintenance activities.

A distinguishing feature of the various software development life cycle models is the way in which software requirements are managed. Linear development models typically develop a complete set of software requirements, to the extent possible, during project initiation and planning. The software requirements are then rigorously controlled. Changes to the software requirements are based on change requests that are processed by a change control board (see Requesting, Evaluating and Approving Software Changes in the Change Control Board in the Software Configuration Management KA). An incremental model produces successive increments of working, deliverable software based on partitioning of the software requirements to be implemented in each of the increments. The software requirements may be rigorously controlled, as in a linear model, or there may be some flexibility in revising the software requirements as the software product evolves. Agile models may define product scope and high-level features initially; however, agile models are designed to facilitate evolution of the software requirements during the project.

It must be emphasized that the continuum of SDLCs from linear to agile is not a thin, straight line. Elements of different approaches may be incorporated into a specific model; for example, an incremental software development life cycle model may incorporate sequential software requirements and design phases but permit considerable flexibility in revising the software requirements and architecture during software construction.

2.3. Software Process Adaptation
[1*, s2.7] [2*, p51]

Predefined SDLCs, SPLCs, and individual software processes often need to be adapted (or "tailored") to better serve local needs. Organizational context, innovations in technology, project size, product criticality, regulatory requirements, industry practices, and corporate culture may determine needed adaptations. Adaptation of individual software processes and software life cycle models (development and product) may consist of adding more details to software processes, activities, tasks, and procedures to address critical concerns. It may consist of using an alternate set of activities that achieves the purpose and outcomes of the software process. Adaptation may also include omitting software processes or activities from a development or product life cycle model that are clearly inapplicable to the scope of work to be accomplished.

2.4. Practical Considerations
[2*, p188–190]

In practice, software processes and activities are often interleaved, overlapped, and applied concurrently. Software life cycle models that specify discrete software processes, with rigorously specified entry and exit criteria and prescribed boundaries and interfaces, should be recognized as idealizations that must be adapted to reflect the realities of software development and maintenance within the organizational context and business environment.

Another practical consideration: software processes (such as configuration management,

construction, and testing) can be adapted to facilitate operation, support, maintenance, migration, and retirement of the software.

Additional factors to be considered when defining and tailoring a software life cycle model include required conformance to standards, directives, and policies; customer demands; criticality of the software product; and organizational maturity and competencies. Other factors include the nature of the work (e.g., modification of existing software versus new development) and the application domain (e.g., aerospace versus hotel management).

3. Software Process Assessment and Improvement
[2*, p188, p194] [3*, c26] [4*, p397, c15]

This topic addresses software process assessment models, software process assessment methods, software process improvement models, and continuous and staged process ratings. Software process assessments are used to evaluate the form and content of a software process, which may be specified by a standardized set of criteria. In some instances, the terms "process appraisal" and "capability evaluation" are used instead of process assessment. Capability evaluations are typically performed by an acquirer (or potential acquirer) or by an external agent on behalf of an acquirer (or potential acquirer). The results are used as an indicator of whether the software processes used by a supplier (or potential supplier) are acceptable to the acquirer. Performance appraisals are typically performed within an organization to identify software processes in need of improvement or to determine whether a process (or processes) satisfies the criteria at a given level of process capability or maturity.

Process assessments are performed at the levels of entire organizations, organizational units within organizations, and individual projects. Assessment may involve issues such as assessing whether software process entry and exit criteria are being met, to review risk factors and risk management, or to identify lessons learned. Process assessment is carried out using both an assessment model and an assessment method. The model can provide a norm for a benchmarking comparison among projects within an organization and among organizations.

A process audit differs from a process assessment. Assessments are performed to determine levels of capability or maturity and to identify software processes to be improved. Audits are typically conducted to ascertain compliance with policies and standards. Audits provide management visibility into the actual operations being performed in the organization so that accurate and meaningful decisions can be made concerning issues that are impacting a development project, a maintenance activity, or a software-related topic.

Success factors for software process assessment and improvement within software engineering organizations include management sponsorship, planning, training, experienced and capable leaders, team commitment, expectation management, the use of change agents, plus pilot projects and experimentation with tools. Additional factors include independence of the assessor and the timeliness of the assessment.

3.1. Software Process Assessment Models
[2*, s4.5, s4.6] [3*, s26.5] [4*, p44–48]

Software process assessment models typically include assessment criteria for software processes that are regarded as constituting good practices. These practices may address software development processes only, or they may also include topics such as software maintenance, software project management, systems engineering, or human resources management.

3.2. Software Process Assessment Methods
[1*, p322–331] [3*, s26.3]
[4*, p44–48, s16.4] [6]

A software process assessment method can be qualitative or quantitative. Qualitative assessments rely on the judgment of experts; quantitative assessments assign numerical scores to software processes based on analysis of objective evidence that indicates attainment of the goals and outcomes of a defined software process. For example, a quantitative assessment of the software inspection process might be performed by

examining the procedural steps followed and results obtained plus data concerning defects found and time required to find and fix the defects as compared to software testing.

A typical method of software process assessment includes planning, fact-finding (by collecting evidence through questionnaires, interviews, and observation of work practices), collection and validation of process data, and analysis and reporting. Process assessments may rely on the subjective, qualitative judgment of the assessor, or on the objective presence or absence of defined artifacts, records, and other evidence.

The activities performed during a software process assessment and the distribution of effort for assessment activities are different depending on the purpose of the software process assessment. Software process assessments may be undertaken to develop capability ratings used to make recommendations for process improvements or may be undertaken to obtain a process maturity rating in order to qualify for a contract or award.

The quality of assessment results depends on the software process assessment method, the integrity and quality of the obtained data, the assessment team's capability and objectivity, and the evidence examined during the assessment. The goal of a software process assessment is to gain insight that will establish the current status of a process or processes and provide a basis for process improvement; performing a software process assessment by following a checklist for conformance without gaining insight adds little value.

3.3. Software Process Improvement Models
[2*, p187–188] [3*, s26.5] [4*, s2.7]

Software process improvement models emphasize iterative cycles of continuous improvement. A software process improvement cycle typically involves the subprocesses of measuring, analyzing, and changing. The Plan-Do-Check-Act model is a well-known iterative approach to software process improvement. Improvement activities include identifying and prioritizing desired improvements (planning); introducing an improvement, including change management and training (doing); evaluating the improvement as compared to previous or exemplary process results and costs (checking); and making further modifications (acting). The Plan-Do-Check-Act process improvement model can be applied, for example, to improve software processes that enhance defect prevention.

3.4. Continuous and Staged Software Process Ratings

[1*, p28–34] [3*, s26.5] [4*, p39–45]

Software process capability and software process maturity are typically rated using five or six levels to characterize the capability or maturity of the software processes used within an organization.

A *continuous* rating system involves assigning a rating to each software process of interest; a *staged* rating system is established by assigning the same maturity rating to all of the software processes within a specified process level. A representation of continuous and staged process levels is provided in Table 8.1. Continuous models typically use a level 0 rating; staged models typically do not.

Table 8.1. Software Process Rating Levels

Level	Continuous Representation of Capability Levels	Staged Representation of Maturity Levels
0	Incomplete	
1	Performed	Initial
2	Managed	Managed
3	Defined	Defined
4		Quantitatively Managed
5		Optimizing

In Table 8.1, level 0 indicates that a software process is incompletely performed or may not be performed. At level 1, a software process is being performed (capability rating), or the software processes in a maturity level 1 group are being performed but on an ad hoc, informal basis. At level 2, a software process (capability rating) or the processes in maturity level 2 are being performed in a manner that provides management

visibility into intermediate work products and can exert some control over transitions between processes. At level 3, a single software process or the processes in a maturity level 3 group plus the process or processes in maturity level 2 are well defined (perhaps in organizational policies and procedures) and are being repeated across different projects. Level 3 of process capability or maturity provides the basis for process improvement across an organization because the process is (or processes are) conducted in a similar manner. This allows collection of performance data in a uniform manner across multiple projects. At maturity level 4, quantitative measures can be applied and used for process assessment; statistical analysis may be used. At maturity level 5, the mechanisms for continuous process improvements are applied.

Continuous and staged representations can be used to determine the order in which software processes are to be improved. In the continuous representation, the different capability levels for different software processes provide a guideline for determining the order in which software processes will be improved. In the staged representation, satisfying the goals of a set of software processes within a maturity level is accomplished for that maturity level, which provides a foundation for improving all of the software processes at the next higher level.

4. Software Measurement

[3*, s26.2] [4*, s18.1.1]

This topic addresses software process and product measurement, quality of measurement results, software information models, and software process measurement techniques (see Measurement in the Engineering Foundations KA).

Before a new process is implemented or a current process is modified, measurement results for the current situation should be obtained to provide a baseline for comparison between the current situation and the new situation. For example, before introducing the software inspection process, effort required to fix defects discovered by testing should be measured. Following an initial start-up period after the inspection process is introduced, the combined effort of inspection plus testing can be compared to the previous amount of effort required for testing alone. Similar considerations apply if a process is changed.

4.1. Software Process and Product Measurement
[1*, s6.3, p273] [3*, s26.2, p638]

Software process and product measurement are concerned with determining the efficiency and effectiveness of a software process, activity, or task. The *efficiency* of a software process, activity, or task is the ratio of resources actually consumed to resources expected or desired to be consumed in accomplishing a software process, activity, or task (see Efficiency in the Software Engineering Economics KA). Effort (or equivalent cost) is the primary measure of resources for most software processes, activities, and tasks; it is measured in units such as person-hours, person-days, staff-weeks, or staff-months of effort or in equivalent monetary units—such as euros or dollars.

Effectiveness is the ratio of actual output to expected output produced by a software process, activity, or task; for example, actual number of defects detected and corrected during software testing to expected number of defects to be detected and corrected—perhaps based on historical data for similar projects (see Effectiveness in the Software Engineering Economics KA). Note that measurement of software process effectiveness requires measurement of the relevant product attributes; for example, measurement of software defects discovered and corrected during software testing.

One must take care when measuring product attributes for the purpose of determining process effectiveness. For example, the number of defects detected and corrected by testing may not achieve the expected number of defects and thus provide a misleadingly low effectiveness measure, either because the software being tested is of better-than-usual quality or perhaps because introduction of a newly introduced upstream inspection process has reduced the remaining number of defects in the software.

Product measures that may be important in determining the effectiveness of software processes include product complexity, total defects, defect density, and the quality of requirements, design documentation, and other related work products.

Also note that efficiency and effectiveness are independent concepts. An effective software process can be inefficient in achieving a desired software process result; for example, the amount of effort expended to find and fix software defects could be very high and result in low efficiency, as compared to expectations.

An efficient process can be ineffective in accomplishing the desired transformation of input work products into output work products; for example, failure to find and correct a sufficient number of software defects during the testing process.

Causes of low efficiency and/or low effectiveness in the way a software process, activity, or task is executed might include one or more of the following problems: deficient input work products, inexperienced personnel, lack of adequate tools and infrastructure, learning a new process, a complex product, or an unfamiliar product domain. The efficiency and effectiveness of software process execution are also affected (either positively or negatively) by factors such as turnover in software personnel, schedule changes, a new customer representative, or a new organizational policy.

In software engineering, productivity in performing a process, activity, or task is the ratio of output produced divided by resources consumed; for example, the number of software defects discovered and corrected divided by person-hours of effort (see Productivity in the Software Engineering Economics KA). Accurate measurement of productivity must include total effort used to satisfy the exit criteria of a software process, activity, or task; for example, the effort required to correct defects discovered during software testing must be included in software development productivity.

Calculation of productivity must account for the context in which the work is accomplished. For example, the effort to correct discovered defects will be included in the productivity calculation of a software team if team members correct the defects they find—as in unit testing by software developers or in a cross-functional agile team. Or the productivity calculation may include either the effort of the software

developers or the effort of an independent testing team, depending on who fixes the defects
found by the independent testers. Note that this
example refers to the effort of teams of developers or teams of testers and not to individuals.
Software productivity calculated at the level of
individuals can be misleading because of the
many factors that can affect the individual productivity of software engineers.

Standardized definitions and counting rules
for measurement of software processes and work
products are necessary to provide standardized
measurement results across projects within an
organization, to populate a repository of historical data that can be analyzed to identify software
processes that need to be improved, and to build
predictive models based on accumulated data. In
the example above, definitions of software defects
and staff-hours of testing effort plus counting
rules for defects and effort would be necessary to
obtain satisfactory measurement results.

The extent to which the software process is
institutionalized is important; failure to institu-
tionalize a software process may explain why
"good" software processes do not always produce anticipated results. Software processes may
be institutionalized by adoption within the local
organizational unit or across larger units of an
enterprise.

4.2. Quality of Measurement Results
[4*, s3.4–3.7]

The quality of process and product measurement
results is primarily determined by the reliability
and validity of the measured results. Measurements that do not satisfy these quality criteria
can result in incorrect interpretations and faulty
software process improvement initiatives. Other
desirable properties of software measurements
include ease of collection, analysis, and presentation plus a strong correlation between cause and
effect.

The Software Engineering Measurement topic
in the Software Engineering Management KA
describes a process for implementing a software
measurement program.

4.3. Software Information Models
[1*, p310–311] [3*, p712–713] [4*, s19.2]

Software information models allow modeling,
analysis, and prediction of software process and
software product attributes to provide answers to
relevant questions and achieve process and product
improvement goals. Needed data can be collected
and retained in a repository; the data can be analyzed and models can be constructed. Validation
and refinement of software information models
occur during software projects and after projects
are completed to ensure that the level of accuracy
is sufficient and that their limitations are known
and understood. Software information models may
also be developed for contexts other than software
projects; for example, a software information
model might be developed for processes that apply
across an organization, such as software configuration management or software quality assurance
processes at the organizational level.

Analysis-driven software information model
building involves the development, calibration,
and evaluation of a model. A software information model is developed by establishing a
hypothesized transformation of input variables
into desired outputs; for example, product size
and complexity might be transformed into estimated effort needed to develop a software product using a regression equation developed from
observed data from past projects. A model is
calibrated by adjusting parameters in the model
to match observed results from past projects; for
example, the exponent in a nonlinear regression
model might be changed by applying the regression equation to a different set of past projects
other than the projects used to develop the model.

A model is evaluated by comparing computed
results to actual outcomes for a different set of
similar data. There are three possible evaluation
outcomes:

1. results computed for a different data set vary
   widely from actual outcomes for that data
   set, in which case the derived model is not
   applicable for the new data set and should
   not be applied to analyze or make predictions
   for future projects;

2. results computed for a new data set are close to actual outcomes for that data set, in which case minor adjustments are made to the parameters of the model to improve agreement;

3. results computed for the new data set and subsequent data sets are very close and no adjustments to the model are needed.

Continuous evaluation of the model may indicate a need for adjustments over time as the context in which the model is applied changes.

The Goals/Questions/Metrics (GQM) method was originally intended for establishing measurement activities, but it can also be used to guide analysis and improvement of software processes.

It can be used to guide analysis-driven software information model building; results obtained from the software information model can be used to guide process improvement.

The following example illustrates application of the GQM method:

- Goal: Reduce the average change request processing time by 10% within six months.
- Question 1-1: What is the baseline change request processing time?
- Metric 1-1-1: Average of change request processing times on starting date
- Metric 1-1-2: Standard deviation of change request processing times on starting date
- Question 1-2: What is the current change request processing time?
- Metric 1-2-1: Average of change request processing times currently
- Metric 1-2-2: Standard deviation of change request processing times currently

4.4. Software Process Measurement Techniques
[1*, c8]

Software process measurement techniques are used to collect process data and work product data, transform the data into useful information, and analyze the information to identify process activities that are candidates for improvement. In some cases, new software processes may be needed.

Process measurement techniques also provide the information needed to measure the effects of process improvement initiatives. Process measurement techniques can be used to collect both quantitative and qualitative data.

4.4.1. Quantitative Process Measurement Techniques
[4*, s5.1, s5.7, s9.8]

The purpose of quantitative process measurement techniques is to collect, transform, and analyze quantitative process and work product data that can be used to indicate where process improvements are needed and to assess the results of process improvement initiatives. Quantitative process measurement techniques are used to collect and analyze data in numerical form to which mathematical and statistical techniques can be applied.

Quantitative process data can be collected as a byproduct of software processes. For example, the number of defects discovered during software testing and the staff-hours expended can be collected by direct measurement, and the productivity of defect discovery can be derived by calculating defects discovered per staff-hour.

Basic tools for quality control can be used to analyze quantitative process measurement data (e.g., check sheets, Pareto diagrams, histograms, scatter diagrams, run charts, control charts, and cause-and-effect diagrams) (see Root Cause Analysis in the Engineering Foundations KA). In addition, various statistical techniques can be used that range from calculation of medians and means to multivariate analysis methods (see Statistical Analysis in the Engineering Foundations KA).

Data collected using quantitative process measurement techniques can also be used as inputs to simulation models (see Modeling, Prototyping, and Simulation in the Engineering Foundations KA); these models can be used to assess the impact of various approaches to software process improvement.

Orthogonal Defect Classification (ODC) can be used to analyze quantitative process measurement data. ODC can be used to group detected defects into categories and link the defects in each category to the software process or software processes where a group of defects originated (see Defect Characterization in the Software Quality KA). Software interface defects, for example, may have originated during an inadequate software design process; improving the software design process will reduce the number of software interface defects. ODC can provide quantitative data for applying root cause analysis.

Statistical Process Control can be used to track process stability, or the lack of process stability, using control charts.

4.4.2. Qualitative Process Measurement Techniques

[1*, s6.4]

Qualitative process measurement techniques—including interviews, questionnaires, and expert judgment—can be used to augment quantitative process measurement techniques. Group consensus techniques, including the Delphi technique, can be used to obtain consensus among groups of stakeholders.

5. Software Engineering Process Tools

[1*, s8.7]

Software process tools support many of the notations used to define, implement, and manage individual software processes and software life cycle models. They include editors for notations such as data-flow diagrams, state charts, BPMN, IDEF0 diagrams, Petri nets, and UML activity diagrams. In some cases, software process tools allow different types of analyses and simulations (for example, discrete event simulation). In addition, general purpose business tools, such as a spreadsheet, may be useful.

Computer-Assisted Software Engineering (CASE) tools can reinforce the use of integrated processes, support the execution of process definitions, and provide guidance to humans in performing well-defined processes. Simple tools such as word processors and spreadsheets can be used to prepare textual descriptions of processes, activities, and tasks; these tools also support traceability among the inputs and outputs of multiple software processes (such as stakeholder needs analysis, software requirements specification, software architecture, and software detailed design) as well as the results of software processes such as documentation, software components, test cases, and problem reports.

Most of the knowledge areas in this *Guide* describe specialized tools that can be used to manage the processes within that KA. In particular, see the Software Configuration Management KA for a discussion of software configuration management tools that can be used to manage the construction, integration, and release processes for software products. Other tools, such as those for requirements management and testing, are described in the appropriate KAs.

Software process tools can support projects that involve geographically dispersed (virtual) teams. Increasingly, software process tools are available through cloud computing facilities as well as through dedicated infrastructures.

A project control panel or dashboard can display selected process and product attributes for software projects and indicate measurements that are within control limits and those needing corrective action.

MATRIX OF TOPICS VS. REFERENCE MATERIAL

	Fairley 2009 [1*]	Moore 2009 [2*]	Sommerville 2011 [3*]	Kan 2003 [4*]
1. Software Process Definition	p177	p295	p28–29, p36, c5	
1.1. Software Process Management			s26.1	p453–454
1.2. Software Process Infrastructure		p183, p186		p437–438
2. Software Life Cycles	c2	p190		
2.1. Categories of Software Processes	preface	p294–295	c22, c23, c24	
2.2. Software Life Cycle Models	c2	s3.2	s2.1	
2.3. Software Process Adaptation	s2.7	p51		
2.4. Practical Considerations		p188–190		
3. Software Process Assessment and Improvement		p188, p194	c26	p397, c15
3.1. Software Process Assessment Models		s4.5, s4.6	s26.5	p44–48
3.2. Software Process Assessment Methods	p322–331		s26.3	p44–48, s16.4
3.3. Software Process Improvement Models		p187–188	s26.5	s2.7
3.4. Continuous and Staged Ratings	p28–34		s26.5	p39–45
4. Software Measurement			s26.2	s18.1.1
4.1. Software Process and Product Measurement	s6.3, p273		s26.2, p638	
4.2. Quality of Measurement Results				s3.4, s3.5, s3.6, s3.7
4.3. Software Information Models	p310–311		p. 712–713	s19.2
4.4. Software Process Measurement Techniques	s6.4, c8			s5.1, s5.7, s9.8
5. Software Engineering Process Tools	s8.7			

FURTHER READINGS

Software Extension to the Guide to the Project Management Body of Knowledge® (SWX) [5].

SWX provides adaptations and extensions to the generic practices of project management documented in the *PMBOK® Guide* for managing software projects. The primary contribution of this extension to the *PMBOK® Guide* is description of processes that are applicable for managing adaptive life cycle software projects.

D. Gibson, D. Goldenson, and K. Kost, "Performance Results of CMMI-Based Process Improvement" [6].

This technical report summarizes publicly available empirical evidence about the performance results that can occur as a consequence of CMMI-based process improvement. The report contains a series of brief case descriptions that were created with collaboration from representatives from 10 organizations that have achieved notable quantitative performance results through their CMMI-based improvement efforts.

CMMI® for Development, Version 1.3 [7].

CMMI® for Development, Version 1.3 provides an integrated set of process guidelines for developing and improving products and services. These guidelines include best practices for developing and improving products and services to meet the needs of customers and end users.

ISO/IEC 15504-1:2004 Information technology—Process assessment—Part 1: Concepts and vocabulary [8].

This standard, commonly known as SPICE (Software Process Improvement and Capability Determination), includes multiple parts. Part 1 provides concepts and vocabulary for software development processes and related business-management functions. Other parts of 15504 define the requirements and procedures for performing process assessments.

REFERENCES

[1*] R.E. Fairley, *Managing and Leading Software Projects*, Wiley-IEEE Computer Society Press, 2009.

[2*] J.W. Moore, *The Road Map to Software Engineering: A Standards-Based Guide*, Wiley-IEEE Computer Society Press, 2006.

[3*] I. Sommerville, *Software Engineering*, 9th ed., Addison-Wesley, 2011.

[4*] S.H. Kan, *Metrics and Models in Software Quality Engineering*, 2nd ed., Addison-Wesley, 2002.

[5] Project Management Institute and IEEE Computer Society, *Software Extension to the PMBOK® Guide Fifth Edition*, ed: Project Management Institute, 2013.

[6] D. Gibson, D. Goldenson, and K. Kost, "Performance Results of CMMI-Based Process Improvement," Software Engineering Institute, 2006; http://resources.sei.cmu.edu/library/asset-view.cfm?assetID=8065.

[7] CMMI Product Team, "CMMI for Development, Version 1.3," Software Engineering Institute, 2010; http://resources.sei.cmu.edu/library/asset-view.cfm?assetID=9661.

[8] *ISO/IEC 15504-1:2004, Information Technology—Process Assessment—Part 1: Concepts and Vocabulary*, ISO/IEC, 2004.

CHAPTER 9

SOFTWARE ENGINEERING MODELS AND METHODS

ACRONYMS

3GL	3rd Generation Language
BNF	Backus-Naur Form
FDD	Feature-Driven Development
IDE	Integrated Development Environment
PBI	Product Backlog Item
RAD	Rapid Application Development
UML	Unified Modeling Language
XP	eXtreme Programming

INTRODUCTION

Software engineering models and methods impose structure on software engineering with the goal of making that activity systematic, repeatable, and ultimately more success-oriented. Using models provides an approach to problem solving, a notation, and procedures for model construction and analysis. Methods provide an approach to the systematic specification, design, construction, test, and verification of the end-item software and associated work products.

Software engineering models and methods vary widely in scope—from addressing a single software life cycle phase to covering the complete software life cycle. The emphasis in this knowledge area (KA) is on software engineering models and methods that encompass multiple software life cycle phases, since methods specific for single life cycle phases are covered by other KAs.

BREAKDOWN OF TOPICS FOR SOFTWARE ENGINEERING MODELS AND METHODS

This chapter on software engineering models and methods is divided into four main topic areas:

- *Modeling*: discusses the general practice of modeling and presents topics in modeling principles; properties and expression of models; modeling syntax, semantics, and pragmatics; and preconditions, postconditions, and invariants.
- *Types of Models*: briefly discusses models and aggregation of submodels and provides some general characteristics of model types commonly found in the software engineering practice.
- *Analysis of Models*: presents some of the common analysis techniques used in modeling to verify completeness, consistency, correctness, traceability, and interaction.
- *Software Engineering Methods*: presents a brief summary of commonly used software engineering methods. The discussion guides the reader through a summary of heuristic methods, formal methods, prototyping, and agile methods.

The breakdown of topics for the Software Engineering Models and Methods KA is shown in Figure 9.1.

1. Modeling

Modeling of software is becoming a pervasive technique to help software engineers understand,

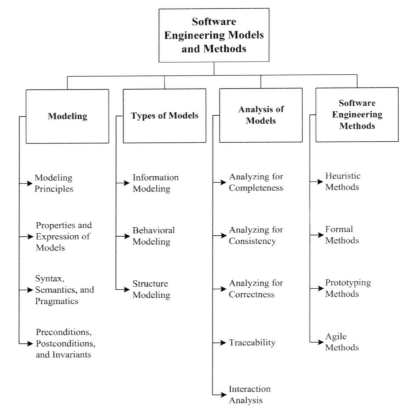

Figure 9.1. Breakdown of Topics for the Software Engineering Models and Methods KA

engineer, and communicate aspects of the software to appropriate stakeholders. Stakeholders are those persons or parties who have a stated or implied interest in the software (for example, user, buyer, supplier, architect, certifying authority, evaluator, developer, software engineer, and perhaps others).

While there are many modeling languages, notations, techniques, and tools in the literature and in practice, there are unifying general concepts that apply in some form to them all. The following sections provide background on these general concepts.

1.1. Modeling Principles
[1*, c2s2, c5s1, c5s2] [2*, c2s2] [3*, c5s0]

Modeling provides the software engineer with an organized and systematic approach for representing significant aspects of the software under study, facilitating decision-making about the software or elements of it, and communicating those

significant decisions to others in the stakeholder communities. There are three general principles guiding such modeling activities:

- *Model the Essentials*: good models do not usually represent every aspect or feature of the software under every possible condition. Modeling typically involves developing only those aspects or features of the software that need specific answers, abstracting away any nonessential information. This approach keeps the models manageable and useful.
- *Provide Perspective*: modeling provides views of the software under study using a defined set of rules for expression of the model within each view. This perspective-driven approach provides dimensionality to the model (for example, a structural view, behavioral view, temporal view, organizational view, and other views as relevant). Organizing information into views focuses the software modeling efforts on specific

concerns relevant to that view using the appropriate notation, vocabulary, methods, and tools.

- *Enable Effective Communications*: modeling employs the application domain vocabulary of the software, a modeling language, and semantic expression (in other words, meaning within context). When used rigorously and systematically, this modeling results in a reporting approach that facilitates effective communication of software information to project stakeholders.

A model is an *abstraction* or simplification of a software component. A consequence of using abstraction is that no single abstraction completely describes a software component. Rather, the model of the software is represented as an aggregation of abstractions, which—when taken together—describe only selected aspects, perspectives, or views—only those that are needed to make informed decisions and respond to the reasons for creating the model in the first place. This simplification leads to a set of assumptions about the context within which the model is placed that should also be captured in the model. Then, when reusing the model, these assumptions can be validated first to establish the relevancy of the reused model within its new use and context.

1.2. Properties and Expression of Models
[1*, c5s2, c5s3] [3*, c4s1.1p7, c4s6p3, c5s0p3]

Properties of models are those distinguishing features of a particular model used to characterize its completeness, consistency, and correctness within the chosen modeling notation and tooling used. Properties of models include the following:

- *Completeness*: the degree to which all requirements have been implemented and verified within the model.
- *Consistency*: the degree to which the model contains no conflicting requirements, assertions, constraints, functions, or component descriptions.
- *Correctness*: the degree to which the model satisfies its requirements and design specifications and is free of defects.

Models are constructed to represent real-world objects and their behaviors to answer specific questions about how the software is expected to operate. Interrogating the models—either through exploration, simulation, or review—may expose areas of uncertainty within the model and the software to which the model refers. These uncertainties or unanswered questions regarding the requirements, design, and/or implementation can then be handled appropriately.

The primary expression element of a model is an entity. An entity may represent concrete artifacts (for example, processors, sensors, or robots) or abstract artifacts (for example, software modules or communication protocols). Model entities are connected to other entities using relations (in other words, lines or textual operators on target entities). Expression of model entities may be accomplished using textual or graphical modeling languages; both modeling language types connect model entities through specific language constructs. The meaning of an entity may be represented by its shape, textual attributes, or both. Generally, textual information adheres to language-specific syntactic structure. The precise meanings related to the modeling of context, structure, or behavior using these entities and relations is dependent on the modeling language used, the design rigor applied to the modeling effort, the specific view being constructed, and the entity to which the specific notation element may be attached. Multiple views of the model may be required to capture the needed semantics of the software.

When using models supported with automation, models may be checked for completeness and consistency. The usefulness of these checks depends greatly on the level of semantic and syntactic rigor applied to the modeling effort in addition to explicit tool support. Correctness is typically checked through simulation and/or review.

1.3. Syntax, Semantics, and Pragmatics
[2* c2s2.2.2p6] [3*, c5s0]

Models can be surprisingly deceptive. The fact that a model is an abstraction with missing information can lead one into a false sense of completely understanding the software from a single model. A complete model ("complete" being relative to the modeling effort) may be a union of multiple submodels and any special function models. Examination and decision-making relative to a single model within this collection of submodels may be problematic.

Understanding the precise meanings of modeling constructs can also be difficult. Modeling languages are defined by syntactic and semantic rules. For textual languages, syntax is defined using a notation grammar that defines valid language constructs (for example, Backus-Naur Form (BNF)). For graphical languages, syntax is defined using graphical models called metamodels. As with BNF, metamodels define the valid syntactical constructs of a graphical modeling language; the metamodel defines how these constructs can be composed to produce valid models.

Semantics for modeling languages specify the meaning attached to the entities and relations captured within the model. For example, a simple diagram of two boxes connected by a line is open to a variety of interpretations. Knowing that the diagram on which the boxes are placed and connected is an object diagram or an activity diagram can assist in the interpretation of this model.

As a practical matter, there is usually a good understanding of the semantics of a specific software model due to the modeling language selected, how that modeling language is used to express entities and relations within that model, the experience base of the modeler(s), and the context within which the modeling has been undertaken and so represented. Meaning is communicated through the model even in the presence of incomplete information through abstraction; pragmatics explains how meaning is embodied in the model and its context and communicated effectively to other software engineers.

There are still instances, however, where caution is needed regarding modeling and semantics. For example, any model parts imported from another model or library must be examined for semantic assumptions that conflict in the new modeling environment; this may not be obvious. The model should be checked for documented assumptions. While modeling syntax may be identical, the model may mean something quite different in the new environment, which is a different context. Also, consider that as software matures and changes are made, semantic discord

can be introduced, leading to errors. With many software engineers working on a model part over time coupled with tool updates and perhaps new requirements, there are opportunities for portions of the model to represent something different from the original author's intent and initial model context.

1.4. Preconditions, Postconditions, and Invariants
[2*, c4s4] [4*, c10s4p2, c10s5p2p4]

When modeling functions or methods, the software engineer typically starts with a set of assumptions about the state of the software prior to, during, and after the function or method executes. These assumptions are essential to the correct operation of the function or method and are grouped, for discussion, as a set of preconditions, postconditions, and invariants.

- *Preconditions*: a set of conditions that must be satisfied prior to execution of the function or method. If these preconditions do not hold prior to execution of the function or method, the function or method may produce erroneous results.
- *Postconditions*: a set of conditions that is guaranteed to be true after the function or method has executed successfully. Typically, the postconditions represent how the state of the software has changed, how parameters passed to the function or method have changed, how data values have changed, or how the return value has been affected.
- *Invariants*: a set of conditions within the operational environment that persist (in other words, do not change) before and after execution of the function or method. These invariants are relevant and necessary to the software and the correct operation of the function or method.

2. Types of Models

A typical model consists of an aggregation of submodels. Each submodel is a partial description and is created for a specific purpose; it may be comprised of one or more diagrams. The collection of submodels may employ multiple modeling languages or a single modeling language. The Unified Modeling Language (UML) recognizes a rich collection of modeling diagrams. Use of these diagrams, along with the modeling language constructs, brings about three broad model types commonly used: information models, behavioral models, and structure models (see section 1.1).

2.1. Information Modeling
[1*, c7s2.2] [3*, c8s1]

Information models provide a central focus on data and information. An information model is an abstract representation that identifies and defines a set of concepts, properties, relations, and constraints on data entities. The semantic or conceptual information model is often used to provide some formalism and context to the software being modeled as viewed from the problem perspective, without concern for how this model is actually mapped to the implementation of the software. The semantic or conceptual information model is an abstraction and, as such, includes only the concepts, properties, relations, and constraints needed to conceptualize the real-world view of the information. Subsequent transformations of the semantic or conceptual information model lead to the elaboration of logical and then physical data models as implemented in the software.

2.2. Behavioral Modeling
[1*, c7s2.1, c7s2.3, c7s2.4] [2*, c9s2]
[3*, c5s4]

Behavioral models identify and define the functions of the software being modeled. Behavioral models generally take three basic forms: state machines, control-flow models, and data-flow models. State machines provide a model of the software as a collection of defined states, events, and transitions. The software transitions from one state to the next by way of a guarded or unguarded triggering event that occurs in the modeled environment. Control-flow models depict how a sequence of events causes processes to be activated or deactivated. Data-flow behavior is typified as a sequence of steps where data moves through processes toward data stores or data sinks.

2.3. Structure Modeling
[1*, c7s2.5, c7s3.1, c7s3.2] [3*, c5s3] [4*, c4]

Structure models illustrate the physical or logical composition of software from its various component parts. Structure modeling establishes the defined boundary between the software being implemented or modeled and the environment in which it is to operate. Some common structural constructs used in structure modeling are composition, decomposition, generalization, and specialization of entities; identification of relevant relations and cardinality between entities; and the definition of process or functional interfaces. Structure diagrams provided by the UML for structure modeling include class, component, object, deployment, and packaging diagrams.

3. Analysis of Models

The development of models affords the software engineer an opportunity to study, reason about, and understand the structure, function, operational usage, and assembly considerations associated with software. Analysis of constructed models is needed to ensure that these models are complete, consistent, and correct enough to serve their intended purpose for the stakeholders.

The sections that follow briefly describe the analysis techniques generally used with software models to ensure that the software engineer and other relevant stakeholders gain appropriate value from the development and use of models.

3.1. Analyzing for Completeness
[3*, c4s1.1p7, c4s6] [5*, p8–11]

In order to have software that fully meets the needs of the stakeholders, completeness is critical—from the requirements elicitation process to code implementation. Completeness is the degree to which all of the specified requirements have been implemented and verified. Models may be checked for completeness by a modeling tool that uses techniques such as structural analysis and state-space reachability analysis (which ensure that all paths in the state models are reached by some set of correct inputs); models may also be checked for completeness manually by using inspections or other review techniques (see the Software Quality KA). Errors and warnings generated by these analysis tools and found by inspection or review indicate probable needed corrective actions to ensure completeness of the models.

3.2. Analyzing for Consistency
[3*, c4s1.1p7, c4s6] [5*, p8–11]

Consistency is the degree to which models contain no conflicting requirements, assertions, constraints, functions, or component descriptions. Typically, consistency checking is accomplished with the modeling tool using an automated analysis function; models may also be checked for consistency manually using inspections or other review techniques (see the Software Quality KA). As with completeness, errors and warnings generated by these analysis tools and found by inspection or review indicate the need for corrective action.

3.3. Analyzing for Correctness
[5*, p8–11]

Correctness is the degree to which a model satisfies its software requirements and software design specifications, is free of defects, and ultimately meets the stakeholders' needs. Analyzing for correctness includes verifying syntactic correctness of the model (that is, correct use of the modeling language grammar and constructs) and verifying semantic correctness of the model (that is, use of the modeling language constructs to correctly represent the meaning of that which is being modeled). To analyze a model for syntactic and semantic correctness, one analyzes it—either automatically (for example, using the modeling tool to check for model syntactic correctness) or manually (using inspections or other review techniques)—searching for possible defects and then removing or repairing the confirmed defects before the software is released for use.

3.4. Traceability
[3*, c4s7.1, c4s7.2]

Developing software typically involves the use, creation, and modification of many work products such as planning documents, process specifications, software requirements, diagrams, designs and pseudo-code, handwritten and tool-generated code, manual and automated test cases and reports, and files and data. These work products may be related through various dependency relationships (for example, uses, implements, and tests). As software is being developed, managed, maintained, or extended, there is a need to map and control these traceability relationships to demonstrate software requirements consistency with the software model (see Requirements Tracing in the Software Requirements KA) and the many work products. Use of traceability typically improves the management of software work products and software process quality; it also provides assurances to stakeholders that all requirements have been satisfied. Traceability enables change analysis once the software is developed and released, since relationships to software work products can easily be traversed to assess change impact. Modeling tools typically provide some automated or manual means to specify and manage traceability links between requirements, design, code, and/or test entities as may be represented in the models and other software work products. (For more information on traceability, see the Software Configuration Management KA).

3.5. Interaction Analysis
[2*, c10, c11] [3*, c29s1.1, c29s5] [4*, c5]

Interaction analysis focuses on the communications or control flow relations between entities used to accomplish a specific task or function within the software model. This analysis examines the dynamic behavior of the interactions between different portions of the software model, including other software layers (such as the operating system, middleware, and applications). It may also be important for some software applications to examine interactions between the computer software application and the user interface software. Some software modeling environments provide simulation facilities to study aspects of the dynamic behavior of modeled software. Stepping through the simulation provides an analysis option for the software engineer to review the interaction design and verify that the different parts of the software work together to provide the intended functions.

4. Software Engineering Methods

Software engineering methods provide an organized and systematic approach to developing software for a target computer. There are numerous methods from which to choose, and it is important for the software engineer to choose an appropriate method or methods for the software development task at hand; this choice can have a dramatic effect on the success of the software project. Use of these software engineering methods coupled with people of the right skill set and tools enable the software engineers to visualize the details of the software and ultimately transform the representation into a working set of code and data.

Selected software engineering methods are discussed below. The topic areas are organized into discussions of Heuristic Methods, Formal Methods, Prototyping Methods, and Agile Methods.

4.1. Heuristic Methods
[1*, c13, c15, c16] [3*, c2s2.2, c5s4.1, c7s1,]

Heuristic methods are those experience-based software engineering methods that have been and are fairly widely practiced in the software industry. This topic area contains three broad discussion categories: structured analysis and design methods, data modeling methods, and object-oriented analysis and design methods.

- *Structured Analysis and Design Methods*: The software model is developed primarily from a functional or behavioral viewpoint, starting from a high-level view of the software (including data and control elements) and then progressively decomposing or refining the model components through increasingly detailed designs. The detailed design eventually converges to very specific details or specifications of the software that must be coded (by hand, automatically generated, or both), built, tested, and verified.
- *Data Modeling Methods*: The data model is constructed from the viewpoint of the data or information used. Data tables and relationships define the data models. This data modeling method is used primarily for defining and analyzing data requirements supporting database designs or data repositories typically found in business software, where data is actively managed as a business systems resource or asset.
- *Object-Oriented Analysis and Design Methods*: The object-oriented model is represented as a collection of objects that encapsulate data and relationships and interact with other objects through methods. Objects may be real-world items or virtual items. The software model is constructed using diagrams to constitute selected views of the software. Progressive refinement of the software models leads to a detailed design. The detailed design is then either evolved through successive iteration or transformed (using some mechanism) into the implementation view of the model, where the code and packaging approach for eventual software product release and deployment is expressed.

4.2. Formal Methods
[1*, c18] [3*, c27] [5*, p8–24]

Formal methods are software engineering methods used to specify, develop, and verify the software through application of a rigorous mathematically based notation and language. Through use of a specification language, the software model can be checked for consistency (in other words, lack of ambiguity), completeness, and correctness in a systematic and automated or semi-automated fashion. This topic is related to the Formal Analysis section in the Software Requirements KA.

This section addresses specification languages, program refinement and derivation, formal verification, and logical inference.

- *Specification Languages*: Specification languages provide the mathematical basis for a formal method; specification languages are formal, higher level computer languages (in other words, not a classic 3rd Generation Language (3GL) programming language) used during the software specification, requirements analysis, and/ or design stages to describe specific input/ output behavior. Specification languages are not directly executable languages; they are typically comprised of a notation and syntax, semantics for use of the notation, and a set of allowed relations for objects.

- *Program Refinement and Derivation*: Program refinement is the process of creating a lower level (or more detailed) specification using a series of transformations. It is through successive transformations that the software engineer derives an executable representation of a program. Specifications may be refined, adding details until the model can be formulated in a 3GL programming language or in an executable portion of the chosen specification language. This specification refinement is made possible by defining specifications with precise semantic properties; the specifications must set out not only the relationships between entities but also the exact runtime meanings of those relationships and operations.

- *Formal Verification*: Model checking is a formal verification method; it typically involves performing a state-space exploration or reachability analysis to demonstrate that the represented software design has or preserves certain model properties of interest. An example of model checking is an analysis that verifies correct program behavior under all possible interleaving of event or message arrivals. The use of formal verification requires a rigorously specified model of the software and its operational environment; this model often takes the form of a finite state machine or other formally defined automaton.

- *Logical Inference*: Logical inference is a method of designing software that involves specifying preconditions and postconditions around each significant block of the design, and—using mathematical logic—developing the proof that those preconditions and postconditions must hold under all inputs. This provides a way for the software engineer to predict software behavior without having to execute the software. Some Integrated Development Environments (IDEs) include ways to represent these proofs along with the design or code.

4.3. Prototyping Methods
[1*, c12s2] [3*, c2s3.1] [6*, c7s3p5]

Software prototyping is an activity that generally creates incomplete or minimally functional versions of a software application, usually for trying out specific new features, soliciting feedback on software requirements or user interfaces, further exploring software requirements, software design, or implementation options, and/or gaining some other useful insight into the software. The software engineer selects a prototyping method to understand the least understood aspects or components of the software first; this approach is in contrast with other software engineering methods that usually begin development with the most understood portions first. Typically, the prototyped product does not become the final software product without extensive development rework or refactoring.

This section discusses prototyping styles, targets, and evaluation techniques in brief.

- *Prototyping Style*: This addresses the various approaches to developing prototypes. Prototypes can be developed as throwaway code or paper products, as an evolution of a working design, or as an executable specification. Different prototyping life cycle processes are typically used for each style. The style chosen is based on the type of results the project needs, the quality of the results needed, and the urgency of the results.

- *Prototyping Target*: The target of the prototype activity is the specific product being served by the prototyping effort. Examples of prototyping targets include a requirements specification, an architectural design element or component, an algorithm, or a human-machine user interface.

- *Prototyping Evaluation Techniques*: A prototype may be used or evaluated in a number of ways by the software engineer or other project stakeholders, driven primarily by the underlying reasons that led to prototype development in the first place. Prototypes may be evaluated or tested against the actual implemented software or against a target set of requirements (for example, a requirements prototype); the prototype may also serve as a model for a future software development effort (for example, as in a user interface specification).

4.4. Agile Methods
[3*, c3] [6*, c7s3p7] [7*, c6, App. A]

Agile methods were born in the 1990s from the need to reduce the apparent large overhead associated with heavyweight, plan-based methods used in large-scale software-development projects. Agile methods are considered lightweight methods in that they are characterized by short, iterative development cycles, self-organizing teams, simpler designs, code refactoring, test-driven development, frequent customer involvement, and an emphasis on creating a demonstrable working product with each development cycle.

Many agile methods are available in the literature; some of the more popular approaches, which are discussed here in brief, include Rapid Application Development (RAD), eXtreme Programming (XP), Scrum, and Feature-Driven Development (FDD).

- *RAD:* Rapid software development methods are used primarily in data-intensive, business-systems application development. The RAD method is enabled with special-purpose database development tools used by software engineers to quickly develop, test, and deploy new or modified business applications.
- *XP:* This approach uses stories or scenarios for requirements, develops tests first, has direct customer involvement on the team (typically defining acceptance tests), uses pair programming, and provides for continuous code refactoring and integration. Stories are decomposed into tasks, prioritized, estimated, developed, and tested. Each increment of software is tested with automated and manual tests; an increment may be released frequently, such as every couple of weeks or so.

- *Scrum:* This agile approach is more project management-friendly than the others. The scrum master manages the activities within the project increment; each increment is called a sprint and lasts no more than 30 days. A Product Backlog Item (PBI) list is developed from which tasks are identified, defined, prioritized, and estimated. A working version of the software is tested and released in each increment. Daily scrum meetings ensure work is managed to plan.
- *FDD:* This is a model-driven, short, iterative software development approach using a five-phase process: (1) develop a product model to scope the breadth of the domain, (2) create the list of needs or features, (3) build the feature development plan, (4) develop designs for iteration-specific features, and (5) code, test, and then integrate the features. FDD is similar to an incremental software development approach; it is also similar to XP, except that code ownership is assigned to individuals rather than the team. FDD emphasizes an overall architectural approach to the software, which promotes building the feature correctly the first time rather than emphasizing continual refactoring.

There are many more variations of agile methods in the literature and in practice. Note that there will always be a place for heavyweight, plan-based software engineering methods as well as places where agile methods shine. There are new methods arising from combinations of agile and plan-based methods where practitioners are defining new methods that balance the features needed in both heavyweight and lightweight methods based primarily on prevailing organizational business needs. These business needs, as typically represented by some of the project stakeholders, should and do drive the choice in using one software engineering method over another or in constructing a new method from the best features of a combination of software engineering methods.

MATRIX OF TOPICS VS. REFERENCE MATERIAL

	Budgen 2003 [1*]	Mellor and Balcer 2002 [2*]	Sommerville 2011 [3*]	Page-Jones 1999 [4*]	Wing 1990 [5*]	Brookshear 2008 [6*]	Boehm and Turner 2003 [7*]
1. Modeling							
1.1. Modeling Principles	c2s2, c5s1, c5s2	c2s2	c5s0				
1.2. Properties and Expression of Models	c5s2, c5s3		c4s1.1p7, c4s6p3, c5s0p3				
1.3. Syntax, Semantics, and Pragmatics		c2s2.2.2 p6	c5s0				
1.4. Preconditions, Postconditions, and Invariants		c4s4		c10s4p2, c10s5 p2p4			
2. Types of Models							
2.1. Information Modeling	c7s2.2		c8s1				
2.2. Behavioral Modeling	c7s2.1, c7s2.3, c7s2.4	c9s2	c5s4				
2.3. Structure Modeling	c7s2.5, c7s3.1, c7s3.2		c5s3	c4			
3. Analysis of Models							
3.1. Analyzing for Completeness			c4s1.1p7, c4s6			pp8–11	
3.2. Analyzing for Consistency			c4s1.1p7, c4s6			pp8–11	
3.3. Analyzing for Correctness						pp8–11	
3.4. Traceability			c4s7.1, c4s7.2				
3.5. Interaction Analysis		c10, c11	c29s1.1, c29s5	c5			

	Budgen 2003 [1*]	Mellor and Balcer 2002 [2*]	Sommerville 2011 [3*]	Page-Jones 1999 [4*]	Wing 1990 [5*]	Brookshear 2008 [6*]	Boehm and Turner 2003 [7*]
4. Software Engineering Methods							
4.1. Heuristic Methods	c13, c15, c16		c2s2.2, c7s1, c5s4.1				
4.2. Formal Methods	c18		c27		pp8–24		
4.3. Prototyping Methods	c12s2		c2s3.1			c7s3p5	
4.4. Agile Methods			c3			c7s3p7	c6, app. A

REFERENCES

[1*] D. Budgen, *Software Design*, 2nd ed., Addison-Wesley, 2003.

[2*] S.J. Mellor and M.J. Balcer, *Executable UML: A Foundation for Model-Driven Architecture*, 1st ed., Addison-Wesley, 2002.

[3*] I. Sommerville, *Software Engineering*, 9th ed., Addison-Wesley, 2011.

[4*] M. Page-Jones, *Fundamentals of Object-Oriented Design in UML*, 1st ed., Addison-Wesley, 1999.

[5*] J.M. Wing, "A Specifier's Introduction to Formal Methods," *Computer*, vol. 23, no. 9, 1990, pp. 8, 10–23.

[6*] J.G. Brookshear, *Computer Science: An Overview*, 10th ed., Addison-Wesley, 2008.

[7*] B. Boehm and R. Turner, *Balancing Agility and Discipline: A Guide for the Perplexed*, Addison-Wesley, 2003.

CHAPTER 10

SOFTWARE QUALITY

ACRONYMS

CMMI	Capability Maturity Model Integration
CoSQ	Cost of Software Quality
COTS	Commercial Off-the-Shelf Software
FMEA	Failure Mode and Effects Analysis
FTA	Fault Tree Analysis
PDCA	Plan-Do-Check-Act
PDSA	Plan-Do-Study-Act
QFD	Quality Function Deployment
SPI	Software Process Improvement
SQA	Software Quality Assurance
SQC	Software Quality Control
SQM	Software Quality Management
TQM	Total Quality Management
V&V	Verification and Validation

INTRODUCTION

What is software quality, and why is it so important that it is included in many knowledge areas (KAs) of the *SWEBOK Guide*?

One reason is that the term *software quality* is overloaded. Software quality may refer: to desirable characteristics of software products, to the extent to which a particular software product possess those characteristics, and to processes, tools, and techniques used to achieve those characteristics. Over the years, authors and organizations have defined the term quality differently. To Phil Crosby, it was "conformance to requirements" [1]. Watts Humphrey refers to it as "achieving excellent levels of "fitness for use" [2]. Meanwhile, IBM coined the phrase "market-driven

quality," where the "customer is the final arbiter" [3*, p8].

More recently, software quality is defined as the "capability of software product to satisfy stated and implied needs under specified conditions" [4] and as "the degree to which a software product meets established requirements; however, quality depends upon the degree to which those established requirements accurately represent stakeholder needs, wants, and expectations" [5]. Both definitions embrace the premise of conformance to requirements. Neither refers to types of requirements (e.g., functional, reliability, performance, dependability, or any other characteristic). Significantly, however, these definitions emphasize that quality is dependent upon requirements.

These definitions also illustrate another reason for the prevalence of software quality throughout this *Guide*: a frequent ambiguity of *software quality* versus *software quality requirements* ("the *-ilities*" is a common shorthand). Software quality requirements are actually attributes of (or constraints on) functional requirements (what the system does). Software requirements may also specify resource usage, a communication protocol, or many other characteristics. This KA attempts clarity by using *software quality* in the broadest sense from the definitions above and by using *software quality requirements* as constraints on functional requirements. Software quality is achieved by conformance to all requirements regardless of what characteristic is specified or how requirements are grouped or named.

Software quality is also considered in many of the SWEBOK KAs because it is a basic parameter of a software engineering effort. For all engineered products, the primary goal is delivering maximum stakeholder value, while balancing the constraints of development cost and schedule; this is sometimes characterized as "fitness for

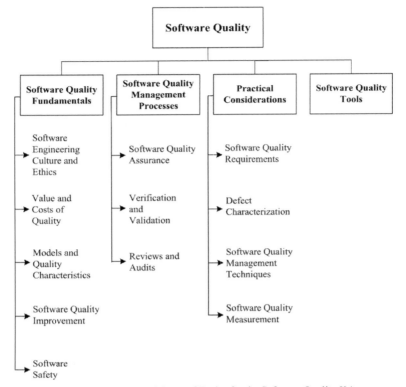

Figure 10.1. Breakdown of Topics for the Software Quality KA

use." Stakeholder value is expressed in requirements. For software products, stakeholders could value price (what they pay for the product), lead time (how fast they get the product), and software quality.

This KA addresses definitions and provides an overview of practices, tools, and techniques for defining software quality and for appraising the state of software quality during development, maintenance, and deployment. Cited references provide additional details.

BREAKDOWN OF TOPICS FOR SOFTWARE QUALITY

The breakdown of topics for the Software Quality KA is presented in Figure 10.1.

1. Software Quality Fundamentals

Reaching agreement on what constitutes quality for all stakeholders and clearly communicating that agreement to software engineers require that the many aspects of quality be formally defined and discussed.

A software engineer should understand quality concepts, characteristics, values, and their application to the software under development or maintenance. The important concept is that the software requirements define the required quality attributes of the software. Software requirements influence the measurement methods and acceptance criteria for assessing the degree to which the software and related documentation achieve the desired quality levels.

1.1. Software Engineering Culture and Ethics
[3*, c1s4] [6*, c2s3.5]

Software engineers are expected to share a commitment to software quality as part of their culture. A healthy software engineering culture includes many characteristics, including the understanding that tradeoffs among cost, schedule, and quality are a basic tenant of the engineering of any product. A strong software engineering ethic assumes that engineers accurately report information, conditions, and outcomes related to quality.

Ethics also play a significant role in software quality, the culture, and the attitudes of software engineers. The IEEE Computer Society and the ACM have developed a code of ethics and professional practice (see Codes of Ethics and Professional Conduct in the Software Engineering Professional Practice KA).

1.2. Value and Costs of Quality
[7*, c17, c22]

Defining and then achieving software quality is not simple. Quality characteristics may or may not be required, or they may be required to a greater or lesser degree, and tradeoffs may be made among them. To help determine the level of software quality, i.e., achieving stakeholder value, this section presents cost of software quality (CoSQ): a set of measurements derived from the economic assessment of software quality development and maintenance processes. The CoSQ measurements are examples of process measurements that may be used to infer characteristics of a product.

The premise underlying the CoSQ is that the level of quality in a software product can be inferred from the cost of activities related to dealing with the consequences of poor quality. Poor quality means that the software product does not fully "satisfy stated and implied needs" or "established requirements." There are four cost of quality categories: prevention, appraisal, internal failure, and external failure.

Prevention costs include investments in software process improvement efforts, quality infrastructure, quality tools, training, audits, and management reviews. These costs are usually not specific to a project; they span the organization. Appraisal costs arise from project activities that find defects. These appraisal activities can be categorized into costs of reviews (design, peer) and costs of testing (software unit testing, software integration, system level testing, acceptance testing); appraisal costs would be extended to subcontracted software suppliers. Costs of internal failures are those that are incurred to fix defects found during appraisal activities and discovered prior to delivery of the software product to the customer. External failure costs include activities to respond to software problems discovered after delivery to the customer.

Software engineers should be able to use CoSQ methods to ascertain levels of software quality and should also be able to present quality alternatives and their costs so that tradeoffs between cost, schedule, and delivery of stakeholder value can be made.

1.3. Models and Quality Characteristics
[3*, c24s1] [7*, c2s4] [8*, c17]

Terminology for software quality characteristics differs from one taxonomy (or model of software quality) to another, each model perhaps having a different number of hierarchical levels and a different total number of characteristics. Various authors have produced models of software quality characteristics or attributes that can be useful for discussing, planning, and rating the quality of software products. ISO/IEC 25010: 2011 [4] defines product quality and quality in use as two related quality models. Appendix B in the *SWEBOK Guide* provides a list of applicable standards for each KA. Standards for this KA cover various ways of characterizing software quality.

1.3.1. Software Process Quality

Software quality management and software engineering process quality have a direct bearing on the quality of the software product.

Models and criteria that evaluate the capabilities of software organizations are primarily project organization and management considerations and, as such, are covered in the Software Engineering Management and Software Engineering Process KAs.

It is not possible to completely distinguish process quality from product quality because process outcomes include products. Determining whether a process has the capability to consistently produce products of desired quality is not simple.

The software engineering process, discussed in the Software Engineering Process KA, influences the quality characteristics of software products, which in turn affect quality as perceived by stakeholders.

1.3.2. Software Product Quality

The software engineer, first of all, must determine the real purpose of the software. In this regard, stakeholder requirements are paramount, and they include quality requirements in addition to functional requirements. Thus, software engineers have a responsibility to elicit quality requirements that may not be explicit at the outset and to understand their importance as well as the level of difficulty in attaining them. All software development processes (e.g., eliciting requirements, designing, constructing, building, checking, improving quality) are designed with these quality requirements in mind and may carry additional development costs if attributes such as safety, security, and dependability are important. The additional development costs help ensure that quality obtained can be traded off against the anticipated benefits.

The term work-product means any artifact that is the outcome of a process used to create the final software product. Examples of a work-product include a system/subsystem specification, a software requirements specification for a software component of a system, a software design description, source code, software test documentation, or reports. While some treatments of quality are described in terms of final software and system performance, sound engineering practice requires that intermediate work-products relevant to quality be evaluated throughout the software engineering process.

1.4. Software Quality Improvement
[3*, c1s4] [9*, c24] [10*, c11s2.4]

The quality of software products can be improved through preventative processes or an iterative process of continual improvement, which requires management control, coordination, and feedback from many concurrent processes: (1) the software life cycle processes, (2) the process of fault/defect detection, removal, and prevention, and (3) the quality improvement process.

The theory and concepts behind quality improvement—such as building in quality through the prevention and early detection of defects, continual improvement, and stakeholder focus—are pertinent to software engineering. These concepts are based on the work of experts in quality who have stated that the quality of a product is directly linked to the quality of the process used to create it. Approaches such as the Deming improvement cycle of Plan-Do-Check-Act (PDCA), evolutionary delivery, kaizen, and quality function deployment (QFD) offer techniques to specify quality objectives and determine whether they are met. The Software Engineering Institute's IDEAL is another method [7*]. Quality management is now recognized by the *SWEBOK Guide* as an important discipline.

Management sponsorship supports process and product evaluations and the resulting findings. Then an improvement program is developed identifying detailed actions and improvement projects to be addressed in a feasible time frame. Management support implies that each improvement project has enough resources to achieve the goal defined for it. Management sponsorship is solicited frequently by implementing proactive communication activities.

1.5. Software Safety
[9*, c11s3]

Safety-critical systems are those in which a system failure could harm human life, other living things, physical structures, or the environment. The software in these systems is safety-critical. There are increasing numbers of applications of safety-critical software in a growing number of industries. Examples of systems with safety-critical software include mass transit systems, chemical manufacturing plants, and medical devices. The failure of software in these systems could have catastrophic effects. There are industry standards, such as DO-178C [11], and emerging processes, tools, and techniques for developing safetycritical software. The intent of these standards, tools, and techniques is to reduce the risk of injecting faults into the software and thus improve software reliability.

Safety-critical software can be categorized as direct or indirect. Direct is that software embedded in a safety-critical system, such as the flight control computer of an aircraft. Indirect includes software applications used to develop safety-critical software. Indirect software is included in software engineering environments and software test environments.

Three complementary techniques for reducing the risk of failure are avoidance, detection and removal, and damage limitation. These techniques impact software functional requirements, software performance requirements, and development processes. Increasing levels of risk imply increasing levels of software quality assurance and control techniques such as inspections. Higher risk levels may necessitate more thorough inspections of requirements, design, and code or the use of more formal analytical techniques. Another technique for managing and controlling software risk is building assurance cases. An assurance case is a reasoned, auditable artifact created to support the contention that its claim or claims are satisfied. It contains the following and their relationships: one or more claims about properties; arguments that logically link the evidence and any assumptions to the claims; and a body of evidence and assumptions supporting these arguments [12].

2. Software Quality Management Processes

Software quality management is the collection of all processes that ensure that software products, services, and life cycle process implementations meet organizational software quality objectives and achieve stakeholder satisfaction [13, 14]. SQM defines processes, process owners, requirements for the processes, measurements of the processes and their outputs, and feedback channels throughout the whole software life cycle.

SQM comprises four subcategories: software quality planning, software quality assurance (SQA), software quality control (SQC), and software process improvement (SPI). Software quality planning includes determining which quality standards are to be used, defining specific quality goals, and estimating the effort and schedule of software quality activities. In some cases, software quality planning also includes defining the software quality processes to be used. SQA activities define and assess the adequacy of software processes to provide evidence that establishes confidence that the software processes are appropriate for and produce software products of suitable quality for their intended purposes [5]. SQC activities examine specific project artifacts (documents and executables) to determine whether they comply with standards established for the project (including requirements, constraints, designs, contracts, and plans). SQC evaluates intermediate products as well as the final products.

The fourth SQM category dealing with improvement has various names within the software industry, including SPI, software quality improvement, and software corrective and preventive action. The activities in this category seek to improve process effectiveness, efficiency, and other characteristics with the ultimate goal of improving software quality. Although SPI could be included in any of the first three categories, an increasing number of organizations organize SPI into a separate category that may span across many projects (see the Software Engineering Process KA).

Software quality processes consist of tasks and techniques to indicate how software plans (e.g., software management, development, quality management, or configuration management plans) are being implemented and how well the intermediate and final products are meeting their specified requirements. Results from these tasks are assembled in reports for management before corrective action is taken. The management of an SQM process is tasked with ensuring that the results of these reports are accurate.

Risk management can also play an important role in delivering quality software. Incorporating disciplined risk analysis and management techniques into the software life cycle processes can help improve product quality (see the Software Engineering Management KA for related material on risk management).

2.1. Software Quality Assurance
[7*, c4–c6, c11, c12, c26–27]

To quell a widespread misunderstanding, software quality assurance is not testing. software quality assurance (SQA) is a set of activities that define and assess the adequacy of software processes to provide evidence that establishes confidence that the software processes are appropriate and produce software products of suitable quality for their intended purposes. A key attribute of SQA is the objectivity of the SQA function with respect to the project. The SQA function may also be organizationally independent of the project; that is, free from technical, managerial, and financial pressures from the project [5]. SQA has two aspects: product assurance and process assurance, which are explained in section 2.3.

The software quality plan (in some industry sectors it is termed the software quality assurance plan) defines the activities and tasks employed to ensure that software developed for a specific product satisfies the project's established requirements and user needs within project cost and schedule constraints and is commensurate with project risks. The SQAP first ensures that quality targets are clearly defined and understood.

The SQA plan's quality activities and tasks are specified with their costs, resource requirements, objectives, and schedule in relation to related objectives in the software engineering management, software development, and software maintenance plans. The SQA plan should be consistent with the software configuration management plan (see the Software Configuration Management KA). The SQA plan identifies documents, standards, practices, and conventions governing the project and how these items are checked and monitored to ensure adequacy and compliance. The SQA plan also identifies measures; statistical techniques; procedures for problem reporting and corrective action; resources such as tools, techniques, and methodologies; security for physical media; training; and SQA reporting and documentation. Moreover, the SQA plan addresses the software quality assurance activities of any other type of activity described in the software plans—such as procurement of supplier software for the project, commercial off-the-shelf software (COTS) installation, and service after delivery of the software. It can also contain acceptance criteria as well as reporting and management activities that are critical to software quality.

2.2. Verification & Validation
[9*, c2s2.3, c8, c15s1.1, c21s3.3]

As stated in [15],

> The purpose of V&V is to help the development organization build quality into the system during the life cycle. V&V processes provide an objective assessment of products and processes throughout the life cycle. This assessment demonstrates whether the requirements are correct, complete, accurate, consistent, and testable. The V&V processes determine whether the development products of a given activity conform to the requirements of that activity and whether the product satisfies its intended use and user needs.

Verification is an attempt to ensure that the product is built correctly, in the sense that the output products of an activity meet the specifications imposed on them in previous activities. Validation is an attempt to ensure that the right product is built—that is, the product fulfills its specific intended purpose. Both the verification process and the validation process begin early in the development or maintenance phase. They provide an examination of key product features in relation to both the product's immediate predecessor and the specifications to be met.

The purpose of planning V&V is to ensure that each resource, role, and responsibility is clearly assigned. The resulting V&V plan documents describe the various resources and their roles and activities, as well as the techniques and tools to be used. An understanding of the different purposes of each V&V activity helps in the careful planning of the techniques and resources needed to fulfill their purposes. The plan also addresses the management, communication, policies, and procedures of the V&V activities and their interaction, as well as defect reporting and documentation requirements.

2.3. Reviews and Audits
[9*, c24s3] [16*]

Reviews and audit processes are broadly defined as static—meaning that no software programs or models are executed—examination of software engineering artifacts with respect to standards that have been established by the organization or project for those artifacts. Different types of reviews and audits are distinguished by their purpose, levels of independence, tools and techniques, roles, and by the subject of the activity. Product assurance and process assurance audits are typically conducted by software quality assurance (SQA) personnel who are independent of development teams. Management reviews are conducted by organizational or project management. The engineering staff conducts technical reviews.

- Management reviews evaluate actual project results with respect to plans.
- Technical reviews (including inspections, walkthrough, and desk checking) examine engineering work-products.
- Process assurance audits. SQA process assurance activities make certain that the processes used to develop, install, operate, and maintain software conform to contracts, comply with any imposed laws, rules, and regulations and are adequate, efficient and effective for their intended purpose [5].
- Product assurance audits. SQA product assurance activities make certain to provide evidence that software products and related documentation are identified in and comply with contracts; and ensure that nonconformances are identified and addressed [5].

2.3.1. Management Reviews

As stated in [16*],

> The purpose of a management review is to monitor progress, determine the status of plans and schedules, and evaluate the effectiveness of management processes, tools and techniques. Management reviews compare actual project results against plans to determine the status of projects or maintenance efforts. The main parameters of management reviews are project cost, schedule, scope, and quality. Management reviews evaluate decisions about corrective actions, changes in the allocation of resources, or changes to the scope of the project.

Inputs to management reviews may include audit reports, progress reports, V&V reports, and plans of many types, including risk management, project management, software configuration management, software safety, and risk assessment, among others. (Refer to the Software Engineering Management and the Software Configuration Management KAs for related material.)

2.3.2. Technical Reviews

As stated in [16*],

> The purpose of a technical review is to evaluate a software product by a team of qualified personnel to determine its suitability for its intended use and identify discrepancies from specifications and standards. It provides management with evidence to confirm the technical status of the project.

Although any work-product can be reviewed, technical reviews are performed on the main software engineering work-products of software requirements and software design.

Purpose, roles, activities, and most importantly the level of formality distinguish different types of technical reviews. Inspections are the most formal, walkthroughs less, and pair reviews or desk checks are the least formal.

Examples of specific roles include a decision maker (i.e., software lead), a review leader, a recorder, and checkers (technical staff members who examine the work-products). Reviews are also distinguished by whether meetings (face to face or electronic) are included in the process. In some review methods checkers solitarily examine work-products and send their results back to a coordinator. In other methods checkers work cooperatively in meetings. A technical review may require that mandatory inputs be in place in order to proceed:

- Statement of objectives
- Specific software product
- Specific project management plan
- Issues list associated with this product
- Technical review procedure.

The team follows the documented review procedure. The technical review is completed once all the activities listed in the examination have been completed.

Technical reviews of source code may include a wide variety of concerns such as analysis of algorithms, utilization of critical computer resources, adherence to coding standards, structure and organization of code for testability, and safety-critical considerations.

Note that technical reviews of source code or design models such as UML are also termed static analysis (see topic 3, Practical Considerations).

2.3.3. Inspections

"The purpose of an inspection is to detect and identify software product anomalies" [16*]. Some important differentiators of inspections as compared to other types of technical reviews are these:

1. Rules. Inspections are based upon examining a work-product with respect to a defined set of criteria specified by the organization. Sets of rules can be defined for different types of workproducts (e.g., rules for requirements, architecture descriptions, source code).
2. Sampling. Rather that attempt to examine every word and figure in a document, the inspection process allows checkers to evaluate defined subsets (samples) of the documents under review.
3. Peer. Individuals holding management positions over members of the inspection team do not participate in the inspection. This is a key distinction between peer review and management review.
4. Led. An impartial moderator who is trained in inspection techniques leads inspection meetings.
5. Meeting. The inspection process includes meetings (face to face or electronic) conducted by a moderator according to a formal procedure in which inspection team members report the anomalies they have found and other issues.

Software inspections always involve the author of an intermediate or final product; other reviews might not. Inspections also include an inspection leader, a recorder, a reader, and a few (two to five) checkers (inspectors). The members of an inspection team may possess different expertise, such as domain expertise, software design method expertise, or programming language expertise. Inspections are usually conducted on one relatively small section of the product at a time (samples). Each team member examines the software product and other review inputs prior to the review meeting, perhaps by applying an analytical technique (see section 3.3.3) to a small section of the product or to the entire product with a focus on only one aspect—e.g., interfaces. During the inspection, the moderator conducts the session and verifies that everyone has prepared for the inspection and conducts the session. The inspection recorder documents anomalies found. A set of rules, with criteria and questions germane to the issues of interest, is a common tool used in inspections. The resulting list often classifies the anomalies (see section 3.2, Defect Characterization) and is reviewed for completeness and accuracy by the team. The inspection exit decision corresponds to one of the following options:

1. Accept with no or, at most, minor reworking
2. Accept with rework verification
3. Reinspect.

2.3.4. Walkthroughs

As stated in [16*],

> The purpose of a systematic walk-through is to evaluate a software product. A walk-through may be conducted for the purpose of educating an audience regarding a software product.

Walkthroughs are distinguished from inspections. The main difference is that the author presents the work-product to the other participants in a meeting (face to face or electronic). Unlike an inspection, the meeting participants may not have necessarily seen the material prior to the meeting. The meetings may be conducted less formally. The author takes the role of explaining and showing the material to participants and solicits feedback. Like inspections, walkthroughs may be conducted on any type of work-product including project plan, requirements, design, source code, and test reports.

2.3.5. Process Assurance and Product Assurance Audits

As stated in [16*],

> The purpose of a software audit is to provide an independent evaluation of the conformance of software products and processes to applicable regulations, standards, guidelines, plans, and procedures.

Process assurance audits determine the adequacy of plans, schedules, and requirements to achieve project objectives [5]. The audit is a formally organized activity with participants having specific roles—such as lead auditor, another auditor, a recorder, or an initiator—and including a representative of the audited organization. Audits identify instances of nonconformance and produce a report requiring the team to take corrective action.

While there may be many formal names for reviews and audits, such as those identified in the standard [16*], the important point is that they can occur on almost any product at any stage of the development or maintenance process.

3. Practical Considerations

3.1. Software Quality Requirements
[9*, c11s1] [18*, c12]
[17*, c15s3.2.2, c15s3.3.1, c16s9.10]

3.1.1. Influence Factors

Various factors influence planning, management, and selection of SQM activities and techniques, including

- the domain of the system in which the software resides; the system functions could be safety-critical, mission-critical, business-critical, security-critical
- the physical environment in which the software system resides
- system and software functional (what the system does) and quality (how well the system performs its functions) requirements
- the commercial (external) or standard (internal) components to be used in the system

- the specific software engineering standards applicable
- the methods and software tools to be used for development and maintenance and for quality evaluation and improvement
- the budget, staff, project organization, plans, and scheduling of all processes
- the intended users and use of the system
- the integrity level of the system.

Information on these factors influences how the SQM processes are organized and documented, how specific SQM activities are selected, what resources are needed, and which of those resources impose bounds on the efforts.

3.1.2. Dependability

In cases where system failure may have extremely severe consequences, overall dependability (hardware, software, and human or operational) is the main quality requirement over and above basic functionality. This is the case for the following reasons: system failures affect a large number of people; users often reject systems that are unreliable, unsafe, or insecure; system failure costs may be enormous; and undependable systems may cause information loss. System and software dependability include such characteristics as availability, reliability, safety, and security. When developing dependable software, tools and techniques can be applied to reduce the risk of injecting faults into the intermediate deliverables or the final software product. Verification, validation, and testing processes, techniques, methods, and tools identify faults that impact dependability as early as possible in the life cycle. Additionally, mechanisms may need to be in place in the software to guard against external attacks and to tolerate faults.

3.1.3. Integrity Levels of Software

Defining integrity levels is a method of risk management.

> Software integrity levels are a range of values that represent software complexity, criticality, risk, safety level, security level,

desired performance, reliability, or other project-unique characteristics that define the importance of the software to the user and acquirer. The characteristics used to determine software integrity level vary depending on the intended application and use of the system. The software is a part of the system, and its integrity level is to be determined as a part of that system.

The assigned software integrity levels may change as the software evolves. Design, coding, procedural, and technology features implemented in the system or software can raise or lower the assigned software integrity levels. The software integrity levels established for a project result from agreements among the acquirer, supplier, developer, and independent assurance authorities. A software integrity level scheme is a tool used in determining software integrity levels. [5]

As noted in [17*], "the integrity levels can be applied during development to allocate additional verification and validation efforts to high-integrity components."

3.2. Defect Characterization
[3*, c3s3, c8s8, c10s2]

Software quality evaluation (i.e., software quality control) techniques find defects, faults and failures. Characterizing these techniques leads to an understanding of the product, facilitates corrections to the process or the product, and informs management and other stakeholders of the status of the process or product. Many taxonomies exist and, while attempts have been made to gain consensus, the literature indicates that there are quite a few in use. Defect characterization is also used in audits and reviews, with the review leader often presenting a list of issues provided by team members for consideration at a review meeting.

As new design methods and languages evolve, along with advances in overall software technologies, new classes of defects appear, and a great deal of effort is required to interpret previously defined classes. When tracking defects, the software engineer is interested in not only the number of defects but also the types. Information alone, without some classification, may not be sufficient to identify the underlying causes of the defects.

Specific types of problems need to be grouped to identify trends over time. The point is to establish a defect taxonomy that is meaningful to the organization and to software engineers.

Software quality control activities discover information at all stages of software development and maintenance. In some cases, the word *defect* is overloaded to refer to different types of anomalies. However, different engineering cultures and standards may use somewhat different meanings for these terms. The variety of terms prompts this section to provide a widely used set of definitions [19]:

- *Computational Error*: "the difference between a computed, observed, or measured value or condition and the true, specified, or theoretically correct value or condition."
- *Error*: "A human action that produces an incorrect result." A slip or mistake that a person makes. Also called human error.
- *Defect*: An "imperfection or deficiency in a work product where that work product does not meet its requirements or specifications and needs to be either repaired or replaced." A defect is caused by a person committing an error.
- *Fault*: A defect in source code. An "incorrect step, process, or data definition in computer program." The encoding of a human error in source code. Fault is the formal name of a bug.
- *Failure*: An "event in which a system or system component does not perform a required function within specified limits." A failure is produced when a fault is encountered by the processor under specified conditions.

Using these definitions three widely used software quality measurements are defect density (number of defects per unit size of documents), fault density (number of faults per 1K lines of code), and failure intensity (failures per use-hour or per test-hour). Reliability models are built from failure data collected during software testing or from software in service and thus can be used to estimate the probability of future failures and to assist in decisions on when to stop testing.

One probable action resulting from SQM findings is to remove the defects from the product under examination (e.g., find and fix bugs, create new build). Other activities attempt to eliminate the causes of the defects—for example, root cause analysis (RCA). RCA activities include analyzing and summarizing the findings to find root causes and using measurement techniques to improve the product and the process as well as to track the defects and their removal. Process improvement is primarily discussed in the Software Engineering Process KA, with the SQM process being a source of information.

Data on inadequacies and defects found by software quality control techniques may be lost unless they are recorded. For some techniques (e.g., technical reviews, audits, inspections), recorders are present to set down such information, along with issues and decisions. When automated tools are used (see topic 4, Software Quality Tools), the tool output may provide the defect information. Reports about defects are provided to the management of the organization.

3.3. Software Quality Management Techniques
[7*, c7s3] [8*, c17] [9*, c12s5, c15s1, p417] [16*]

Software quality control techniques can be categorized in many ways, but a straightforward approach uses just two categories: static and dynamic. Dynamic techniques involve executing the software; static techniques involve analyzing documents and source code but not executing the software.

3.3.1. Static Techniques

Static techniques examine software documentation (including requirements, interface specifications, designs, and models) and software source code without executing the code. There are many tools and techniques for statically examining software work-products (see section 2.3.2). In addition, tools that analyze source code control flow and search for dead code are considered to be static analysis tools because they do not involve executing the software code.

Other, more formal, types of analytical techniques are known as formal methods. They are notably used to verify software requirements and designs. They have mostly been used in the verification of crucial parts of critical systems, such as specific security and safety requirements. (See also Formal Methods in the Software Engineering Models and Methods KA.)

3.3.2. Dynamic Techniques

Dynamic techniques involve executing the software code. Different kinds of dynamic techniques are performed throughout the development and maintenance of software. Generally, these are testing techniques, but techniques such as simulation and model analysis may be considered dynamic (see the Software Engineering Models and Methods KA). Code reading is considered a static technique, but experienced software engineers may execute the code as they read through it. Code reading may utilize dynamic techniques. This discrepancy in categorizing indicates that people with different roles and experience in the organization may consider and apply these techniques differently.

Different groups may perform testing during software development, including groups independent of the development team. The Software Testing KA is devoted entirely to this subject.

3.3.3. Testing

Two types of testing may fall under V&V because of their responsibility for the quality of the materials used in the project:

- Evaluation and tests of tools to be used on the project
- Conformance tests (or review of conformance tests) of components and COTS products to be used in the product.

Sometimes an independent (third-party or IV&V) organization may be tasked to perform testing or to monitor the test process V&V may be called upon to evaluate the testing itself: adequacy of plans, processes, and procedures, and adequacy and accuracy of results.

The third party is not the developer, nor is it associated with the development of the product. Instead, the third party is an independent facility, usually accredited by some body of authority. Their purpose is to test a product for conformance to a specific set of requirements (see the Software Testing KA).

3.4. Software Quality Measurement
[3*, c4] [8*, c17] [9*, p90]

Software quality measurements are used to support decision-making. With the increasing sophistication of software, questions of quality go beyond whether or not the software works to how well it achieves measurable quality goals.

Decisions supported by software quality measurement include determining levels of software quality (notably because models of software product quality include measures to determine the degree to which the software product achieves quality goals); managerial questions about effort, cost, and schedule; determining when to stop testing and release a product (see Termination under section 5.1, Practical Considerations, in the Software Testing KA); and determining the efficacy of process improvement efforts.

The cost of SQM processes is an issue frequently raised in deciding how a project or a software development and maintenance group should be organized. Often, generic models of cost are used, which are based on when a defect is found and how much effort it takes to fix the defect relative to finding the defect earlier in the development process. Software quality measurement data collected internally may give a better picture of cost within this project or organization.

While the software quality measurement data may be useful in itself (e.g., the number of defective requirements or the proportion of defective requirements), mathematical and graphical techniques can be applied to aid in the interpretation of the measures (see the Engineering Foundations KA). These techniques include

- descriptive statistics based (e.g., Pareto analysis, run charts, scatter plots, normal distribution)
- statistical tests (e.g., the binomial test, chi-squared test)
- trend analysis (e.g., control charts; see *The Quality Toolbox* in the list of further readings)
- prediction (e.g., reliability models).

Descriptive statistics-based techniques and tests often provide a snapshot of the more troublesome areas of the software product under examination. The resulting charts and graphs are visualization aids, which the decision makers can use to focus resources and conduct process improvements where they appear to be most needed. Results from trend analysis may indicate that a schedule is being met, such as in testing, or that certain classes of faults may become more likely to occur unless some corrective action is taken in development. The predictive techniques assist in estimating testing effort and schedule and in predicting failures. More discussion on measurement in general appears in the Software Engineering Process and Software Engineering Management KAs. More specific information on testing measurement is presented in the Software Testing KA.

Software quality measurement includes measuring defect occurrences and applying statistical methods to understand the types of defects that occur most frequently. This information may be used by software process improvement for determining methods to prevent, reduce, or eliminate their recurrence. They also aid in understanding trends, how well detection and containment techniques are working, and how well the development and maintenance processes are progressing.

From these measurement methods, defect profiles can be developed for a specific application domain. Then, for the next software project within that organization, the profiles can be used to guide the SQM processes—that is, to expend the effort where problems are most likely to occur. Similarly, benchmarks, or defect counts typical of that domain, may serve as one aid in determining when the product is ready for delivery. Discussion on using data from SQM to improve development and maintenance processes appears in the Software Engineering Management and Software Engineering Process KAs.

4. Software Quality Tools

Software quality tools include static and dynamic analysis tools. Static analysis tools input source code, perform syntactical and semantic analysis without executing the code, and present results to users. There is a large variety in the depth, thoroughness, and scope of static analysis tools that can be applied to artifacts including models, in addition to source code. (See the Software Construction, Software Testing, and Software Maintenance KAs for descriptions of dynamic analysis tools.)

Categories of static analysis tools include the following:

- Tools that facilitate and partially automate reviews and inspections of documents and code. These tools can route work to different participants in order to partially automate and control a review process. They allow users to enter defects found during inspections and reviews for later removal.
- Some tools help organizations perform software safety hazard analysis. These tools provide, e.g., automated support for failure mode and effects analysis (FMEA) and fault tree analysis (FTA).

- Tools that support tracking of software problems provide for entry of anomalies discovered during software testing and subsequent analysis, disposition, and resolution. Some tools include support for workflow and for tracking the status of problem resolution.
- Tools that analyze data captured from software engineering environments and software test environments and produce visual displays of quantified data in the form of graphs, charts, and tables. These tools sometimes include the functionality to perform statistical analysis on data sets (for the purpose of discerning trends and making forecasts). Some of these tools provide defect and removal injection rates; defect densities; yields; distribution of defect injection and removal for each of the life cycle phases.

MATRIX OF TOPICS VS. REFERENCE MATERIAL

	Kan 2002 [3*]	Bott et al. 2000 [6*]	Galin 2004 [7*]	Naik and Tripathy 2008 [8*]	Sommerville 2011 [9*]	Voland 2003 [10*]	IEEE Std. 1028-2008 [16*]	Moore 2006 [17*]	Wiegers 2003 [18*]
1. Software Quality Fundamentals									
1.1. Software Engineering Culture and Ethics	c1s4	c2s3.5							
1.2. Value and Cost of Quality			c17, c22						
1.3. Models and Quality Characteristics	c24s1		c2s4	c17					
1.4. Software Quality Improvement	c1s4				c24	c11 s2.4			
1.5. Software Safety					c11s3				
2. Software Quality Management Processes									
2.1. Software Quality Assurance			c4–c6, c11, c26–27						
2.2. Verification and Validation					c2 s2.3, c8, c15 s1.1, c21 s3.3				
2.3. Reviews and Audits					c24s3		*		

	Kan 2002 [3*]	Bott et al. 2000 [6*]	Galin 2004 [7*]	Naik and Tripathy 2008 [8*]	Sommerville 2011 [9*]	Voland 2003 [10*]	IEEE Std. 1028-2008 [16*]	Moore 2006 [17*]	Wiegers 2003 [18*]
3. Software Quality Practical Considerations									
3.1. Software Quality Requirements					c11s1			c15 s3.2.2, c15 s3.3.1, c16 s9.10	c12
3.2. Defect Characterization	c3s3, c8s8, c10s2								
3.3. SQM Techniques			c7s3	c17	c12s5, c15s1, p417		*		
3.4. Software Quality Measurement	c4			c17	p90				
4. Software Quality Tools									

FURTHER READINGS

N. Leveson, *Safeware: System Safety and Computers* [20].

This book describes the importance of software safety practices and how these practices can be incorporated into software development projects.

T. Gilb, *Principles of Software Engineering Management* [21].

This is one of the first books on iterative and incremental development techniques. The Evo Method defines quantified goals, frequent time-boxed iterations, measurements of progress toward goals, and adaptation of plans based on actual results.

T. Gilb and D. Graham, *Software Inspection* [22].

This book introduces measurement and statistical sampling for reviews and defects. It presents techniques that produce quantified results for reducing defects, improving productivity, tracking projects, and creating documentation.

K.E. Wiegers, *Peer Reviews in Software: A Practical Guide* [23].

This book provides clear, succinct explanations of different peer review methods distinguished by level of formality and effectiveness. Pragmatic guidance for implementing the methods and how to select which methods are appropriate for given circumstances is provided.

N.R. Tague, *The Quality Toolbox*, 2nd ed., [24].

Provides a pragmatic how-to explanation of a comprehensive set of methods, tools, and techniques for solving quality improvement problems. Includes the seven basic quality control tools and many others.

IEEE Std. P730-2013 Draft Standard for Software Quality Assurance Processes [5].

This draft standard expands the SQA processes identified in IEEE/ISO/IEC 12207-2008. P730 establishes standards for initiating, planning, controlling, and executing the software quality assurance processes of a software development or maintenance project. Approval of this draft standard is expected in 2014.

REFERENCES

[1] P.B. Crosby, *Quality Is Free*, McGraw-Hill, 1979.

[2] W. Humphrey, *Managing the Software Process*, Addison-Wesley, 1989.

[3*] S.H. Kan, *Metrics and Models in Software Quality Engineering*, 2nd ed., Addison-Wesley, 2002.

[4] *ISO/IEC 25010:2011 Systems and Software Engineering—Systems and Software Quality Requirements and Evaluation (SQuaRE)—Systems and Software Quality Models*, ISO/IEC, 2011.

[5] *IEEE P730™/D8 Draft Standard for Software Quality Assurance Processes*, IEEE, 2012.

[6*] F. Bott et al., *Professional Issues in Software Engineering*, 3rd ed., Taylor & Francis, 2000.

[7*] D. Galin, *Software Quality Assurance: From Theory to Implementation*, Pearson Education Limited, 2004.

[8*] S. Naik and P. Tripathy, *Software Testing and Quality Assurance: Theory and Practice*, Wiley-Spektrum, 2008.

[9*] P. Clements et al., *Documenting Software Architectures: Views and Beyond*, 2nd ed., Pearson Education, 2010.

[10*] G. Voland, *Engineering by Design*, 2nd ed., Prentice Hall, 2003.

[11] *RTCA DO-178C, Software Considerations in Airborne Systems and Equipment Certification*, Radio Technical Commission for Aeronautics, 2011.

[12] *IEEE Std. 15026.1-2011 Trial-Use Standard Adoption of ISO/IEC TR 15026-1:2010 Systems and Software Engineering— Systems and Software Assurance—Part 1: Concepts and Vocabulary*, IEEE, 2011.

[13] *IEEE Std. 12207-2008 (a.k.a. ISO/IEC 12207:2008) Standard for Systems and Software Engineering—Software Life Cycle Processes*, IEEE, 2008.

[14] *ISO 9000:2005 Quality Management Systems—Fundamentals and Vocabulary*, ISO, 2005.

[15] *IEEE Std. 1012-2012 Standard for System and Software Verification and Validation*, IEEE, 2012.

[16*] *IEEE Std. 1028-2008, Software Reviews and Audits*, IEEE, 2008.

[17*] J.W. Moore, *The Road Map to Software Engineering: A Standards-Based Guide*, Wiley-IEEE Computer Society Press, 2006.

[18*] K.E. Wiegers, *Software Requirements*, 2nd ed., Microsoft Press, 2003.

[19] *ISO/IEC/IEEE 24765:2010 Systems and Software Engineering—Vocabulary*, ISO/IEC/IEEE, 2010.

[20] N. Leveson, *Safeware: System Safety and Computers*, Addison-Wesley Professional, 1995.

[21] T. Gilb, *Principles of Software Engineering Management*, Addison-Wesley Professional, 1988.

[22] T. Gilb and D. Graham, *Software Inspection*, Addison-Wesley Professional, 1993.

[23] K. Wiegers, *Peer Reviews in Software: A Practical Guide*, Addison-Wesley Professional, 2001.

[24] N.R. Tague, *The Quality Toolbox*, 2nd ed., ASQ Quality Press, 2010.

CHAPTER 11

SOFTWARE ENGINEERING PROFESSIONAL PRACTICE

ACRONYMS

ACM	Association for Computing Machinery
BCS	British Computer Society
CSDA	Certified Software Development Associate
CSDP	Certified Software Development Professional
IEC	International Electrotechnical Commission
IEEE CS	IEEE Computer Society
IFIP	International. Federation for Information Processing
IP	Intellectual Property
ISO	International Organization for Standardization
NDA	Non-Disclosure Agreement
WIPO	World Intellectual Property Organization
WTO	World Trade Organization

INTRODUCTION

The Software Engineering Professional Practice knowledge area (KA) is concerned with the knowledge, skills, and attitudes that software engineers must possess to practice software engineering in a professional, responsible, and ethical manner. Because of the widespread applications of software products in social and personal life, the quality of software products can have profound impact on our personal well-being and societal harmony. Software engineers must handle unique engineering problems, producing

software with known characteristics and reliability. This requirement calls for software engineers who possess a proper set of knowledge, skills, training, and experience in professional practice.

The term "professional practice" refers to a way of conducting services so as to achieve certain standards or criteria in both the process of performing a service and the end product resulting from the service. These standards and criteria can include both technical and nontechnical aspects. The concept of professional practice can be viewed as being more applicable within those professions that have a generally accepted body of knowledge; codes of ethics and professional conduct with penalties for violations; accepted processes for accreditation, certification, and licensing; and professional societies to provide and administer all of these. Admission to these professional societies is often predicated on a prescribed combination of education and experience.

A software engineer maintains a professional practice by performing all work in accordance with generally accepted practices, standards, and guidelines notably set forth by the applicable professional society. For example, the Association for Computing Machinery (ACM) and IEEE Computer Society (IEEE CS) have established a Software Engineering Code of Ethics and Professional Practice. Both the British Computer Society (BCS) and the International Federation for Information Processing (IFIP) have established similar professional practice standards. ISO/IEC and IEEE have further provided internationally accepted software engineering standards (see Appendix B of this *Guide*). IEEE CS has established two international certification programs (CSDA, CSDP) and a corresponding *Guide to the Software Engineering Body of Knowledge* (*SWEBOK Guide*). All of these are

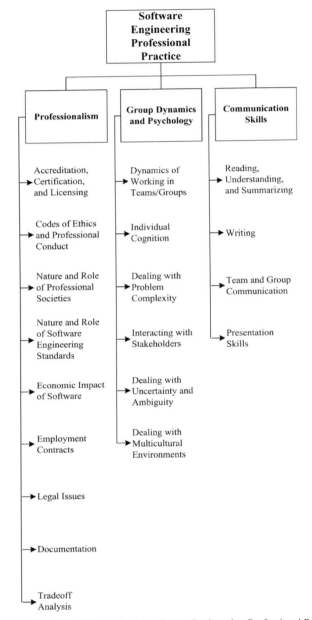

Figure 11.1. Breakdown of Topics for the Software Engineering Professional Practice KA

elements that lay the foundation for of the professional practice of software engineering.

BREAKDOWN OF TOPICS FOR SOFTWARE ENGINEERING PROFESSIONAL PRACTICE

The Software Engineering Professional Practice KA's breakdown of topics is shown in Figure 11.1. The subareas presented in this KA are professionalism, group dynamics and psychology, and communication skills.

1. Professionalism

A software engineer displays professionalism notably through adherence to codes of ethics and professional conduct and to standards and practices that are established by the engineer's professional community.

The professional community is often represented by one or more professional societies; those societies publish codes of ethics and professional conduct as well as criteria for admittance to the community. Those criteria form the basis for accreditation and licensing activities and may be used as a measure to determine engineering competence or negligence.

1.1. Accreditation, Certification, and Licensing
[1*, cls4.1, cls5.1–cls5.4]

1.1.1. Accreditation

Accreditation is a process to certify the competency, authority, or credibility of an organization. Accredited schools or programs are assured to adhere to particular standards and maintain certain qualities. In many countries, the basic means by which engineers acquire knowledge is through completion of an accredited course of study. Often, engineering accreditation is performed by a government organization, such as the ministry of education. Such countries with government accreditations include China, France, Germany, Israel, Italy, and Russia.

In other countries, however, the accreditation process is independent of government and performed by private membership associations. For example, in the United States, engineering accreditation is performed by an organization known as ABET. An organization known as CSAB serving as a participating body of ABET is the lead society within ABET for the accreditation of degree programs in software engineering.

While the process of accreditation may be different for each country and jurisdiction, the general meaning is the same. For an institution's course of study to be accredited means that "the accreditation body recognizes an educational institution as maintaining standards that qualify the graduates for admission to higher or more specialized institutions or for professional practice" [2].

1.1.2. Certification

Certification refers to the confirmation of a person's particular characteristics. A common type of certification is professional certification, where a person is certified as being able to complete an activity in a certain discipline at a stated level of competency. Professional certification also can also verify the holder's ability to meet professional standards and to apply professional judgment in solving or addressing problems. Professional certification can also involve the verification of prescribed knowledge, the mastering of best practice and proven methodologies, and the amount of professional experience.

An engineer usually obtains certification by passing an examination in conjunction with other experience-based criteria. These examinations are often administered by nongovernmental organizations, such as professional societies.

In software engineering, certification testifies to one's qualification as a software engineer. For example, the IEEE CS has enacted two certification programs (CSDA and CSDP) designed to confirm a software engineer's knowledge of standard software engineering practices and to advance one's career. A lack of certification does not exclude the individual from working as a software engineer. Currently certification in software engineering is completely voluntary. In fact, most software engineers are not certified under any program.

1.1.3. Licensing

"Licensing" is the action of giving a person the authorization to perform certain kinds of activities and take responsibility for resultant engineering products. The noun "license" refers to both that authorization and the document recording that authorization. Governmental authorities or statutory bodies usually issue licenses.

Obtaining a license to practice requires not only that an individual meets a certain standard, but also that they do so with a certain ability to practice or operate. Sometimes there is an entry-level requirement which sets the minimum skills and capabilities to practice, but as the professional moves through his or her career, the required skills and capabilities change and evolve.

In general, engineers are licensed as a means of protecting the public from unqualified individuals. In some countries, no one can practice as a professional engineer unless licensed; or further, no company may offer "engineering services" unless at least one licensed engineer is employed there.

1.2. Codes of Ethics and Professional Conduct
[1*, c1s6–c1s9] [3*, c8] [4*, c1s2] [5*, c33] [6*]

Codes of ethics and professional conduct comprise the values and behavior that an engineer's professional practice and decisions should embody.

The professional community establishes codes of ethics and professional conduct. They exist in the context of, and are adjusted to agree with, societal norms and local laws. Therefore, codes of ethics and professional conduct present guidance in the face of conflicting imperatives.

Once established, codes of ethics and professional conduct are enforced by the profession, as represented by professional societies or by a statutory body.

Violations may be acts of commission, such as concealing inadequate work, disclosing confidential information, falsifying information, or misrepresenting one's abilities. They may also occur through omission, including failure to disclose risks or to provide important information, failure to give proper credit or to acknowledge references, and failure to represent client interests. Violations of codes of ethics and professional conduct may result in penalties and possible expulsion from professional status.

A code of ethics and professional conduct for software engineering was approved by the ACM Council and the IEEE CS Board of Governors in 1999 [6*]. According to the short version of this code:

> Software engineers shall commit themselves to making the analysis, specification, design, development, testing and maintenance of software a beneficial and respected profession. In accordance with their commitment to the health, safety and welfare of the public, software engineers shall adhere to the eight principles concerning the public, client and employer, product, judgment, management, profession, colleagues, and self, respectively.

Since standards and codes of ethics and professional conduct may be introduced, modified, or replaced at any time, individual software engineers bear the responsibility for their own continuing study to stay current in their professional practice.

1.3. Nature and Role of Professional Societies
[1*, c1s1–c1s2] [4*, c1s2] [5*, c35s1]

Professional societies are comprised of a mix of practitioners and academics. These societies serve to define, advance, and regulate their corresponding professions. Professional societies help to establish professional standards as well as codes of ethics and professional conduct. For this reason, they also engage in related activities, which include

- establishing and promulgating a body of generally accepted knowledge;
- accrediting, certifying, and licensing;
- dispensing disciplinary actions;
- advancing the profession through conferences, training, and publications.

Participation in professional societies assists the individual engineer in maintaining and sharpening their professional knowledge and relevancy and in expanding and maintaining their professional network.

1.4. Nature and Role of Software Engineering Standards
[1*, c5s3.2, c10s2.1] [5*, c32s6] [7*, c1s2]

Software engineering standards cover a remarkable variety of topics. They provide guidelines for the practice of software engineering and processes to be used during development, maintenance, and support of software. By establishing a consensual body of knowledge and experience, software engineering standards establish a basis upon which further guidelines may be developed. Appendix B of this *Guide* provides guidance on IEEE and ISO/IEC software engineering standards that support the knowledge areas of this *Guide*.

The benefits of software engineering standards are many and include improving software quality, helping avoid errors, protecting both software producers and users, increasing professional discipline, and helping technology transition.

1.5. Economic Impact of Software
[3*, c10s8] [4*, c1s1.1] [8*, c1]

Software has economic effects at the individual, business, and societal levels. Software "success" may be determined by the suitability of a product for a recognized problem as well as by its effectiveness when applied to that problem.

At the individual level, an engineer's continuing employment may depend on their ability and willingness to interpret and execute tasks in meeting customers' or employers' needs and expectations. The customer or employer's financial situation may in turn be positively or negatively affected by the purchase of software.

At the business level, software properly applied to a problem can eliminate months of work and translate to elevated profits or more effective organizations. Moreover, organizations that acquire or provide successful software may be a boon to the society in which they operate by providing both employment and improved services. However, the development or acquisition costs of software can also equate to those of any major acquisition.

At the societal level, direct impacts of software success or failure include or exclude accidents, interruptions, and loss of service. Indirect impacts include the success or failure of the organization that acquired or produced the software, increased or decreased societal productivity, harmonious or disruptive social order, and even the saving or loss of property and life.

1.6. Employment Contracts
[1*, c7]

Software engineering services may be provided under a variety of client-engineer relationships. The software engineering work may be solicited as company-to-customer supplier, engineer-to-customer consultancy, direct hire, or even volunteering. In all of these situations, the customer and supplier agree that a product or service will be provided in return for some sort of

consideration. Here, we are most concerned with the engineer-to-customer arrangement and its attendant agreements or contracts, whether they are of the direct-hire or consultant variety, and the issues they typically address.

A common concern in software engineering contracts is confidentiality. Employers derive commercial advantage from intellectual property, so they strive to protect that property from disclosure. Therefore, software engineers are often required to sign non-disclosure (NDA) or intellectual property (IP) agreements as a precondition to work. These agreements typically apply to information the software engineer could only gain through association with the customer. The terms of these agreements may extend past termination of the association.

Another concern is IP ownership. Rights to software engineering assets—products, innovations, inventions, discoveries, and ideas—may reside with the employer or customer, either under explicit contract terms or relevant laws, if those assets are obtained during the term of the software engineer's relationship with that employer or customer. Contracts differ in the ownership of assets created using non-employer-owned equipment or information.

Finally, contracts can also specify among other elements the location at which work is to be performed; standards to which that work will be held; the system configuration to be used for development; limitations of the software engineer's and employer's liability; a communication matrix and/or escalation plan; and administrative details such as rates, frequency of compensation, working hours, and working conditions.

1.7. Legal Issues
[1*, c6, c11] [3*, c5s3–c5s4] [9*, c1s10]

Legal issues surrounding software engineering professional practice notably include matters related to standards, trademarks, patents, copyrights, trade secrets, professional liability, legal requirements, trade compliance, and cybercrime. It is therefore beneficial to possess knowledge of these issues and their applicability.

Legal issues are jurisdictionally based; software engineers must consult attorneys who specialize in the type and jurisdiction of any identified legal issues.

1.7.1. Standards

Software engineering standards establish guidelines for generally accepted practices and minimum requirements for products and services provided by a software engineer. Appendix B of this *Guide* provides guidance on software engineering standards that are applicable to each KA.

Standards are valuable sources of requirements and assistance during the everyday conduct of software engineering activities. Adherence to standards facilitates discipline by enumerating minimal characteristics of products and practice. That discipline helps to mitigate subconscious assumptions or overconfidence in a design. For these reasons, organizations performing software engineering activities often include conformance to standards as part of their organizational policies. Further, adherence to standards is a major component of defense from legal action or from allegations of malpractice.

1.7.2. Trademarks

A trademark relates to any word, name, symbol, or device that is used in business transactions. It is used "to indicate the source or origin of the goods" [2].

Trademark protection protects names, logos, images, and packaging. However, if a name, image, or other trademarked asset becomes a generic term, then trademark protection is nullified.

The World Intellectual Property Organization (WIPO) is the authority that frames the rules and regulations on trademarks. WIPO is the United Nations agency dedicated to the use of intellectual property as a means of stimulating innovation and creativity.

1.7.3. Patents

Patents protect an inventor's right to manufacture and sell an idea. A patent consists of a set of exclusive rights granted by a sovereign government to an individual, group of individuals, or organization for a limited period of time. Patents are an old form of idea-ownership protection and date back to the 15th century.

Application for a patent entails careful records of the process that led to the invention. Patent attorneys are helpful in writing patent disclosure claims in a manner most likely to protect the software engineer's rights.

Note that, if inventions are made during the course of a software engineering contract, ownership may belong to the employer or customer or be jointly held, rather than belong to the software engineer.

There are rules concerning what is and is not patentable. In many countries, software code is not patentable, although software algorithms may be. Existing and filed patent applications can be searched at WIPO.

1.7.4. Copyrights

Most governments in the world give exclusive rights of an original work to its creator, usually for a limited time, enacted as a copyright. Copyrights protect the way an idea is presented—not the idea itself. For example, they may protect the particular wording of an account of an historical event, whereas the event itself is not protected. Copyrights are long-term and renewable; they date back to the 17th century.

1.7.5. Trade Secrets

In many countries, an intellectual asset such as a formula, algorithm, process, design, method, pattern, instrument, or compilation of information may be considered a "trade secret," provided that these assets are not generally known and may provide a business some economic advantage. The designation of "trade secret" provides legal protection if the asset is stolen. This protection is not subject to a time limit. However, if another party derives or discovers the same asset legally, then the asset is no longer protected and the other party will also possess all rights to use it.

1.7.6. Professional Liability

It is common for software engineers to be concerned with matters of professional liability. As an individual provides services to a client or employer, it is vital to adhere to standards and generally accepted practices, thereby protecting against allegations or proceedings of or related to malpractice, negligence, or incompetence.

For engineers, including software engineers, professional liability is related to product liability. Under the laws and rules governing in their jurisdiction, engineers may be held to account for failing to fully and conscientiously follow recommended practice; this is known as "negligence." They may also be subject to laws governing "strict liability" and either implied or express warranty, where, by selling the product, the engineer is held to warrant that the product is both suitable and safe for use. In some countries (for example, in the US), "privity" (the idea that one could only sue the person selling the product) is no longer a defense against liability actions.

Legal suits for liability can be brought under tort law in the US allowing anyone who is harmed to recover their loss even if no guarantees were made. Because it is difficult to measure the suitability or safety of software, failure to take due care can be used to prove negligence on the part of software engineers. A defense against such an allegation is to show that standards and generally accepted practices were followed in the development of the product.

1.7.7. Legal Requirements

Software engineers must operate within the confines of local, national, and international legal frameworks. Therefore, software engineers must be aware of legal requirements for

- registration and licensing—including examination, education, experience, and training requirements;
- contractual agreements;
- noncontractual legalities, such as those governing liability;
- Basic information on the international legal framework can be accessed from the World Trade Organization (WTO).

1.7.8. Trade Compliance

All software professionals must be aware of legal restrictions on import, export, or reexport of goods, services, and technology in the jurisdictions in which they work. The considerations include export controls and classification, transfer of goods, acquisition of necessary governmental licenses for foreign use of hardware and software, services and technology by sanctioned nation, enterprise or individual entities, and import restrictions and duties. Trade experts should be consulted for detailed compliance guidance.

1.7.9. Cybercrime

Cybercrime refers to any crime that involves a computer, computer software, computer networks, or embedded software controlling a system. The computer or software may have been used in the commission of a crime or it may have been the target. This category of crime includes fraud, unauthorized access, spam, obscene or offensive content, threats, harassment, theft of sensitive personal data or trade secrets, and use of one computer to damage or infiltrate other networked computers and automated system controls.

Computer and software users commit fraud by altering electronic data to facilitate illegal activity. Forms of unauthorized access include hacking, eavesdropping, and using computer systems in a way that is concealed from their owners.

Many countries have separate laws to cover cybercrimes, but it has sometimes been difficult to prosecute cybercrimes due to a lack of precisely framed statutes. The software engineer has a professional obligation to consider the threat of cybercrime and to understand how the software system will protect or endanger software and user information from accidental or malicious access, use, modification, destruction, or disclosure.

1.8. Documentation
[1*, c10s5.8] [3*, c1s5] [5*, c32]

Providing clear, thorough, and accurate documentation is the responsibility of each software engineer. The adequacy of documentation is judged by different criteria based on the needs of the various stakeholder audiences.

Good documentation complies with accepted standards and guidelines. In particular, software engineers should document

- relevant facts,
- significant risks and tradeoffs, and
- warnings of undesirable or dangerous consequences from use or misuse of the software.

Software engineers should avoid

- certifying or approving unacceptable products,
- disclosing confidential information, or
- falsifying facts or data.

In addition, software engineers and their managers should notably provide the following documentation for use by other elements of the software development organization:

- software requirements specifications, software design documents, details on the software engineering tools used, software test specifications and results, and details on the adopted software engineering methods;
- problems encountered during the development process.

For external stakeholders (customer, users, others) software documentation should notably provide

- information needed to determine if the software is likely to meet the customer's and users' needs,
- description of the safe, and unsafe, use of the software,
- description of the protection of sensitive information created by or stored using the software, and
- clear identification of warnings and critical procedures.

Use of software may include installation, operation, administration, and performance of other functions by various groups of users and support personnel. If the customer will acquire ownership of the software source code or the right to modify the code, the software engineer should provide documentation of the functional specifications, the software design, the test suite, and the necessary operating environment for the software.

The minimum length of time documents should be kept is the duration of the software products' life cycle or the time required by relevant organizational or regulatory requirements.

1.9. Tradeoff Analysis
[3*, c1s2, c10] [9*, c9s5.10]

Within the practice of software engineering, a software engineer often has to choose between alternative problem solutions. The outcome of these choices is determined by the software engineer's professional evaluation of the risks, costs, and benefits of alternatives, in cooperation with stakeholders. The software engineer's evaluation is called "tradeoff analysis." Tradeoff analysis notably enables the identification of competing and complementary software requirements in order to prioritize the final set of requirements defining the software to be constructed (see Requirements Negotiation in the Software Requirements KA and Determination and Negotiation of Requirements in the Software Engineering Management KA).

In the case of an ongoing software development project that is late or over budget, tradeoff analysis is often conducted to decide which software requirements can be relaxed or dropped given the effects thereof.

A first step in a tradeoff analysis is establishing design goals (see Engineering Design in the Engineering Foundations KA) and setting the relative importance of those goals. This permits identification of the solution that most nearly meets those goals; this means that the way the goals are stated is critically important.

Design goals may include minimization of monetary cost and maximization of reliability, performance, or some other criteria on a wide range of dimensions. However, it is difficult to formulate a tradeoff analysis of cost against risk, especially where primary production and secondary risk-based costs must be traded against each other.

A software engineer must conduct a tradeoff analysis in an ethical manner—notably by being objective and impartial when selecting criteria for comparison of alternative problem solutions and when assigning weights or importance to these criteria. Any conflict of interest must be disclosed up front.

2. Group Dynamics and Psychology

Engineering work is very often conducted in the context of teamwork. A software engineer must be able to interact cooperatively and constructively with others to first determine and then meet both needs and expectations. Knowledge of group dynamics and psychology is an asset when interacting with customers, coworkers, suppliers, and subordinates to solve software engineering problems.

2.1. Dynamics of Working in Teams/Groups
[3*, cls6] [9*, cls3.5, c10]

Software engineers must work with others. On one hand, they work internally in engineering teams; on the other hand, they work with customers, members of the public, regulators, and other stakeholders. Performing teams—those that demonstrate consistent quality of work and progress toward goals—are cohesive and possess a cooperative, honest, and focused atmosphere. Individual and team goals are aligned so that the members naturally commit to and feel ownership of shared outcomes.

Team members facilitate this atmosphere by being intellectually honest, making use of group thinking, admitting ignorance, and acknowledging mistakes. They share responsibility, rewards, and workload fairly. They take care to communicate clearly, directly to each other and in documents, as well as in source code, so that information is accessible to everyone. Peer reviews about work products are framed in a constructive and nonpersonal way (see Reviews and Audits in the Software Quality KA). This allows all the members to pursue a cycle of continuous improvement and growth without personal risk. In general, members of cohesive teams demonstrate respect for each other and their leader.

One point to emphasize is that software engineers must be able to work in multidisciplinary environments and in varied application domains. Since today software is everywhere, from a phone to a car, software is impacting people's lives far beyond the more traditional concept of software made for information management in a business environment.

2.2. Individual Cognition
[3*, cls6.5] [5*, c33]

Engineers desire to solve problems. The ability to solve problems effectively and efficiently is what every engineer strives for. However, the limits and processes of individual cognition affect problem solving. In software engineering, notably due to the highly abstract nature of software itself, individual cognition plays a very prominent role in problem solving.

In general, an individual's (in particular, a software engineer's) ability to decompose a problem and creatively develop a solution can be inhibited by

- need for more knowledge,
- subconscious assumptions,
- volume of data,
- fear of failure or consequence of failure,
- culture, either application domain or organizational,
- lack of ability to express the problem,
- perceived working atmosphere, and
- emotional status of the individual.

The impact of these inhibiting factors can be reduced by cultivating good problem solving habits that minimize the impact of misleading assumptions. The ability to focus is vital, as is intellectual humility: both allow a software engineer to suspend personal considerations and consult with others freely, which is especially important when working in teams.

There is a set of basic methods engineers use to facilitate problem solving (see Problem Solving Techniques in the Computing Foundations KA). Breaking down problems and solving them one piece at a time reduces cognitive overload. Taking advantage of professional curiosity and pursuing continuous professional development through training and study add skills and knowledge to the software engineer's portfolio; reading, networking, and experimenting with new tools, techniques, and methods are all valid means of professional development.

2.3. Dealing with Problem Complexity
[3*, c3s2] [5*, c33]

Many, if not most, software engineering problems are too complex and difficult to address as a whole or to be tackled by individual software engineers. When such circumstances arise, the usual means to adopt is teamwork and problem decomposition (see Problem Solving Techniques in the Computing Foundations KA).

Teams work together to deal with complex and large problems by sharing burdens and drawing upon each other's knowledge and creativity. When software engineers work in teams, different views and abilities of the individual engineers complement each other and help build a solution that is otherwise difficult to come by. Some specific teamwork examples to software engineering are pair programming (see Agile Methods in the Software Engineering Models and Methods KA) and code review (see Reviews and Audits in the Software Quality KA).

2.4. Interacting with Stakeholders
[9*, c2s3.1]

Success of a software engineering endeavor depends upon positive interactions with stakeholders. They should provide support, information, and feedback at all stages of the software life cycle process. For example, during the early stages, it is critical to identify all stakeholders and discover how the product will affect them, so that sufficient definition of the stakeholder requirements can be properly and completely captured.

During development, stakeholders may provide feedback on specifications and/or early versions of the software, change of priority, as well as clarification of detailed or new software requirements. Last, during software maintenance and until the end of product life, stakeholders provide feedback on evolving or new requirements as well problem reports so that the software may be extended and improved.

Therefore, it is vital to maintain open and productive communication with stakeholders for the duration of the software product's lifetime.

2.5. Dealing with Uncertainty and Ambiguity
[4*, c24s4, c26s2] [9*, c9s4]

As with engineers of other fields, software engineers must often deal with and resolve uncertainty and ambiguities while providing services and developing products. The software engineer must attack and reduce or eliminate any lack of clarity that is an obstacle to performing work.

Often, uncertainty is simply a reflection of lack of knowledge. In this case, investigation through recourse to formal sources such as textbooks and professional journals, interviews with stakeholders, or consultation with teammates and peers can overcome it.

When uncertainty or ambiguity cannot be overcome easily, software engineers or organizations may choose to regard it as a project risk. In this case, work estimates or pricing are adjusted to mitigate the anticipated cost of addressing it (see Risk Management in the Software Engineering Management KA).

2.6. Dealing with Multicultural Environments
[9*, c10s7]

Multicultural environments can have an impact on the dynamics of a group. This is especially true when the group is geographically separated or communication is infrequent, since such separation elevates the importance of each contact. Intercultural communication is even more difficult if the difference in time zones make oral communication less frequent.

Multicultural environments are quite prevalent in software engineering, perhaps more than in other fields of engineering, due to the strong trend of international outsourcing and the easy shipment of software components instantaneously across the globe. For example, it is rather common for a software project to be divided into pieces across national and cultural borders, and it is also quite common for a software project team to consist of people from diverse cultural backgrounds.

For a software project to be a success, team members must achieve a level of tolerance, acknowledging that some rules depend on societal norms and that not all societies derive the same solutions and expectations.

This tolerance and accompanying understanding can be facilitated by the support of leadership and management. More frequent communication, including face-to-face meetings, can help to mitigate geographical and cultural divisions, promote cohesiveness, and raise productivity. Also, being able to communicate with teammates in their native language could be very beneficial.

3. Communication Skills

It is vital that a software engineer communicate well, both orally and in reading and writing. Successful attainment of software requirements and deadlines depends on developing clear understanding between the software engineer and customers, supervisors, coworkers, and suppliers. Optimal problem solving is made possible through the ability to investigate, comprehend, and summarize information. Customer product acceptance and safe product usage depend on the provision of relevant training and documentation. It follows that the software engineer's own career success is affected by the ability to consistently provide oral and written communication effectively and on time.

3.1. Reading, Understanding, and Summarizing
[5*, c33s3]

Software engineers are able to read and understand technical material. Technical material includes reference books, manuals, research papers, and program source code.

Reading is not only a primary way of improving skills, but also a way of gathering information necessary for the completion of engineering goals. A software engineer sifts through accumulated information, filtering out the pieces that will be most helpful. Customers may request that a software engineer summarize the results of such information gathering for them, simplifying or explaining it so that they may make the final choice between competing solutions.

Reading and comprehending source code is also a component of information gathering and problem solving. When modifying, extending, or rewriting software, it is critical to understand both its implementation directly derived from the presented code and its design, which must often be inferred.

3.2. Writing
[3*, c1s5]

Software engineers are able to produce written products as required by customer requests or generally accepted practice. These written products may include source code, software project plans, software requirement documents, risk analyses, software design documents, software test plans, user manuals, technical reports and evaluations, justifications, diagrams and charts, and so forth.

Writing clearly and concisely is very important because often it is the primary method of communication among relevant parties. In all cases, written software engineering products must be written so that they are accessible, understandable and relevant for their intended audience(s).

3.3. Team and Group Communication
[3*, c1s6.8] [4*, c22s3] [5*, c27s1]
[9*, c10s4]

Effective communication among team and group members is essential to a collaborative software engineering effort. Stakeholders must be consulted, decisions must be made, and plans must be generated. The greater the number of team and group members, the greater the need to communicate.

The number of communication paths, however, grows quadratically with the addition of each team member. Further, team members are unlikely to communicate with anyone perceived to be removed from them by more than two degrees (levels). This problem can be more serious when software engineering endeavors or organizations are spread across national and continental borders.

Some communication can be accomplished in writing. Software documentation is a common substitute for direct interaction. Email is another but, although it is useful, it is not always enough; also, if one sends too many messages, it becomes difficult to identify the important information. Increasingly, organizations are using enterprise collaboration tools to share information. In addition, the use of electronic information stores, accessible to all team members, for organizational policies, standards, common engineering procedures, and project-specific information, can be most beneficial.

Some software engineering teams focus on face-to-face interaction and promote such interaction by office space arrangement. Although private offices improve individual productivity, colocating team members in physical or virtual forms and providing communal work areas is important to collaborative efforts.

3.4. Presentation Skills
[3*, c1s5] [4*, c22] [9*, c10s7–c10s8]

Software engineers rely on their presentation skills during software life cycle processes. For example, during the software requirements phase, software engineers may walk customers and teammates through software requirements and conduct formal requirements reviews (see Requirement Reviews in the Software Requirements KA). During and after software design, software construction, and software maintenance, software engineers lead reviews, product walkthroughs (see Review and Audits in the Software Quality KA), and training. All of these require the ability to present technical information to groups and solicit ideas or feedback.

The software engineer's ability to convey concepts effectively in a presentation therefore influences product acceptance, management, and customer support; it also influences the ability of stakeholders to comprehend and assist in the product effort. This knowledge needs to be archived in the form of slides, knowledge write-up, technical whitepapers, and any other material utilized for knowledge creation.

MATRIX OF TOPICS VS. REFERENCE MATERIAL

	Bott et al. 2000 [1*]	Voland 2003 [3*]	Sommerville 2011 [4*]	McConnell 2004 [5*]	IEEE-CS/ACM 1999 [6*]	Moore 2006 [7*]	Tockey 2004 [8*]	Fairley 2009 [9*]
1. Professionalism								
1.1. Accreditation, Certification, and Licensing	c1s4.1, c1s5.1–c1s5.4							
1.2. Codes of Ethics and Professional Conduct	c1s6–c1s9	c8	c1s2	c33	*			
1.3. Nature and Role of Professional Societies	c1s1–c1s2		c1s2	c35s1				
1.4. Nature and Role of Software Engineering Standards	c5s3.2, c10s2.1			c32s6		c1s2		
1.5. Economic Impact of Software		c10s8	c1s1.1				c1	
1.6. Employment Contracts	c7							
1.7. Legal Issues	c6, c11	c5s3–c5s4						c1s10
1.8. Documentation	c10s5.8	c1s5		c32				
1.9. Tradeoff Analysis		c1s2, c10						c9s5.10
2. Group Dynamics and Psychology								
2.1. Dynamics of Working in Teams/Groups		c1s6						c1s3.5, c10
2.2. Individual Cognition		c1s6.5		c33				
2.3. 2.3 Dealing with Problem Complexity		c3s2		c33				
2.4. Interacting with Stakeholders								c2s3.1

	Bott et al. 2000 [1*]	Voland 2003 [3*]	Sommerville 2011 [4*]	McConnell 2004 [5*]	IEEE-CS/ACM 1999 [6*]	Moore 2006 [7*]	Tockey 2004 [8*]	Fairley 2009 [9*]
2.5. Dealing with Uncertainty and Ambiguity			c24s4, c26s2					c9s4
2.6. Dealing with Multicultural Environments								c10s7
3. Communication Skills								
3.1. Reading, Understanding, and Summarizing				c33s3				
3.2. Writing		c1s5						
3.3. Team and Group Communication		c1s6.8	c22s3	c27s1				c10s4
3.4. Presentation Skills		c1s5	c22					c10s7– c10s8

FURTHER READINGS

Gerald M. Weinberg, *The Psychology of Computer Programming* [10].

This was the first major book to address programming as an individual and team effort and became a classic in the field.

Kinney and Lange, P.A., *Intellectual Property Law for Business Lawyers* [11].

This book covers IP laws in the US. It not only talks about what the IP law is; it also explains why it looks the way it does.

REFERENCES

[1*] F. Bott et al., *Professional Issues in Software Engineering*, 3rd ed., Taylor & Francis, 2000.

[2] *Merriam-Webster's Collegiate Dictionary*, 11th ed., 2003.

[3*] G. Voland, *Engineering by Design*, 2nd ed., Prentice Hall, 2003.

[4*] I. Sommerville, *Software Engineering*, 9th ed., Addison-Wesley, 2011.

[5*] S. McConnell, *Code Complete*, 2nd ed., Microsoft Press, 2004.

[6*] IEEE CS/ACM Joint Task Force on Software Engineering Ethics and Professional Practices, "Software Engineering Code of Ethics and Professional Practice (Version 5.2)," 1999; www.acm.org/serving/se/code.htm.

[7*] J.W. Moore, *The Road Map to Software Engineering: A Standards-Based Guide*, Wiley-IEEE Computer Society Press, 2006.

[8*] S. Tockey, *Return on Software: Maximizing the Return on Your Software Investment*, Addison-Wesley, 2004.

[9*] R.E. Fairley, *Managing and Leading Software Projects*, Wiley-IEEE Computer Society Press, 2009.

[10] G.M. Weinberg, *The Psychology of Computer Programming: Silver Anniversary Edition*, Dorset House, 1998.

[11] Kinney and Lange, P.A., *Intellectual Property Law for Business Lawyers*, Thomson West, 2013.

CHAPTER 12

SOFTWARE ENGINEERING ECONOMICS

ACRONYMS

EVM	Earned Value Management
IRR	Internal Rate of Return
MARR	Minimum Acceptable Rate of Return
SDLC	Software Development Life Cycle
SPLC	Software Product Life Cycle
ROI	Return on Investment
ROCE	Return on Capital Employed
TCO	Total Cost of Ownership

INTRODUCTION

Software engineering economics is about making decisions related to software engineering in a business context. The success of a software product, service, and solution depends on good business management. Yet, in many companies and organizations, software business relationships to software development and engineering remain vague. This knowledge area (KA) provides an overview on software engineering economics.

Economics is the study of value, costs, resources, and their relationship in a given context or situation. In the discipline of software engineering, activities have costs, but the resulting software itself has economic attributes as well. Software engineering economics provides a way to study the attributes of software and software processes in a systematic way that relates them to economic measures. These economic measures can be weighed and analyzed when making decisions that are within the scope of a software organization and those within the integrated scope of an entire producing or acquiring business.

Software engineering economics is concerned with aligning software technical decisions with the business goals of the organization. In all types of organizations—be it "for-profit," "not-for-profit," or governmental—this translates into sustainably staying in business. In "for-profit" organizations this additionally relates to achieving a tangible return on the invested capital—both assets and capital employed. This KA has been formulated in a way to address all types of organizations independent of focus, product and service portfolio, or capital ownership and taxation restrictions.

Decisions like "Should we use a specific component?" may look easy from a technical perspective, but can have serious implications on the business viability of a software project and the resulting product. Often engineers wonder whether such concerns apply at all, as they are "only engineers." Economic analysis and decision-making are important engineering considerations because engineers are capable of evaluating decisions both technically and from a business perspective. The contents of this knowledge area are important topics for software engineers to be aware of even if they are never actually involved in concrete business decisions; they will have a well-rounded view of business issues and the role technical considerations play in making business decisions. Many engineering proposals and decisions, such as make versus buy, have deep intrinsic economic impacts that should be considered explicitly.

This KA first covers the foundations, key terminology, basic concepts, and common practices of software engineering economics to indicate how decision-making in software engineering includes, or should include a business perspective. It then provides a life cycle perspective, highlights risk and uncertainty management, and shows how economic analysis methods are used. Some practical considerations finalize the knowledge area.

Figure 12.1. Breakdown of Topics for the Software Engineering Economics KA

BREAKDOWN OF TOPICS FOR SOFTWARE ENGINEERING ECONOMICS

The breakdown of topics for the Software Engineering Economics KA is shown in Figure 12.1.

1. Software Engineering Economics Fundamentals

1.1. Finance

[1*, c2]

Finance is the branch of economics concerned with issues such as allocation, management, acquisition, and investment of resources. Finance is an element of every organization, including software engineering organizations.

The field of finance deals with the concepts of time, money, risk, and how they are interrelated. It also deals with how money is spent and budgeted. Corporate finance is concerned with providing the funds for an organization's activities. Generally, this involves balancing risk and profitability, while attempting to maximize an organization's wealth and the value of its stock. This holds primarily for "for-profit" organizations, but also applies to "not-for-profit" organizations. The latter needs finances to ensure sustainability, while not targeting tangible profit. To do this, an organization must

- identify organizational goals, time horizons, risk factors, tax considerations, and financial constraints;
- identify and implement the appropriate business strategy, such as which portfolio and investment decisions to take, how to manage cash flow, and where to get the funding;
- measure financial performance, such as cash flow and ROI (see section 4.3, Return on Investment), and take corrective actions in case of deviation from objectives and strategy.

1.2. Accounting

[1*, c15]

Accounting is part of finance. It allows people whose money is being used to run an organization to know the results of their investment: did they get the profit they were expecting? In "for-profit" organizations, this relates to the tangible ROI (see section 4.3, Return on Investment), while in "not-for-profit" and governmental organizations as well as "for-profit" organizations, it translates into sustainably staying in business. The primary role of accounting is to measure the organization's actual financial performance and to communicate financial information about a business entity to stakeholders, such as shareholders, financial auditors, and investors. Communication is generally in the form of financial statements that show in money terms the economic resources to be controlled. It is important to select the right information that is both relevant and reliable to the user. Information and its timing are partially governed by risk management and governance policies. Accounting systems are also a rich source of historical data for estimating.

1.3. Controlling

[1*, c15]

Controlling is an element of finance and accounting. Controlling involves measuring and correcting the performance of finance and accounting. It ensures that an organization's objectives and plans are accomplished. Controlling cost is a specialized branch of controlling used to detect variances of actual costs from planned costs.

1.4. Cash Flow

[1*, c3]

Cash flow is the movement of money into or out of a business, project, or financial product over a given period. The concepts of cash flow instances and cash flow streams are used to describe the business perspective of a proposal. To make a meaningful business decision about any specific proposal, that proposal will need to be evaluated from a business perspective. In a proposal to develop and launch product X, the payment for new software licenses is an example of an outgoing cash flow instance. Money would need to be spent to carry out that proposal. The sales income from product X in the 11th month after market launch is an example of an incoming cash flow

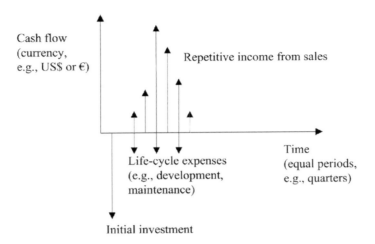

Figure 12.2. A Cash Flow Diagram

instance. Money would be coming in because of carrying out the proposal.

The term *cash flow stream* refers to the set of cash flow instances over time that are caused by carrying out some given proposal. The cash flow stream is, in effect, the complete financial picture of that proposal. How much money goes out? When does it go out? How much money comes in? When does it come in? Simply, if the cash flow stream for Proposal A is more desirable than the cash flow stream for Proposal B, then—all other things being equal—the organization is better off carrying out Proposal A than Proposal B. Thus, the cash flow stream is an important input for investment decision-making. A cash flow instance is a specific amount of money flowing into or out of the organization at a specific time as a direct result of some activity.

A cash flow diagram is a picture of a cash flow stream. It gives the reader a quick overview of the financial picture of the subject organization or project. Figure 12.2 shows an example of a cash flow diagram for a proposal.

1.5. Decision-Making Process

[1*, c2, c4]

If we assume that candidate solutions solve a given technical problem equally well, why should the organization care which one is chosen? The answer is that there is usually a large difference in the costs and incomes from the different

solutions. A commercial, off-the-shelf, object-request broker product might cost a few thousand dollars, but the effort to develop a homegrown service that gives the same functionality could easily cost several hundred times that amount.

If the candidate solutions all adequately solve the problem from a technical perspective, then the selection of the most appropriate alternative should be based on commercial factors such as optimizing total cost of ownership (TCO) or maximizing the short-term return on investment (ROI). Life cycle costs such as defect correction, field service, and support duration are also relevant considerations. These costs need to be factored in when selecting among acceptable technical approaches, as they are part of the lifetime ROI (see section 4.3, Return on Investment).

A systematic process for making decisions will achieve transparency and allow later justification. Governance criteria in many organizations demand selection from at least two alternatives. A systematic process is shown in Figure 12.3. It starts with a business challenge at hand and describes the steps to identify alternative solutions, define selection criteria, evaluate the solutions, implement one selected solution, and monitor the performance of that solution.

Figure 12.3 shows the process as mostly stepwise and serial. The real process is more fluid. Sometimes the steps can be done in a different order and often several of the steps can be done in parallel. The important thing is to be sure that

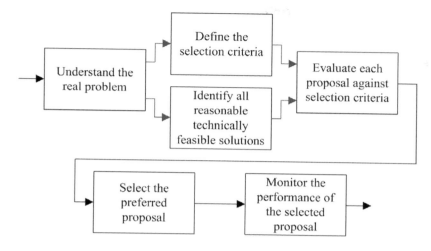

Figure 12.3. The Basic Business Decision-Making Process

none of the steps are skipped or curtailed. It's also important to understand that this same process applies at all levels of decision making: from a decision as big as determining whether a software project should be done at all, to a deciding on an algorithm or data structure to use in a software module. The difference is how financially significant the decision is and, therefore, how much effort should be invested in making that decision. The project-level decision is financially significant and probably warrants a relatively high level of effort to make the decision. Selecting an algorithm is often much less financially significant and warrants a much lower level of effort to make the decision, even though the same basic decision-making process is being used.

More often than not, an organization could carry out more than one proposal if it wanted to, and usually there are important relationships among proposals. Maybe Proposal Y can only be carried out if Proposal X is also carried out. Or maybe Proposal P cannot be carried out if Proposal Q is carried out, nor could Q be carried out if P were. Choices are much easier to make when there are mutually exclusive paths—for example, either A or B or C or whatever is chosen. In preparing decisions, it is recommended to turn any given set of proposals, along with their various interrelationships, into a set of mutually exclusive alternatives. The choice can then be made among these alternatives.

1.6. Valuation

[1*, c5, c8]

In an abstract sense, the decision-making process—be it financial decision making or other—is about maximizing value. The alternative that maximizes total value should always be chosen. A financial basis for value-based comparison is comparing two or more cash flows. Several bases of comparison are available, including

- present worth
- future worth
- annual equivalent
- internal rate of return
- (discounted) payback period.

Based on the time-value of money, two or more cash flows are equivalent only when they equal the same amount of money at a common point in time. Comparing cash flows only makes sense when they are expressed in the same time frame.

Note that value can't always be expressed in terms of money. For example, whether an item is a brand name or not can significantly affect its perceived value. Relevant values that can't be expressed in terms of money still need to be expressed in similar terms so that they can be evaluated objectively.

1.7. Inflation

[1*, c13]

Inflation describes long-term trends in prices. Inflation means that the same things cost more than they did before. If the planning horizon of a business decision is longer than a few years, or if the inflation rate is over a couple of percentage points annually, it can cause noticeable changes in the value of a proposal. The present time value therefore needs to be adjusted for inflation rates and also for exchange rate fluctuations.

1.8. Depreciation

[1*, c14]

Depreciation involves spreading the cost of a tangible asset across a number of time periods; it is used to determine how investments in capitalized assets are charged against income over several years. Depreciation is an important part of determining after-tax cash flow, which is critical for accurately addressing profit and taxes. If a software product is to be sold after the development costs are incurred, those costs should be capitalized and depreciated over subsequent time periods. The depreciation expense for each time period is the capitalized cost of developing the software divided across the number of periods in which the software will be sold. A software project proposal may be compared to other software and nonsoftware proposals or to alternative investment options, so it is important to determine how those other proposals would be depreciated and how profits would be estimated.

1.9. Taxation

[1*, c16, c17]

Governments charge taxes in order to finance expenses that society needs but that no single organization would invest in. Companies have to pay income taxes, which can take a substantial portion of a corporation's gross profit. A decision analysis that does not account for taxation can lead to the wrong choice. A proposal with a high pretax profit won't look nearly as profitable in posttax terms. Not accounting for taxation can also lead to unrealistically high expectations about how profitable a proposed product might be.

1.10. Time-Value of Money

[1*, c5, c11]

One of the most fundamental concepts in finance—and therefore, in business decisions—is that money has time-value: its value changes over time. A specific amount of money right now almost always has a different value than the same amount of money at some other time. This concept has been around since the earliest recorded human history and is commonly known as *time-value*. In order to compare proposals or portfolio elements, they should be normalized in cost, value, and risk to the net present value. Currency exchange variations over time need to be taken into account based on historical data. This is particularly important in cross-border developments of all kinds.

1.11. Efficiency

[2*, c1]

Economic efficiency of a process, activity, or task is the ratio of resources actually consumed to resources expected to be consumed or desired to be consumed in accomplishing the process, activity, or task. Efficiency means "doing things right." An efficient behavior, like an effective behavior, delivers results—but keeps the necessary effort to a minimum. Factors that may affect efficiency in software engineering include product complexity, quality requirements, time pressure, process capability, team distribution, interrupts, feature churn, tools, and programming language.

1.12. Effectiveness

[2*, c1]

Effectiveness is about having impact. It is the relationship between achieved objectives to defined objectives. Effectiveness means "doing the right things." Effectiveness looks only at whether defined objectives are reached—not at how they are reached.

1.13. Productivity

[2*, c23]

Productivity is the ratio of output over input from an economic perspective. Output is the value delivered. Input covers all resources (e.g., effort) spent to generate the output. Productivity combines efficiency and effectiveness from a value-oriented perspective: maximizing productivity is about generating highest value with lowest resource consumption.

2. Life Cycle Economics

2.1. Product

[2*, c22] [3*, c6]

A product is an economic good (or output) that is created in a process that transforms product factors (or inputs) to an output. When sold, a product is a deliverable that creates both a value and an experience for its users. A product can be a combination of systems, solutions, materials, and services delivered internally (e.g., in-house IT solution) or externally (e.g., software application), either as-is or as a component for another product (e.g., embedded software).

2.2. Project

[2*, c22] [3*, c1]

A project is "a temporary endeavor undertaken to create a unique product, service, or result".[1] In software engineering, different project types are distinguished (e.g., product development, outsourced services, software maintenance, service creation, and so on). During its life cycle, a software product may require many projects. For example, during the product conception phase, a project might be conducted to determine the customer need and market requirements; during maintenance, a project might be conducted to produce a next version of a product.

2.3. Program

A program is "a group of related projects, subprograms, and program activities managed in a coordinated way to obtain benefits not available

from managing them individually."[2] Programs are often used to identify and manage different deliveries to a single customer or market over a time horizon of several years.

2.4. Portfolio

Portfolios are "projects, programs, subportfolios, and operations managed as a group to achieve strategic objectives."[3] Portfolios are used to group and then manage simultaneously all assets within a business line or organization. Looking to an entire portfolio makes sure that impacts of decisions are considered, such as resource allocation to a specific project—which means that the same resources are not available for other projects.

2.5. Product Life Cycle

[2*, c2] [3*, c2]

A software product life cycle (SPLC) includes all activities needed to define, build, operate, maintain, and retire a software product or service and its variants. The SPLC activities of "operate," "maintain," and "retire" typically occur in a much longer time frame than initial software development (the software development life cycle—SDLC—see Software Life Cycle Models in the Software Engineering Process KA). Also the operate-maintain-retire activities of an SPLC typically consume more total effort and other resources than the SDLC activities (see Majority of Maintenance Costs in the Software Maintenance KA). The value contributed by a software product or associated services can be objectively determined during the "operate and maintain" time frame. Software engineering economics should be concerned with all SPLC activities, including the activities after initial product release.

2.6. Project Life Cycle

[2*, c2] [3*, c2]

Project life cycle activities typically involve five process groups—Initiating, Planning, Executing, Monitoring and Controlling, and Closing [4]

---

1   Project Management Institute, Inc., *PMI Lexicon of Project Management Terms,* 2012, www.pmi.org/PMBOK-Guide-and-Standards/~/media/Registered/PMI_Lexicon_Final.ashx.

2   Ibid.
3   Ibid.

(see the Software Engineering Management KA). The activities within a software project life cycle are often interleaved, overlapped, and iterated in various ways [3*, c2] [5] (see the Software Engineering Process KA). For instance, agile product development within an SPLC involves multiple iterations that produce increments of deliverable software. An SPLC should include risk management and synchronization with different suppliers (if any), while providing auditable decision-making information (e.g., complying with product liability needs or governance regulations). The software project life cycle and the software product life cycle are interrelated; an SPLC may include several SDLCs.

2.7. Proposals

[1*, c3]

Making a business decision begins with the notion of a *proposal*. Proposals relate to reaching a business objective—at the project, product, or portfolio level. A proposal is a single, separate option that is being considered, like carrying out a particular software development project or not. Another proposal could be to enhance an existing software component, and still another might be to redevelop that same software from scratch. Each proposal represents a unit of choice—either you can choose to carry out that proposal or you can choose not to. The whole purpose of business decision-making is to figure out, given the current business circumstances, which proposals should be carried out and which shouldn't.

2.8. Investment Decisions

[1*, c4]

Investors make investment decisions to spend money and resources on achieving a target objective. Investors are either inside (e.g., finance, board) or outside (e.g., banks) the organization. The target relates to some economic criteria, such as achieving a high return on the investment, strengthening the capabilities of the organization, or improving the value of the company. Intangible aspects such as goodwill, culture, and competences should be considered.

2.9. Planning Horizon

[1*, c11]

When an organization chooses to invest in a particular proposal, money gets tied up in that proposal—so-called "frozen assets." The economic impact of frozen assets tends to start high and decreases over time. On the other hand, operating and maintenance costs of elements associated with the proposal tend to start low but increase over time. The total cost of the proposal—that is, owning and operating a product—is the sum of those two costs. Early on, frozen asset costs dominate; later, the operating and maintenance costs dominate. There is a point in time where the sum of the costs is minimized; this is called the *minimum cost lifetime.*

To properly compare a proposal with a four-year life span to a proposal with a six-year life span, the economic effects of either cutting the six-year proposal by two years or investing the profits from the four-year proposal for another two years need to be addressed. The planning horizon, sometimes known as the study period, is the consistent time frame over which proposals are considered. Effects such as software lifetime will need to be factored into establishing a planning horizon. Once the planning horizon is established, several techniques are available for putting proposals with different life spans into that planning horizon.

2.10. Price and Pricing

[1*, c13]

A price is what is paid in exchange for a good or service. Price is a fundamental aspect of financial modeling and is one of the four Ps of the marketing mix. The other three Ps are product, promotion, and place. Price is the only revenue-generating element amongst the four Ps; the rest are costs.

Pricing is an element of finance and marketing. It is the process of determining what a company will receive in exchange for its products. Pricing factors include manufacturing cost, market placement, competition, market condition, and quality of product. Pricing applies prices to products and services based on factors such as fixed amount, quantity break, promotion or sales campaign, specific vendor quote, shipment or invoice date, combination of multiple orders, service offerings, and many others. The needs of the consumer can be converted into demand only if the consumer has the willingness and capacity to buy the product. Thus, pricing is very important in marketing. Pricing is initially done during the project initiation phase and is a part of "go" decision making.

2.11. Cost and Costing

[1*, c15]

A cost is the value of money that has been used up to produce something and, hence, is not available for use anymore. In economics, a cost is an alternative that is given up as a result of a decision.

A sunk cost is the expenses before a certain time, typically used to abstract decisions from expenses in the past, which can cause emotional hurdles in looking forward. From a traditional economics point of view, sunk costs should not be considered in decision making. Opportunity cost is the cost of an alternative that must be forgone in order to pursue another alternative.

Costing is part of finance and product management. It is the process to determine the cost based on expenses (e.g., production, software engineering, distribution, rework) and on the target cost to be competitive and successful in a market. The target cost can be below the actual estimated cost. The planning and controlling of these costs (called *cost management*) is important and should always be included in costing.

An important concept in costing is the total cost of ownership (TCO). This holds especially for software, because there are many not-so-obvious costs related to SPLC activities after initial product development. TCO for a software product is defined as the total cost for acquiring, activating, and keeping that product running. These costs can be grouped as direct and indirect costs. TCO is an accounting method that is crucial in making sound economic decisions.

2.12. Performance Measurement

[3*, c7, c8]

Performance measurement is the process whereby an organization establishes and measures the parameters used to determine whether programs, investments, and acquisitions are achieving the desired results. It is used to evaluate whether performance objectives are actually achieved; to control budgets, resources, progress, and decisions; and to improve performance.

2.13. Earned Value Management

[3*, c8]

Earned value management (EVM) is a project management technique for measuring progress based on created value. At a given moment, the results achieved to date in a project are compared with the projected budget and the planned schedule progress for that date. Progress relates already-consumed resources and achieved results at a given point in time with the respective planned values for the same date. It helps to identify possible performance problems at an early stage. A key principle in EVM is tracking cost and schedule variances via comparison of planned versus actual schedule and budget versus actual cost. EVM tracking gives much earlier visibility to deviations and thus permits corrections earlier than classic cost and schedule tracking that only looks at delivered documents and products.

2.14. Termination Decisions

[1*, c11, c12] [2*, c9]

Termination means to end a project or product. Termination can be preplanned for the end of a long product lifetime (e.g., when foreseeing that a product will reach its lifetime) or can come rather spontaneously during product development (e.g., when project performance targets are not achieved). In both cases, the decision should be carefully prepared, considering always the alternatives of continuing versus terminating. Costs of different alternatives must be estimated—covering topics such as replacement, information collection, suppliers, alternatives, assets, and utilizing resources for other opportunities. Sunk costs should not be considered in such decision making because they have been spent and will not reappear as a value.

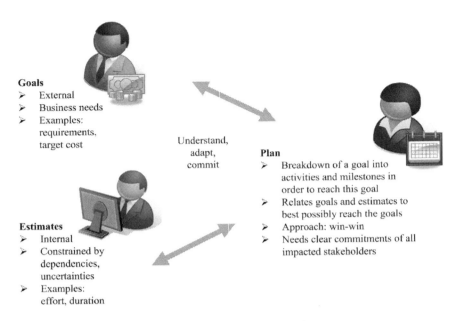

Goals
➢ External
➢ Business needs
➢ Examples:
  requirements,
  target cost

Understand,
adapt,
commit

Plan
➢ Breakdown of a goal into
  activities and milestones in
  order to reach this goal
➢ Relates goals and estimates to
  best possibly reach the goals
➢ Approach: win-win
➢ Needs clear commitments of all
  impacted stakeholders

Estimates
➢ Internal
➢ Constrained by
  dependencies,
  uncertainties
➢ Examples:
  effort, duration

Figure 12.4. Goals, Estimates, and Plans

2.15. Replacement and Retirement Decisions
[1*, c12] [2*, c9]

A replacement decision is made when an organization already has a particular asset and they are considering replacing it with something else; for example, deciding between maintaining and supporting a legacy software product or redeveloping it from the ground up. Replacement decisions use the same business decision process as described above, but there are additional challenges: sunk cost and salvage value. Retirement decisions are also about getting out of an activity altogether, such as when a software company considers not selling a software product anymore or a hardware manufacturer considers not building and selling a particular model of computer any longer. Retirement decision can be influenced by lock-in factors such as technology dependency and high exit costs.

3. Risk and Uncertainty

3.1. Goals, Estimates, and Plans
[3*, c6]

Goals in software engineering economics are mostly business goals (or business objectives).

A business goal relates business needs (such as increasing profitability) to investing resources (such as starting a project or launching a product with a given budget, content, and timing). Goals apply to operational planning (for instance, to reach a certain milestone at a given date or to extend software testing by some time to achieve a desired quality level—see Key Issues in the Software Testing KA) and to the strategic level (such as reaching a certain profitability or market share in a stated time period).

An estimate is a well-founded evaluation of resources and time that will be needed to achieve stated goals (see Effort, Schedule, and Cost Estimation in the Software Engineering Management KA and Maintenance Cost Estimation in the Software Maintenance KA). A software estimate is used to determine whether the project goals can be achieved within the constraints on schedule, budget, features, and quality attributes. Estimates are typically internally generated and are not necessarily visible externally. Estimates should not be driven exclusively by the project goals because this could make an estimate overly optimistic. Estimation is a periodic activity; estimates should be continually revised during a project.

A plan describes the activities and milestones that are necessary in order to reach the goals of a project (see Software Project Planning in the Software Engineering Management KA). The plan should be in line with the goal and the estimate, which is not necessarily easy and obvious—such as when a software project with given requirements would take longer than the target date foreseen by the client. In such cases, plans demand a review of initial goals as well as estimates and the underlying uncertainties and inaccuracies. Creative solutions with the underlying rationale of achieving a win-win position are applied to resolve conflicts.

To be of value, planning should involve consideration of the project constraints and commitments to stakeholders. Figure 12.4 shows how goals are initially defined. Estimates are done based on the initial goals. The plan tries to match the goals and the estimates. This is an iterative process, because an initial estimate typically does not meet the initial goals.

3.2. Estimation Techniques

[3*, c6]

Estimations are used to analyze and forecast the resources or time necessary to implement requirements (see Effort, Schedule, and Cost Estimation in the Software Engineering Management KA and Maintenance Cost Estimation in the Software Maintenance KA). Five families of estimation techniques exist:

- Expert judgment
- Analogy
- Estimation by parts
- Parametric methods
- Statistical methods.

No single estimation technique is perfect, so using multiple estimation technique is useful. Convergence among the estimates produced by different techniques indicates that the estimates are probably accurate. Spread among the estimates indicates that certain factors might have been overlooked. Finding the factors that caused the spread and then reestimating again to produce results that converge could lead to a better estimate.

3.3. Addressing Uncertainty

[3*, c6]

Because of the many unknown factors during project initiation and planning, estimates are inherently uncertain; that uncertainty should be addressed in business decisions. Techniques for addressing uncertainty include

- consider ranges of estimates
- analyze sensitivity to changes of assumptions
- delay final decisions.

3.4. Prioritization

[3*, c6]

Prioritization involves ranking alternatives based on common criteria to deliver the best possible value. In software engineering projects, software requirements are often prioritized in order to deliver the most value to the client within constraints of schedule, budget, resources, and technology, or to provide for building product increments, where the first increments provide the highest value to the customer (see Requirements Classification and Requirements Negotiation in the Software Requirements KA and Software Life Cycle Models in the Software Engineering Process KA).

3.5. Decisions under Risk

[1*, c24] [3*, c9]

Decisions under risk techniques are used when the decision maker can assign probabilities to the different possible outcomes (see Risk Management in the Software Engineering Management KA). The specific techniques include

- expected value decision making
- expectation variance and decision making
- Monte Carlo analysis
- decision trees
- expected value of perfect information.

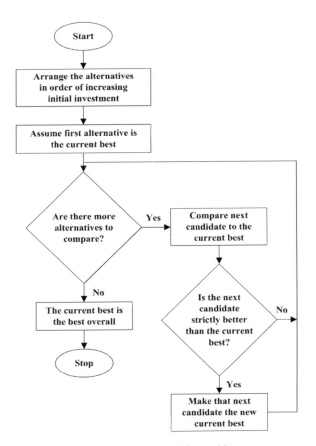

Figure 12.5. The for-profit decision-making process

3.6. Decisions under Uncertainty
[1*, c25] [3*, c9]

Decisions under uncertainty techniques are used when the decision maker cannot assign probabilities to the different possible outcomes because needed information is not available (see Risk Management in the Software Engineering Management KA). Specific techniques include

- Laplace Rule
- Maximin Rule
- Maximax Rule
- Hurwicz Rule
- Minimax Regret Rule.

4. Economic Analysis Methods

4.1. For-Profit Decision Analysis
[1*, c10]

Figure 12.5 describes a process for identifying the best alternative from a set of mutually exclusive alternatives. Decision criteria depend on the business objectives and typically include ROI (see section 4.3, Return on Investment) or Return on Capital Employed (ROCE) (see section 4.4, Return on Capital Employed).

For-profit decision techniques don't apply for government and nonprofit organizations. In these cases, organizations have different goals—which means that a different set of decision techniques are needed, such as cost-benefit or cost-effectiveness analysis.

4.2. Minimum Acceptable Rate of Return

[1*, c10]

The minimum acceptable rate of return (MARR) is the lowest internal rate of return the organization would consider to be a good investment. Generally speaking, it wouldn't be smart to invest in an activity with a return of 10% when there's another activity that's known to return 20%. The MARR is a statement that an organization is confident it can achieve at least that rate of return. The MARR represents the organization's opportunity cost for investments. By choosing to invest in some activity, the organization is explicitly deciding to not invest that same money somewhere else. If the organization is already confident it can get some known rate of return, other alternatives should be chosen only if their rate of return is at least that high. A simple way to account for that opportunity cost is to use the MARR as the interest rate in business decisions. An alternative's present worth evaluated at the MARR shows how much more or less (in present-day cash terms) that alternative is worth than investing at the MARR.

4.3. Return on Investment

[1*, c10]

Return on investment (ROI) is a measure of the profitability of a company or business unit. It is defined as the ratio of money gained or lost (whether realized or unrealized) on an investment relative to the amount of money invested. The purpose of ROI varies and includes, for instance, providing a rationale for future investments and acquisition decisions.

4.4. Return on Capital Employed

The return on capital employed (ROCE) is a measure of the profitability of a company or business unit. It is defined as the ratio of a gross profit before taxes and interest (EBIT) to the total assets minus current liabilities. It describes the return on the used capital.

4.5. Cost-Benefit Analysis

[1*, c18]

Cost-benefit analysis is one of the most widely used methods for evaluating individual proposals. Any proposal with a benefit-cost ratio of less than 1.0 can usually be rejected without further analysis because it would cost more than the benefit. Proposals with a higher ratio need to consider the associated risk of an investment and compare the benefits with the option of investing the money at a guaranteed interest rate (see section 4.2, Minimum Acceptable Rate of Return).

4.6. Cost-Effectiveness Analysis

[1*, c18]

Cost-effectiveness analysis is similar to cost-benefit analysis. There are two versions of cost-effectiveness analysis: the *fixed-cost* version maximizes the benefit given some upper bound on cost; the *fixed-effectiveness* version minimizes the cost needed to achieve a fixed goal.

4.7. Break-Even Analysis

[1*, c19]

Break-even analysis identifies the point where the costs of developing a product and the revenue to be generated are equal. Such an analysis can be used to choose between different proposals at different estimated costs and revenue. Given estimated costs and revenue of two or more proposals, break-even analysis helps in choosing among them.

4.8. Business Case

[1*, c3]

The business case is the consolidated information summarizing and explaining a business proposal from different perspectives for a decision maker (cost, benefit, risk, and so on). It is often used to assess the potential value of a product, which can be used as a basis in the investment decision-making process. As opposed to a mere profit-loss calculation, the business case is a "case" of plans and analyses that is owned by the product manager and used in support of achieving the business objectives.

4.9. Multiple Attribute Evaluation

[1*, c26]

The topics discussed so far are used to make decisions based on a single decision criterion: money. The alternative with the best present worth, the best ROI, and so forth is the one selected. Aside from technical feasibility, money is almost always the most important decision criterion, but it's not always the only one. Quite often there are other criteria, other "attributes," that need to be considered, and those attributes can't be cast in terms of money. Multiple attribute decision techniques allow other, nonfinancial criteria to be factored into the decision.

There are two families of multiple attribute decision techniques that differ in how they use the attributes in the decision. One family is the "compensatory," or single-dimensioned, techniques. This family collapses all of the attributes onto a single figure of merit. The family is called compensatory because, for any given alternative, a lower score in one attribute can be compensated by—or traded off against—a higher score in other attributes. The compensatory techniques include

- nondimensional scaling
- additive weighting
- analytic hierarchy process.

In contrast, the other family is the "noncompensatory," or fully dimensioned, techniques. This family does not allow tradeoffs among the attributes. Each attribute is treated as a separate entity in the decision process. The noncompensatory techniques include

- dominance
- satisficing
- lexicography.

4.10. Optimization Analysis

[1*, c20]

The typical use of optimization analysis is to study a cost function over a range of values to find the point where overall performance is best. Software's classic space-time tradeoff is an example of optimization; an algorithm that runs faster will often use more memory. Optimization balances the value of the faster runtime against the cost of the additional memory.

Real options analysis can be used to quantify the value of project choices, including the value of delaying a decision. Such options are difficult to compute with precision. However, awareness that choices have a monetary value provides insight in the timing of decisions such as increasing project staff or lengthening time to market to improve quality.

5. Practical Considerations

5.1. The "Good Enough" Principle

[1*, c21]

Often software engineering projects and products are not precise about the targets that should be achieved. Software requirements are stated, but the marginal value of adding a bit more functionality cannot be measured. The result could be late delivery or too-high cost. The "good enough" principle relates marginal value to marginal cost and provides guidance to determine criteria when a deliverable is "good enough" to be delivered. These criteria depend on business objectives and on prioritization of different alternatives, such as ranking software requirements, measurable quality attributes, or relating schedule to product content and cost.

The RACE principle (reduce accidents and control essence) is a popular rule towards good enough software. Accidents imply unnecessary overheads such as gold-plating and rework due to late defect removal or too many requirements changes. Essence is what customers pay for. Software engineering economics provides the mechanisms to define criteria that determine when a deliverable is "good enough" to be delivered. It also highlights that both words are relevant: "good" and "enough." Insufficient quality or insufficient quantity is not good enough.

Agile methods are examples of "good enough" that try to optimize value by reducing the overhead of delayed rework and the gold plating that results from adding features that have low marginal value for the users (see Agile Methods in the Software Engineering Models and Methods KA and Software Life Cycle Models in the Software Engineering Process KA). In agile methods, detailed planning and lengthy development phases are replaced by incremental planning and frequent delivery of small increments of a deliverable product that is tested and evaluated by user representatives.

5.2. Friction-Free Economy

Economic friction is everything that keeps markets from having perfect competition. It involves distance, cost of delivery, restrictive regulations, and/or imperfect information. In high-friction markets, customers don't have many suppliers from which to choose. Having been in a business for a while or owning a store in a good location determines the economic position. It's hard for new competitors to start business and compete. The marketplace moves slowly and predictably. Friction-free markets are just the reverse. New competitors emerge and customers are quick to respond. The marketplace is anything but predictable. Theoretically, software and IT are friction-free. New companies can easily create products and often do so at a much lower cost than established companies, since they need not consider any legacies. Marketing and sales can be done via the Internet and social networks, and basically free distribution mechanisms can enable a ramp up to a global business. Software engineering economics aims to provide foundations to judge how a software business performs and how friction-free a market actually is. For instance, competition among software app developers is inhibited when apps must be sold through an app store and comply with that store's rules.

5.3. Ecosystems

An ecosystem is an environment consisting of all the mutually dependent stakeholders, business units, and companies working in a particular area.

In a typical ecosystem, there are producers and consumers, where the consumers add value to the consumed resources. Note that a consumer is not the end user but an organization that uses the product to enhance it. A software ecosystem is, for instance, a supplier of an application working with companies doing the installation and support in different regions. Neither one could exist without the other. Ecosystems can be permanent or temporary. Software engineering economics provides the mechanisms to evaluate alternatives in establishing or extending an ecosystem—for instance, assessing whether to work with a specific distributor or have the distribution done by a company doing service in an area.

5.4. Offshoring and Outsourcing

Offshoring means executing a business activity beyond sales and marketing outside the home country of an enterprise. Enterprises typically either have their offshoring branches in low-cost countries or they ask specialized companies abroad to execute the respective activity. Offshoring should therefore not be confused with outsourcing. Offshoring within a company is called captive offshoring. Outsourcing is the result-oriented relationship with a supplier who executes business activities for an enterprise when, traditionally, those activities were executed inside the enterprise. Outsourcing is site-independent. The supplier can reside in the neighborhood of the enterprise or offshore (outsourced offshoring). Software engineering economics provides the basic criteria and business tools to evaluate different sourcing mechanisms and control their performance. For instance, using an outsourcing supplier for software development and maintenance might reduce the cost per hour of software development, but increase the number of hours and capital expenses due to an increased need for monitoring and communication. (For more information on offshoring and outsourcing, see "Outsourcing" in Management Issues in the Software Maintenance KA.)

MATRIX OF TOPICS VS. REFERENCE MATERIAL

	Tockey 2005 [1*]	Sommerville 2011 [2*]	Fairley 2009 [3*]
1. Software Engineering Economics Fundamentals			
1.1. Finance	c2		
1.2. Accounting	c15		
1.3. Controlling	c15		
1.4. Cash Flow	c3		
1.5. Decision-Making Process	c2, c4		
1.6. Valuation	c5, c8		
1.7. Inflation	c13		
1.8. Depreciation	c14		
1.9. Taxation	c16, c17		
1.10. Time-Value of Money	c5, c11		
1.11. Efficiency		c1	
1.12. Effectiveness		c1	
1.13. Productivity		c23	
2. Life Cycle Economics			
2.1. Product		c22	c6
2.2. Project		c22	c1
2.3. Program			
2.4. Portfolio			
2.5. Product Life Cycle		c2	c2
2.6. Project Life Cycle		c2	c2
2.7. Proposals	c3		
2.8. Investment Decisions	c4		
2.9. Planning Horizon	c11		
2.10. Price and Pricing	c13		
2.11. Cost and Costing	c15		
2.12. Performance Measurement			c7, c8
2.13. Earned Value Management			c8
2.14. Termination Decisions	c11, c12	c9	
2.15. Replacement and Retirement Decisions	c12	c9	

	Tockey 2005 [1*]	Sommerville 2011 [2*]	Fairley 2009 [3*]
3. Risk and Uncertainty			
3.1. Goals, Estimates, and Plans			c6
3.2. Estimation Techniques			c6
3.3. Addressing Uncertainty			c6
3.4. Prioritization			c6
3.5. Decisions under Risk	c24		c9
3.6. Decisions under Uncertainty	c25		c9
4. Economic Analysis Methods			
4.1. For-Profit Decision Analysis	c10		
4.2. Minimum Acceptable Rate of Return	c10		
4.3. Return on Investment	c10		
4.4. Return on Capital Employed			
4.5. Cost-Benefit Analysis	c18		
4.6. Cost-Effectiveness Analysis	c18		
4.7. Break-Even Analysis	c19		
4.8. Business Case	c3		
4.9. Multiple Attribute Evaluation	c26		
4.10. Optimization Analysis	c20		
5. Practical Considerations			
5.1. The "Good Enough" Principle	c21		
5.2. Friction-Free Economy			
5.3. Ecosystems			
5.4. Offshoring and Outsourcing			

FURTHER READINGS

A Guide to the Project Management Body of Knowledge (PMBOK® Guide) [4].

The *PMBOK® Guide* provides guidelines for managing individual projects and defines project management related concepts. It also describes the project management life cycle and its related processes, as well as the project life cycle. It is a globally recognized guide for the project management profession.

Software Extension to the Guide to the Project Management Body of Knowledge (SWX) [5].

SWX provides adaptations and extensions to the generic practices of project management documented in the *PMBOK® Guide* for managing software projects. The primary contribution of this extension to the *PMBOK® Guide* is description of processes that are applicable for managing adaptive life cycle software projects.

B.W. Boehm, *Software Engineering Economics* [6].

This book is the classic reading on software engineering economics. It provides an overview of business thinking in software engineering. Although the examples and figures are dated, it still is worth reading.

C. Ebert and R. Dumke, *Software Measurement* [7].

This book provides an overview on quantitative methods in software engineering, starting with measurement theory and proceeding to performance management and business decision making.

D.J. Reifer, *Making the Software Business Case: Improvement by the Numbers* [8].

This book is a classic reading on making a business case in the software and IT businesses. Many useful examples illustrate how the business case is formulated and quantified.

REFERENCES

[1*] S. Tockey, *Return on Software: Maximizing the Return on Your Software Investment*, Addison-Wesley, 2004.

[2*] J.H. Allen et al., *Software Security Engineering: A Guide for Project Managers*, Addison-Wesley, 2008.

[3*] R.E. Fairley, *Managing and Leading Software Projects*, Wiley-IEEE Computer Society Press, 2009.

[4] Project Management Institute, *A Guide to the Project Management Body of Knowledge (PMBOK(R) Guide)*, 5th ed., Project Management Institute, 2013.

[5] Project Management Institute and IEEE Computer Society, *Software Extension to the PMBOK® Guide Fifth Edition*, ed: Project Management Institute, 2013.

[6] B.W. Boehm, *Software Engineering Economics*, Prentice-Hall, 1981.

[7] C. Ebert and R. Dumke, *Software Measurement*, Springer, 2007.

[8] D.J. Reifer, *Making the Software Business Case: Improvement by the Numbers*, Addison Wesley, 2002.

CHAPTER 13

COMPUTING FOUNDATIONS

ACRONYMS

AOP	Aspect-Oriented Programming
ALU	Arithmetic and Logic Unit
API	Application Programming Interface
ATM	Asynchronous Transfer Mode
B/S	Browser-Server
CERT	Computer Emergency Response Team
COTS	Commercial Off-The-Shelf
CRUD	Create, Read, Update, Delete
C/S	Client-Server
CS	Computer Science
DBMS	Database Management System
FPU	Float Point Unit
I/O	Input and Output
ISA	Instruction Set Architecture
ISO	International Organization for Standardization
ISP	Internet Service Provider
LAN	Local Area Network
MUX	Multiplexer
NIC	Network Interface Card
OOP	Object-Oriented Programming
OS	Operating System
OSI	Open Systems Interconnection
PC	Personal Computer
PDA	Personal Digital Assistant
PPP	Point-to-Point Protocol
RFID	Radio Frequency Identification
RAM	Random Access Memory
ROM	Read Only Memory

SCSI	Small Computer System Interface
SQL	Structured Query Language
TCP	Transport Control Protocol
UDP	User Datagram Protocol
VPN	Virtual Private Network
WAN	Wide Area Network

INTRODUCTION

The scope of the Computing Foundations knowledge area (KA) encompasses the development and operational environment in which software evolves and executes. Because no software can exist in a vacuum or run without a computer, the core of such an environment is the computer and its various components. Knowledge about the computer and its underlying principles of hardware and software serves as a framework on which software engineering is anchored. Thus, all software engineers must have good understanding of the Computing Foundations KA.

It is generally accepted that software engineering builds on top of computer science. For example, "Software Engineering 2004: Curriculum Guidelines for Undergraduate Degree Programs in Software Engineering" [1] clearly states, "One particularly important aspect is that *software engineering builds on computer science and mathematics*" (italics added).

Steve Tockey wrote in his book *Return on Software*:

> Both computer science and software engineering deal with computers, computing, and software. The science of computing, as a body of knowledge, is at the core of both.

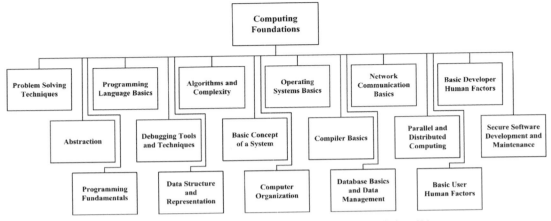

Figure 13.1. Breakdown of Topics for the Computing Foundations KA

… Software engineering is concerned with the application of computers, computing, and software to practical purposes, specifically the design, construction, and operation of efficient and economical software systems.

Thus, at the core of software engineering is an understanding of computer science.

While few people will deny the role computer science plays in the development of software engineering both as a discipline and as a body of knowledge, the importance of computer science to software engineering cannot be overemphasized; thus, this Computing Foundations KA is being written.

The majority of topics discussed in the Computing Foundations KA are also topics of discussion in basic courses given in computer science undergraduate and graduate programs. Such courses include programming, data structure, algorithms, computer organization, operating systems, compilers, databases, networking, distributed systems, and so forth. Thus, when breaking down topics, it can be tempting to decompose the Computing Foundations KA according to these often-found divisions in relevant courses.

However, a purely course-based division of topics suffers serious drawbacks. For one, not all courses in computer science are related or equally important to software engineering. Thus, some topics that would otherwise be covered in a computer science course are not covered in this KA. For example, computer graphics—while an important course in a computer science degree program—is not included in this KA.

Second, some topics discussed in this guideline do not exist as standalone courses in undergraduate or graduate computer science programs. Consequently, such topics may not be adequately covered in a purely course-based breakdown. For example, abstraction is a topic incorporated into several different computer science courses; it is unclear which course abstraction should belong to in a course-based breakdown of topics.

The Computing Foundations KA is divided into seventeen different topics. A topic's direct usefulness to software engineers is the criterion used for selecting topics for inclusion in this KA (see Figure 13.1). The advantage of this topic-based breakdown is its foundation on the belief that Computing Foundations—if it is to be grasped firmly—must be considered as a collection of logically connected topics undergirding software engineering in general and software construction in particular.

The Computing Foundations KA is related closely to the Software Design, Software Construction, Software Testing, Software Maintenance, Software Quality, and Mathematical Foundations KAs.

BREAKDOWN OF TOPICS FOR COMPUTING FOUNDATIONS

The breakdown of topics for the Computing Foundations KA is shown in Figure 13.1.

1. Problem Solving Techniques

[2*, s3.2, c4] [3*, c5]

The concepts, notions, and terminology introduced here form an underlying basis for understanding the role and scope of problem solving techniques.

1.1. Definition of Problem Solving

Problem solving refers to the thinking and activities conducted to answer or derive a solution to a problem. There are many ways to approach a problem, and each way employs different tools and uses different processes. These different ways of approaching problems gradually expand and define themselves and finally give rise to different disciplines. For example, software engineering focuses on solving problems using computers and software.

While different problems warrant different solutions and may require different tools and processes, the methodology and techniques used in solving problems do follow some guidelines and can often be generalized as problem solving techniques. For example, a general guideline for solving a generic engineering problem is to use the three-step process given below [2*].

- Formulate the real problem.
- Analyze the problem.
- Design a solution search strategy.

1.2. Formulating the Real Problem

Gerard Voland writes, "It is important to recognize that a specific problem should be formulated if one is to develop a specific solution" [2*]. This formulation is called the problem statement, which explicitly specifies what both the problem and the desired outcome are.

Although there is no universal way of stating a problem, in general a problem should be expressed in such a way as to facilitate the development of solutions. Some general techniques to help one formulate the real problem include statement-restatement, determining the source and the cause, revising the statement, analyzing present and desired state, and using the fresh eye approach.

1.3. Analyze the Problem

Once the problem statement is available, the next step is to analyze the problem statement or situation to help structure our search for a solution. Four types of analysis include *situation analysis,* in which the most urgent or critical aspects of a situation are identified first; *problem analysis,* in which the cause of the problem must be determined; *decision analysis,* in which the action(s) needed to correct the problem or eliminate its cause must be determined; and *potential problem analysis,* in which the action(s) needed to prevent any reoccurrences of the problem or the development of new problems must be determined.

1.4. Design a Solution Search Strategy

Once the problem analysis is complete, we can focus on structuring a search strategy to find the solution. In order to find the "best" solution (here, "best" could mean different things to different people, such as faster, cheaper, more usable, different capabilities, etc.), we need to eliminate paths that do not lead to viable solutions, design tasks in a way that provides the most guidance in searching for a solution, and use various attributes of the final solution state to guide our choices in the problem solving process.

1.5. Problem Solving Using Programs

The uniqueness of computer software gives problem solving a flavor that is distinct from general engineering problem solving. To solve a problem using computers, we must answer the following questions.

- How do we figure out what to tell the computer to do?
- How do we convert the problem statement into an algorithm?
- How do we convert the algorithm into machine instructions?

The first task in solving a problem using a computer is to determine what to tell the computer to do. There may be many ways to tell the story, but all should take the perspective of a computer such that the computer can eventually solve the problem. In general, a problem should be expressed in such a way as to facilitate the development of algorithms and data structures for solving it.

The result of the first task is a problem statement. The next step is to convert the problem statement into algorithms that solve the problem. Once an algorithm is found, the final step converts the algorithm into machine instructions that form the final solution: software that solves the problem.

Abstractly speaking, problem solving using a computer can be considered as a process of problem transformation—in other words, the step-by-step transformation of a problem statement into a problem solution. To the discipline of software engineering, the ultimate objective of problem solving is to transform a problem expressed in natural language into electrons running around a circuit. In general, this transformation can be broken into three phases:

a) Development of algorithms from the problem statement.
b) Application of algorithms to the problem.
c) Transformation of algorithms to program code.

The conversion of a problem statement into algorithms and algorithms into program codes usually follows a "stepwise refinement" (a.k.a. systematic decomposition) in which we start with a problem statement, rewrite it as a task, and recursively decompose the task into a few simpler subtasks until the task is so simple that solutions to it are straightforward. There are three basic ways of decomposing: sequential, conditional, and iterative.

2. Abstraction

[3*, s5.2–5.4]

Abstraction is an indispensible technique associated with problem solving. It refers to both the process and result of generalization by reducing the information of a concept, a problem, or an observable phenomenon so that one can focus on the "big picture." One of the most important skills in any engineering undertaking is framing the levels of abstraction appropriately.

"Through abstraction," according to Voland, "we view the problem and its possible solution paths from a higher level of conceptual understanding. As a result, we may become better prepared to recognize possible relationships between different aspects of the problem and thereby generate more creative design solutions" [2*]. This is particularly true in computer science in general (such as hardware vs. software) and in software engineering in particular (data structure vs. data flow, and so forth).

2.1. Levels of Abstraction

When abstracting, we concentrate on one "level" of the big picture at a time with confidence that we can then connect effectively with levels above and below. Although we focus on one level, abstraction does not mean knowing nothing about the neighboring levels. Abstraction levels do not necessarily correspond to discrete components in reality or in the problem domain, but to well-defined standard interfaces such as programming APIs. The advantages that standard interfaces provide include portability, easier software/hardware integration and wider usage.

2.2. Encapsulation

Encapsulation is a mechanism used to implement abstraction. When we are dealing with one level of abstraction, the information concerning the levels below and above that level is encapsulated. This information can be the concept, problem, or observable phenomenon; or it may be the permissible operations on these relevant entities. Encapsulation usually comes with some degree of information hiding in which some or all of the underlying details are hidden from the level above the interface provided by the abstraction. To an object, information hiding means we don't need to know the details of how the object is represented or how the operations on those objects are implemented.

2.3. Hierarchy

When we use abstraction in our problem formulation and solution, we may use different abstractions at different times—in other words, we work on different levels of abstraction as the situation calls. Most of the time, these different levels of abstraction are organized in a hierarchy. There are many ways to structure a particular hierarchy and the criteria used in determining the specific content of each layer in the hierarchy varies depending on the individuals performing the work.

Sometimes, a hierarchy of abstraction is sequential, which means that each layer has one and only one predecessor (lower) layer and one and only one successor (upper) layer—except the upmost layer (which has no successor) and the bottommost layer (which has no predecessor). Sometimes, however, the hierarchy is organized in a tree-like structure, which means each layer can have more than one predecessor layer but only one successor layer. Occasionally, a hierarchy can have a many-to-many structure, in which each layer can have multiple predecessors and successors. At no time, shall there be any loop in a hierarchy.

A hierarchy often forms naturally in task decomposition. Often, a task analysis can be decomposed in a hierarchical fashion, starting with the larger tasks and goals of the organization and breaking each of them down into smaller subtasks that can again be further subdivided This continuous division of tasks into smaller ones would produce a hierarchical structure of tasks-subtasks.

2.4. Alternate Abstractions

Sometimes it is useful to have multiple alternate abstractions for the same problem so that one can keep different perspectives in mind. For example, we can have a class diagram, a state chart, and a sequence diagram for the same software at the same level of abstraction. These alternate abstractions do not form a hierarchy but rather complement each other in helping understanding the problem and its solution. Though beneficial, it is as times difficult to keep alternate abstractions in sync.

3. Programming Fundamentals

[3*, c6–19]

Programming is composed of the methodologies or activities for creating computer programs that perform a desired function. It is an indispensible part in software construction. In general, programming can be considered as the process of designing, writing, testing, debugging, and maintaining the source code. This source code is written in a programming language.

The process of writing source code often requires expertise in many different subject areas—including knowledge of the application domain, appropriate data structures, specialized algorithms, various language constructs, good programming techniques, and software engineering.

3.1. The Programming Process

Programming involves design, writing, testing, debugging, and maintenance. *Design* is the conception or invention of a scheme for turning a customer requirement for computer software into operational software. It is the activity that links application requirements to coding and debugging. *Writing* is the actual coding of the design in an appropriate programming language. *Testing* is the activity to verify that the code one writes actually does what it is supposed to do. *Debugging* is the activity to find and fix bugs (faults) in the source code (or design). *Maintenance* is the activity to update, correct, and enhance existing programs. Each of these activities is a huge topic and often warrants the explanation of an entire KA in the *SWEBOK Guide* and many books.

3.2. Programming Paradigms

Programming is highly creative and thus somewhat personal. Different people often write different programs for the same requirements. This diversity of programming causes much difficulty in the construction and maintenance of large complex software. Various programming paradigms have been developed over the years to put some standardization into this highly creative and personal activity. When one programs, he or she can use one of several programming paradigms to write the code. The major types of programming paradigms are discussed below.

Unstructured Programming: In unstructured programming, a programmer follows his/her hunch to write the code in whatever way he/she likes as long as the function is operational. Often, the practice is to write code to fulfill a specific utility without regard to anything else. Programs written this way exhibit no particular structure—thus the name "unstructured programming." Unstructured programming is also sometimes called ad hoc programming.

Structured/Procedural/ Imperative Programming: A hallmark of structured programming is the use of well-defined control structures, including procedures (and/or functions) with each procedure (or function) performing a specific task. Interfaces exist between procedures to facilitate correct and smooth calling operations of the programs. Under structured programming, programmers often follow established protocols and rules of thumb when writing code. These protocols and rules can be numerous and cover almost the entire scope of programming—ranging from the simplest issue (such as how to name variables, functions, procedures, and so forth) to more complex issues (such as how to structure an interface, how to handle exceptions, and so forth).

Object-Oriented Programming: While procedural programming organizes programs around procedures, object-oriented programming (OOP) organize a program around objects, which are abstract data structures that combine both data and methods used to access or manipulate the data. The primary features of OOP are that objects representing various abstract and concrete entities are created and these objects interact with each other to collectively fulfill the desired functions.

Aspect-Oriented Programming: Aspect-oriented programming (AOP) is a programming paradigm that is built on top of OOP. AOP aims to isolate secondary or supporting functions from the main program's business logic by focusing on the cross sections (concerns) of the objects. The primary motivation for AOP is to resolve the object tangling and scattering associated with OOP, in which the interactions among objects become very complex. The essence of AOP is the greatly emphasized separation of concerns, which separates noncore functional concerns or logic into various aspects.

Functional Programming: Though less popular, functional programming is as viable as the other paradigms in solving programming problems. In functional programming, all computations are treated as the evaluation of mathematical functions. In contrast to the imperative programming that emphasizes changes in state, functional programming emphasizes the application of functions, avoids state and mutable data, and provides referential transparency.

4. Programming Language Basics

[4*, c6]

Using computers to solve problems involves programming—which is writing and organizing instructions telling the computer what to do at each step. Programs must be written in some programming language with which and through which we describe necessary computations. In other words, we use the facilities provided by a programming language to describe problems, develop algorithms, and reason about problem solutions. To write any program, one must understand at least one programming language.

4.1. Programming Language Overview

A programming language is designed to express computations that can be performed by a computer. In a practical sense, a programming language is a notation for writing programs and thus should be able to express most data structures and algorithms. Some, but not all, people restrict the term "programming language" to those languages that can express all possible algorithms.

Not all languages have the same importance and popularity. The most popular ones are often defined by a specification document established by a well-known and respected organization. For example, the C programming language is specified by an ISO standard named ISO/IEC 9899. Other languages, such as Perl and Python, do not enjoy such treatment and often have a dominant implementation that is used as a reference.

4.2. Syntax and Semantics of Programming Languages

Just like natural languages, many programming languages have some form of written specification of their syntax (form) and semantics (meaning). Such specifications include, for example, specific requirements for the definition of variables and constants (in other words, declaration and types) and format requirements for the instructions themselves.

In general, a programming language supports such constructs as variables, data types, constants, literals, assignment statements, control statements, procedures, functions, and comments. The syntax and semantics of each construct must be clearly specified.

4.3. Low-Level Programming Languages

Programming language can be classified into two classes: low-level languages and high-level languages. Low-level languages can be understood by a computer with no or minimal assistance and typically include machine languages and assembly languages. A machine language uses ones and zeros to represent instructions and variables, and is directly understandable by a computer. An assembly language contains the same instructions as a machine language but the instructions and variables have symbolic names that are easier for humans to remember.

Assembly languages cannot be directly understood by a computer and must be translated into a machine language by a utility program called an *assembler*. There often exists a correspondence between the instructions of an assembly language and a machine language, and the translation from assembly code to machine code is straightforward. For example, "add r1, r2, r3" is an assembly instruction for adding the content of register r2 and r3 and storing the sum into register r1. This instruction can be easily translated into machine code "0001 0001 0010 0011." (Assume the operation code for addition is 0001, see Figure 13.2).

add	r1,	r2,	r3
0001	0001	0010	0011

Figure 13.2. Assembly-to-Binary Translations

One common trait shared by these two types of language is their close association with the specifics of a type of computer or instruction set architecture (ISA).

4.4. High-Level Programming Languages

A high-level programming language has a strong abstraction from the details of the computer's ISA. In comparison to low-level programming languages, it often uses natural-language elements and is thus much easier for humans to understand. Such languages allow symbolic naming of variables, provide expressiveness, and enable abstraction of the underlying hardware. For example, while each microprocessor has its own ISA, code written in a high-level programming language is usually portable between many different hardware platforms. For these reasons, most programmers use and most software are written in high-level programming languages. Examples of high-level programming languages include C, C++, C#, and Java.

4.5. Declarative vs. Imperative Programming Languages

Most programming languages (high-level or low-level) allow programmers to specify the individual instructions that a computer is to execute. Such programming languages are called imperative programming languages because one has to specify every step clearly to the computer. But some programming languages allow programmers to only describe the function to be performed without specifying the exact instruction sequences to be executed. Such programming languages are called declarative programming languages. Declarative languages are high-level languages. The actual implementation of the computation written in such a language is hidden from the programmers and thus is not a concern for them.

The key point to note is that declarative programming only describes *what* the program should accomplish without describing *how* to accomplish it. For this reason, many people believe declarative programming facilitates easier software development. Declarative programming languages include Lisp (also a functional programming language) and Prolog, while imperative programming languages include C, C++, and JAVA.

5. Debugging Tools and Techniques

[3*, c23]

Once a program is coded and compiled (compilation will be discussed in section 10), the next step is debugging, which is a methodical process of finding and reducing the number of bugs or faults in a program. The purpose of debugging is to find out why a program doesn't work or produces a wrong result or output. Except for very simple programs, debugging is always necessary.

5.1. Types of Errors

When a program does not work, it is often because the program contains bugs or errors that can be either syntactic errors, logical errors, or data errors. Logical errors and data errors are also known as two categories of "faults" in software engineering terminology (see topic 1.1, Testing-Related Terminology, in the Software Testing KA).

Syntax errors are simply any error that prevents the translator (compiler/interpreter) from successfully parsing the statement. Every statement in a program must be parse-able before its meaning can be understood and interpreted (and, therefore, executed). In high-level programming languages, syntax errors are caught during the compilation or translation from the high-level language into machine code. For example, in the C/C++ programming language, the statement "123=constant;" contains a syntax error that will be caught by the compiler during compilation.

Logic errors are semantic errors that result in incorrect computations or program behaviors. Your program is legal, but wrong! So the results do not match the problem statement or user expectations. For example, in the C/C++ programming language, the inline function "int f(int x) {return f(x-1);}" for computing factorial x! is legal but logically incorrect. This type of error cannot be caught by a compiler during compilation and is often discovered through tracing the execution of the program (Modern static checkers do identify some of these errors. However, the point remains that these are not machine checkable in general).

Data errors are input errors that result either in input data that is different from what the program expects or in the processing of wrong data.

5.2. Debugging Techniques

Debugging involves many activities and can be static, dynamic, or postmortem. *Static debugging* usually takes the form of code review, while *dynamic debugging* usually takes the form of tracing and is closely associated with testing. *Postmortem debugging* is the act of debugging the core dump (memory dump) of a process. Core dumps are often generated after a process has terminated due to an unhandled exception. All three techniques are used at various stages of program development.

The main activity of dynamic debugging is tracing, which is executing the program one piece at a time, examining the contents of registers and memory, in order to examine the results at each step. There are three ways to trace a program.

- *Single-stepping:* execute one instruction at a time to make sure each instruction is executed correctly. This method is tedious but useful in verifying each step of a program.
- *Breakpoints:* tell the program to stop executing when it reaches a specific instruction. This technique lets one quickly execute selected code sequences to get a high-level overview of the execution behavior.
- *Watch points:* tell the program to stop when a register or memory location changes or when it equals to a specific value. This technique is useful when one doesn't know where or when a value is changed and when this value change likely causes the error.

5.3. Debugging Tools

Debugging can be complex, difficult, and tedious. Like programming, debugging is also highly creative (sometimes more creative than programming). Thus some help from tools is in order. For dynamic debugging, *debuggers* are widely used and enable the programmer to monitor the execution of a program, stop the execution, restart the execution, set breakpoints, change values in memory, and even, in some cases, go back in time.

For static debugging, there are many *static code analysis tools*, which look for a specific set of known problems within the source code.

Both commercial and free tools exist in various languages. These tools can be extremely useful when checking very large source trees, where it is impractical to do code walkthroughs. The UNIX *lint* program is an early example.

6. Data Structure and Representation

[5*, s2.1–2.6]

Programs work on data. But data must be expressed and organized within computers before being processed by programs. This organization and expression of data for programs' use is the subject of data structure and representation. Simply put, a data structure tries to store and organize data in a computer in such a way that the data can be used efficiently. There are many types of data structures and each type of structure is suitable for some kinds of applications. For example, B/B+ trees are well suited for implementing massive file systems and databases.

6.1. Data Structure Overview

Data structures are computer representations of data. Data structures are used in almost every program. In a sense, no meaningful program can be constructed without the use of some sort of data structure. Some design methods and programming languages even organize an entire software system around data structures. Fundamentally, data structures are abstractions defined on a collection of data and its associated operations.

Often, data structures are designed for improving program or algorithm efficiency. Examples of such data structures include stacks, queues, and heaps. At other times, data structures are used for conceptual unity (abstract data type), such as the name and address of a person. Often, a data structure can determine whether a program runs in a few seconds or in a few hours or even a few days.

From the perspective of physical and logical ordering, a data structure is either linear or nonlinear. Other perspectives give rise to different classifications that include homogeneous vs. heterogeneous, static vs. dynamic, persistent vs. transient, external vs. internal, primitive vs. aggregate, recursive vs. nonrecursive; passive vs. active; and stateful vs. stateless structures.

6.2. Types of Data Structure

As mentioned above, different perspectives can be used to classify data structures. However, the predominant perspective used in classification centers on physical and logical ordering between data items. This classification divides data structures into linear and nonlinear structures. Linear structures organize data items in a single dimension in which each data entry has one (physical or logical) predecessor and one successor with the exception of the first and last entry. The first entry has no predecessor and the last entry has no successor. Nonlinear structures organize data items in two or more dimensions, in which case one entry can have multiple predecessors and successors. Examples of linear structures include lists, stacks, and queues. Examples of nonlinear structures include heaps, hash tables, and trees (such as binary trees, balance trees, B-trees, and so forth).

Another type of data structure that is often encountered in programming is the compound structure. A compound data structure builds on top of other (more primitive) data structures and, in some way, can be viewed as the same structure as the underlying structure. Examples of compound structures include sets, graphs, and partitions. For example, a partition can be viewed as a set of sets.

6.3. Operations on Data Structures

All data structures support some operations that produce a specific structure and ordering, or retrieve relevant data from the structure, store data into the structure, or delete data from the structure. Basic operations supported by all data structures include create, read, update, and delete (CRUD).

- Create: Insert a new data entry into the structure.
- Read: Retrieve a data entry from the structure.
- Update: Modify an existing data entry.
- Delete: Remove a data entry from the structure.

Some data structures also support additional operations:

- Find a particular element in the structure.
- Sort all elements according to some ordering.
- Traverse all elements in some specific order.
- Reorganize or rebalance the structure.

Different structures support different operations with different efficiencies. The difference between operation efficiency can be significant. For example, it is easy to retrieve the last item inserted into a stack, but finding a particular element within a stack is rather slow and tedious.

7. Algorithms and Complexity
[5*, s1.1–1.3, s3.3–3.6, s4.1–4.8, s5.1–5.7, s6.1–6.3, s7.1–7.6, s11.1, s12.1]

Programs are not random pieces of code: they are meticulously written to perform user-expected actions. The guide one uses to compose programs are algorithms, which organize various functions into a series of steps and take into consideration the application domain, the solution strategy, and the data structures being used. An algorithm can be very simple or very complex.

7.1. Overview of Algorithms

Abstractly speaking, algorithms guide the operations of computers and consist of a sequence of actions composed to solve a problem. Alternative definitions include but are not limited to:

- An algorithm is any well-defined computational procedure that takes some value or set of values as input and produces some value or set of values as output.
- An algorithm is a sequence of computational steps that transform the input into the output.
- An algorithm is a tool for solving a well-specified computation problem.

Of course, different definitions are favored by different people. Though there is no universally accepted definition, some agreement exists that an algorithm needs to be correct, finite (in other words, terminate eventually or one must be able to write it in a finite number of steps), and unambiguous.

7.2. Attributes of Algorithms

The attributes of algorithms are many and often include modularity, correctness, maintainability, functionality, robustness, user-friendliness (i.e. easy to be understood by people), programmer time, simplicity, and extensibility. A commonly emphasized attribute is "performance" or "efficiency" by which we mean both time and resource-usage efficiency while generally emphasizing the time axis. To some degree, efficiency determines if an algorithm is feasible or impractical. For example, an algorithm that takes one hundred years to terminate is virtually useless and is even considered incorrect.

7.3. Algorithmic Analysis

Analysis of algorithms is the theoretical study of computer-program performance and resource usage; to some extent it determines the goodness of an algorithm. Such analysis usually abstracts away the particular details of a specific computer and focuses on the asymptotic, machine-independent analysis.

There are three basic types of analysis. In *worst-case analysis,* one determines the maximum time or resources required by the algorithm on any input of size n. In *average-case analysis,* one determines the expected time or resources required by the algorithm over all inputs of size n; in performing average-case analysis, one often needs to make assumptions on the statistical distribution of inputs. The third type of analysis is the *best-case analysis,* in which one determines the minimum time or resources required by the algorithm on any input of size n. Among the three types of analysis, average-case analysis is the most relevant but also the most difficult to perform.

Besides the basic analysis methods, there are also the *amortized analysis,* in which one determines the maximum time required by an algorithm over a sequence of operations; and the *competitive analysis,* in which one determines the relative performance merit of an algorithm against the optimal algorithm (which may not be known) in the same category (for the same operations).

7.4. Algorithmic Design Strategies

The design of algorithms generally follows one of the following strategies: brute force, divide and conquer, dynamic programming, and greedy selection. The *brute force strategy* is actually a no-strategy. It exhaustively tries every possible way to tackle a problem. If a problem has a solution, this strategy is guaranteed to find it; however, the time expense may be too high. The *divide and conquer strategy* improves on the brute force strategy by dividing a big problem into smaller, homogeneous problems. It solves the big problem by recursively solving the smaller problems and combing the solutions to the smaller problems to form the solution to the big problem. The underlying assumption for divide and conquer is that smaller problems are easier to solve.

The *dynamic programming strategy* improves on the divide and conquer strategy by recognizing that some of the sub-problems produced by division may be the same and thus avoids solving the same problems again and again. This elimination of redundant subproblems can dramatically improve efficiency.

The *greedy selection strategy* further improves on dynamic programming by recognizing that not all of the sub-problems contribute to the solution of the big problem. By eliminating all but one sub-problem, the greedy selection strategy achieves the highest efficiency among all algorithm design strategies. Sometimes the use of *randomization* can improve on the greedy selection strategy by eliminating the complexity in determining the greedy choice through coin flipping or randomization.

7.5. Algorithmic Analysis Strategies

The analysis strategies of algorithms include *basic counting analysis,* in which one actually counts the number of steps an algorithm takes to complete its task; *asymptotic analysis,* in which one only considers the order of magnitude of the number of steps an algorithm takes to complete its task; *probabilistic analysis,* in which one makes use of probabilities in analyzing the average performance of an algorithm; *amortized analysis,* in which one uses the methods of aggregation, potential, and accounting to analyze the worst performance of an algorithm on a sequence of operations; and *competitive analysis,* in which one uses methods such as potential and accounting to analyze the relative performance of an algorithm to the optimal algorithm.

For complex problems and algorithms, one may need to use a combination of the aforementioned analysis strategies.

8. Basic Concept of a System

[6*, c10]

Ian Sommerville writes, "a system is a purposeful collection of interrelated components that work together to achieve some objective" [6*]. A system can be very simple and include only a few components, like an ink pen, or rather complex, like an aircraft. Depending on whether humans are part of the system, systems can be divided into technical computer-based systems and sociotechnical systems. A technical computer-based system functions without human involvement, such as televisions, mobile phones, thermostat, and some software; a sociotechnical system will not function without human involvement. Examples of such system include manned space vehicles, chips embedded inside a human, and so forth.

8.1. Emergent System Properties

A system is more than simply the sum of its parts. Thus, the properties of a system are not simply the sum of the properties of its components. Instead, a system often exhibits properties that are properties of the system as a whole. These properties are called *emergent properties* because they develop only after the integration of constituent parts in the system. Emergent system properties can be either functional or nonfunctional. Functional properties describe the things that a system does. For example, an aircraft's functional properties include flotation on air, carrying people or cargo, and use as a weapon of mass destruction. Nonfunctional properties describe how the system behaves in its operational environment. These can include such qualities as consistency, capacity, weight, security, etc.

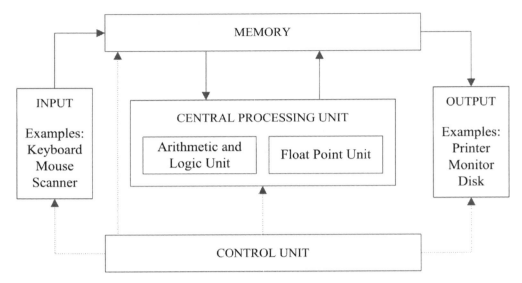

Figure 13.3. Basic Components of a Computer System Based on the von Neumann Model

8.2. Systems Engineering

"Systems engineering is the interdisciplinary approach governing the total technical and managerial effort required to transform a set of customer needs, expectations, and constraints into a solution and to support that solution throughout its life." [7]. The life cycle stages of systems engineering vary depending on the system being built but, in general, include system requirements definition, system design, sub-system development, system integration, system testing, system installation, system evolution, and system decommissioning.

Many practical guidelines have been produced in the past to aid people in performing the activities of each phase. For example, system design can be broken into smaller tasks of identification of subsystems, assignment of system requirements to subsystems, specification of subsystem functionality, definition of sub-system interfaces, and so forth.

8.3. Overview of a Computer System

Among all the systems, one that is obviously relevant to the software engineering community is the computer system. A computer is a machine that executes programs or software. It consists of a purposeful collection of mechanical, electrical, and electronic components with each component performing a preset function. Jointly, these components are able to execute the instructions that are given by the program.

Abstractly speaking, a computer receives some input, stores and manipulates some data, and provides some output. The most distinct feature of a computer is its ability to store and execute sequences of instructions called *programs*. An interesting phenomenon concerning the computer is the universal equivalence in functionality. According to Turing, all computers with a certain minimum capability are equivalent in their ability to perform computation tasks. In other words, given enough time and memory, all computers—ranging from a netbook to a supercomputer—are capable of computing exactly the same things, irrespective of speed, size, cost, or anything else.

Most computer systems have a structure that is known as the "von Neumann model," which consists of five components: a *memory* for storing instructions and data, a *central processing unit* for performing arithmetic and logical operations, a *control unit* for sequencing and interpreting instructions, *input* for getting external information into the memory, and *output* for producing results for the user. The basic components of a computer system based on the von Neumann model are depicted in Figure 13.3.

9. Computer Organization

[8*, c1–c4]

From the perspective of a computer, a wide semantic gap exists between its intended behavior and the workings of the underlying electronic devices that actually do the work within the computer. This gap is bridged through computer organization, which meshes various electrical, electronic, and mechanical devices into one device that forms a computer. The objects that computer organization deals with are the devices, connections, and controls. The abstraction built in computer organization is the computer.

9.1. Computer Organization Overview

A computer generally consists of a CPU, memory, input devices, and output devices. Abstractly speaking, the organization of a computer can be divided into four levels (Figure 13.4). The *macro architecture* level is the formal specification of all the functions a particular machine can carry out and is known as the instruction set architecture (ISA). The *micro architecture* level is the implementation of the ISA in a specific CPU—in other words, the way in which the ISA's specifications are actually carried out. The *logic circuits* level is the level where each functional component of the micro architecture is built up of circuits that make decisions based on simple rules. The *devices* level is the level where, finally, each logic circuit is actually built of electronic devices such as complementary metal-oxide semiconductors (CMOS), n-channel metal oxide semiconductors (NMOS), or gallium arsenide (GaAs) transistors, and so forth.

Macro Architecture Level (ISA)
Micro Architecture Level
Logic Circuits Level
Devices Level

Figure 13.4. Machine Architecture Levels

Each level provides an abstraction to the level above and is dependent on the level below. To a programmer, the most important abstraction is the ISA, which specifies such things as the native data types, instructions, registers, addressing modes, the memory architecture, interrupt and exception handling, and the I/Os. Overall, the ISA specifies the ability of a computer and what can be done on the computer with programming.

9.2. Digital Systems

At the lowest level, computations are carried out by the electrical and electronic devices within a computer. The computer uses circuits and memory to hold charges that represents the presence or absence of voltage. The presence of voltage is equal to a 1 while the absence of voltage is a zero. On disk the polarity of the voltage is represented by 0s and 1s that in turn represents the data stored. Everything—including instruction and data—is expressed or encoded using digital zeros and ones. In this sense, a computer becomes a digital system. For example, decimal value 6 can be encoded as 110, the addition instruction may be encoded as 0001, and so forth. The component of the computer such as the control unit, ALU, memory and I/O use the information to compute the instructions.

9.3. Digital Logic

Obviously, logics are needed to manipulate data and to control the operation of computers. This logic, which is behind a computer's proper function, is called *digital logic* because it deals with the operations of digital zeros and ones. Digital logic specifies the rules both for building various digital devices from the simplest elements (such as transistors) and for governing the operation of digital devices. For example, digital logic spells out what the value will be if a zero and one is ANDed, ORed, or exclusively ORed together. It also specifies how to build decoders, multiplexers (MUX), memory, and adders that are used to assemble the computer.

9.4. Computer Expression of Data

As mentioned before, a computer expresses data with electrical signals or digital zeros and ones. Since there are only two different digits used in data expression, such a system is called a *binary expression system*. Due to the inherent nature of a binary system, the maximum numerical value expressible by an n-bits binary code is $2^n - 1$. Specifically, binary number $a_n a_{n-1}...a_1 a_0$ corresponds to $a_n \times 2^n + a_{n-1} \times 2^{n-1} + ... + a_1 \times 2^1 + a_0 \times 2^0$. Thus, the numerical value of the binary expression of 1011 is $1 \times 8 + 0 \times 4 + 1 \times 2 + 1 \times 1 = 11$. To express a nonnumerical value, we need to decide the number of zeros and ones to use and the order in which those zeros and ones are arranged.

Of course, there are different ways to do the encoding, and this gives rise to different data expression schemes and subschemes. For example, integers can be expressed in the form of unsigned, one's complement, or two's complement. For characters, there are ASCII, Unicode, and IBM's EBCDIC standards. For floating point numbers, there are IEEE-754 FP 1, 2, and 3 standards.

9.5. The Central Processing Unit (CPU)

The central processing unit is the place where instructions (or programs) are actually executed. The execution usually takes several steps, including fetching the program instruction, decoding the instruction, fetching operands, performing arithmetic and logical operations on the operands, and storing the result. The main components of a CPU consist of registers where instructions and data are often read from and written to, the arithmetic and logic unit (ALU) that performs the actual arithmetic (such as addition, subtraction, multiplication, and division) and logic (such as AND, OR, shift, and so forth) operations, the control unit that is responsible for producing proper signals to control the operations, and various (data, address, and control) buses that link the components together and transport data to and from these components.

9.6. Memory System Organization

Memory is the storage unit of a computer. It concerns the assembling of a large-scale memory system from smaller and single-digit storage units. The main topics covered by memory system architecture include the following:

- Memory cells and chips
- Memory boards and modules
- Memory hierarchy and cache
- Memory as a subsystem of the computer.

Memory cells and chips deal with single-digital storage and the assembling of single-digit units into one-dimensional memory arrays as well as the assembling of one-dimensional storage arrays into multi-dimensional storage memory chips. *Memory boards and modules* concern the assembling of memory chips into memory systems, with the focus being on the organization, operation, and management of the individual chips in the system. *Memory hierarchy and cache* are used to support efficient memory operations. *Memory as a sub-system* deals with the interface between the memory system and other parts of the computer.

9.7. Input and Output (I/O)

A computer is useless without I/O. Common input devices include the keyboard and mouse; common output devices include the disk, the screen, the printer, and speakers. Different I/O devices operate at different data rates and reliabilities. How computers connect and manage various input and output devices to facilitate the interaction between computers and humans (or other computers) is the focus of topics in I/O. The main issues that must be resolved in input and output are the ways I/O can and should be performed.

In general, I/O is performed at both hardware and software levels. Hardware I/O can be performed in any of three ways. *Dedicated I/O* dedicates the CPU to the actual input and output operations during I/O; *memory-mapped I/O* treats I/O operations as memory operations; and *hybrid I/O* combines dedicated I/O and memory-mapped I/O into a single holistic I/O operation mode.

Coincidentally, software I/O can also be performed in one of three ways. *Programmed I/O* lets the CPU wait while the I/O device is doing I/O; *interrupt-driven I/O* lets the CPU's handling of I/O be driven by the I/O device; and *direct memory access (DMA)* lets I/O be handled by a secondary CPU embedded in a DMA device (or channel). (Except during the initial setup, the main CPU is not disturbed during a DMA I/O operation.)

Regardless of the types of I/O scheme being used, the main issues involved in I/O include *I/O addressing* (which deals with the issue of how to identify the I/O device for a specific I/O operation), *synchronization* (which deals with the issue of how to make the CPU and I/O device work in harmony during I/O), and *error detection and correction* (which deals with the occurrence of transmission errors).

10. Compiler Basics

[4*, s6.4] [8*, s8.4]

10.1. Compiler/Interpreter Overview

Programmers usually write programs in high level language code, which the CPU cannot execute; so this source code has to be converted into machine code to be understood by a computer. Due to the differences between different ISAs, the translation must be done for each ISA or specific machine language under consideration.

The translation is usually performed by a piece of software called a compiler or an interpreter. This process of translation from a high-level language to a machine language is called compilation, or, sometimes, interpretation.

10.2. Interpretation and Compilation

There are two ways to translate a program written in a higher-level language into machine code: interpretation and compilation. *Interpretation* translates the source code one statement at a time into machine language, executes it on the spot, and then goes back for another statement. Both the high-level-language source code and the interpreter are required every time the program is run.

Compilation translates the high-level-language source code into an entire machine-language program (an executable image) by a program called a compiler. After compilation, only the executable image is needed to run the program. Most application software is sold in this form.

While both compilation and interpretation convert high level language code into machine code,

there are some important differences between the two methods. First, a compiler makes the conversion just once, while an interpreter typically converts it every time a program is executed. Second, interpreting code is slower than running the compiled code, because the interpreter must analyze each statement in the program when it is executed and then perform the desired action, whereas the compiled code just performs the action within a fixed context determined by the compilation. Third, access to variables is also slower in an interpreter because the mapping of identifiers to storage locations must be done repeatedly at runtime rather than at compile time.

The primary tasks of a compiler may include preprocessing, lexical analysis, parsing, semantic analysis, code generation, and code optimization. Program faults caused by incorrect compiler behavior can be very difficult to track down. For this reason, compiler implementers invest a lot of time ensuring the correctness of their software.

10.3. The Compilation Process

Compilation is a complex task. Most compilers divide the compilation process into many phases. A typical breakdown is as follows:

- Lexical Analysis
- Syntax Analysis or Parsing
- Semantic Analysis
- Code Generation

Lexical analysis partitions the input text (the source code), which is a sequence of characters, into separate *comments*, which are to be ignored in subsequent actions, and *basic symbols, which have lexical meanings.* These basic symbols must correspond to some terminal symbols of the grammar of the particular programming language. Here terminal symbols refer to the elementary symbols (or tokens) in the grammar that cannot be changed.

Syntax analysis is based on the results of the lexical analysis and discovers the structure in the program and determines whether or not a text conforms to an expected format. *Is this a textually correct C++ program?* or *Is this entry textually correct?* are typical questions that can be answered by syntax analysis. Syntax analysis determines if the source code of a program is correct and converts it into a more structured representation (parse tree) for semantic analysis or transformation.

Semantic analysis adds semantic information to the parse tree built during the syntax analysis and builds the symbol table. It performs various semantic checks that include type checking, object binding (associating variable and function references with their definitions), and definite assignment (requiring all local variables to be initialized before use). If mistakes are found, the semantically incorrect program statements are rejected and flagged as errors.

Once semantic analysis is complete, the phase of *code generation* begins and transforms the intermediate code produced in the previous phases into the native machine language of the computer under consideration. This involves resource and storage decisions—such as deciding which variables to fit into registers and memory and the selection and scheduling of appropriate machine instructions, along with their associated addressing modes.

It is often possible to combine multiple phases into one pass over the code in a compiler implementation. Some compilers also have a preprocessing phase at the beginning or after the lexical analysis that does necessary housekeeping work, such as processing the program instructions for the compiler (directives). Some compilers provide an optional optimization phase at the end of the entire compilation to optimize the code (such as the rearrangement of instruction sequence) for efficiency and other desirable objectives requested by the users.

11. Operating Systems Basics

[4*, c3]

Every system of meaningful complexity needs to be managed. A computer, as a rather complex electrical-mechanical system, needs its own manager for managing the resources and activities occurring on it. That manager is called an *operating system* (OS).

11.1. Operating Systems Overview

Operating systems is a collection of software and firmware, that controls the execution of computer programs and provides such services as computer resource allocation, job control, input/output control, and file management in a computer system. Conceptually, an operating system is a computer program that manages the hardware resources and makes it easier to use by applications by presenting nice abstractions. This nice abstraction is often called the virtual machine and includes such things as processes, virtual memory, and file systems. An OS hides the complexity of the underlying hardware and is found on all modern computers.

The principal roles played by OSs are management and illusion. *Management* refers to the OS's management (allocation and recovery) of physical resources among multiple competing users/applications/tasks. *Illusion* refers to the nice abstractions the OS provides.

11.2. Tasks of an Operating System

The tasks of an operating system differ significantly depending on the machine and time of its invention. However, modern operating systems have come to agreement as to the tasks that must be performed by an OS. These tasks include CPU management, memory management, disk management (file system), I/O device management, and security and protection. Each OS task manages one type of physical resource.

Specifically, CPU management deals with the allocation and releases of the CPU among competing programs (called processes/threads in OS jargon), including the operating system itself. The main abstraction provided by CPU management is the process/thread model. Memory management deals with the allocation and release of memory space among competing processes, and the main abstraction provided by memory management is virtual memory. Disk management deals with the sharing of magnetic or optical or solid state disks among multiple programs/users and its main abstraction is the file system. I/O device management deals with the allocation and releases of various I/O devices among competing processes.

Security and protection deal with the protection of computer resources from illegal use.

11.3. Operating System Abstractions

The arsenal of OSs is abstraction. Corresponding to the five physical tasks, OSs use five abstractions: process/thread, virtual memory, file systems, input/output, and protection domains. The overall OS abstraction is the virtual machine.

For each task area of OS, there is both a physical reality and a conceptual abstraction. The physical reality refers to the hardware resource under management; the conceptual abstraction refers to the interface the OS presents to the users/programs above. For example, in the thread model of the OS, the physical reality is the CPU and the abstraction is multiple CPUs. Thus, a user doesn't have to worry about sharing the CPU with others when working on the abstraction provided by an OS. In the virtual memory abstraction of an OS, the physical reality is the physical RAM or ROM (whatever), the abstraction is multiple unlimited memory space. Thus, a user doesn't have to worry about sharing physical memory with others or about limited physical memory size.

Abstractions may be virtual or transparent; in this context virtual applies to something that appears to be there, but isn't (like usable memory beyond physical), whereas transparent applies to something that is there, but appears not to be there (like fetching memory contents from disk or physical memory).

11.4. Operating Systems Classification

Different operating systems can have different functionality implementation. In the early days of the computer era, operating systems were relatively simple. As time goes on, the complexity and sophistication of operating systems increases significantly. From a historical perspective, an operating system can be classified as one of the following.

- *Batching OS:* organizes and processes work in batches. Examples of such OSs include IBM's FMS, IBSYS, and University of Michigan's UMES.

- *Multiprogrammed batching OS:* adds multitask capability into earlier simple batching OSs. An example of such an OS is IBM's OS/360.
- *Time-sharing OS:* adds multi-task and interactive capabilities into the OS. Examples of such OSs include UNIX, Linux, and NT.
- *Real-time OS:* adds timing predictability into the OS by scheduling individual tasks according to each task's completion deadlines. Examples of such OS include VxWorks (WindRiver) and DART (EMC).
- *Distributed OS:* adds the capability of managing a network of computers into the OS.
- *Embedded OS:* has limited functionality and is used for embedded systems such as cars and PDAs. Examples of such OSs include Palm OS, Windows CE, and TOPPER.

Alternatively, an OS can be classified by its applicable target machine/environment into the following.

- *Mainframe OS:* runs on the mainframe computers and include OS/360, OS/390, AS/400, MVS, and VM.
- *Server OS:* runs on workstations or servers and includes such systems as UNIX, Windows, Linux, and VMS.
- *Multicomputer OS:* runs on multiple computers and include such examples as Novell Netware.
- *Personal computers OS:* runs on personal computers and include such examples as DOS, Windows, Mac OS, and Linux.
- *Mobile device OS:* runs on personal devices such as cell phones, IPAD and include such examples of iOS, Android, Symbian, etc.

12. Database Basics and Data Management
[4*, c9]

A database consists of an organized collection of data for one or more uses. In a sense, a database is a generalization and expansion of data structures. But the difference is that a database is usually external to individual programs and permanent in existence compared to data structures. Databases are used when the data volume is large or logical relations between data items are important. The factors considered in database design include performance, concurrency, integrity, and recovery from hardware failures.

12.1. Entity and Schema

The things a database tries to model and store are called entities. Entities can be real-world objects such as persons, cars, houses, and so forth, or they may be abstract concepts such as persons, salary, names, and so forth. An entity can be primitive such as a name or composite such as an employee that consists of a name, identification number, salary, address, and so forth.

The single most important concept in a database is the *schema*, which is a description of the entire database structure from which all other database activities are built. A schema defines the relationships between the various entities that compose a database. For example, a schema for a company payroll system would consist of such things as employee ID, name, salary rate, address, and so forth. Database software maintains the database according to the schema.

Another important concept in database is the *database model* that describes the type of relationship among various entities. The commonly used models include relational, network, and object models.

12.2. Database Management Systems (DBMS)

Database Management System (DBMS) components include database applications for the storage of structured and unstructured data and the required database management functions needed to view, collect, store, and retrieve data from the databases. A DBMS controls the creation, maintenance, and use of the database and is usually categorized according to the database model it supports—such as the relational, network, or object model. For example, a relational database management system (RDBMS) implements features of the relational model. An object database management system (ODBMS) implements features of the object model.

12.3. Database Query Language

Users/applications interact with a database through a database query language, which is a specialized programming language tailored to database use. The database model tends to determine the query languages that are available to access the database. One commonly used query language for the relational database is the structured query language, more commonly abbreviated as SQL. A common query language for object databases is the object query language (abbreviated as OQL). There are three components of SQL: Data Definition Language (DDL), Data Manipulation Language (DML), and Data Control Language (DCL). An example of an DML query may look like the following:

```
SELECT Component_No, Quantity
FROM COMPONENT
WHERE Item_No = 100
```

The above query selects all the Component_No and its corresponding quantity from a database table called COMPONENT, where the Item_No equals to 100.

12.4. Tasks of DBMS Packages

A DBMS system provides the following capabilities:

- *Database development* is used to define and organize the content, relationships, and structure of the data needed to build a database.
- *Database interrogation* is used for accessing the data in a database for information retrieval and report generation. End users can selectively retrieve and display information and produce printed reports. This is the operation that most users know about databases.
- *Database Maintenance* is used to add, delete, update, and correct the data in a database.
- *Application Development* is used to develop prototypes of data entry screens, queries, forms, reports, tables, and labels for a prototyped application. It also refers to the use of 4th Generation Language or application generators to develop or generate program code.

12.5. Data Management

A database must manage the data stored in it. This management includes both organization and storage.

The organization of the actual data in a database depends on the database model. In a relational model, data are organized as tables with different tables representing different entities or relations among a set of entities. The storage of data deals with the storage of these database tables on disks. The common ways for achieving this is to use files. Sequential, indexed, and hash files are all used in this purpose with different file structures providing different access performance and convenience.

12.6. Data Mining

One often has to know what to look for before querying a database. This type of "pinpointing" access does not make full use of the vast amount of information stored in the database, and in fact reduces the database into a collection of discrete records. To take full advantage of a database, one can perform statistical analysis and pattern discovery on the content of a database using a technique called *data mining*. Such operations can be used to support a number of business activities that include, but are not limited to, marketing, fraud detection, and trend analysis.

Numerous ways for performing data mining have been invented in the past decade and include such common techniques as class description, class discrimination, cluster analysis, association analysis, and outlier analysis.

13. Network Communication Basics
[8*, c12]

A computer network connects a collection of computers and allows users of different computers to share resources with other users. A network facilitates the communications between all the connected computers and may give the illusion of a single, omnipresent computer. Every computer or device connected to a network is called a *network node*.

A number of computing paradigms have emerged to benefit from the functions and capabilities provided by computer networks. These paradigms include distributed computing, grid computing, Internet computing, and cloud computing.

13.1. Types of Network

Computer networks are not all the same and may be classified according to a wide variety of characteristics, including the network's connection method, wired technologies, wireless technologies, scale, network topology, functions, and speed. But the classification that is familiar to most is based on the scale of networking.

- *Personal Area Network/Home Network* is a computer network used for communication among computer(s) and different information technological devices close to one person. The devices connected to such a network may include PCs, faxes, PDAs, and TVs. This is the base on which the Internet of Things is built.
- *Local Area Network* (LAN) connects computers and devices in a limited geographical area, such as a school campus, computer laboratory, office building, or closely positioned group of buildings.
- *Campus Network* is a computer network made up of an interconnection of local area networks (LANs) within a limited geographical area.
- *Wide area network* (WAN) is a computer network that covers a large geographic area, such as a city or country or even across intercontinental distances. A WAN limited to a city is sometimes called a Metropolitan Area Network.
- *Internet* is the global network that connects computers located in many (perhaps all) countries.

Other classifications may divide networks into control networks, storage networks, virtual private networks (VPN), wireless networks, point-to-point networks, and Internet of Things.

13.2. Basic Network Components

All networks are made up of the same basic hardware components, including computers, network interface cards (NICs), bridges, hubs, switches, and routers. All these components are called *nodes* in the jargon of networking. Each component performs a distinctive function that is essential for the packaging, connection, transmission, amplification, controlling, unpacking, and interpretation of the data. For example, a repeater amplifies the signals, a switch performs many-to-many connections, a hub performs one-to-many connections, an interface card is attached to the computer and performs data packing and transmission, a bridge connects one network with another, and a router is a computer itself and performs data analysis and flow control to regulate the data from the network.

The functions performed by various network components correspond to the functions specified by one or more levels of the seven-layer Open Systems Interconnect (OSI) networking model, which is discussed below.

13.3. Networking Protocols and Standards

Computers communicate with each other using protocols, which specify the format and regulations used to pack and un-pack data. To facilitate easier communication and better structure, network protocols are divided into different layers with each layer dealing with one aspect of the communication. For example, the physical layers deal with the physical connection between the parties that are to communicate, the data link layer deals with the raw data transmission and flow control, and the network layer deals with the packing and un-packing of data into a particular format that is understandable by the relevant parties. The most commonly used OSI networking model organizes network protocols into seven layers, as depicted in Figure 13.5.

One thing to note is that not all network protocols implement all layers of the OSI model. For example, the TCP/IP protocol implements neither the presentation layer nor the session layer.

There can be more than one protocol for each layer. For example, UDP and TCP both work on the transport layer above IP's network layer, providing best-effort, unreliable transport (UDP) vs. reliable transport function (TCP). Physical layer protocols include token ring, Ethernet, fast Ethernet, gigabit Ethernet, and wireless Ethernet. Data

link layer protocols include frame-relay, asynchronous transfer mode (ATM), and Point-to-Point Protocol (PPP). Application layer protocols include Fibre channel, Small Computer System Interface (SCSI), and Bluetooth. For each layer or even each individual protocol, there may be standards established by national or international organizations to guide the design and development of the corresponding protocols.

Application Layer
Presentation Layer
Session Layer
Transport Layer
Network Layer
Data link Layer
Physical Layer

Figure 13.5. The Seven-Layer OSI Networking Model

13.4. The Internet

The Internet is a global system of interconnected governmental, academic, corporate, public, and private computer networks. In the public domain access to the internet is through organizations known as internet service providers (ISP). The ISP maintains one or more switching centers called a point of presence, which actually connects the users to the Internet.

13.5. Internet of Things

The Internet of Things refers to the networking of everyday objects—such as cars, cell phones, PDAs, TVs, refrigerators, and even buildings—using wired or wireless networking technologies. The function and purpose of *Internet of Things* is to interconnect all things to facilitate autonomous and better living. Technologies used in the Internet of Things include RFID, wireless and wired networking, sensor technology, and much software of course. As the paradigm of Internet of Things is still taking shape, much work is needed for Internet of Things to gain wide spread acceptance.

13.6. *Virtual Private Network (VPN)*

A virtual private network is a preplanned virtual connection between nodes in a LAN/WAN or on the internet. It allows the network administrator to separate network traffic into user groups that have a common affinity for each other such as all users in the same organization, or workgroup. This circuit type may improve performance and security between nodes and allows for easier maintenance of circuits when troubleshooting.

14. Parallel and Distributed Computing

[8*, c9]

Parallel computing is a computing paradigm that emerges with the development of multi-functional units within a computer. The main objective of parallel computing is to execute several tasks simultaneously on different functional units and thus improve throughput or response or both. Distributed computing, on the other hand, is a computing paradigm that emerges with the development of computer networks. Its main objective is to either make use of multiple computers in the network to accomplish things otherwise not possible within a single computer or improve computation efficiency by harnessing the power of multiple computers.

14.1. *Parallel and Distributed Computing Overview*

Traditionally, parallel computing investigates ways to maximize concurrency (the simultaneous execution of multiple tasks) within the boundary of a computer. Distributed computing studies distributed systems, which consists of multiple *autonomous* computers that communicate through a computer network. Alternatively, distributed computing can also refer to the use of distributed systems to solve computational or transactional problems. In the former definition, distributed computing investigates the protocols, mechanisms, and strategies that provide the foundation for distributed computation; in the latter definition, distributed computing studies the ways of dividing a problem into many tasks and assigning such tasks to various computers involved in the computation.

Fundamentally, distributed computing is another form of parallel computing, albeit on a grander scale. In distributed computing, the functional units are not ALU, FPU, or separate cores, but individual computers. For this reason, some people regard distributed computing as being the same as parallel computing. Because both distributed and parallel computing involve some form of concurrency, they are both also called concurrent computing.

14.2. *Difference between Parallel and Distributed Computing*

Though parallel and distributed computing resemble each other on the surface, there is a subtle but real distinction between them: parallel computing does not necessarily refer to the execution of programs on different computers— instead, they can be run on different processors within a single computer. In fact, consensus among computing professionals limits the scope of parallel computing to the case where a shared memory is used by all processors involved in the computing, while distributed computing refers to computations where private memory exists for each processor involved in the computations.

Another subtle difference between parallel and distributed computing is that parallel computing necessitates concurrent execution of several tasks while distributed computing does not have this necessity.

Based on the above discussion, it is possible to classify concurrent systems as being "parallel" or "distributed" based on the existence or nonexistence of shared memory among all the processor: parallel computing deals with computations within a single computer; distributed computing deals with computations within a set of computers. According to this view, multicore computing is a form of parallel computing.

14.3. *Parallel and Distributed Computing Models*

Since multiple computers/processors/cores are involved in distributed/parallel computing, some coordination among the involved parties is necessary to ensure correct behavior of the system.

Different ways of coordination give rise to different computing models. The most common models in this regard are the shared memory (parallel) model and the message-passing (distributed) model.

In a *shared memory (parallel)* model, all computers have access to a shared central memory where local caches are used to speed up the processing power. These caches use a protocol to insure the localized data is fresh and up to date, typically the MESI protocol. The algorithm designer chooses the program for execution by each computer. Access to the central memory can be synchronous or asynchronous, and must be coordinated such that coherency is maintained. Different access models have been invented for such a purpose.

In a *message-passing (distributed)* model, all computers run some programs that collectively achieve some purpose. The system must work correctly regardless of the structure of the network. This model can be further classified into client-server (C/S), browser-server (B/S), and n-tier models. In the C/S model, the server provides services and the client requests services from the server. In the B/S model, the server provides services and the client is the browser. In the n-tier model, each tier (i.e. layer) provides services to the tier immediately above it and requests services from the tier immediately below it. In fact, the n-tier model can be seen as a chain of client-server models. Often, the tiers between the bottommost tier and the topmost tier are called *middleware,* which is a distinct subject of study in its own right.

14.4. Main Issues in Distributed Computing

Coordination among all the components in a distributed computing environment is often complex and time-consuming. As the number of cores/CPUs/computers increases, the complexity of distributed computing also increases. Among the many issues faced, memory coherency and consensus among all computers are the most difficult ones. Many computation paradigms have been invented to solve these problems and are the main discussion issues in distributed/parallel computing.

15. Basic User Human Factors

[3*, c8] [9*, c5]

Software is developed to meet human desires or needs. Thus, all software design and development must take into consideration human-user factors such as how people use software, how people view software, and what humans expect from software. There are numerous factors in the human-machine interaction, and ISO 9241 document series define all the detailed standards of such interactions.[10] But the basic human-user factors considered here include input/output, the handling of error messages, and the robustness of the software in general.

15.1. Input and Output

Input and output are the interfaces between users and software. Software is useless without input and output. Humans design software to process some input and produce desirable output. All software engineers must consider input and output as an integral part of the software product they engineer or develop. Issues considered for input include (but are not limited to):

- What input is required?
- How is the input passed from users to computers?
- What is the most convenient way for users to enter input?
- What format does the computer require of the input data?

The designer should request the minimum data from human input, only when the data is not already stored in the system. The designer should format and edit the data at the time of entry to reduce errors arising from incorrect or malicious data entry.

For output, we need to consider what the users wish to see:

- In what format would users like to see output?
- What is the most pleasing way to display output?

If the party interacting with the software isn't human but another software or computer or control system, then we need to consider the input/output type and format that the software should produce to ensure proper data exchange between systems.

There are many rules of thumb for developers to follow to produce good input/output for a software. These rules of thumb include simple and natural dialogue, speaking users' language, minimizing user memory load, consistency, minimal surprise, conformance to standards (whether agreed to or not: e.g., automobiles have a standard interface for accelerator, brake, steering).

15.2. Error Messages

It is understandable that most software contains faults and fails from time to time. But users should be notified if there is anything that impedes the smooth execution of the program. Nothing is more frustrating than an unexpected termination or behavioral deviation of software without any warning or explanation. To be user friendly, the software should report all error conditions to the users or upper-level applications so that some measure can be taken to rectify the situation or to exit gracefully. There are several guidelines that define what constitutes a good error message: error messages should be clear, to the point, and timely.

First, error messages should clearly explain what is happening so that users know what is going on in the software. Second, error messages should pinpoint the cause of the error, if at all possible, so that proper actions can be taken. Third, error messages should be displayed right when the error condition occurs. According to Jakob Nielsen, "Good error messages should be expressed in plain language (no codes), precisely indicate the problem, and constructively suggest a solution" [9*]. Fourth, error messages should not overload the users with too much information and cause them to ignore the messages all together.

However, messages relating to security access errors should not provide extra information that would help unauthorized persons break in.

15.3. Software Robustness

Software robustness refers to the ability of software to tolerate erroneous inputs. Software is said to be robust if it continues to function even when erroneous inputs are given. Thus, it is unacceptable for software to simply crash when encountering an input problem as this may cause unexpected consequences, such as the loss of valuable data. Software that exhibits such behavior is considered to lack robustness.

Nielsen gives a simpler description of software robustness: "The software should have a low error rate, so that users make few errors during the use of the system and so that if they do make errors they can easily recover from them. Further, catastrophic errors must not occur" [9*].

There are many ways to evaluate the robustness of software and just as many ways to make software more robust. For example, to improve robustness, one should always check the validity of the inputs and return values before progressing further; one should always throw an exception when something unexpected occurs, and one should never quit a program without first giving users/applications a chance to correct the condition.

16. Basic Developer Human Factors
[3*, c31–32]

Developer human factors refer to the considerations of human factors taken when developing software. Software is developed by humans, read by humans, and maintained by humans. If anything is wrong, humans are responsible for correcting those wrongs. Thus, it is essential to write software in a way that is easily understandable by humans or, at the very least, by other software developers. A program that is easy to read and understand exhibits readability.

The means to ensure that software meet this objective are numerous and range from proper architecture at the macro level to the particular coding style and variable usage at the micro level. But the two prominent factors are *structure* (or program layouts) and *comments* (documentation).

16.1. Structure

Well-structured programs are easier to understand and modify. If a program is poorly structured, then no amount of explanation or comments is sufficient to make it understandable. The ways to organize a program are numerous and range from the proper use of white space, indentation, and parentheses to nice arrangements of groupings, blank lines, and braces. Whatever style one chooses, it should be consistent across the entire program.

16.2. Comments

To most people, programming is coding. These people do not realize that programming also includes writing comments and that comments are an integral part of programming. True, comments are not used by the computer and certainly do not constitute final instructions for the computer, but they improve the readability of the programs by explaining the meaning and logic of the statements or sections of code. It should be remembered that programs are not only meant for computers, they are also read, written, and modified by humans.

The types of comments include repeat of the code, explanation of the code, marker of the code, summary of the code, description of the code's intent, and information that cannot possibly be expressed by the code itself. Some comments are good, some are not. The good ones are those that explain the intent of the code and justify why this code looks the way it does. The bad ones are repeat of the code and stating irrelevant information. The best comments are self-documenting code. If the code is written in such a clear and precise manner that its meaning is self-proclaimed, then no comment is needed. But this is easier said than done. Most programs are not self-explanatory and are often hard to read and understand if no comments are given.

Here are some general guidelines for writing good comments:

- Comments should be consistent across the entire program.
- Each function should be associated with comments that explain the purpose of the function and its role in the overall program.
- Within a function, comments should be given for each logical section of coding to explain the meaning and purpose (intention) of the section.
- Comments should stipulate what freedom does (or does not) the maintaining programmers have with respect to making changes to that code.
- Comments are seldom required for individual statements. If a statement needs comments, one should reconsider the statement.

17. Secure Software Development and Maintenance

[11*, c29]

Due to increasing malicious activities targeted at computer systems, security has become a significant issue in the development of software. In addition to the usual correctness and reliability, software developers must also pay attention to the security of the software they develop. Secure software development builds security in software by following a set of established and/or recommended rules and practices in software development. Secure software maintenance complements secure software development by ensuring the no security problems are introduced during software maintenance.

A generally accepted view concerning software security is that it is much better to design security into software than to patch it in after software is developed. To design security into software, one must take into consideration every stage of the software development lifecycle. In particular, secure software development involves *software requirements security*, software *design security*, *software construction security,* and *software testing security*. In addition, security must also be taken into consideration when performing software maintenance as security faults and loopholes can be and often are introduced during maintenance.

17.1. Software Requirements Security

Software requirements security deals with the clarification and specification of security policy and objectives into software requirements, which lays the foundation for security considerations in the software development. Factors to consider in this phase include software requirements and threats/risks. The former refers to the specific functions that are required for the sake of security; the latter refers to the possible ways that the security of software is threatened.

17.2. Software Design Security

Software Design security deals with the design of software modules that fit together to meet the security objectives specified in the security requirements. This step clarifies the details of security considerations and develops the specific steps for implementation. Factors considered may include frameworks and access modes that set up the overall security monitoring/enforcement strategies, as well as the individual policy enforcement mechanisms.

17.3. Software Construction Security

Software construction security concerns the question of how to write actual programming code for specific situations such that security considerations are taken care of. The term "Software Construction Security" could mean different things for different people. It can mean the way a specific function is coded, such that the coding itself is secure, or it can mean the coding of security into software.

Most people entangle the two together without distinction. One reason for such entanglement is that it is not clear how one can make sure that a specific coding is secure. For example, in C programming language, the expression of $i<<1$ (shift the binary representation of i's value to the left by one bit) and $2*i$ (multiply the value of variable i by constant 2) mean the same thing semantically, but do they have the same security ramification? The answer could be different for different combinations of ISAs and compilers. Due to this lack of understanding, software construction security—in its current state of existence—mostly refers to the second aspect mentioned above: the coding of security into software.

Coding of security into software can be achieved by following recommended rules. A few such rules follow:

- Structure the process so that all sections requiring extra privileges are modules. The modules should be as small as possible and should perform only those tasks that require those privileges.
- Ensure that any assumptions in the program are validated. If this is not possible, document them for the installers and maintainers so they know the assumptions that attackers will try to invalidate.
- Ensure that the program does not share objects in memory with any other program.
- The error status of every function must be checked. Do not try to recover unless neither the cause of the error nor its effects affect any security considerations. The program should restore the state of the software to the state it had before the process began, and then terminate.

17.4. Software Testing Security

Software testing security determines that software protects data and maintains security specification as given. For more information, please refer to the Software Testing KA.

17.5. Build Security into Software Engineering Process

Software is only as secure as its development process goes. To ensure the security of software, security must be built into the software engineering process. One trend that emerges in this regard is the Secure Development Lifecycle (SDL) concept, which is a classical spiral model that takes a holistic view of security from the perspective of software lifecycle and ensures that security is inherent in software design and development, not an afterthought later in production. The SDL process is claimed to reduce software maintenance costs and increase reliability of software concerning software security related faults.

17.6. Software Security Guidelines

Although there are no bulletproof ways for secure software development, some general guidelines do exist that can be used to aid such effort. These guidelines span every phase of the software development lifecycle. Some reputable guidelines are published by the Computer Emergency Response Team (CERT) and below are its top 10 software security practices (the details can be found in [12]:

1. Validate input.
2. Heed compiler warnings.
3. Architect and design for security policies.
4. Keep it simple.
5. Default deny.
6. Adhere to the principle of least privilege.
7. Sanitize data sent to other software.
8. Practice defense in depth.
9. Use effective quality assurance techniques.
10. Adopt a software construction security standard.

MATRIX OF TOPICS VS. REFERENCE MATERIAL

	Voland 2003 [2*]	McConnell 2004 [3*]	Brookshear 2008 [4*]	Horowitz et al. 2007 [5*]	Sommerville 2011 [6*]	Null and Lobur 2006 [8*]	Nielsen 1993 [9*]	Bishop 2002 [11*]
1. Problem Solving Techniques	s3.2, s4.2							
1.1. Definition of Problem Solving	s3.2							
1.2. Formulating the Real Problem	s3.2							
1.3. Analyze the Problem	s3.2							
1.4. Design a Solution Search Strategy	s4.2							
1.5. Problem Solving Using Programs		c5						
2. Abstraction		s5.2–5.4						
2.1. Levels of Abstraction		s5.2–5.3						
2.2. Encapsulation		s5.3						
2.3. Hierarchy		s5.2						
3. Programming Fundamentals		c6–19						
3.1. The Programming Process		c6–c19						
3.2. Programming Paradigms		c6–c19						
3.3. Defensive Programming		c8						
4. Programming Language Basics			c6					
4.1. Programming Language Overview			s6.1					
4.2. Syntax and Semantics of Programming Language			s6.2					

	Voland 2003 [2*]	McConnell 2004 [3*]	Brookshear 2008 [4*]	Horowitz et al. 2007 [5*]	Sommerville 2011 [6*]	Null and Lobur 2006 [8*]	Nielsen 1993 [9*]	Bishop 2002 [11*]
4.3. Low Level Programming Language			s6.5–6.7					
4.4. High Level Programing Language			s6.5–6.7					
4.5. Declarative vs. Imperative Programming Language			s6.5–6.7					
5. Debugging Tools and Techniques		c23						
5.1. Types of Errors		s23.1						
5.2. Debugging Techniques:		s23.2						
5.3. Debugging Tools		s23.5						
6. Data Structure and Representation				s2.1–2.6				
6.1. Data Structure Overview				s2.1–2.6				
6.2. Types of Data Structure				s2.1–2.6				
6.3. Operations on Data Structures				s2.1–2.6				
7. Algorithms and Complexity				s1.1–1.3, s3.3–3.6, s4.1–4.8, s5.1–5.7, s6.1–6.3, s7.1–7.6, s11.1, s12.1				

	Voland 2003 [2*]	McConnell 2004 [3*]	Brookshear 2008 [4*]	Horowitz et al. 2007 [5*]	Sommerville 2011 [6*]	Null and Lobur 2006 [8*]	Nielsen 1993 [9*]	Bishop 2002 [11*]
7.1. Overview of Algorithms				s1.1–1.2				
7.2. Attributes of Algorithms				s1.3				
7.3. Algorithmic Analysis				s1.3				
7.4. Algorithmic Design Strategies				s3.3–3.6, s4.1–4.8, s5.1–5.7, s6.1–6.3, s7.1–7.6, s11.1, s12.1				
7.5. Algorithmic Analysis Strategies				s3.3–3.6, s4.1–4.8, s5.1–5.7, s6.1–6.3, s7.1–7.6, s11.1, s12.1				
8. Basic Concept of a System					c10			
8.1. Emergent System Properties					s10.1			
8.2. System Engineering					s10.2			
8.3. Overview of a Computer System								

	Voland 2003 [2*]	McConnell 2004 [3*]	Brookshear 2008 [4*]	Horowitz et al. 2007 [5*]	Sommerville 2011 [6*]	Null and Lobur 2006 [8*]	Nielsen 1993 [9*]	Bishop 2002 [11*]
9. Computer Organization						c1–4		
9.1. Computer Organization Overview						s1.1–1.2		
9.2. Digital Systems						c3		
9.3. Digital Logic						c3		
9.4. Computer Expression of Data						c2		
9.5. The Central Processing Unit (CPU)						s4.1–4.2		
9.6. Memory System Organization						s4.6		
9.7. Input and Output (I/O)						s4.5		
10. Compiler Basics			s6.4			s8.4		
10.1. Compiler Overview						s8.4		
10.2. Interpretation and Compilation						s8.4		
10.3. The Compilation Process			s6.4			s8.4		
11. Operating Systems Basics			c3					
11.1. Operating Systems Overview			s3.2					
11.2. Tasks of Operating System			s3.3					
11.3. Operating System Abstractions			s3.2					
11.4. Operating Systems Classification			s3.1					

	Voland 2003 [2*]	McConnell 2004 [3*]	Brookshear 2008 [4*]	Horowitz et al. 2007 [5*]	Sommerville 2011 [6*]	Null and Lobur 2006 [8*]	Nielsen 1993 [9*]	Bishop 2002 [11*]
12. Database Basics and Data Management			c9					
12.1. Entity and Schema			s9.1					
12.2. Database Management Systems (DBMS)			s9.1					
12.3. Database Query Language			s9.2					
12.4. Tasks of DBMS Packages			s9.2					
12.5. Data Management			s9.5					
12.6. Data Mining			s9.6					
13. Network Communication Basics						c12		
13.1. Types of Network						s12.2–12.3		
13.2. Basic Network Components						s12.6		
13.3. Networking Protocols and Standards						s12.4–12.5		
13.4. The Internet								
13.5. Internet of Things						s12.8		
13.6. Virtual Private Network								
14. Parallel and Distributed Computing						c9		
14.1. Parallel and Distributed Computing Overview						s9.4.1–9.4.3		

	Voland 2003 [2*]	McConnell 2004 [3*]	Brookshear 2008 [4*]	Horowitz et al. 2007 [5*]	Sommerville 2011 [6*]	Null and Lobur 2006 [8*]	Nielsen 1993 [9*]	Bishop 2002 [11*]
14.2. Differences between Parallel and Distributed Computing						s9.4.4–9.4.5		
14.3. Parallel and Distributed Computing Models						s9.4.4–9.4.5		
14.4. Main Issues in Distributed Computing								
15. Basic User Human Factors		c8					c5	
15.1. Input and Output							s5.1, s5.3	
15.2. Error Messages							s5.2, s5.8	
15.3. Software Robustness							s5.5–5.6	
16. Basic Developer Human Factors		c31–32						
16.1. Structure		c31						
16.2. Comments		c32						
17. Secure Software Development and Maintenance								c29
17.1. Two Aspects of Secure Coding								s29.1
17.2. Coding Security into Software								s29.4
17.3. Requirement Security								s29.2
17.4. Design Security								s29.3
17.5. Implementation Security								s29.5

REFERENCES

[1] Joint Task Force on Computing Curricula, IEEE Computer Society and Association for Computing Machinery, *Software Engineering 2004: Curriculum Guidelines for Undergraduate Degree Programs in Software Engineering*, 2004; http://sites. computer.org/ccse/SE2004Volume.pdf.

[2*] G. Voland, *Engineering by Design*, 2nd ed., Prentice Hall, 2003.

[3*] S. McConnell, *Code Complete*, 2nd ed., Microsoft Press, 2004.

[4*] J.G. Brookshear, *Computer Science: An Overview*, 10th ed., Addison-Wesley, 2008.

[5*] E. Horowitz et al., *Computer Algorithms*, 2nd ed., Silicon Press, 2007.

[6*] I. Sommerville, *Software Engineering*, 9th ed., Addison-Wesley, 2011.

[7] *ISO/IEC/IEEE 24765:2010 Systems and Software Engineering—Vocabulary*, ISO/IEC/IEEE, 2010.

[8*] L. Null and J. Lobur, *The Essentials of Computer Organization and Architecture*, 2nd ed., Jones and Bartlett Publishers, 2006.

[9*] J. Nielsen, *Usability Engineering*, Morgan Kaufmann, 1993.

[10] ISO 9241-420:2011 Ergonomics of Human-System Interaction, ISO, 2011.

[11*] M. Bishop, *Computer Security: Art and Science*, Addison-Wesley, 2002.

[12] R.C. Seacord, *The CERT C Secure Coding Standard*, Addison-Wesley Professional, 2008.

CHAPTER 14

MATHEMATICAL FOUNDATIONS

INTRODUCTION

Software professionals live with programs. In a very simple language, one can program only for something that follows a well-understood, non-ambiguous logic. The Mathematical Foundations knowledge area (KA) helps software engineers comprehend this logic, which in turn is translated into programming language code. The mathematics that is the primary focus in this KA is quite different from typical arithmetic, where numbers are dealt with and discussed. Logic and reasoning are the essence of mathematics that a software engineer must address.

Mathematics, in a sense, is the study of formal systems. The word "formal" is associated with preciseness, so there cannot be any ambiguous or erroneous interpretation of the fact. Mathematics is therefore the study of any and all certain truths about any concept. This concept can be about numbers as well as about symbols, images, sounds, video—almost anything. In short, not only numbers and numeric equations are subject to preciseness. On the contrary, a software engineer needs to have a precise abstraction on a diverse application domain.

The *SWEBOK Guide*'s Mathematical Foundations KA covers basic techniques to identify a set of rules for reasoning in the context of the system under study. Anything that one can deduce following these rules is an absolute certainty within the context of that system. In this KA, techniques that can represent and take forward the reasoning and judgment of a software engineer in a precise (and therefore mathematical) manner are defined and discussed. The language and methods of logic that are discussed here allow us to describe mathematical proofs to infer conclusively the absolute truth of certain concepts beyond the numbers. In

short, you can write a program for a problem only if it follows some logic. The objective of this KA is to help you develop the skill to identify and describe such logic. The emphasis is on helping you understand the basic concepts rather than on challenging your arithmetic abilities.

BREAKDOWN OF TOPICS FOR MATHEMATICAL FOUNDATIONS

The breakdown of topics for the Mathematical Foundations KA is shown in Figure 14.1.

1. Set, Relations, Functions

[1*, c2]

Set. A set is a collection of objects, called elements of the set. A set can be represented by listing its elements between braces, e.g., S = {1, 2, 3}.

The symbol $\in$ is used to express that an element belongs to a set, or—in other words—is a member of the set. Its negation is represented by $\notin$, e.g., $1 \in$ S, but $4 \notin$ S.

In a more compact representation of set using set builder notation, {x | P(x)} is the set of all x such that P(x) for any proposition P(x) over any universe of discourse. Examples for some important sets include the following:

N = {0, 1, 2, 3, ...} = the set of nonnegative integers.
Z = {..., −3, −2, −1, 0, 1, 2, 3, ...} = the set of integers.

Finite and Infinite Set. A set with a finite number of elements is called a finite set. Conversely, any set that does not have a finite number of elements in it is an *infinite set*. The set of all natural numbers, for example, is an infinite set.

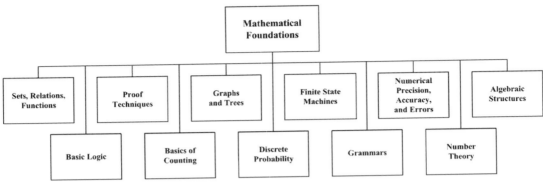

Figure 14.1. Breakdown of Topics for the Mathematical Foundations KA

Cardinality. The cardinality of a finite set S is the number of elements in S. This is represented |S|, e.g., if S = {1, 2, 3}, then |S| = 3.

Universal Set. In general S = {x ∈ U | p(x)}, where U is the universe of discourse in which the predicate P(x) must be interpreted. The "universe of discourse" for a given predicate is often referred to as the universal set. Alternately, one may define universal set as the set of all elements.

Set Equality. Two sets are equal if and only if they have the same elements, i.e.:

$$X = Y \equiv \forall p \, (p \in X \leftrightarrow p \in Y).$$

Subset. X is a subset of set Y, or X is contained in Y, if all elements of X are included in Y. This is denoted by X ⊆ Y. In other words, X ⊆ Y if and only if ∀p (p ∈ X → p ∈ Y).

For example, if X = {1, 2, 3} and Y = {1, 2, 3, 4, 5}, then X ⊆ Y.

If X is not a subset of Y, it is denoted as X ⊄ Y.

Proper Subset. X is a proper subset of Y (denoted by X ⊂ Y) if X is a subset of Y but not equal to Y, i.e., there is some element in Y that is not in X.

In other words, X ⊂ Y if (X ⊆ Y) ∧ (X ≠ Y).

For example, if X = {1, 2, 3}, Y = {1, 2, 3, 4}, and Z = {1, 2, 3}, then X ⊂ Y, but X is not a proper subset of Z. Sets X and Z are equal sets.

If X is not a proper subset of Y, it is denoted as X ⊄ Y.

Superset. If X is a subset of Y, then Y is called a *superset* of X. This is denoted by Y ⊇ X, i.e., Y ⊇ X if and only if X ⊆ Y.

For example, if X = {1, 2, 3} and Y = {1, 2, 3, 4, 5}, then Y ⊇ X.

Empty Set. A set with no elements is called an *empty set*. An empty set, denoted by ∅, is also referred to as a null or void set.

Power Set. The set of all subsets of a set X is called the *power set* of X. It is represented as ℘(X).

For example, if X = {a, b, c}, then ℘(X) = {∅, {a}, {b}, {c}, {a, b}, {a, c}, {b, c}, {a, b, c}}. If |X| = n, then |℘(X)| = 2^n.

Venn Diagrams. Venn diagrams are graphic representations of sets as enclosed areas in the plane.

For example, in Figure 14.2, the rectangle represents the universal set and the shaded region represents a set X.

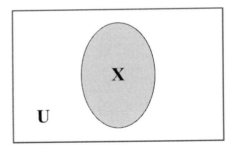

Figure 14.2. Venn Diagram for Set X

1.1. Set Operations

Intersection. The intersection of two sets X and Y, denoted by X ∩ Y, is the set of common elements in both X and Y.

In other words, X ∩ Y = {p | (p ∈ X) ∧ (p ∈ Y)}.

As, for example, {1, 2, 3} ∩ {3, 4, 6} = {3}

If X ∩ Y = f, then the two sets X and Y are said to be a disjoint pair of sets.

A Venn diagram for set intersection is shown in Figure 14.3. The common portion of the two sets represents the set intersection.

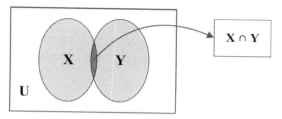

Figure 14.3. Intersection of Sets X and Y

Union. The union of two sets X and Y, denoted by $X \cup Y$, is the set of all elements either in X, or in Y, or in both.

In other words, $X \cup Y = \{p \mid (p \in X) \vee (p \in Y)\}$.

As, for example, $\{1, 2, 3\} \cup \{3, 4, 6\} = \{1, 2, 3, 4, 6\}$.

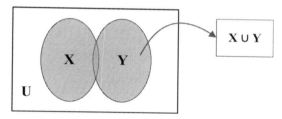

Figure 14.4. Union of Sets X and Y

It may be noted that $|X \cup Y| = |X| + |Y| - |X \cap Y|$.

A Venn diagram illustrating the union of two sets is represented by the shaded region in Figure 14.4.

Complement. The set of elements in the universal set that do not belong to a given set X is called its complement set X'.

In other words, $X' = \{p \mid (p \in U) \wedge (p \notin X)\}$.

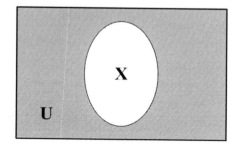

Figure 14.5. Venn Diagram for Complement Set of X

The shaded portion of the Venn diagram in Figure 14.5 represents the complement set of X.

Set Difference or Relative Complement. The set of elements that belong to set X but not to set Y builds the set difference of Y from X. This is represented by X − Y.

In other words, $X - Y = \{p \mid (p \in X) \wedge (p \notin Y)\}$.
As, for example, $\{1, 2, 3\} - \{3, 4, 6\} = \{1, 2\}$.
It may be proved that $X - Y = X \cap Y'$.

Set difference X − Y is illustrated by the shaded region in Figure 14.6 using a Venn diagram.

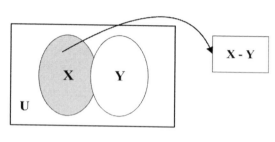

Figure 14.6. Venn Diagram for X − Y

Cartesian Product. An ordinary pair $\{p, q\}$ is a set with two elements. In a set, the order of the elements is irrelevant, so $\{p, q\} = \{q, p\}$.

In an ordered pair (p, q), the order of occurrences of the elements is relevant. Thus, $(p, q) \neq (q, p)$ unless $p = q$. In general $(p, q) = (s, t)$ if and only if $p = s$ and $q = t$.

Given two sets X and Y, their Cartesian product $X \times Y$ is the set of all ordered pairs (p, q) such that $p \in X$ and $q \in Y$.

In other words, $X \times Y = \{(p, q) \mid (p \in X) \wedge (q \in Y)\}$.

As for example, $\{a, b\} \times \{1, 2\} = \{(a, 1), (a, 2), (b, 1), (b, 2)\}$

1.2. Properties of Set

Some of the important properties and laws of sets are mentioned below.

1. Associative Laws:
$$X \cup (Y \cup Z) = (X \cup Y) \cup Z$$
$$X \cap (Y \cap Z) = (X \cap Y) \cap Z$$

2. Commutative Laws:
   $$X \cup Y = Y \cup X \qquad X \cap Y = Y \cap X$$

3. Distributive Laws:
   $$X \cup (Y \cap Z) = (X \cup Y) \cap (X \cup Z)$$
   $$X \cap (Y \cup Z) = (X \cap Y) \cup (X \cap Z)$$

4. Identity Laws:
   $$X \cup \varnothing = X \qquad X \cap U = X$$

5. Complement Laws:
   $$X \cup X' = U \qquad X \cap X' = \varnothing$$

6. Idempotent Laws:
   $$X \cup X = X \qquad X \cap X = X$$

7. Bound Laws:
   $$X \cup U = U \qquad X \cap \varnothing = \varnothing$$

8. Absorption Laws:
   $$X \cup (X \cap Y) = X \qquad X \cap (X \cup Y) = X$$

9. De Morgan's Laws:
   $$(X \cup Y)' = X' \cap Y' \qquad (X \cap Y)' = X' \cup Y'$$

1.3. Relation and Function

A relation is an association between two sets of information. For example, let's consider a set of residents of a city and their phone numbers. The pairing of names with corresponding phone numbers is a relation. This pairing is *ordered* for the entire relation. In the example being considered, for each pair, either the name comes first followed by the phone number or the reverse. The set from which the first element is drawn is called the *domain set* and the other set is called the *range set*. The domain is what you start with and the range is what you end up with.

A function is a *well-behaved* relation. A relation R(X, Y) is well behaved if the function maps every element of the domain set X to a single element of the range set Y. Let's consider domain set X as a set of persons and let range set Y store their phone numbers. Assuming that a person may have more than one phone number, the relation being considered is not a function. However, if we draw a relation between names of residents and their date of births with the name set as domain, then

this becomes a well-behaved relation and hence a function. This means that, while all functions are relations, not all relations are functions. In case of a function given an x, one gets one and exactly one y for each ordered pair (x, y).

For example, let's consider the following two relations.

A: $\{(3, -9), (5, 8), (7, -6), (3, 9), (6, 3)\}$.
B: $\{(5, 8), (7, 8), (3, 8), (6, 8)\}$.

Are these functions as well?

In case of relation A, the domain is all the x-values, i.e., $\{3, 5, 6, 7\}$, and the range is all the y-values, i.e., $\{-9, -6, 3, 8, 9\}$.

Relation A is not a function, as there are two different range values, -9 and 9, for the same x-value of 3.

In case of relation B, the domain is same as that for A, i.e., $\{3, 5, 6, 7\}$. However, the range is a single element $\{8\}$. This qualifies as an example of a function even if all the x-values are mapped to the same y-value. Here, each x-value is distinct and hence the function is well behaved. Relation B may be represented by the equation $y = 8$.

The characteristic of a function may be verified using a vertical line test, which is stated below:

Given the graph of a relation, if one can draw a vertical line that crosses the graph in more than one place, then the relation is not a function.

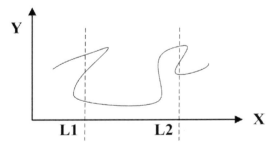

Figure 14.7. Vertical Line Test for Function

In this example, both lines L1 and L2 cut the graph for the relation thrice. This signifies that for the same x-value, there are three different y-values for each of case. Thus, the relation is not a function.

2. Basic Logic

[1*, c1]

2.1. Propositional Logic

A proposition is a statement that is either true or false, but not both. Let's consider declarative sentences for which it is meaningful to assign either of the two status values: *true* or *false*. Some examples of propositions are given below.

1. The sun is a star
2. Elephants are mammals.
3. $2 + 3 = 5$.

However, $a + 3 = b$ is not a proposition, as it is neither true nor false. It depends on the values of the variables a and b.

The Law of Excluded Middle: For every proposition p, either p is true or p is false.

The Law of Contradiction: For every proposition p, it is not the case that p is both true and false.

Propositional logic is the area of logic that deals with propositions. A truth table displays the relationships between the truth values of propositions.

A Boolean variable is one whose value is either true or false. Computer bit operations correspond to logical operations of Boolean variables.

The basic logical operators including negation ($\neg$ p), conjunction (p $\wedge$ q), disjunction (p $\vee$ q), exclusive or (p $\oplus$ q), and implication (p $\rightarrow$ q) are to be studied. Compound propositions may be formed using various logical operators.

A compound proposition that is always true is a tautology. A compound proposition that is always false is a contradiction. A compound proposition that is neither a tautology nor a contradiction is a contingency.

Compound propositions that always have the same truth value are called logically equivalent (denoted by $\equiv$). Some of the common equivalences are:

Identity laws:
$$p \wedge T \equiv p \qquad p \vee F \equiv p$$

Domination laws:
$$p \vee T \equiv T \qquad p \wedge F \equiv F$$

Idempotent laws:
$$p \vee p \equiv p \qquad p \wedge p \equiv p$$

Double negation law:
$$\neg (\neg p) \equiv p$$

Commutative laws:
$$p \vee q \equiv q \vee p \qquad p \wedge q \equiv q \wedge p$$

Associative laws:
$$(p \vee q) \vee r \equiv p \vee (q \vee r)$$
$$(p \wedge q) \wedge r \equiv p \wedge (q \wedge r)$$

Distributive laws:
$$p \vee (q \wedge r) \equiv (p \vee q) \wedge (p \vee r)$$
$$p \wedge (q \vee r) \equiv (p \wedge q) \vee (p \wedge r)$$

De Morgan's laws:
$$\neg (p \wedge q) \equiv \neg p \vee \neg q \qquad \neg (p \vee q) \equiv \neg p \wedge \neg q$$

2.2. Predicate Logic

A predicate is a verb phrase template that describes a property of objects or a relationship among objects represented by the variables. For example, in the sentence, *The flower is red,* the template *is red* is a predicate. It describes the property of a flower. The same predicate may be used in other sentences too.

Predicates are often given a name, e.g., "Red" or simply "R" can be used to represent the predicate *is red*. Assuming R as the name for the predicate *is red*, sentences that assert an object is of the color red can be represented as $R(x)$, where x represents an arbitrary object. $R(x)$ reads as x *is red*.

Quantifiers allow statements about entire collections of objects rather than having to enumerate the objects by name.

The Universal quantifier $\forall x$ asserts that a sentence is true for all values of variable x.

For example, $\forall x$ Tiger(x) $\rightarrow$ Mammal(x) means all tigers are mammals.

The Existential quantifier $\exists x$ asserts that a sentence is true for at least one value of variable x.

For example, $\exists x$ Tiger(x) $\rightarrow$ Man-eater(x) means there exists at least one tiger that is a man-eater.

Thus, while universal quantification uses implication, the existential quantification naturally uses conjunction.

A variable *x* that is introduced into a logical expression by a quantifier is bound to the closest enclosing quantifier.

A variable is said to be a free variable if it is not bound to a quantifier.

Similarly, in a block-structured programming language, a variable in a logical expression refers to the closest quantifier within whose scope it appears.

For example, in $\exists x\ (Cat(x) \wedge \forall x\ (Black(x)))$, x in Black(x) is universally quantified. The expression implies that cats exist and everything is black.

Propositional logic falls short in representing many assertions that are used in computer science and mathematics. It also fails to compare equivalence and some other types of relationship between propositions.

For example, the assertion *a is greater than 1* is not a proposition because one cannot infer whether it is true or false without knowing the value of *a*. Thus, propositional logic cannot deal with such sentences. However, such assertions appear quite often in mathematics and we want to infer on those assertions. Also, the pattern involved in the following two logical equivalences cannot be captured by propositional logic: "*Not all men are smokers*" and "*Some men don't smoke.*" Each of these two propositions is treated independently in propositional logic. There is no mechanism in propositional logic to find out whether or not the two are equivalent to one another. Hence, in propositional logic, each equivalent proposition is treated individually rather than dealing with a general formula that covers all equivalences collectively.

Predicate logic is supposed to be a more powerful logic that addresses these issues. In a sense, predicate logic (also known as first-order logic or predicate calculus) is an extension of propositional logic to formulas involving terms and predicates.

3. Proof Techniques

[1*, c1]

A proof is an argument that rigorously establishes the truth of a statement. Proofs can themselves be represented formally as discrete structures.

Statements used in a proof include axioms and postulates that are essentially the underlying assumptions about mathematical structures, the hypotheses of the theorem to be proved, and previously proved theorems.

A theorem is a statement that can be shown to be true.

A lemma is a simple theorem used in the proof of other theorems.

A corollary is a proposition that can be established directly from a theorem that has been proved.

A conjecture is a statement whose truth value is unknown.

When a conjecture's proof is found, the conjecture becomes a theorem. Many times conjectures are shown to be false and, hence, are not theorems.

3.1. Methods of Proving Theorems

Direct Proof. Direct proof is a technique to establish that the implication $p \rightarrow q$ is true by showing that q must be true when p is true.

For example, to show that if n is odd then n^2-1 is even, suppose n is odd, i.e., $n = 2k + 1$ for some integer k:

$$\therefore n^2 = (2k + 1)^2 = 4k^2 + 4k + 1.$$

As the first two terms of the Right Hand Side (RHS) are even numbers irrespective of the value of k, the Left Hand Side (LHS) (i.e., n^2) is an odd number. Therefore, n^2-1 is even.

Proof by Contradiction. A proposition p is true by contradiction if proved based on the truth of the implication $\neg p \rightarrow q$ where q is a contradiction.

For example, to show that the sum of $2x + 1$ and $2y - 1$ is even, assume that the sum of $2x + 1$ and $2y - 1$ is odd. In other words, $2(x + y)$, which is a multiple of 2, is odd. This is a contradiction. Hence, the sum of $2x + 1$ and $2y - 1$ is even.

An inference rule is a pattern establishing that if a set of premises are all true, then it can be deduced that a certain conclusion statement is true. The reference rules of addition, simplification, and conjunction need to be studied.

Proof by Induction. Proof by induction is done in two phases. First, the proposition is established to be true for a base case—typically for the positive integer 1. In the second phase, it is established that if the proposition holds for an arbitrary positive integer k, then it must also hold for the next greater integer, $k + 1$. In other words, proof by induction is based on the rule of inference that tells us that the truth of an infinite sequence of propositions P(n), $\forall n \in [1 \ldots \infty]$ is established if P(1) is true, and secondly, $\forall k \in [2 \ldots n]$ if P(k) $\rightarrow$ P(k + 1).

It may be noted here that, for a proof by mathematical induction, it is not assumed that P(k) is true for all positive integers k. Proving a theorem or proposition only requires us to establish that if it is assumed P(k) is true for any arbitrary positive integer k, then P(k + 1) is also true. The correctness of mathematical induction as a valid proof technique is beyond discussion of the current text. Let us prove the following proposition using induction.

Proposition: *The sum of the first n positive odd integers P(n) is n².*

Basis Step: The proposition is true for n = 1 as P(1) = 1^2 = 1. The basis step is complete.

Inductive Step: The induction hypothesis (IH) is that the proposition is true for n = k, k being an arbitrary positive integer k.

$\therefore 1 + 3 + 5 + \ldots + (2k - 1) = k^2$

Now, it's to be shown that P(k) $\rightarrow$ P(k + 1).

$P(k + 1) = 1 + 3 + 5 + \ldots + (2k - 1) + (2k + 1)$
$= P(k) + (2k + 1)$
$= k^2 + (2k + 1) \text{ [using IH]}$
$= k^2 + 2k + 1$
$= (k + 1)^2$

Thus, it is shown that if the proposition is true for n = k, then it is also true for n = k + 1.

The basis step together with the inductive step of the proof show that P(1) is true and the conditional statement P(k) $\rightarrow$ P(k + 1) is true for all positive integers k. Hence, the proposition is proved.

4. Basics of Counting

[1*c6]

The sum rule states that if a task t_1 can be done in n_1 ways and a second task t_2 can be done in n_2 ways, and if these tasks cannot be done at the same time, then there are $n_1 + n_2$ ways to do either task.

- If A and B are disjoint sets, then $|A \cup B| = |A| + |B|$.
- In general if A1, A2, ..., An are disjoint sets, then $|A1 \cup A2 \cup \ldots \cup An| = |A1| + |A2| + \ldots + |An|$.

For example, if there are 200 athletes doing sprint events and 30 athletes who participate in the long jump event, then how many ways are there to pick one athlete who is either a sprinter or a long jumper?

Using the sum rule, the answer would be 200 + 30 = 230.

The product rule states that if a task t_1 can be done in n_1 ways and a second task t_2 can be done in n_2 ways after the first task has been done, then there are $n_1 * n_2$ ways to do the procedure.

- If A and B are disjoint sets, then $|A \times B| = |A| * |B|$.
- In general if A1, A2, ..., An are disjoint sets, then $|A1 \times A2 \times \ldots \times An| = |A1| * |A2| * \ldots * |An|$.

For example, if there are 200 athletes doing sprint events and 30 athletes who participate in the long jump event, then how many ways are there to pick two athletes so that one is a sprinter and the other is a long jumper?

Using the product rule, the answer would be 200 * 30 = 6000.

The *principle of inclusion-exclusion* states that if a task t_1 can be done in n_1 ways and a second task t_2 can be done in n_2 ways at the same time with t_1, then to find the total number of ways the two tasks can be done, subtract the number of ways to do both tasks from $n_1 + n_2$.

- If A and B are not disjoint, $|A \cup B| = |A| + |B| - |A \cap B|$.

In other words, the principle of inclusion-exclusion aims to ensure that the objects in the intersection of two sets are not counted more than once.

Recursion is the general term for the practice of defining an object in terms of itself. There are recursive algorithms, recursively defined functions, relations, sets, etc.

A recursive function is a function that calls itself. For example, we define f(n) = 3 * f(n − 1) for all n ∈ N and n ≠ 0 and f(0) = 5.

An algorithm is recursive if it solves a problem by reducing it to an instance of the same problem with a smaller input.

A phenomenon is said to be random if individual outcomes are uncertain but the long-term pattern of many individual outcomes is predictable.

The probability of any outcome for a random phenomenon is the proportion of times the outcome would occur in a very long series of repetitions.

The probability P(A) of any event A satisfies 0 ≤ P(A) ≤ 1. Any probability is a number between 0 and 1. If S is the sample space in a probability model, the P(S) = 1. All possible outcomes together must have probability of 1.

Two events A and B are disjoint if they have no outcomes in common and so can never occur together. If A and B are two disjoint events, P(A or B) = P(A) + P(B). This is known as the addition rule for disjoint events.

If two events have no outcomes in common, the probability that one or the other occurs is the sum of their individual probabilities.

Permutation is an arrangement of objects in which the order matters without repetition. One can choose r objects in a particular order from a total of n objects by using ^nP_r ways, where, ^np_r = n! / (n − r)!. Various notations like ^nP_r and P(n, r) are used to represent the number of permutations of a set of n objects taken r at a time.

Combination is a selection of objects in which the order does not matter without repetition. This is different from a permutation because the order does not matter. If the order is only changed (and not the members) then no new combination is formed. One can choose r objects in any order from a total of n objects by using ^nC_r ways, where, ^nC_r = n! / [r! * (n − r)!].

5. Graphs and Trees

[1*, c10, c11]

5.1. Graphs

A graph G = (V, E) where V is the set of vertices (nodes) and E is the set of edges. Edges are also referred to as arcs or links.

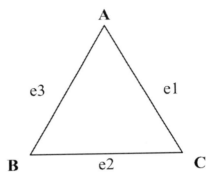

Figure 14.8. Example of a Graph

F is a function that maps the set of edges E to a set of ordered or unordered pairs of elements V. For example, in Figure 14.8, G = (V, E) where V = {A, B, C}, E = {e1, e2, e3}, and F = {(e1, (A, C)), (e2, (C, B)), (e3, (B, A))}.

The graph in Figure 14.8 is a simple graph that consists of a set of vertices or nodes and a set of edges connecting unordered pairs.

The edges in simple graphs are undirected. Such graphs are also referred to as undirected graphs.

For example, in Figure 14.8, (e1, (A, C)) may be replaced by (e1, (C, A)) as the pair between vertices A and C is unordered. This holds good for the other two edges too.

In a multigraph, more than one edge may connect the same two vertices. Two or more connecting edges between the same pair of vertices may reflect multiple associations between the same two vertices. Such edges are called parallel or multiple edges.

For example, in Figure 14.9, the edges e3 and e4 are both between A and B. Figure 14.9 is a multigraph where edges e3 and e4 are multiple edges.

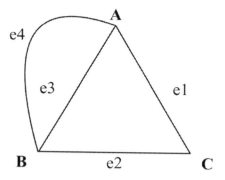

Figure 14.9. Example of a Multigraph

In a *pseudograph*, edges connecting a node to itself are allowed. Such edges are called loops.

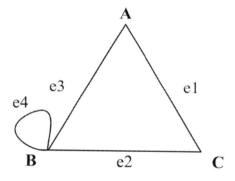

Figure 14.10. Example of a Pseudograph

For example, in Figure 14.10, the edge e4 both starts and ends at B. Figure 14.10 is a pseudograph in which e4 is a loop.

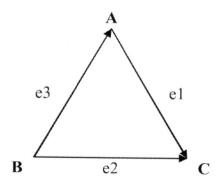

Figure 14.11. Example of a Directed Graph

A directed graph G = (V, E) consists of a set of vertices V and a set of edges E that are ordered pairs of elements of V. A directed graph may contain loops.

For example, in Figure 14.11, G = (V, E) where V = {A, B, C}, E = {e1, e2, e3}, and F = {(e1, (A, C)), (e2, (B, C)), (e3, (B, A))}.

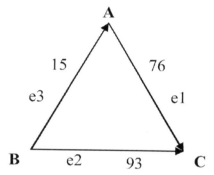

Figure 14.12. Example of a Weighted Graph

In a weighted graph G = (V, E), each edge has a weight associated with it. The weight of an edge typically represents the numeric value associated with the relationship between the corresponding two vertices.

For example, in Figure 14.12, the weights for the edges e1, e2, and e3 are taken to be 76, 93, and 15 respectively. If the vertices A, B, and C represent three cities in a state, the weights, for example, could be the distances in miles between these cities.

Let G = (V, E) be an undirected graph with edge set E. Then, for an edge e ∈ E where e = {u, v}, the following terminologies are often used:

- u, v are said to be *adjacent* or *neighbors* or *connected*.
- edge e is *incident* with vertices u and v.
- edge e *connects* u and v.
- vertices u and v are *endpoints* for edge e.

If vertex v ∈ V, the set of vertices in the undirected graph G(V, E), then:

- the *degree* of v, deg(v), is its number of incident edges, except that any self-loops are counted twice.

- a vertex with degree 0 is called an *isolated vertex*.
- a vertex of degree 1 is called a *pendant vertex*.

Let G(V, E) be a directed graph. If e(u, v) is an edge of G, then the following terminologies are often used:

- u is *adjacent to* v, and v is *adjacent from* u.
- e *comes from* u and *goes to* v.
- e *connects* u to v, or e *goes from* u to v.
- the *initial vertex* of e is u.
- the *terminal vertex* of e is v.

If vertex v is in the set of vertices for the directed graph G(V, E), then

- *in-degree* of v, $\deg^-(v)$, is the number of edges going to v, i.e., for which v is the terminal vertex.
- *out-degree* of v, $\deg^+(v)$, is the number of edges coming from v, i.e., for which v is the initial vertex.
- *degree* of v, $\deg(v) = \deg^-(v) + \deg^+(v)$, is the sum of vs in-degree and out-degree.
- a loop at a vertex contributes 1 to both in-degree and out-degree of this vertex.

It may be noted that, following the definitions above, the degree of a node is unchanged whether we consider its edges to be directed or undirected.

In an undirected graph, a path of length n from u to v is a sequence of n adjacent edges from vertex u to vertex v.

- A path is a *circuit* if u=v.
- A path *traverses* the vertices along it.
- A path is *simple* if it contains no edge more than once.

A cycle on n vertices C_n for any n ≥ 3 is a simple graph where V = {v_1, v_2, ..., v_n} and E = {{v_1, v_2}, {v_2, v_3}, ... , {v_{n-1}, v_n}, {v_n, v_1}}.

For example, Figure 14.13 illustrates two cycles of length 3 and 4.

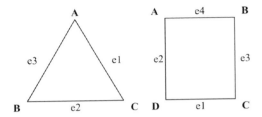

Figure 14.13. Example of Cycles C_3 and C_4

An adjacency list is a table with one row per vertex, listing its adjacent vertices. The adjacency listing for a directed graph maintains a listing of the terminal nodes for each of the vertex in the graph.

Vertex	Adjacency List
A	B, C
B	A, B, C
C	A, B

Figure 14.14. Adjacency Lists for Graphs in Figures 14.10 and 14.11

For example, Figure 14.14 illustrates the adjacency lists for the pseudograph in Figure 14.10 and the directed graph in Figure 14.11. As the out-degree of vertex C in Figure 14.11 is zero, there is no entry against C in the adjacency list.

Different representations for a graph—like adjacency matrix, incidence matrix, and adjacency lists—need to be studied.

5.2. Trees

A tree T(N, E) is a hierarchical data structure of n = |N| nodes with a specially designated root node R while the remaining n − 1 nodes form subtrees under the root node R. The number of edges |E| in a tree would always be equal to |N| − 1.

The subtree at node X is the subgraph of the tree consisting of node X and its descendants and all edges incident to those descendants. As an alternate to this recursive definition, a tree may be defined as a connected undirected graph with no simple circuits.

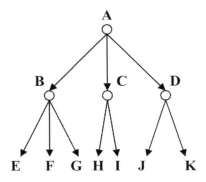

Figure 14.15. Example of a Tree

However, one should remember that a tree is strictly hierarchical in nature as compared to a graph, which is flat. In case of a tree, an ordered pair is built between two nodes as parent and child. Each child node in a tree is associated with only one parent node, whereas this restriction becomes meaningless for a graph where no parent-child association exists.

An undirected graph is a tree if and only if there is a unique simple path between any two of its vertices.

Figure 14.15 presents a tree T(N, E) where the set of nodes N = {A, B, C, D, E, F, G, H, I, J, K}. The edge set E is {(A, B), (A, C), (A, D), (B, E), (B, F), (B, G), (C, H), (C, I), (D, J), (D, K)}.

The parent of a nonroot node v is the unique node u with a directed edge from u to v. Each node in the tree has a unique parent node except the root of the tree.

For example, in Figure 14.15, root node A is the parent node for nodes B, C, and D. Similarly, B is the parent of E, F, G, and so on. The root node A does not have any parent.

A node that has children is called an internal node.

For example, in Figure 14.15, node A or node B are examples of internal nodes.

The degree of a node in a tree is the same as its number of children.

For example, in Figure 14.15, root node A and its child B are both of degree 3. Nodes C and D have degree 2.

The distance of a node from the root node in terms of number of hops is called its *level*. Nodes in a tree are at different levels. The root node is at level 0. Alternately, the level of a node X is the length of the unique path from the root of the tree to node X.

For example, root node A is at level 0 in Figure 14.15. Nodes B, C, and D are at level 1. The remaining nodes in Figure 14.15 are all at level 2.

The height of a tree is the maximum of the levels of nodes in the tree.

For example, in Figure 14.15, the height of the tree is 2.

A node is called a *leaf* if it has no children. The degree of a leaf node is 0.

For example, in Figure 14.15, nodes E through K are all leaf nodes with degree 0.

The ancestors or predecessors of a nonroot node X are all the nodes in the path from root to node X.

For example, in Figure 14.15, nodes A and D form the set of ancestors for J.

The successors or descendents of a node X are all the nodes that have X as its ancestor. For a tree with n nodes, all the remaining n − 1 nodes are successors of the root node.

For example, in Figure 14.15, node B has successors in E, F, and G.

If node X is an ancestor of node Y, then node Y is a successor of X.

Two or more nodes sharing the same parent node are called *sibling* nodes.

For example, in Figure 14.15, nodes E and G are siblings. However, nodes E and J, though from the same level, are not sibling nodes.

Two sibling nodes are of the same level, but two nodes in the same level are not necessarily siblings.

A tree is called an *ordered tree* if the relative position of occurrences of children nodes is significant.

For example, a family tree is an ordered tree if, as a rule, the name of an elder sibling appears always before (i.e., on the left of) the younger sibling.

In an unordered tree, the relative position of occurrences between the siblings does not bear any significance and may be altered arbitrarily.

A binary tree is formed with zero or more nodes where there is a root node R and all the remaining nodes form a pair of ordered subtrees under the root node.

In a binary tree, no internal node can have more than two children. However, one must consider that besides this criterion in terms of the degree of internal nodes, a binary tree is always ordered. If the positions of the left and right subtrees for any node in the tree are swapped, then a new tree is derived.

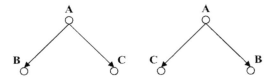

Figure 14.16. Examples of Binary Trees

For example, in Figure 14.16, the two binary trees are different as the positions of occurrences of the children of A are different in the two trees.

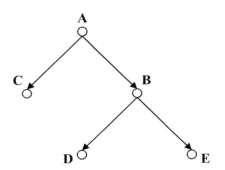

Figure 14.17. Example of a Full Binary Tree

According to [1*], a binary tree is called a full binary tree if every internal node has exactly two children.

For example, the binary tree in Figure 14.17 is a full binary tree, as both of the two internal nodes A and B are of degree 2.

A full binary tree following the definition above is also referred to as a *strictly binary tree*.

For example, both binary trees in Figure 14.18 are complete binary trees. The tree in Figure 14.18(a) is a complete as well as a full binary tree. A complete binary tree has all its levels, except possibly the last one, filled up to capacity. In case the last level of a complete binary tree is not full, nodes occur from the leftmost positions available.

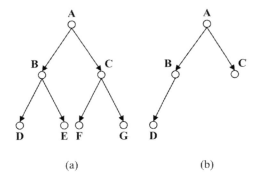

(a)   (b)

Figure 14.18. Example of Complete Binary Trees

Interestingly, following the definitions above, the tree in Figure 14.18(b) is a complete but not full binary tree as node B has only one child in D. On the contrary, the tree in Figure 14.17 is a full —but not complete—binary tree, as the children of B occur in the tree while the children of C do not appear in the last level.

A binary tree of height H is balanced if all its leaf nodes occur at levels H or H − 1.

For example, all three binary trees in Figures 14.17 and 14.18 are balanced binary trees.

There are at most 2^H leaves in a binary tree of height H. In other words, if a binary tree with L leaves is full and balanced, then its height is $H = \lceil \log_2 L \rceil$.

For example, this statement is true for the two trees in Figures 14.17 and 14.18(a) as both trees are full and balanced. However, the expression above does not match for the tree in Figure 14.18(b) as it is not a full binary tree.

A binary search tree (BST) is a special kind of binary tree in which each node contains a distinct key value, and the key value of each node in the tree is less than every key value in its right subtree and greater than every key value in its left subtree.

A traversal algorithm is a procedure for systematically visiting every node of a binary tree. Tree traversals may be defined recursively.

If T is binary tree with root R and the remaining nodes form an ordered pair of nonnull left subtree T_L and nonnull right subtree T_R below R, then the preorder traversal function PreOrder(T) is defined as:

$$PreOrder(T) = R, PreOrder(T_L), PreOrder(T_R)$$
... eqn. 1

The recursive process of finding the preorder traversal of the subtrees continues till the subtrees are found to be Null. Here, commas have been used as delimiters for the sake of improved readability.

The postorder and in-order may be similarly defined using eqn. 2 and eqn. 3 respectively.

PostOrder(T) = PostOrder(T_L), PostOrder(T_R), R ... eqn 2

InOrder(T) = InOrder(T_L), R, InOrder(T_R) ... eqn 3

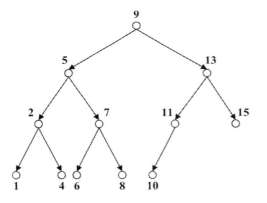

Figure 14.19. A Binary Search Tree

For example, the tree in Figure 14.19 is a binary search tree (BST). The preorder, postorder, and in-order traversal outputs for the BST are given below in their respective order.

Preorder output: 9, 5, 2, 1, 4, 7, 6, 8, 13, 11, 10, 15

Postorder output: 1, 4, 2, 6, 8, 7, 5, 10, 11, 15, 13, 9

In-order output: 1, 2, 4, 5, 6, 7, 8, 9, 10, 11, 13, 15

Further discussion on trees and their usage has been included in section 6, Data Structure and Representation, of the Computing Foundations KA.

6. Discrete Probability

[1*, c7]

Probability is the mathematical description of randomness. Basic definition of probability and randomness has been defined in section 4 of this KA. Here, let us start with the concepts behind probability distribution and discrete probability.

A probability model is a mathematical description of a random phenomenon consisting of two parts: a sample space S and a way of assigning probabilities to events. The sample space defines the set of all possible outcomes, whereas an event is a subset of a sample space representing a possible outcome or a set of outcomes.

A random variable is a function or rule that assigns a number to each outcome. Basically, it is just a symbol that represents the outcome of an experiment.

For example, let X be the number of heads when the experiment is flipping a coin n times. Similarly, let S be the speed of a car as registered on a radar detector.

The values for a random variable could be discrete or continuous depending on the experiment.

A discrete random variable can hold all possible outcomes without missing any, although it might take an infinite amount of time.

A continuous random variable is used to measure an uncountable number of values even if an infinite amount of time is given.

For example, if a random variable X represents an outcome that is a real number between 1 and 100, then X may have an infinite number of values. One can never list all possible outcomes for X even if an infinite amount of time is allowed. Here, X is a continuous random variable. On the contrary, for the same interval of 1 to 100, another random variable Y can be used to list all the integer values in the range. Here, Y is a discrete random variable.

An upper-case letter, say X, will represent the *name* of the random variable. Its lower-case counterpart, x, will represent the *value* of the random variable.

The probability that the random variable X will equal x is:

P(X = x) or, more simply, P(x).

A probability distribution (density) function is a table, formula, or graph that describes the values of a random variable and the probability associated with these values.

Probabilities associated with discrete random variables have the following properties:

i. $0 \leq P(x) \leq 1$ for all x
ii. $\Sigma P(x) = 1$

A discrete probability distribution can be represented as a discrete random variable.

X	1	2	3	4	5	6
P(x)	1/6	1/6	1/6	1/6	1/6	1/6

Figure 14.20. A Discrete Probability Function for a Rolling Die

The mean μ of a probability distribution model is the sum of the product terms for individual events and its outcome probability. In other words, for the possible outcomes $x_1, x_2, \ldots, x_n$ in a sample space S if p_k is the probability of outcome x_k, the mean of this probability would be $\mu = x_1 p_1 + x_2 p_2 + \ldots + x_n p_n$.

For example, the mean of the probability density for the distribution in Figure 14.20 would be

$$1 * (1/6) + 2 * (1/6) + 3 * (1/6) + 4 * (1/6) + 5 * (1/6) + 6 * (1/6)$$
$$= 21 * (1/6) = 3.5$$

Here, the sample space refers to the set of all possible outcomes.

The variance s^2 of a discrete probability model is: $s^2 = (x_1 - \mu)^2 p_1 + (x_2 - \mu)^2 p_2 + \ldots + (x_k - \mu)^2 p_k$. The *standard deviation*s is the square root of the variance.

For example, for the probability distribution in Figure 14.20, the variation σ^2 would be

$$s^2 = [(1 - 3.5)^2 * (1/6) + (2 - 3.5)^2 * (1/6) + (3 - 3.5)^2 * (1/6) + (4 - 3.5)^2 * (1/6) + (5 - 3.5)^2 * (1/6) + (6 - 3.5)^2 * (1/6)]$$
$$= (6.25 + 2.25 + 0.25 + 0.5 + 2.25 + 6.25) * (1/6)$$
$$= 17.5 * (1/6)$$
$$= 2.90$$

$\therefore$ standard deviation s =

These numbers indeed aim to derive the average value from repeated experiments. This is based on the single most important phenomenon of probability, i.e., the average value from repeated experiments is likely to be close to the expected value of one experiment. Moreover, the average value is more likely to be closer to the expected value of any one experiment as the number of experiments increases.

7. Finite State Machines

[1*, c13]

A computer system may be abstracted as a mapping from state to state driven by inputs. In other words, a system may be considered as a transition function T: $S \times I \rightarrow S \times O$, where S is the set of states and I, O are the input and output functions.

If the state set S is finite (not infinite), the system is called a *finite state machine* (FSM).

Alternately, a finite state machine (FSM) is a mathematical abstraction composed of a finite number of states and transitions between those states. If the domain $S \times I$ is reasonably small, then one can specify T explicitly using diagrams similar to a flow graph to illustrate the way logic flows for different inputs. However, this is practical only for machines that have a very small information capacity.

An FSM has a finite internal memory, an input feature that reads symbols in a sequence and one at a time, and an output feature.

The operation of an FSM begins from a start state, goes through transitions depending on input to different states, and can end in any valid state. However, only a few of all the states mark a successful flow of operation. These are called *accept states*.

The information capacity of an FSM is $C = \log |S|$. Thus, if we represent a machine having an information capacity of C bits as an FSM, then its state transition graph will have $|S| = 2^C$ nodes.

A finite state machine is formally defined as $M = (S, I, O, f, g, s_0)$.

S is the state set;
I is the set of input symbols;
O is the set of output symbols;
f is the state transition function;

g is the output function; and s_0 is the initial state.

Given an input $x \in I$ on state S_k, the FSM makes a transition to state S_h following state transition function f and produces an output $y \in O$ using the output function g.

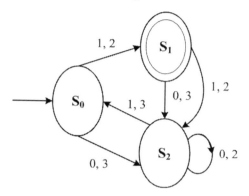

Figure 14.21. Example of an FSM

For example, Figure 14.21 illustrates an FSM with S_0 as the start state and S_1 as the final state. Here, $S = \{S_0, S_1, S_2\}$; $I = \{0, 1\}$; $O = \{2, 3\}$; $f(S_0, 0) = S_2$, $f(S_0, 1) = S_1$, $f(S_1, 0) = S_2$, $f(S_1, 1) = S_2$, $f(S_2, 0) = S_2$, $f(S_2, 1) = S_0$; $g(S_0, 0) = 3$, $g(S_0, 1) = 2$, $g(S_1, 0) = 3$, $g(S_1, 1) = 2$, $g(S_2, 0) = 2$, $g(S_2, 1) = 3$.

Current State	Input	
	0	1
S_0	S_2	S_1
S_1	S_2	S_2
S_2	S_2	S_0

(a)

Current State	Output		State	
	Input		Input	
	0	1	0	1
S_0	3	2	S_2	S_1
S_1	3	2	S_2	S_2
S_2	2	3	S_2	S_0

(b)

Figure 14.22. Tabular Representation of an FSM

The state transition and output values for different inputs on different states may be represented using a state table. The state table for the FSM in Figure 14.21 is shown in Figure 14.22. Each pair against an input symbol represents the new state and the output symbol.

For example, Figures 14.22(a) and 14.22(b) are two alternate representations of the FSM in Figure 14.21.

8. Grammars

[1*, c13]

The grammar of a natural language tells us whether a combination of words makes a valid sentence. Unlike natural languages, a formal language is specified by a well-defined set of rules for syntaxes. The valid sentences of a formal language can be described by a grammar with the help of these rules, referred to as *production rules*.

A formal language is a set of finite-length words or strings over some finite alphabet, and a grammar specifies the rules for formation of these words or strings. The entire set of words that are valid for a grammar constitutes the language for the grammar. Thus, the grammar G is any compact, precise mathematical definition of a language L as opposed to just a raw listing of all of the language's legal sentences or examples of those sentences.

A grammar implies an algorithm that would generate all legal sentences of the language. There are different types of grammars.

A phrase-structure or Type-0 grammar G = (V, T, S, P) is a 4-tuple in which:

- V is the vocabulary, i.e., set of words.
- $T \subseteq V$ is a set of words called terminals.
- $S \in N$ is a special word called the start symbol.
- P is the set of productions rules for substituting one sentence fragment for another.

There exists another set $N = V - T$ of words called nonterminals. The nonterminals represent concepts like *noun*. Production rules are applied on strings containing nonterminals until no more nonterminal symbols are present in the string. The start symbol S is a nonterminal.

The language generated by a formal grammar G, denoted by L(G), is the set of all strings over the set of alphabets V that can be generated, starting with the start symbol, by applying production rules until all the nonterminal symbols are replaced in the string.

For example, let G = ({S, A, a, b}, {a, b}, S, {S → aA, S → b, A → aa}). Here, the set of terminals are N = {S, A}, where S is the start symbol. The three production rules for the grammar are given as P1: S → aA; P2: S → b; P3: A → aa.

Applying the production rules in all possible ways, the following words may be generated from the start symbol.

S → aA	(using P1 on start symbol)
→ aaa	(using P3)
S → b	(using P2 on start symbol)

Nothing else can be derived for G. Thus, the language of the grammar G consists of only two words: L(G) = {aaa, b}.

8.1. Language Recognition

Formal grammars can be classified according to the types of productions that are allowed. The Chomsky hierarchy (introduced by Noam Chomsky in 1956) describes such a classification scheme.

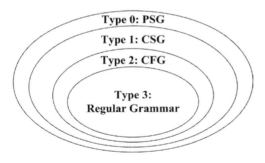

Figure 14.23. Chomsky Hierarchy of Grammars

As illustrated in Figure 14.23, we infer the following on different types of grammars:

1. Every regular grammar is a context-free grammar (CFG).
2. Every CFG is a context-sensitive grammar (CSG).

3. Every CSG is a phrase-structure grammar (PSG).

Context-Sensitive Grammar: All fragments in the RHS are either longer than the corresponding fragments in the LHS or empty, i.e., if b → a, then |b| < |a| or a = ∅.

A formal language is context-sensitive if a context-sensitive grammar generates it.

Context-Free Grammar: All fragments in the LHS are of length 1, i.e., if A → a, then |A| = 1 for all A ∈ N.

The term context-free derives from the fact that A can always be replaced by a, regardless of the context in which it occurs.

A formal language is context-free if a context-free grammar generates it. Context-free languages are the theoretical basis for the syntax of most programming languages.

Regular Grammar. All fragments in the RHS are either single terminals or a pair built by a terminal and a nonterminal; i.e., if A → a, then either a ∈ T, or a = cD, or a = Dc for c ∈ T, D ∈ N.

If a = cD, then the grammar is called a right linear grammar. On the other hand, if a = Dc, then the grammar is called a left linear grammar. Both the right linear and left linear grammars are regular or Type-3 grammar.

The language L(G) generated by a regular grammar G is called a regular language.

A regular expression A is a string (or pattern) formed from the following six pieces of information: a ∈ S, the set of alphabets, e, 0 and the operations, OR (+), PRODUCT (.), CONCATENATION (*). The language of G, L(G) is equal to all those strings that match G, L(G) = {x ∈ S*|x matches G}.

For any a ∈ S, L(a) = a; L(e) = {ε}; L(0) = 0.
+ functions as an or, L(A + B) = L(A) ∪ L(B).
. creates a product structure, L(AB) = L(A) . L(B).
* denotes concatenation, L(A*) = {$x_1 x_2 \ldots x_n$ | x_i ∈ L(A) and n ³ 0}

For example, the regular expression (ab)* matches the set of strings: {e, ab, abab, ababab, abababab, …}.

For example, the regular expression (aa)* matches the set of strings on one letter *a* that have even length.

For example, the regular expression (aaa)* + (aaaaa)* matches the set of strings of length equal to a multiple of 3 or 5.

9. Numerical Precision, Accuracy, and Errors
[2*, c2]

The main goal of numerical analysis is to develop efficient algorithms for computing precise numerical values of functions, solutions of algebraic and differential equations, optimization problems, etc.

A matter of fact is that all digital computers can only store finite numbers. In other words, there is no way that a computer can represent an infinitely large number—be it an integer, rational number, or any real or all complex numbers (see section 10, Number Theory). So the mathematics of approximation becomes very critical to handle all the numbers in the finite range that a computer can handle.

Each number in a computer is assigned a location or word, consisting of a specified number of binary digits or bits. A k bit word can store a total of $N = 2^k$ different numbers.

For example, a computer that uses 32 bit arithmetic can store a total of $N = 2^{32} \approx 4.3 \times 10^9$ different numbers, while another one that uses 64 bits can handle $N' = 2^{64} \approx 1.84 \times 10^{19}$ different numbers. The question is how to distribute these N numbers over the real line for maximum efficiency and accuracy in practical computations.

One evident choice is to distribute them evenly, leading to fixed-point arithmetic. In this system, the first bit in a word is used to represent a sign and the remaining bits are treated for integer values. This allows representation of the integers from $1 - \frac{1}{2}N$, i.e., $= 1 - 2^{k-1}$ to 1. As an approximating method, this is not good for noninteger numbers.

Another option is to space the numbers closely together—say with a uniform gap of 2^{-n}—and so distribute the total N numbers uniformly over the interval $-2^{-n-1}N < x \leq 2^{-n-1}N$. Real numbers lying between the gaps are represented by either *rounding* (meaning the closest exact representative)

or *chopping* (meaning the exact representative immediately below —or above, if negative—the number).

Numbers lying beyond the range must be represented by the largest (or largest negative) number that can be represented. This becomes a symbol for overflow. Overflow occurs when a computation produces a value larger than the maximum value in the range.

When processing speed is a significant bottleneck, the use of the fixed-point representations is an attractive and faster alternative to the more cumbersome floating-point arithmetic most commonly used in practice.

Let's define a couple of very important terms: *accuracy* and *precision* as associated with numerical analysis.

Accuracy is the closeness with which a measured or computed value agrees with the true value.

Precision, on the other hand, is the closeness with which two or more measured or computed values for the same physical substance agree with each other. In other words, precision is the closeness with which a number represents an exact value.

Let x be a real number and let x* be an approximation. The *absolute error* in the approximation $x^* \approx x$ is defined as $| x^* - x |$. The *relative error* is defined as the ratio of the absolute error to the size of x, i.e., $|x^* - x| / | x |$, which assumes x ^{1} 0; otherwise, relative error is not defined.

For example, 1000000 is an approximation to 1000001 with an absolute error of 1 and a relative error of 10^{-6}, while 10 is an approximation of 11 with an absolute error of 1 and a relative error of 0.1. Typically, relative error is more intuitive and the preferred determiner of the size of the error. The present convention is that errors are always ≥ 0, and are = 0 if and only if the approximation is exact.

An approximation x* has k significant decimal digits if its relative error is $< 5 \times 10^{-k-1}$. This means that the first k digits of x* following its first nonzero digit are the same as those of x.

Significant digits are the digits of a number that are known to be correct. In a measurement, one uncertain digit is included.

For example, measurement of length with a ruler of 15.5 mm with ±0.5 mm maximum allowable error has 2 significant digits, whereas a measurement of the same length using a caliper and recorded as 15.47 mm with ±0.01 mm maximum allowable error has 3 significant digits.

10. Number Theory

[1*, c4]

Number theory is one of the oldest branches of pure mathematics and one of the largest. Of course, it concerns questions about numbers, usually meaning whole numbers and fractional or rational numbers. The different types of numbers include integer, real number, natural number, complex number, rational number, etc.

10.1. Divisibility

Let's start this section with a brief description of each of the above types of numbers, starting with the natural numbers.

Natural Numbers. This group of numbers starts at 1 and continues: 1, 2, 3, 4, 5, and so on. Zero is not in this group. There are no negative or fractional numbers in the group of natural numbers. The common mathematical symbol for the set of all natural numbers is N.

Whole Numbers. This group has all of the natural numbers in it plus the number 0.

Unfortunately, not everyone accepts the above definitions of natural and whole numbers. There seems to be no general agreement about whether to include 0 in the set of natural numbers.

Many mathematicians consider that, in Europe, the sequence of natural numbers traditionally started with 1 (0 was not even considered to be a number by the Greeks). In the 19th century, set theoreticians and other mathematicians started the convention of including 0 in the set of natural numbers.

Integers. This group has all the whole numbers in it and their negatives. The common mathematical symbol for the set of all integers is Z, i.e., Z = {..., −3, −2, −1, 0, 1, 2, 3, ...}.

Rational Numbers. These are any numbers that can be expressed as a ratio of two integers. The common symbol for the set of all rational numbers is Q.

Rational numbers may be classified into three types, based on how the decimals act. The decimals either do not exist, e.g., 15, or, when decimals do exist, they may terminate, as in 15.6, or they may repeat with a pattern, as in 1.666..., (which is 5/3).

Irrational Numbers. These are numbers that cannot be expressed as an integer divided by an integer. These numbers have decimals that never terminate and never repeat with a pattern, e.g., PI or $\sqrt{2}$.

Real Numbers. This group is made up of all the rational and irrational numbers. The numbers that are encountered when studying algebra are real numbers. The common mathematical symbol for the set of all real numbers is R.

Imaginary Numbers. These are all based on the imaginary number i. This imaginary number is equal to the square root of −1. Any real number multiple of i is an imaginary number, e.g., i, $5i$, $3.2i$, $-2.6i$, etc.

Complex Numbers. A complex number is a combination of a real number and an imaginary number in the form $a + bi$. The real part is a, and b is called the imaginary part. The common mathematical symbol for the set of all complex numbers is **C**.

For example, $2 + 3i$, $3 - 5i$, $7.3 + 0i$, and $0 + 5i$.

Consider the last two examples:

$7.3 + 0i$ is the same as the real number 7.3. Thus, all real numbers are complex numbers with zero for the imaginary part.

Similarly, $0 + 5i$ is just the imaginary number $5i$. Thus, all imaginary numbers are complex numbers with zero for the real part.

Elementary number theory involves divisibility among integers. Let $a, b \in Z$ with $a \neq 0$. The expression $a|b$, i.e., *a divides b* if $\exists c \in Z$: $b = ac$, i.e., there is an integer c such that c times a equals b.

For example, $3|{-}12$ is true, but $3|7$ is false.

If a divides b, then we say that a is a factor of b or a is a divisor of b, and b is a multiple of a.

b is even if and only if $2|b$.

Let $a, d \in Z$ with $d > 1$. Then *a mod d* denotes that the remainder r from the division algorithm with dividend a and divisor d, i.e., the remainder when a is divided by d. We can compute *(a mod d)* by: $a - d * \lfloor a/d \rfloor$, where $\lfloor a/d \rfloor$ represents the floor of the real number.

Let $Z^+ = \{n \in Z \mid n > 0\}$ and $a, b \in Z$, $m \in Z^+$, then a is congruent to b *modulo m*, written as $a \equiv b \ (mod \ m)$, if and only if $m \mid a - b$.

Alternately, a is congruent to b *modulo* m if and only if $(a-b) \bmod m = 0$.

10.2. Prime Number, GCD

An integer $p > 1$ is prime if and only if it is not the product of any two integers greater than 1, i.e., p is prime if $p > 1 \wedge \exists \neg a, b \in N: a > 1, b > 1, a * b = p$.

The only positive factors of a prime p are 1 and p itself. For example, the numbers 2, 13, 29, 61, etc. are prime numbers. Nonprime integers greater than 1 are called composite numbers. A composite number may be composed by multiplying two integers greater than 1.

There are many interesting applications of prime numbers; among them are the public-key cryptography scheme, which involves the exchange of public keys containing the product $p*q$ of two random large primes p and q (a private key) that must be kept secret by a given party.

The greatest common divisor gcd(a, b) of integers a, b is the greatest integer d that is a divisor both of a and of b, i.e.,

$$d = \gcd(a, b) \text{ for } \max(d: d|a \wedge d|b)$$

For example, gcd(24, 36) = 12.

Integers a and b are called relatively prime or coprime if and only if their GCD is 1.

For example, neither 35 nor 6 are prime, but they are coprime as these two numbers have no common factors greater than 1, so their GCD is 1.

A set of integers $X = \{i_1, i_2, \ldots\}$ is relatively prime if all possible pairs $i_h, i_k, h \neq k$ drawn from the set X are relatively prime.

11. Algebraic Structures

This section introduces a few representations used in higher algebra. An algebraic structure consists of one or two sets closed under some operations and satisfying a number of axioms, including none.

For example, group, monoid, ring, and lattice are examples of algebraic structures. Each of these is defined in this section.

11.1. Group

A set S closed under a binary operation • forms a group if the binary operation satisfies the following four criteria:

- Associative: $\forall a, b, c \in S$, the equation $(a \bullet b) \bullet c = a \bullet (b \bullet c)$ holds.
- Identity: There exists an identity element $I \in S$ such that for all $a \in S$, $I \bullet a = a \bullet I = a$.
- Inverse: Every element $a \in S$, has an inverse $a' \in S$ with respect to the binary operation, i.e., $a \bullet a' = I$; for example, the set of integers Z with respect to the addition operation is a group. The identity element of the set is 0 for the addition operation. $\forall x \in Z$, the inverse of x would be $-x$, which is also included in Z.
- Closure property: $\forall a, b \in S$, the result of the operation $a \bullet b \in S$.
- A group that is commutative, i.e., $a \bullet b = b \bullet a$, is known as a commutative or Abelian group.

The set of natural numbers N (with the operation of addition) is not a group, since there is no inverse for any $x > 0$ in the set of natural numbers. Thus, the third rule (of inverse) for our operation is violated. However, the set of natural number has some structure.

Sets with an associative operation (the first condition above) are called semigroups; if they also have an identity element (the second condition), then they are called monoids.

Our set of natural numbers under addition is then an example of a monoid, a structure that is not quite a group because it is missing the requirement that every element have an inverse under the operation.

A monoid is a set S that is closed under a single associative binary operation • and has an identity element $I \in S$ such that for all $a \in S$, $I \bullet a = a \bullet I = a$. A monoid must contain at least one element.

For example, the set of natural numbers N forms a commutative monoid under addition with identity element 0. The same set of natural numbers N also forms a monoid under multiplication with identity element 1. The set of positive integers P forms a commutative monoid under multiplication with identity element 1.

It may be noted that, unlike those in a group, elements of a monoid need not have inverses. A monoid can also be thought of as a semigroup with an identity element.

A *subgroup* is a group H contained within a bigger one, G, such that the identity element of G is contained in H, and whenever h_1 and h_2 are in H, then so are $h_1 \cdot h_2$ and h_1^{-1}. Thus, the elements of H, equipped with the group operation on G restricted to H, indeed form a group.

Given any subset S of a group G, the subgroup generated by S consists of products of elements of S and their inverses. It is the smallest subgroup of G containing S.

For example, let G be the Abelian group whose elements are $G = \{0, 2, 4, 6, 1, 3, 5, 7\}$ and whose group operation is addition modulo 8. This group has a pair of nontrivial subgroups: $J = \{0, 4\}$ and $H = \{0, 2, 4, 6\}$, where J is also a subgroup of H.

In group theory, a cyclic group is a group that can be generated by a single element, in the sense that the group has an element a (called the *generator* of the group) such that, when written multiplicatively, every element of the group is a power of a.

A group G is cyclic if $G = \{a^n$ for any integer n$\}$.

Since any group generated by an element in a group is a subgroup of that group, showing that the only subgroup of a group G that contains a is G itself suffices to show that G is cyclic.

For example, the group $G = \{0, 2, 4, 6, 1, 3, 5, 7\}$, with respect to addition modulo 8 operation, is cyclic. The subgroups $J = \{0, 4\}$ and $H = \{0, 2, 4, 6\}$ are also cyclic.

11.2. Rings

If we take an Abelian group and define a second operation on it, a new structure is found that is different from just a group. If this second operation is associative and is distributive over the first, then we have a ring.

A ring is a triple of the form (S, +, •), where (S, +) is an Abelian group, (S, •) is a semigroup, and • is distributive over +; i.e., " a, b, c ∈ S, the equation $a \cdot (b + c) = (a \cdot b) + (a \cdot c)$ holds. Further, if • is commutative, then the ring is said to be commutative. If there is an identity element for the • operation, then the ring is said to have an identity.

For example, (Z, +, *), i.e., the set of integers Z, with the usual addition and multiplication operations, is a ring. As (Z, *) is commutative, this ring is a commutative or Abelian ring. The ring has 1 as its identity element.

Let's note that the second operation may not have an identity element, nor do we need to find an inverse for every element with respect to this second operation. As for what distributive means, intuitively it is what we do in elementary mathematics when performing the following change: a * (b + c) = (a * b) + (a * c).

A field is a ring for which the elements of the set, excluding 0, form an Abelian group with the second operation.

A simple example of a field is the field of rational numbers (R, +, *) with the usual addition and multiplication operations. The numbers of the format $a/b \in$ R, where a, b are integers and $b \neq 0$. The additive inverse of such a fraction is simply $-a/b$, and the multiplicative inverse is b/a provided that $a \neq 0$.

MATRIX OF TOPICS VS. REFERENCE MATERIAL

	Rosen 2011 [1*]	Cheney and Kincaid 2007 [2*]
1. Sets, Relations, Functions	c2	
2. Basic Logic	c1	
3. Proof Techniques	c1	
4. Basic Counting	c6	
5. Graphs and Trees	c10, c11	
6. Discrete Probability	c7	
7. Finite State Machines	c13	
8. Grammars	c13	
9. Numerical Precision, Accuracy, and Errors		c2
10. Number Theory	c4	
11. Algebraic Structures		

REFERENCES

[1*] K. Rosen, *Discrete Mathematics and Its Applications*, 7th ed., McGraw-Hill, 2011.

[2*] E.W. Cheney and D.R. Kincaid, *Numerical Mathematics and Computing*, 6th ed., Brooks/Cole, 2007.

ACKNOWLEDGMENTS

The author thankfully acknowledges the contribution of Prof. Arun Kumar Chatterjee, Ex-Head, Department of Mathematics, Manipur University, India, and Prof. Devadatta Sinha, Ex-Head, Department of Computer Science and Engineering, University of Calcutta, India, in preparing this chapter on Mathematical Foundations.

CHAPTER 15

ENGINEERING FOUNDATIONS

ACRONYMS

CAD	Computer-Aided Design
CMMI	Capability Maturity Model Integration
pdf	Probability Density Function
pmf	Probability Mass Function
RCA	Root Cause Analysis
SDLC	Software Development Life Cycle

INTRODUCTION

IEEE defines engineering as "the application of a systematic, disciplined, quantifiable approach to structures, machines, products, systems or processes" [1]. This chapter outlines some of the engineering foundational skills and techniques that are useful for a software engineer. The focus is on topics that support other KAs while minimizing duplication of subjects covered elsewhere in this document.

As the theory and practice of software engineering matures, it is increasingly apparent that software engineering is an engineering discipline that is based on knowledge and skills common to all engineering disciplines. This Engineering Foundations knowledge area (KA) is concerned with the engineering foundations that apply to software engineering and other engineering disciplines. Topics in this KA include empirical methods and experimental techniques; statistical analysis; measurement; engineering design; modeling, prototyping, and simulation; standards; and root cause analysis. Application of this knowledge, as appropriate, will allow software engineers to develop and maintain software more efficiently and effectively. Completing their engineering work efficiently and

effectively is a goal of all engineers in all engineering disciplines.

BREAKDOWN OF TOPICS FOR ENGINEERING FOUNDATIONS

The breakdown of topics for the Engineering Foundations KA is shown in Figure 15.1.

1. Empirical Methods and Experimental Techniques

[2*, c1]

An engineering method for problem solving involves proposing solutions or models of solutions and then conducting experiments or tests to study the proposed solutions or models. Thus, engineers must understand how to create an experiment and then analyze the results of the experiment in order to evaluate the proposed solution. Empirical methods and experimental techniques help the engineer to describe and understand variability in their observations, to identify the sources of variability, and to make decisions.

Three different types of empirical studies commonly used in engineering efforts are designed experiments, observational studies, and retrospective studies. Brief descriptions of the commonly used methods are given below.

1.1. Designed Experiment

A designed or controlled experiment is an investigation of a testable hypothesis where one or more independent variables are manipulated to measure their effect on one or more dependent variables. A precondition for conducting an experiment is the existence of a clear hypothesis. It is important for an engineer to understand how to formulate clear hypotheses.

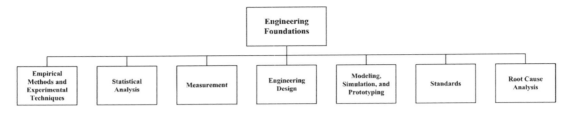

Figure 15.1. Breakdown of Topics for the Engineering Foundations KA

Designed experiments allow engineers to determine in precise terms how the variables are related and, specifically, whether a cause-effect relationship exists between them. Each combination of values of the independent variables is a *treatment*. The simplest experiments have just two treatments representing two levels of a single independent variable (e.g., using a tool vs. not using a tool). More complex experimental designs arise when more than two levels, more than one independent variable, or any dependent variables are used.

1.2. Observational Study

An observational or case study is an empirical inquiry that makes observations of processes or phenomena within a real-life context. While an experiment deliberately ignores context, an observational or case study includes context as part of the observation. A case study is most useful when the focus of the study is on *how* and *why* questions, when the behavior of those involved in the study cannot be manipulated, and when contextual conditions are relevant and the boundaries between the phenomena and context are not clear.

1.3. Retrospective Study

A retrospective study involves the analysis of historical data. Retrospective studies are also known as historical studies. This type of study uses data (regarding some phenomenon) that has been archived over time. This archived data is then analyzed in an attempt to find a relationship between variables, to predict future events, or to identify trends. The quality of the analysis results will depend on the quality of the information contained in the archived data. Historical data may be incomplete, inconsistently measured, or incorrect.

2. Statistical Analysis

[2*, c9s1, c2s1] [3*, c10s3]

In order to carry out their responsibilities, engineers must understand how different product and process characteristics vary. Engineers often come across situations where the relationship between different variables needs to be studied. An important point to note is that most of the studies are carried out on the basis of samples and so the observed results need to be understood with respect to the full population. Engineers must, therefore, develop an adequate understanding of statistical techniques for collecting reliable data in terms of sampling and analysis to arrive at results that can be generalized. These techniques are discussed below.

2.1. Unit of Analysis (Sampling Units), Population, and Sample

Unit of analysis. While carrying out any empirical study, observations need to be made on chosen units called the units of analysis or sampling units. The unit of analysis must be identified and must be appropriate for the analysis. For example, when a software product company wants to find the perceived usability of a software product, the user or the software function may be the unit of analysis.

Population. The set of all respondents or items (possible sampling units) to be studied forms the population. As an example, consider the case of studying the perceived usability of a software product. In this case, the set of all possible users forms the population.

While defining the population, care must be exercised to understand the study and target population. There are cases when the population studied and the population for which the results are being generalized may be different. For example, when the study population consists of only past observations and generalizations are required for the future, the study population and the target population may not be the same.

Sample. A sample is a subset of the population. The most crucial issue towards the selection of a sample is its representativeness, including size. The samples must be drawn in a manner so as to ensure that the draws are independent, and the rules of drawing the samples must be predefined so that the probability of selecting a particular sampling unit is known beforehand. This method of selecting samples is called *probability sampling.*

Random variable. In statistical terminology, the process of making observations or measurements on the sampling units being studied is referred to as conducting the experiment. For example, if the experiment is to toss a coin 10 times and then count the number of times the coin lands on heads, each 10 tosses of the coin is a sampling unit and the number of heads for a given sample is the observation or outcome for the experiment. The outcome of an experiment is obtained in terms of real numbers and defines the random variable being studied. Thus, the attribute of the items being measured at the outcome of the experiment represents the random variable being studied; the observation obtained from a particular sampling unit is a particular realization of the random variable. In the example of the coin toss, the random variable is the number of heads observed for each experiment. In statistical studies, attempts are made to understand population characteristics on the basis of samples.

The set of possible values of a random variable may be finite or infinite but countable (e.g., the set of all integers or the set of all odd numbers). In such a case, the random variable is called a *discrete random variable*. In other cases, the random variable under consideration may take values on a continuous scale and is called a *continuous random variable.*

Event. A subset of possible values of a random variable is called an event. Suppose X denotes some random variable; then, for example, we may define different events such as $X^3 x$ or $X <$ x and so on.

Distribution of a random variable. The range and pattern of variation of a random variable is given by its distribution. When the distribution of a random variable is known, it is possible to compute the chance of any event. Some distributions are found to occur commonly and are used to model many random variables occurring in practice in the context of engineering. A few of the more commonly occurring distributions are given below.

- Binomial distribution: used to model random variables that count the number of successes in *n* trials carried out independently of each other, where each trial results in success or failure. We make an assumption that the chance of obtaining a success remains constant [2*, c3s6].
- Poisson distribution: used to model the count of occurrence of some event over time or space [2*, c3s9].
- Normal distribution: used to model continuous random variables or discrete random variables by taking a very large number of values [2*, c4s6].

Concept of parameters. A statistical distribution is characterized by some parameters. For example, the proportion of success in any given trial is the only parameter characterizing a binomial distribution. Similarly, the Poisson distribution is characterized by a rate of occurrence. A normal distribution is characterized by two parameters: namely, its mean and standard deviation.

Once the values of the parameters are known, the distribution of the random variable is completely known and the chance (probability) of any event can be computed. The probabilities for a discrete random variable can be computed through the probability mass function, called the pmf. The pmf is defined at discrete points and gives the point mass—i.e., the probability that the random variable will take that particular value. Likewise, for a continuous random variable, we have the probability density function, called the pdf. The pdf is very much like density and needs to be integrated over a range to obtain the probability that the continuous random variable lies between certain values. Thus, if the pdf or pmf is known, the chances of the random variable taking certain set of values may be computed theoretically.

Concept of estimation [2*, c6s2, c7s1, c7s3]. The true values of the parameters of a distribution are usually unknown and need to be estimated from the sample observations. The estimates are functions of the sample values and are called statistics. For example, the sample mean is a statistic and may be used to estimate the population mean. Similarly, the rate of occurrence of defects estimated from the sample (rate of defects per line of code) is a statistic and serves as the estimate of the population rate of rate of defects per line of code. The statistic used to estimate some population parameter is often referred to as the *estimator* of the parameter.

A very important point to note is that the results of the estimators themselves are random. If we take a different sample, we are likely to get a different estimate of the population parameter. In the theory of estimation, we need to understand different properties of estimators—particularly, how much the estimates can vary across samples and how to choose between different alternative ways to obtain the estimates. For example, if we wish to estimate the mean of a population, we might use as our estimator a sample mean, a sample median, a sample mode, or the midrange of the sample. Each of these estimators has different statistical properties that may impact the standard error of the estimate.

Types of estimates [2*, c7s3, c8s1]. There are two types of estimates: namely, point estimates and interval estimates. When we use the value of a statistic to estimate a population parameter, we get a point estimate. As the name indicates, a point estimate gives a point value of the parameter being estimated.

Although point estimates are often used, they leave room for many questions. For instance, we are not told anything about the possible size of error or statistical properties of the point estimate. Thus, we might need to supplement a point estimate with the sample size as well as the variance of the estimate. Alternately, we might use an interval estimate. An interval estimate is a random interval with the lower and upper limits of the interval being functions of the sample observations as well as the sample size. The limits are computed on the basis of some assumptions regarding the sampling distribution of the point estimate on which the limits are based.

Properties of estimators. Various statistical properties of estimators are used to decide about the appropriateness of an estimator in a given situation. The most important properties are that an estimator is unbiased, efficient, and consistent with respect to the population.

Tests of hypotheses [2*, c9s1]. A hypothesis is a statement about the possible values of a parameter. For example, suppose it is claimed that a new method of software development reduces the occurrence of defects. In this case, the hypothesis is that the rate of occurrence of defects has reduced. In tests of hypotheses, we decide—on the basis of sample observations—whether a proposed hypothesis should be accepted or rejected.

For testing hypotheses, the null and alternative hypotheses are formed. The null hypothesis is the hypothesis of no change and is denoted as H_0. The alternative hypothesis is written as H_1. It is important to note that the alternative hypothesis may be one-sided or two-sided. For example, if we have the null hypothesis that the population mean is not less than some given value, the alternative hypothesis would be that it is less than that value and we would have a one-sided test. However, if we have the null hypothesis that the population mean is equal to some given value, the alternative hypothesis would be that it is not equal and we would have a two-sided test (because the true value could be either less than or greater than the given value).

In order to test some hypothesis, we first compute some statistic. Along with the computation of the statistic, a region is defined such that in case the computed value of the statistic falls in that region, the null hypothesis is rejected. This region is called the critical region (also known as the confidence interval). In tests of hypotheses, we need to accept or reject the null hypothesis on the basis of the evidence obtained. We note that, in general, the alternative hypothesis is the hypothesis of interest. If the computed value of the statistic does not fall inside the critical region, then we cannot reject the null hypothesis. This indicates that there is not enough evidence to believe that the alternative hypothesis is true.

As the decision is being taken on the basis of sample observations, errors are possible; the types of such errors are summarized in the following table.

Nature	Statistical Decision	
	Accept H_0	Reject H_0
H_0 is true	OK	Type I error (probability = a)
H_0 is false	Type II error (probability = b)	OK

In test of hypotheses, we aim at maximizing the power of the test (the value of $1-b$) while ensuring that the probability of a type I error (the value of a) is maintained within a particular value—typically 5 percent.

It is to be noted that construction of a test of hypothesis includes identifying statistic(s) to estimate the parameter(s) and defining a critical region such that if the computed value of the statistic falls in the critical region, the null hypothesis is rejected.

2.2. Concepts of Correlation and Regression
[2*, c11s2, c11s8]

A major objective of many statistical investigations is to establish relationships that make it possible to predict one or more variables in terms of others. Although it is desirable to predict a quantity exactly in terms of another quantity, it is seldom possible and, in many cases, we have to be satisfied with estimating the average or expected values.

The relationship between two variables is studied using the methods of correlation and regression. Both these concepts are explained briefly in the following paragraphs.

Correlation. The strength of linear relationship between two variables is measured using the correlation coefficient. While computing the correlation coefficient between two variables, we assume that these variables measure two different attributes of the same entity. The correlation coefficient takes a value between -1 to $+1$. The values -1 and $+1$ indicate a situation when the association between the variables is perfect—i.e.,

given the value of one variable, the other can be estimated with no error. A positive correlation coefficient indicates a positive relationship—that is, if one variable increases, so does the other. On the other hand, when the variables are negatively correlated, an increase of one leads to a decrease of the other.

It is important to remember that correlation does not imply causation. Thus, if two variables are correlated, we cannot conclude that one causes the other.

Regression. The correlation analysis only measures the degree of relationship between two variables. The analysis to find the relationship between two variables is called *regression analysis*. The strength of the relationship between two variables is measured using the coefficient of determination. This is a value between 0 and 1. The closer the coefficient is to 1, the stronger the relationship between the variables. A value of 1 indicates a perfect relationship.

3. Measurement
[4*, c3s1, c3s2] [5*, c4s4] [6*, c7s5]
[7*, p442–447]

Knowing what to measure and which measurement method to use is critical in engineering endeavors. It is important that everyone involved in an engineering project understand the measurement methods and the measurement results that will be used.

Measurements can be physical, environmental, economic, operational, or some other sort of measurement that is meaningful for the particular project. This section explores the theory of measurement and how it is fundamental to engineering. Measurement starts as a conceptualization then moves from abstract concepts to definitions of the measurement method to the actual application of that method to obtain a measurement result. Each of these steps must be understood, communicated, and properly employed in order to generate usable data. In traditional engineering, direct measures are often used. In software engineering, a combination of both direct and derived measures is necessary [6*, p273].

The theory of measurement states that measurement is an attempt to describe an underlying real empirical system. Measurement methods define activities that allocate a value or a symbol to an attribute of an entity.

Attributes must then be defined in terms of the operations used to identify and measure them— that is, the measurement methods. In this approach, a measurement method is defined to be a precisely specified operation that yields a number (called the *measurement result)* when measuring an attribute. It follows that, to be useful, the measurement method has to be well defined. Arbitrariness in the method will reflect itself in ambiguity in the measurement results.

In some cases—particularly in the physical world—the attributes that we wish to measure are easy to grasp; however, in an artificial world like software engineering, defining the attributes may not be that simple. For example, the attributes of height, weight, distance, etc. are easily and uniformly understood (though they may not be very easy to measure in all circumstances), whereas attributes such as software size or complexity require clear definitions.

Operational definitions. The definition of attributes, to start with, is often rather abstract. Such definitions do not facilitate measurements. For example, we may define a circle as *a line forming a closed loop such that the distance between any point on this line and a fixed interior point called the center is constant.* We may further say that the fixed distance from the center to any point on the closed loop gives the radius of the circle. It may be noted that though the concept has been defined, no means of measuring the radius has been proposed. The operational definition specifies the exact steps or method used to carry out a specific measurement. This can also be called the *measurement method*; sometimes a *measurement procedure* may be required to be even more precise.

The importance of operational definitions can hardly be overstated. Take the case of the apparently simple measurement of height of individuals. Unless we specify various factors like the time when the height will be measured (it is known that the height of individuals vary across various time points of the day), how the variability due to hair would be taken care of, whether the measurement will be with or without shoes, what kind of accuracy is expected (correct up to an inch, 1/2 inch, centimeter, etc.)—even

this simple measurement will lead to substantial variation. Engineers must appreciate the need to define measures from an operational perspective.

3.1. Levels (Scales) of Measurement
[4*, c3s2] [6*, c7s5]

Once the operational definitions are determined, the actual measurements need to be undertaken. It is to be noted that measurement may be carried out in four different scales: namely, nominal, ordinal, interval, and ratio. Brief descriptions of each are given below.

Nominal scale: This is the lowest level of measurement and represents the most unrestricted assignment of numerals. The numerals serve only as labels, and words or letters would serve as well. The nominal scale of measurement involves only classification and the observed sampling units are put into any one of the mutually exclusive and collectively exhaustive categories (classes). Some examples of nominal scales are:

- Job titles in a company
- The software development life cycle (SDLC) model (like waterfall, iterative, agile, etc.) followed by different software projects

In nominal scale, the names of the different categories are just labels and no relationship between them is assumed. The only operations that can be carried out on nominal scale is that of counting the number of occurrences in the different classes and determining if two occurrences have the same nominal value. However, statistical analyses may be carried out to understand how entities belonging to different classes perform with respect to some other response variable.

Ordinal scale: Refers to the measurement scale where the different values obtained through the process of measurement have an implicit ordering. The intervals between values are not specified and there is no objectively defined zero element. Typical examples of measurements in ordinal scales are:

- Skill levels (low, medium, high)
- Capability Maturity Model Integration (CMMI) maturity levels of software development organizations

- Level of adherence to process as measured in a 5-point scale of excellent, above average, average, below average, and poor, indicating the range from total adherence to no adherence at all

Measurement in ordinal scale satisfies the transitivity property in the sense that if A > B and B > C, then A > C. However, arithmetic operations cannot be carried out on variables measured in ordinal scales. Thus, if we measure customer satisfaction on a 5-point ordinal scale of 5 implying a very high level of satisfaction and 1 implying a very high level of dissatisfaction, we cannot say that a score of four is twice as good as a score of two. So, it is better to use terminology such as excellent, above average, average, below average, and poor than ordinal numbers in order to avoid the error of treating an ordinal scale as a ratio scale. It is important to note that ordinal scale measures are commonly misused and such misuse can lead to erroneous conclusions [6*, p274]. A common misuse of ordinal scale measures is to present a mean and standard deviation for the data set, both of which are meaningless. However, we can find the median, as computation of the median involves counting only.

Interval scales: With the interval scale, we come to a form that is quantitative in the ordinary sense of the word. Almost all the usual statistical measures are applicable here, unless they require knowledge of a *true* zero point. The zero point on an interval scale is a matter of convention. Ratios do not make sense, but the difference between levels of attributes can be computed and is meaningful. Some examples of interval scale of measurement follow:

- Measurement of temperature in different scales, such as Celsius and Fahrenheit. Suppose T_1 and T_2 are temperatures measured in some scale. We note that the fact that T_1 is twice T_2 does not mean that one object is twice as hot as another. We also note that the zero points are arbitrary.
- Calendar dates. While the difference between dates to measure the time elapsed is a meaningful concept, the ratio does not make sense.
- Many psychological measurements aspire to create interval scales. Intelligence is often measured in interval scale, as it is not necessary to define what zero intelligence would mean.

If a variable is measured in interval scale, most of the usual statistical analyses like mean, standard deviation, correlation, and regression may be carried out on the measured values.

Ratio scale: These are quite commonly encountered in physical science. These scales of measures are characterized by the fact that operations exist for determining all 4 relations: equality, rank order, equality of intervals, and equality of ratios. Once such a scale is available, its numerical values can be transformed from one unit to another by just multiplying by a constant, e.g., conversion of inches to feet or centimeters. When measurements are being made in ratio scale, existence of a nonarbitrary zero is mandatory. All statistical measures are applicable to ratio scale; logarithm usage is valid only when these scales are used, as in the case of decibels. Some examples of ratio measures are

- the number of statements in a software program
- temperature measured in the Kelvin (K) scale or in Fahrenheit (F).

An additional measurement scale, the absolute scale, is a ratio scale with uniqueness of the measure; i.e., a measure for which no transformation is possible (for example, the number of programmers working on a project).

3.2. Direct and Derived Measures

[6*, c7s5]

Measures may be either direct or derived (sometimes called indirect measures). An example of a direct measure would be a count of how many times an event occurred, such as the number of defects found in a software product. A derived measure is one that combines direct measures in some way that is consistent with the measurement method. An example of a derived measure would be calculating the productivity of a team as the number of lines of code developed per developer-month. In both cases, the measurement method determines how to make the measurement.

3.3. Reliability and Validity

[4*, c3s4, c3s5]

A basic question to be asked for any measurement method is whether the proposed measurement method is truly measuring the concept with good quality. Reliability and validity are the two most important criteria to address this question.

The reliability of a measurement method is the extent to which the application of the measurement method yields consistent measurement results. Essentially, *reliability* refers to the consistency of the values obtained when the same item is measured a number of times. When the results agree with each other, the measurement method is said to be reliable. Reliability usually depends on the operational definition. It can be quantified by using the index of variation, which is computed as the ratio between the standard deviation and the mean. The smaller the index, the more reliable the measurement results.

Validity refers to whether the measurement method really measures what we intend to measure. Validity of a measurement method may be looked at from three different perspectives: namely, construct validity, criteria validity, and content validity.

3.4. Assessing Reliability

[4*, c3s5]

There are several methods for assessing reliability; these include the test-retest method, the alternative form method, the split-halves method, and the internal consistency method. The easiest of these is the test-retest method. In the test-retest method, we simply apply the measurement method to the same subjects twice. The correlation coefficient between the first and second set of measurement results gives the reliability of the measurement method.

4. Engineering Design

[5*, c1s2, c1s3, c1s4]

A product's life cycle costs are largely influenced by the design of the product. This is true for manufactured products as well as for software products.

The design of a software product is guided by the features to be included and the quality attributes to be provided. It is important to note that software engineers use the term "design" within their own context; while there are some commonalities, there are also many differences between engineering design as discussed in this section and software engineering design as discussed in the Software Design KA. The scope of engineering design is generally viewed as much broader than that of software design. The primary aim of this section is to identify the concepts needed to develop a clear understanding regarding the process of engineering design.

Many disciplines engage in problem solving activities where there is a single correct solution. In engineering, most problems have many solutions and the focus is on finding a feasible solution (among the many alternatives) that best meets the needs presented. The set of possible solutions is often constrained by explicitly imposed limitations such as cost, available resources, and the state of discipline or domain knowledge. In engineering problems, sometimes there are also implicit constraints (such as the physical properties of materials or laws of physics) that also restrict the set of feasible solutions for a given problem.

4.1. Engineering Design in Engineering Education

The importance of engineering design in engineering education can be clearly seen by the high expectations held by various accreditation bodies for engineering education. Both the Canadian Engineering Accreditation Board and the Accreditation Board for Engineering and Technology (ABET) note the importance of including engineering design in education programs.

The Canadian Engineering Accreditation Board includes requirements for the amount of engineering design experience/coursework that is necessary for engineering students as well as qualifications for the faculty members who teach such coursework or supervise design projects. Their accreditation criteria states:

Design: An ability to design solutions for complex, open-ended engineering problems and to design systems, components or processes that meet specified needs with appropriate attention to health and safety risks, applicable standards, and economic, environmental, cultural and societal considerations. [8, p12]

In a similar manner, ABET defines engineering design as

the process of devising a system, component, or process to meet desired needs. It is a decision-making process (often iterative), in which the basic sciences, mathematics, and the engineering sciences are applied to convert resources optimally to meet these stated needs. [9, p4]

Thus, it is clear that engineering design is a vital component in the training and education for all engineers. The remainder of this section will focus on various aspects of engineering design.

4.2. Design as a Problem Solving Activity
[5*, c1s4, c2s1, c3s3]

It is to be noted that engineering design is primarily a problem solving activity. Design problems are open ended and more vaguely defined. There are usually several alternative ways to solve the same problem. Design is generally considered to be a *wicked problem*—a term first coined by Horst Rittel in the 1960s when design methods were a subject of intense interest. Rittel sought an alternative to the linear, step-by-step model of the design process being explored by many designers and design theorists and argued that most of the problems addressed by the designers are wicked problems. As explained by Steve McConnell, a wicked problem is one that could be clearly defined only by solving it or by solving part of it. This paradox implies, essentially, that a wicked problem has to be solved once in order to define it clearly and then solved again to create a solution that works. This has been an important insight for software designers for several decades [10*, c5s1].

4.3. Steps Involved in Engineering Design
[7*, c4]

Engineering problem solving begins when a need is recognized and no existing solution will meet that need. As part of this problem solving, the design goals to be achieved by the solution should be identified. Additionally, a set of acceptance criteria must be defined and used to determine how well a proposed solution will satisfy the need. Once a need for a solution to a problem has been identified, the process of engineering design has the following generic steps:

a) define the problem
b) gather pertinent information
c) generate multiple solutions
d) analyze and select a solution
e) implement the solution

All of the engineering design steps are iterative, and knowledge gained at any step in the process may be used to inform earlier tasks and trigger an iteration in the process. These steps are expanded in the subsequent sections.

a. Define the problem. At this stage, the customer's requirements are gathered. Specific information about product functions and features are also closely examined. This step includes refining the problem statement to identify the real problem to be solved and setting the design goals and criteria for success.

The problem definition is a crucial stage in engineering design. A point to note is that this step is deceptively simple. Thus, enough care must be taken to carry out this step judiciously. It is important to identify needs and link the success criteria with the required product characteristics. It is also an engineering task to limit the scope of a problem and its solution through negotiation among the stakeholders.

b. Gather pertinent information. At this stage, the designer attempts to expand his/her knowledge about the problem. This is a vital, yet often neglected, stage. Gathering pertinent information can reveal facts leading to a redefinition of the problem—in particular, mistakes and false starts may be identified. This step may also involve the decomposition of the problem into smaller, more easily solved subproblems.

While gathering pertinent information, care must be taken to identify how a product may be used as well as misused. It is also important to understand the perceived value of the product/service being offered. Included in the pertinent information is a list of constraints that must be satisfied by the solution or that may limit the set of feasible solutions.

c. Generate multiple solutions. During this stage, different solutions to the same problem are developed. It has already been stated that design problems have multiple solutions. The goal of this step is to conceptualize multiple possible solutions and refine them to a sufficient level of detail that a comparison can be done among them.

d. Analyze and select a solution. Once alternative solutions have been identified, they need to be analyzed to identify the solution that best suits the current situation. The analysis includes a functional analysis to assess whether the proposed design would meet the functional requirements. Physical solutions that involve human users often include analysis of the ergonomics or user friendliness of the proposed solution. Other aspects of the solution—such as product safety and liability, an economic or market analysis to ensure a return (profit) on the solution, performance predictions and analysis to meet quality characteristics, opportunities for incorrect data input or hardware malfunctions, and so on—may be studied. The types and amount of analysis used on a proposed solution are dependent on the type of problem and the needs that the solution must address as well as the constraints imposed on the design.

e. Implement the solution. The final phase of the design process is implementation. Implementation refers to development and testing of the proposed solution. Sometimes a preliminary, partial solution called a *prototype* may be developed initially to test the proposed design solution under certain conditions. Feedback resulting from testing a prototype may be used either to

refine the design or drive the selection of an alternative design solution. One of the most important activities in design is documentation of the design solution as well as of the tradeoffs for the choices made in the design of the solution. This work should be carried out in a manner such that the solution to the design problem can be communicated clearly to others.

The testing and verification take us back to the success criteria. The engineer needs to devise tests such that the ability of the design to meet the success criteria is demonstrated. While designing the tests, the engineer must think through different possible failure modes and then design tests based on those failure modes. The engineer may choose to carry out designed experiments to assess the validity of the design.

5. Modeling, Simulation, and Prototyping
[5*, c6] [11*, c13s3] [12*, c2s3.1]

Modeling is part of the abstraction process used to represent some aspects of a system. Simulation uses a model of the system and provides a means of conducting designed experiments with that model to better understand the system, its behavior, and relationships between subsystems, as well as to analyze aspects of the design. Modeling and simulation are techniques that can be used to construct theories or hypotheses about the behavior of the system; engineers then use those theories to make predictions about the system. Prototyping is another abstraction process where a partial representation (that captures aspects of interest) of the product or system is built. A prototype may be an initial version of the system but lacks the full functionality of the final version.

5.1. Modeling

A model is always an abstraction of some real or imagined artifact. Engineers use models in many ways as part of their problem solving activities. Some models are physical, such as a made-to-scale miniature construction of a bridge or building. Other models may be nonphysical representations, such as a CAD drawing of a cog or a mathematical model for a process. Models help engineers reason and understand aspects of a problem. They can also help engineers understand what they do know and what they don't know about the problem at hand.

There are three types of models: iconic, analogic, and symbolic. An iconic model is a visually equivalent but incomplete 2-dimensional or 3-dimensional representation—for example, maps, globes, or built-to-scale models of structures such as bridges or highways. An iconic model actually resembles the artifact modeled.

In contrast, an analogic model is a functionally equivalent but incomplete representation. That is, the model behaves like the physical artifact even though it may not physically resemble it. Examples of analogic models include a miniature airplane for wind tunnel testing or a computer simulation of a manufacturing process.

Finally, a symbolic model is a higher level of abstraction, where the model is represented using symbols such as equations. The model captures the relevant aspects of the process or system in symbolic form. The symbols can then be used to increase the engineer's understanding of the final system. An example is an equation such as $F = Ma$. Such mathematical models can be used to describe and predict properties or behavior of the final system or product.

5.2. Simulation

All simulation models are a specification of reality. A central issue in simulation is to abstract and specify an appropriate simplification of reality. Developing this abstraction is of vital importance, as misspecification of the abstraction would invalidate the results of the simulation exercise. Simulation can be used for a variety of testing purposes.

Simulation is classified based on the type of system under study. Thus, simulation can be either continuous or discrete. In the context of software engineering, the emphasis will be primarily on discrete simulation. Discrete simulations may model event scheduling or process interaction. The main components in such a model include entities, activities and events, resources, the state of the system, a simulation clock, and a random number generator. Output is generated by the simulation and must be analyzed.

An important problem in the development of a discrete simulation is that of initialization. Before a simulation can be run, the initial values of all the state variables must be provided. As the simulation designer may not know what initial values are appropriate for the state variables, these values might be chosen somewhat arbitrarily. For instance, it might be decided that a queue should be initialized as empty and idle. Such a choice of initial condition can have a significant but unrecognized impact on the outcome of the simulation.

5.3. Prototyping

Constructing a prototype of a system is another abstraction process. In this case, an initial version of the system is constructed, often while the system is being designed. This helps the designers determine the feasibility of their design.

There are many uses for a prototype, including the elicitation of requirements, the design and refinement of a user interface to the system, validation of functional requirements, and so on. The objectives and purposes for building the prototype will determine its construction and the level of abstraction used.

The role of prototyping is somewhat different between physical systems and software. With physical systems, the prototype may actually be the first fully functional version of a system or it may be a model of the system. In software engineering, prototypes are also an abstract model of part of the software but are usually not constructed with all of the architectural, performance, and other quality characteristics expected in the finished product. In either case, prototype construction must have a clear purpose and be planned, monitored, and controlled—it is a technique to study a specific problem within a limited context [6*, c2s8].

In conclusion, modeling, simulation, and prototyping are powerful techniques for studying the behavior of a system from a given perspective. All can be used to perform designed experiments to study various aspects of the system. However, these are abstractions and, as such, may not model all attributes of interest.

6. Standards

[5*, c9s3.2] [13*, c1s2]

Moore states that a

> standard can be; (a) an object or measure of comparison that defines or represents the magnitude of a unit; (b) a characterization that establishes allowable tolerances for categories of items; and (c) a degree or level of required excellence or attainment. Standards are definitional in nature, established either to further understanding and interaction or to acknowledge observed (or desired) norms of exhibited characteristics or behavior. [13*, p8]

Standards provide requirements, specifications, guidelines, or characteristics that must be observed by engineers so that the products, processes, and materials have acceptable levels of quality. The qualities that various standards provide may be those of safety, reliability, or other product characteristics. Standards are considered critical to engineers and engineers are expected to be familiar with and to use the appropriate standards in their discipline.

Compliance or conformance to a standard lets an organization say to the public that they (or their products) meet the requirements stated in that standard. Thus, standards divide organizations or their products into those that conform to the standard and those that do not. For a standard to be useful, conformance with the standard must add value—real or perceived—to the product, process, or effort.

Apart from the organizational goals, standards are used for a number of other purposes such as protecting the buyer, protecting the business, and better defining the methods and procedures to be followed by the practice. Standards also provide users with a common terminology and expectations.

There are many internationally recognized standards-making organizations including the International Telecommunications Union (ITU), the International Electrotechnical Commission (IEC), IEEE, and the International Organization for Standardization (ISO). In addition, there are regional and governmentally recognized organizations that generate standards for that region or country. For example, in the United States, there are over 300 organizations that develop standards. These include organizations such as the American National Standards Institute (ANSI), the American Society for Testing and Materials (ASTM), the Society of Automotive Engineers (SAE), and Underwriters Laboratories, Inc. (UL), as well as the US government. For more detail on standards used in software engineering, see Appendix B on standards.

There is a set of commonly used principles behind standards. Standards makers attempt to have consensus around their decisions. There is usually an openness within the community of interest so that once a standard has been set, there is a good chance that it will be widely accepted. Most standards organizations have well-defined processes for their efforts and adhere to those processes carefully. Engineers must be aware of the existing standards but must also update their understanding of the standards as those standards change over time.

In many engineering endeavors, knowing and understanding the applicable standards is critical and the law may even require use of particular standards. In these cases, the standards often represent minimal requirements that must be met by the endeavor and thus are an element in the constraints imposed on any design effort. The engineer must review all current standards related to a given endeavor and determine which must be met. Their designs must then incorporate any and all constraints imposed by the applicable standard. Standards important to software engineers are discussed in more detail in an appendix specifically on this subject.

7. Root Cause Analysis

[4*, c5, c3s7, c9s8] [5*, c9s3, c9s4, c9s5]
[13*, c13s3.4.5]

Root cause analysis (RCA) is a process designed to investigate and identify why and how an undesirable event has happened. Root causes are underlying causes. The investigator should attempt to identify specific underlying causes of the event that has occurred. The primary objective of RCA is to prevent recurrence of the undesirable event. Thus, the more specific the investigator can be about why an event occurred, the easier it will be to prevent recurrence. A common way to identify specific underlying cause(s) is to ask a series of *why* questions.

7.1. Techniques for Conducting Root Cause Analysis

[4*, c5] [5*, c3]

There are many approaches used for both quality control and root cause analysis. The first step in any root cause analysis effort is to identify the real problem. Techniques such as statement-restatement, why-why diagrams, the revision method, present state and desired state diagrams, and the fresh-eye approach are used to identify and refine the real problem that needs to be addressed.

Once the real problem has been identified, then work can begin to determine the cause of the problem. Ishikawa is known for the seven tools for quality control that he promoted. Some of those tools are helpful in identifying the causes for a given problem. Those tools are check sheets or checklists, Pareto diagrams, histograms, run charts, scatter diagrams, control charts, and fishbone or cause-and-effect diagrams. More recently, other approaches for quality improvement and root cause analysis have emerged. Some examples of these newer methods are affinity diagrams, relations diagrams, tree diagrams, matrix charts, matrix data analysis charts, process decision program charts, and arrow diagrams. A few of these techniques are briefly described below.

A fishbone or cause-and-effect diagram is a way to visualize the various factors that affect some characteristic. The main line in the diagram represents the problem and the connecting lines represent the factors that led to or influenced the problem. Those factors are broken down into sub-factors and sub-subfactors until root causes can be identified.

A very simple approach that is useful in quality control is the use of a checklist. Checklists are a list of key points in a process with tasks that must be completed. As each task is completed, it is checked off the list. If a problem occurs, then sometimes the checklist can quickly identify tasks that may have been skipped or only partially completed.

Finally, relations diagrams are a means for displaying complex relationships. They give visual support to cause-and-effect thinking. The diagram relates the specific to the general, revealing key causes and key effects.

Root cause analysis aims at preventing the recurrence of undesirable events. Reduction of variation due to common causes requires utilization of a number of techniques. An important point to note is that these techniques should be used offline and not necessarily in direct response to the occurrence of some undesirable event. Some of the techniques that may be used to reduce variation due to common causes are given below.

1. Cause-and-effect diagrams may be used to identify the sub and sub-sub causes.
2. Fault tree analysis is a technique that may be used to understand the sources of failures.
3. Designed experiments may be used to understand the impact of various causes on the occurrence of undesirable events (see Empirical Methods and Experimental Techniques in this KA).
4. Various kinds of correlation analyses may be used to understand the relationship between various causes and their impact. These techniques may be used in cases when conducting controlled experiments is difficult but data may be gathered (see Statistical Analysis in this KA).

MATRIX OF TOPICS VS. REFERENCE MATERIAL

	Montgomery and Runger 2007 [2*]	Null and Lobur 2006 [3*]	Kan 2002 [4*]	Voland 2003 [5*]	Fairley 2009 [6*]	Tockey 2004 [7*]	McConnell 2004 [10*]	Cheney and Kincaid 2007 [11*]	Sommerville 2011 [12*]	Moore 2006 [13*]
1. Empirical Methods and Experimental Techniques	c1									
1.1. Designed Experiment										
1.2. Observational Study										
1.3. Retrospective Study										
2. Statistical Analysis	c9s1, c2s1	c10s3								
2.1. Concept of Unit of Analysis (Sampling Units), Sample, and Population	c3s6, c3s9, c4s6, c6s2, c7s1, c7s3, c8s1, c9s1									
2.2. Concepts of Correlation and Regression	c11s2, c11s8									
3. Measurement			c3s1, c3s2	c4s4	c7s5					
3.1. Levels (Scales) of Measurement			c3s2		c7s5	p442 –447				
3.2. Direct and Derived Measures										

	Montgomery and Runger 2007 [2*]	Null and Lobur 2006 [3*]	Kan 2002 [4*]	Voland 2003 [5*]	Fairley 2009 [6*]	Tockey 2004 [7*]	McConnell 2004 [10*]	Cheney and Kincaid 2007 [11*]	Sommerville 2011 [12*]	Moore 2006 [13*]
3.3. Reliability and Validity			c3s4, c3s5							
3.4. Assessing Reliability			c3s5							
4. Engineering Design				c1s2, c1s3, c1s4						
4.1. Design in Engineering Education										
4.2. Design as a Problem Solving Activity				c1s4, c2s1, c3s3				c5s1		
4.3. Steps Involved in Engineering Design						c4				
5. Modeling, Prototyping, and Simulation				c6				c13s3	c2 s3.1	
5.1. Modeling										
5.2. Simulation										
5.3. Prototyping										
6. Standards				c9 s3.2						c1s2
7. Root Cause Analysis			c5, c3s7, c9s8	c9s3, c9s4, c9s5						c13 s3.4.5
7.1. Techniques for Conducting Root Cause Analysis			c5	c3						

FURTHER READINGS

A. Abran, *Software Metrics and Software Metrology.* [14]

This book provides very good information on the proper use of the terms measure, measurement method and measurement outcome. It provides strong support material for the entire section on Measurement.

W.G. Vincenti, *What Engineers Know and How They Know It.* [15]

This book provides an interesting introduction to engineering foundations through a series of case studies that show many of the foundational concepts as used in real world engineering applications.

REFERENCES

[1] *ISO/IEC/IEEE 24765:2010 Systems and Software Engineering—Vocabulary*, ISO/IEC/IEEE, 2010.

[2*] D.C. Montgomery and G.C. Runger, *Applied Statistics and Probability for Engineers*, 4th ed., Wiley, 2007.

[3*] L. Null and J. Lobur, *The Essentials of Computer Organization and Architecture*, 2nd ed., Jones and Bartlett Publishers, 2006.

[4*] S.H. Kan, *Metrics and Models in Software Quality Engineering*, 2nd ed., Addison-Wesley, 2002.

[5*] G. Voland, *Engineering by Design*, 2nd ed., Prentice Hall, 2003.

[6*] R.E. Fairley, *Managing and Leading Software Projects*, Wiley-IEEE Computer Society Press, 2009.

[7*] S. Tockey, *Return on Software: Maximizing the Return on Your Software Investment*, Addison-Wesley, 2004.

[8] Canadian Engineering Accreditation Board, Engineers Canada, "Accreditation Criteria and Procedures," Canadian Council of Professional Engineers, 2011; www.engineerscanada.ca/files/w_Accreditation_Criteria_Procedures_2011.pdf.

[9] ABET Engineering Accreditation Commission, "Criteria for Accrediting Engineering Programs, 2012-2013," ABET, 2011; www.abet.org/uploadedFiles/Accreditation/Accreditation_Process/Accreditation_Documents/Current/eac-criteria-2012-2013.pdf.

[10*] S. McConnell, *Code Complete*, 2nd ed., Microsoft Press, 2004.

[11*] E.W. Cheney and D.R. Kincaid, *Numerical Mathematics and Computing*, 6th ed., Brooks/Cole, 2007.

[12*] I. Sommerville, *Software Engineering*, 9th ed., Addison-Wesley, 2011.

[13*] J.W. Moore, *The Road Map to Software Engineering: A Standards-Based Guide*, Wiley-IEEE Computer Society Press, 2006.

[14] A. Abran, *Software Metrics and Software Metrology*, Wiley-IEEE Computer Society Press, 2010.

[15] W.G. Vincenti, *What Engineers Know and How They Know It*, John Hopkins University Press, 1990.

APPENDIX A

KNOWLEDGE AREA DESCRIPTION SPECIFICATIONS

INTRODUCTION

This document presents the specifications provided to the Knowledge Area Editors (KA Editors) regarding the Knowledge Area Descriptions (KA Descriptions) of the Version 3 (V3) edition of the *Guide to the Software Engineering Body of Knowledge (SWEBOK Guide)*. This document will also enable readers, reviewers, and users to clearly understand what specifications were used when developing this version of the *SWEBOK Guide*.

This document begins by situating the *SWEBOK Guide* as a foundational document for the IEEE Computer Society suite of software engineering products and more widely within the software engineering community at large. The role of the baseline and the Change Control Board is then described. Criteria and requirements are defined for the breakdowns of topics, for the rationale underlying these breakdowns and the succinct description of topics, and for reference materials. Important input documents are also identified, and their role within the project is explained. Noncontent issues such as submission format and style guidelines are also discussed.

THE SWEBOK GUIDE IS A FOUNDATIONAL DOCUMENT FOR THE IEEE COMPUTER SOCIETY SUITE OF SOFTWARE ENGINEERING PRODUCTS

The *SWEBOK Guide* is an IEEE Computer Society flagship and structural document for the IEEE Computer Society suite of software engineering products. The *SWEBOK Guide* is also more widely recognized as a foundational document within the software engineering community at large notably through the official recognition of the 2004 Version as ISO/IEC Technical Report 19759:2005. The list of knowledge areas (KAs) and the breakdown of topics within each KA is described and detailed in the introduction of this *SWEBOK Guide*.

Consequently, the *SWEBOK Guide* is foundational to other initiatives within the IEEE Computer Society:

a) The list of KAs and the breakdown of topics within each KA are also adopted by the software engineering certification and associated professional development products offered by the IEEE Computer Society (see www.computer.org/certification).

b) The list of KAs and the breakdown of topics are also foundational to the software engineering curricula guidelines developed or endorsed by the IEEE Computer Society (www.computer.org/portal/web/education/Curricula).

c) The Consolidated Reference List (see Appendix C), meaning the list of recommended reference materials (to the level of section number) that accompanies the breakdown of topics within each KA is also adopted by the software engineering certification and associated professional development products offered by the IEEE Computer Society.

BASELINE AND CHANGE CONTROL BOARD

Due to the structural nature of the *SWEBOK Guide* and its adoption by other products, a baseline was developed at the outset of the project comprised of the list of KAs, the breakdown of topics within each KA, and the Consolidated Reference List.

A Change Control Board (CCB) has been in place for the development of this version to handle all change requests to this baseline coming from the KA Editors, arising during the review process, or otherwise. Change requests must be approved both by the *SWEBOK Guide* Editors and by the CCB before being implemented. This CCB is comprised of members of the initiatives listed above and acting under the authority of the Software and Systems Engineering Committee of the IEEE Computer Society Professional Activities Board.

CRITERIA AND REQUIREMENTS FOR THE BREAKDOWN OF TOPICS WITHIN A KNOWLEDGE AREA

a) KA Editors are instructed to adopt the baseline breakdown of topics.

b) The breakdown of topics is expected to be "reasonable," not "perfect."

c) The breakdown of topics within a KA must decompose the subset of the Software Engineering Body of Knowledge that is "generally recognized." See below for a more detailed discussion of this point.

d) The breakdown of topics within a KA must not presume specific application domains, business needs, sizes of organizations, organizational structures, management philosophies, software life cycle models, software technologies, or software development methods.

e) The breakdown of topics must, as much as possible, be compatible with the various schools of thought within software engineering.

f) The breakdown of topics within a KA must be compatible with the breakdown of software engineering generally found in industry and in the software engineering literature and standards.

g) The breakdown of topics is expected to be as inclusive as possible.

h) The *SWEBOK Guide* adopts the position that even though the following "themes" are common across all Knowledge Areas, they are also an integral part of all Knowledge Areas and therefore must be incorporated into the proposed breakdown of topics of each Knowledge Area. These common themes are measurement, quality (in general), and security.

i) The breakdown of topics should be at most two or three levels deep. Even though no upper or lower limit is imposed on the number of topics within each KA, a reasonable and manageable number of topics is expected to be included in each KA. Emphasis should also be put on the selection of the topics themselves rather than on their organization in an appropriate hierarchy.

j) Topic names must be significant enough to be meaningful even when cited outside the *SWEBOK Guide*.

k) The description of a KA will include a chart (in tree form) describing the knowledge breakdown.

CRITERIA AND REQUIREMENTS FOR DESCRIBING TOPICS

Topics need only be sufficiently described so the reader can select the appropriate reference material according to his/her needs. Topic descriptions must not be prescriptive.

CRITERIA AND REQUIREMENTS FOR REFERENCE MATERIAL

a) KA Editors are instructed to use the references (to the level of section number) allocated to their KA by the Consolidated Reference List as their Recommended References.

b) There are three categories of reference material:

» Recommended References. The set of Recommended References (to the level of section number) is collectively known as the Consolidated Reference List.

» Further Readings.

» Additional references cited in the KA Description (for example, the source of a quotation or reference material in support of a rationale behind a particular argument).

c) The *SWEBOK Guide* is intended by definition to be selective in its choice of topics and associated reference material. The list of reference material should be clearly viewed as an "informed and reasonable selection" rather than as a definitive list.

d) Reference material can be book chapters, refereed journal papers, refereed conference papers, refereed technical or industrial reports, or any other type of recognized artifact. References to another KA, subarea, or topic are also permitted.

e) Reference material must be generally available and must not be confidential in nature.

f) Reference material must be in English.

g) Criteria and requirements for recommended reference material or Consolidated Reference List:

» Collectively the list of Recommended References should be

  i.   complete: covering the entire scope of the *SWEBOK Guide*
  ii. sufficient: providing enough information to describe "generally accepted" knowledge
  iii. consistent: not providing contradictory knowledge nor conflicting practices
  iv. credible: recognized as providing expert treatment
  v.   current: treating the subject in a manner that is commensurate with currently generally accepted knowledge
  vi. succinct: as short as possible (both in number of reference items and in total page count) without failing other objectives.

» Recommended reference material must be identified for each topic. Each recommended reference item may of course cover multiple topics. Exceptionally, a topic may be self-descriptive and not cite a reference material item (for example, a topic that is a definition or a topic for which the description itself without any cited reference material is sufficient for the objectives of the *SWEBOK Guide*).

» Each reference to the recommended reference material should be as precise as possible by identifying what specific chapter or section is relevant.

» A matrix of reference material (to the level of section number) versus topics must be provided.

» A reasonable amount of recommended reference material must be identified for each KA. The following guidelines should be used in determining how much is reasonable:

  i.   If the recommended reference material were written in a coherent manner that followed the proposed breakdown of topics and in a uniform style (for example, in a new book based on the proposed KA description), an average target across all KAs for the number of pages would be 750. However, this target may not be attainable when selecting existing reference material due to differences in style and overlap and redundancy between the selected reference materials.
  ii. In other words, the target for the number of pages for the entire collection of recommended references of the *SWEBOK Guide* is in the range of 10,000 to 15,000 pages.
  iii. Another way of viewing this is that the amount of recommended reference material would be reasonable if it consisted of the study material on this KA for a software engineering licensing exam that a graduate would pass after completing four years of work experience.

h) Additional reference material can be included by the KA Editor in a "Further Readings" list:

» These further readings must be related to the topics in the breakdown rather than, for example, to more advanced topics.

» The list must be annotated (within 1 paragraph per reference) as to why this reference material was included in the list of further readings. Further readings could include: new versions of an existing reference already included in the recommended references, alternative viewpoints on a KA, or a seminal treatment of a KA.

» A general guideline to be followed is 10 or fewer further readings per KA.

» There is no matrix of the reference materials listed in further readings and the breakdown of topics.

i) Criteria and requirements regarding additional references cited in the KA Description:

» The *SWEBOK Guide* is not a research document and its readership will be varied. Therefore, a delicate balance must be maintained between ensuring a high level of readability within the document while maintaining its technical excellence. Additional reference material should therefore only be brought in by the KA Editor if it is necessary to the discussion. Examples are to identify the source of a quotation or to cite reference item in support of a rationale behind a particular and important argument.

COMMON STRUCTURE

KA descriptions should use the following structure:

- Acronyms
- Introduction
- Breakdown of Topics of the KA (including a figure describing the breakdown)
- Matrix of Topics vs. Reference Material
- List of Further Readings
- References

WHAT DO WE MEAN BY "GENERALLY RECOGNIZED KNOWLEDGE"?

The Software Engineering Body of Knowledge is an all-inclusive term that describes the sum of knowledge within the profession of software engineering. However, the *SWEBOK Guide* seeks to identify and describe that subset of the body of knowledge that is generally recognized or, in other words, the core body of knowledge. To better illustrate what "generally recognized" knowledge is relative to other types of knowledge, Figure A.1 proposes a three-category schema for classifying knowledge.

The Project Management Institute in its *Guide to the Project Management Body of Knowledge* defines "generally recognized" knowledge for project management as being:

> that subset of the project management body of knowledge generally recognized as good practice. "Generally recognized" means the knowledge and practices described are applicable to most projects most of the time, and there is consensus about their value and usefulness. "Good practice" means there is general agreement that the application of these skills, tools, and techniques can enhance the chances of success over a wide range of projects. "Good practice" does not mean that the knowledge described should always be applied uniformly to all projects; the organization and/or project management team is responsible for determining what is appropriate for any given project. [1]

"Generally accepted" knowledge could also be viewed as knowledge to be included in the study material of a software engineering licensing exam (in the USA) that a graduate would take after completing four years of work experience. These two definitions should be seen as complementary.

KA Editors are also expected to be somewhat forward looking in their interpretation by taking into consideration not only what is "generally recognized" today and but what they expect will be "generally recognized" in a 3- to 5-year timeframe.

		Generally Recognized Established traditional practices recommended by many organizations
Specialized Practices Used Only for Certain Types of Software		
		Advanced and Research Innovative practices tested and used only by some organizations and concepts still being developed and tested in research organizations

Figure A.1. Categories of Knowledge

LENGTH OF KA DESCRIPTION

KA Descriptions are to be roughly 10 to 20 pages using the formatting template for papers published in conference proceedings of the IEEE Computer Society. This includes text, references, appendices, tables, etc. This, of course, does not include the reference materials themselves.

IMPORTANT RELATED DOCUMENTS

1. *Graduate Software Engineering 2009 (GSwE2009): Curriculum Guidelines for Graduate Degree Programs in Software Engineering*, 2009; www.gswe2009.org. [2]

This document "provides guidelines and recommendations" for defining the curricula of a professional master's level program in software engineering. The *SWEBOK Guide* is identified as a "primary reference" in developing the body of knowledge underlying these guidelines. This document has been officially endorsed by the IEEE Computer Society and sponsored by the Association for Computing Machinery.

2. *IEEE Std. 12207-2008 (a.k.a. ISO/IEC 12207:2008) Standard for Systems and Software Engineering—Software Life Cycle Processes*, IEEE, 2008 [3].

This standard is considered the key standard regarding the definition of life cycle processes and has been adopted by the two main standardization bodies in software engineering: ISO/IEC JTC1/SC7 and the IEEE Computer Society Software

and Systems Engineering Standards Committees. It also has been designated as a pivotal standard by the Software and System Engineering Standards Committee (S2ESC) of the IEEE.

Even though we do not intend that the *Guide to the Software Engineering Body of Knowledge* be fully 12207-conformant, this standard remains a key input to the *SWEBOK Guide*, and special care will be taken throughout the *SWEBOK Guide* regarding the compatibility of the *Guide* with the 12207 standard.

3. J.W. Moore, *The Road Map to Software Engineering: A Standards-Based Guide*, Wiley-IEEE Computer Society Press, 2006. [4*]

This book describes the scope, roles, uses, and development trends of the most widely used software engineering standards. It concentrates on important software engineering activities—quality and project management, system engineering, dependability, and safety. The analysis and regrouping of the standard collections exposes the reader to key relationships between standards.

Even though the *SWEBOK Guide* is not a software engineering standard per se, special care will be taken throughout the document regarding the compatibility of the *Guide* with the current IEEE and ISO/IEC Systems and Software Engineering Standards Collection.

4. *Software Engineering 2004: Curriculum Guidelines for Undergraduate Degree Programs in Software Engineering*, IEEE Computer Society and Association for Computing Machinery, 2004; http://sites.computer.org/ccse/SE2004Volume.pdf. [5]

This document describes curriculum guidelines for an undergraduate degree in software engineering. The *SWEBOK Guide* is identified as being "one of the primary sources" in developing the body of knowledge underlying these guidelines.

5. *ISO/IEC/IEEE 24765:2010 Systems and Software Engineering—Vocabulary*, ISO/IEC/IEEE, 2010; www.computer.org/sevocab. [6]

The hierarchy of references for terminology is *Merriam Webster's Collegiate Dictionary* (11th ed.) [7], IEEE/ISO/IEC 24765 [6], and new proposed definitions if required.

6. "Certification and Training for Software Professionals," IEEE Computer Society, 2013; www.computer.org/certification. [8]

Information on the certification and associated professional development products developed and offered by the IEEE Computer Society for professionals in the field of software engineering can be found on this website. The *SWEBOK Guide* is foundational to these products.

STYLE AND TECHNICAL GUIDELINES

- KA Descriptions should conform to the Word template available at www.computer. org/portal/web/cscps/formatting.
- KA Descriptions are expected to follow the IEEE Computer Society Style Guide (www. computer.org/portal/web/publications/ styleguide).
- Files are to be submitted in Microsoft Word format.
- All citations of reference material are to be produced using EndNote Web as indicated in the instructions provided to KA Editors in this regard.

OTHER DETAILED GUIDELINES

When referencing the *Guide to the Software Engineering Body of Knowledge*, use the title "*SWEBOK Guide.*"

For the purpose of simplicity, avoid footnotes and try to include their content in the main text.

Use explicit references to standards, as opposed to simply inserting numbers referencing items in the bibliography. We believe this approach allows the reader to be better exposed to the source and scope of a standard.

The text accompanying figures and tables should be self-explanatory or have enough related text. This would ensure that the reader knows what the figures and tables mean.

To make sure that some information in the *SWEBOK Guide* does not become rapidly obsolete and due to its generic nature, please avoid directly naming tools and products. Instead, try to name their functions.

EDITING

Editors of the *SWEBOK Guide* as well as professional copy editors will edit KA Descriptions. Editing includes copy editing (grammar, punctuation, and capitalization), style editing (conformance to the Computer Society style guide), and content editing (flow, meaning, clarity, directness, and organization). The final editing will be a collaborative process in which the Editors of the *SWEBOK Guide* and the KA Editors work together to achieve a concise, well-worded, and useful KA Description.

RELEASE OF COPYRIGHT

All intellectual property rights associated with the *SWEBOK Guide* will remain with the IEEE. KA Editors must sign a copyright release form.

It is also understood that the *SWEBOK Guide* will continue to be available free of charge in the public domain in at least one format, provided by the IEEE Computer Society through web technology or by other means.

For more information, see www.computer.org/ copyright.htm.

REFERENCES

[1] Project Management Institute, *A Guide to the Project Management Body of Knowledge (PMBOK(R) Guide)*, 5th ed., Project Management Institute, 2013.

[2] Integrated Software and Systems Engineering Curriculum (iSSEc) Project, *Graduate Software Engineering 2009 (GSwE2009): Curriculum Guidelines for Graduate Degree Programs in Software Engineering*, Stevens Institute of Technology, 2009; www.gswe2009.org.

[3] *IEEE Std. 12207-2008 (a.k.a. ISO/IEC 12207:2008) Standard for Systems and Software Engineering—Software Life Cycle Processes, IEEE, 2008.*

[4*] J.W. Moore, *The Road Map to Software Engineering: A Standards-Based Guide*, Wiley-IEEE Computer Society Press, 2006.

[5] Joint Task Force on Computing Curricula, IEEE Computer Society and Association for Computing Machinery, *Software Engineering 2004: Curriculum Guidelines for Undergraduate Degree Programs in Software Engineering*, 2004; http://sites.computer.org/ccse/SE2004Volume.pdf.

[6] *ISO/IEC/IEEE 24765:2010 Systems and Software Engineering—Vocabulary*, ISO/IEC/IEEE, 2010.

[7] *Merriam-Webster's Collegiate Dictionary*, 11th ed., 2003.

[8] IEEE Computer Society, "Certification and Training for Software Professionals," 2013; www.computer.org/certification.

APPENDIX B

IEEE AND ISO/IEC STANDARDS SUPPORTING THE SOFTWARE ENGINEERING BODY OF KNOWLEDGE (SWEBOK)

Some might say that the supply of software engineering standards far exceeds the demand. One seldom listens to a briefing on the subject without suffering some apparently obligatory joke that there are too many of them. However, the existence of standards takes a very large (possibly infinite) trade space of alternatives and reduces that space to a smaller set of choices—a huge advantage for users. Nevertheless, it can still be difficult to choose from dozens of alternatives, so supplementary guidance, like this appendix, can be helpful. A summary list of the standards mentioned in this appendix appears at the end.

To reduce tedium in reading, a few simplifications and abridgements are made in this appendix:

- ISO/IEC JTC 1/SC 7 maintains nearly two hundred standards on the subject. IEEE maintains about fifty. The two organizations are in the tenth year of a systematic program to coordinate and integrate their collections. In general, this article will focus on the standards that are recognized by both organizations, taking this condition as evidence that wide agreement has been obtained. Other standards will be mentioned briefly.
- Standards tend to have long, taxonomical titles. If there were a single standard for building an automobile, the one for your Camry probably would be titled something like, "Vehicle, internal combustion, four-wheel, passenger, sedan." Also, modern standards organizations provide their standards from databases. Like any database, these sometimes contain errors, particularly for the titles. So this article will often paraphrase the title of the standard or simply use its number. In obtaining a standard of interest, the reader should rely on the number, not the title, given in this article. For reasons of consistency, the article will use the IEEE's convention for the capitalization of titles—nouns, pronouns, adjectives, verbs, adverbs, and first and last words have an initial capital letter—despite the fact that IEEE and ISO/IEC use differing conventions.

- Because these standards are being continually revised to take account of new technologies and usage patterns, this article will be obsolescent before it is published. Therefore, it will occasionally discuss standards that have not yet been published, if they are likely to assume significant importance.
- Explicit trademarks are omitted. Suffice it to say that IEEE places a trademark on all of its standards' designations.

There are some other conventions of interest:

- In both IEEE and ISO/IEC, standards for *systems* engineering are maintained by the same committee as those for *software* engineering. Many of the standards apply to both. So, instead of making fine distinctions, this article will deal with both.
- On the other hand, both S2ESC and SC 7 (see below for descriptions of these organizations) are responsible for standards that don't qualify as "engineering." In the US and many other countries, the services of a licensed engineer are required when a product might affect public safety, health,

and welfare as opposed to affecting merely the pocketbook of the client. This appendix will respect that distinction and ignore standards that appear to be merely economic in consequence.

- User documentation is assumed to be developed similarly to software. For example, a standard concerning the design of user documentation is described in the Software Design KA.
- Some jointly developed standards are explicitly labeled as joint developments, e.g., ISO/IEC/IEEE 24765. In other cases, the standards have different designations in the two organizations. Examples include

  » IEEE Std. 12207:2008 (a.k.a. ISO/IEC 12207:2008), where "a.k.a." ("also known as") is this appendix's abbreviation to note the designation in the other organization;

  » IEEE Std. 15939:2008 Standard Adoption of ISO/IEC 15939:2007, an adoption by IEEE of a standard developed in ISO/IEC;

  » IEEE Std. 1220:2005 (a.k.a. ISO/IEC 26702:2007), a "fast-track" by ISO/IEC of a standard developed in IEEE.

In each of these cases, the standards are substantively identical in the two organizations, differing only in front matter and, occasionally, added informational material.

A summary list of all of the mentioned standards is provided at the end of this appendix.

ISO/IEC JTC 1/SC 7, SOFTWARE AND SYSTEMS ENGINEERING

ISO/IEC JTC 1/SC 7 is the major source of international standards on software and systems engineering. Its name is formed taxonomically. Joint Technical Committee 1 (JTC 1) is a child of the International Organization for Standardization (ISO) and the International Electrotechnical Commission (IEC); it has the scope of "information technology" and subdivides its work among a number of subcommittees; Subcommittee 7 (SC 7) is the one responsible for software and systems engineering. SC 7, and its working groups, meets twice a year, attracting delegations representing the national standards bodies of participating nations. Each nation follows its own procedures for determining national positions and each nation has the responsibility of determining whether an ISO/IEC standard should be adopted as a national standard.

SC 7 creates three types of documents:

- International Standards: Documents containing requirements that must be satisfied in order to claim conformance.
- Technical Specifications (formerly called Technical Reports, type 1 and type 2): Documents published in a preliminary manner while work continues.
- Technical Reports (formerly called Technical Reports, type 3): Documents inherently unsuited to be standards, usually because they are descriptive rather than prescriptive.

The key thing to remember is that only the first category counts as a consensus standard. The reader can easily recognize the others by the suffix TS or TR prepended to the number of the document.

IEEE SOFTWARE AND SYSTEMS ENGINEERING STANDARDS COMMITTEE (S2ESC)

IEEE is the world's largest organization of technical professionals, with about 400,000 members in more than 160 countries. The publication of standards is performed by the IEEE Standards Association (IEEE-SA), but the committees that draft and sponsor the standards are in the various IEEE societies; S2ESC is a part of the IEEE Computer Society. IEEE is a global standards maker because its standards are used in many different countries. Despite its international membership (about 50% non-US), though, the IEEE-SA routinely submits its standards to the American National Standards Institute (ANSI) for endorsement as "American National Standards." Some S2ESC standards are developed within S2ESC, some are developed jointly with SC 7, and some are adopted after being developed by SC 7.

IEEE-SA publishes three types of "standards":

- Standards, with a preponderance of the verb "shall"
- Recommended Practices, with a preponderance of the verb "should"
- Guides, with a preponderance of the verb "may."

All three of these compare to ISO/IEC standards. IEEE-SA does have the concept of a "Trial-Use" standard, which is roughly comparable to an ISO/IEC Technical Specification. However, it has nothing comparable to an ISO/IEC Technical Report; one would look elsewhere in IEEE for documents of this ilk.

THE STANDARDS

The remainder of this article allocates the selected standards to relevant knowledge areas (KAs) of the *SWEBOK Guide*. There is a section for each KA. Within each section, the relevant standards are listed—the ones that principally apply to the KA as well as others that principally apply to other KAs but which are also related to the current one. Following each standard is a brief summary. In most cases, the summary is a quotation or paraphrase of the abstract or other introductory material from the text of the standard.

Most of the standards easily fit into one KA. Some fit into more than one; in such cases, a cross-reference is provided. Two standards apply to all KAs, so they are listed in a category called "General." All of the standards related to computer-aided software engineering (CASE) tools and environments are listed in the Software Engineering Models and Methods KA section.

GENERAL

The first two standards are so central that they could be slotted into all of the KAs. Two more are described in the Software Engineering Process KA, but are mentioned here because they provide a helpful framework and because the descriptions of several other standards refer to them.

ISO/IEC TR 19759 is the *SWEBOK Guide* itself. It's not an IEEE standard because, lacking prescriptive verbs, it doesn't satisfy the criteria for any of the IEEE categories. In ISO/IEC, it is a "technical report"—defined as a document inherently unsuited to be a standard. The 2004 IEEE *SWEBOK Guide* was adopted by ISO/IEC without change. Presumably, ISO/IEC will adopt Version 3 of the *SWEBOK Guide*.

ISO/IEC TR 19759:2005 Software Engineering— *Guide to the Software Engineering Body of Knowledge* (SWEBOK)

Applies to all KAs

ISO/IEC 19759:2005, a *Guide to the Software Engineering Body of Knowledge (SWEBOK)*, identifies and describes that subset of the body of knowledge that is generally accepted, even though software engineers must be knowledgeable not only in software engineering, but also, of course, in other related disciplines. SWEBOK is an all-inclusive term that describes the sum of knowledge within the profession of software engineering.

The text of the *SWEBOK Guide* is freely available at www.swebok.org/. The ISO/IEC adoption of the *Guide* is freely available at http://standards.iso.org/ittf/PubliclyAvailableStandards/index.html.

ISO/IEC/IEEE 24765 provides a shared vocabulary for the systems and software engineering standards of both SC 7 and S2ESC.

ISO/IEC/IEEE 24765:2010 Systems and Software Engineering—Vocabulary

Applies to all KAs

ISO/IEC/IEEE 24765:2010 provides a common vocabulary applicable to all systems and software engineering work. It was prepared to collect and support the standardization of terminology. ISO/IEC/IEEE 24765:2010 is intended to serve as a useful reference for those in the information technology field and to encourage the use of systems and software engineering standards prepared by ISO and liaison organizations IEEE Computer Society and Project Management Institute. ISO/IEC/IEEE 24765:2010 includes references to the active source standards for each definition so that the use of the term can be further explored.

The vocabulary is descriptive, rather than prescriptive; it gathers up all of the definitions from all of the relevant standards, as well as a few other sources, rather than choosing among competing definitions.

The content of the 24765 standard is freely accessible online at www.computer.org/sevocab.

Two standards, 12207 and 15288, provide a complete set of processes for the entire life cycle of a system or a software product. The two standards are aligned for concurrent use on a single project or in a single organization. They are mentioned here because they are often used as a framework for explaining or localizing the role of other standards in the life cycle.

IEEE Std. 12207-2008 (a.k.a. ISO/IEC 12207:2008) Standard for Systems and Software Engineering— Software Life Cycle Processes
    See Software Engineering Process KA

IEEE Std. 15288-2008 (a.k.a. ISO/IEC 15288:2008) Standard for Systems and Software Engineering— System Life Cycle Processes
    See Software Engineering Process KA

SOFTWARE REQUIREMENTS

The primary standard for software and systems requirements engineering is a new one that replaced several existing IEEE standards. It provides a broad view of requirements engineering across the entire life cycle.

ISO/IEC/IEEE 29148:2011 Systems and Software Engineering—Life Cycle Processes—Requirements Engineering

ISO/IEC/IEEE 29148:2011 contains provisions for the processes and products related to the engineering of requirements for systems and software products and services throughout the life cycle.

It defines the construct of a good requirement, provides attributes and characteristics of requirements, and discusses the iterative and recursive application of requirements processes throughout the life cycle. ISO/IEC/IEEE 29148:2011 provides additional guidance in the application of requirements engineering and management processes for requirements-related activities in ISO/IEC 12207:2008 and ISO/IEC 15288:2008. Information items applicable to the engineering of requirements and their content are defined. The content of ISO/IEC/IEEE 29148:2011 can be added to the existing set of requirements-related life cycle processes defined by ISO/IEC 12207:2008 or ISO/IEC 15288:2008, or it can be used independently.

A multipart ISO/IEC standard provides principles and methods for "sizing" software based on its requirements. The functional size is often useful in the denominator of measurements of quality and productivity in software development. It may also play a role in contracting for service-level agreements.

ISO/IEC 14143 [six parts] Information Technology—Software Measurement—Functional Size Measurement

ISO/IEC 14143 describes FSM (functional size measurement). The concepts of functional size measurement (FSM) are designed to overcome the limitations of earlier methods of sizing software by shifting the focus away from measuring how the software is implemented to measuring size in terms of the functions required by the user.

FSM is often known as "function point counting." The four standards listed below are alternative methods for function point counting—all meet the requirements of ISO/IEC 14143. The dominant method, in terms of market share, is the IFPUG method, described in ISO/IEC 20926. Other methods are variations intended to improve the validity of the count in various circumstances. For example, ISO/IEC 19761—COSMIC is notably intended to be used on software with a real-time component.

ISO/IEC 19761:2011 Software Engineering—COSMIC: A Functional Size Measurement Method

ISO/IEC 20926:2009 Software and Systems Engineering—Software Measurement—IFPUG Functional Size Measurement Method

ISO/IEC 20968:2002 Software Engineering—Mk II Function Point Analysis—Counting Practices Manual

ISO/IEC 24570:2005 Software Engineering—NESMA Functional Size Measurement Method Version 2.1—Definitions and Counting Guidelines for the Application of Function Point Analysis

---

Sometimes requirements are described in natural language, but sometimes they are described in formal or semiformal notations. The objective of the Unified Modeling Language (UML) is to provide system architects, software engineers, and software developers with tools for analysis, design, and implementation of software-based systems as well as for modeling business and similar processes. The two parts of ISO/IEC 19505 define UML, revision 2. The older ISO/IEC 19501 is an earlier version of UML. They are mentioned here because they are often used to model requirements.

ISO/IEC 19501:2005 Information Technology—Open Distributed Processing—Unified Modeling Language (UML) Version 1.4.2
　　　　See Software Engineering Models and
　　　　　　　　　　　　　　　　　Methods KA

ISO/IEC 19505:2012 [two parts] Information Technology—Object Management Group Unified Modeling Language (OMG UML)
　　　　See Software Engineering Models and
　　　　　　　　　　　　　　　　　Methods KA

SOFTWARE DESIGN

The software design KA includes both software architectural design (for determining the relationships among the items of the software and detailed design (for describing the individual items). ISO/IEC/IEEE 42010 concerns the description of architecture for systems and software.

ISO/IEC/IEEE 42010:2011 Systems and Software Engineering—Architecture Description

ISO/IEC/IEEE 42010:2011 addresses the creation, analysis, and sustainment of architectures of systems through the use of architecture descriptions. A conceptual model of architecture description is established. The required contents of an architecture description are specified. Architecture viewpoints, architecture frameworks and architecture description languages are introduced for codifying conventions and common practices of architecture description. The required content of architecture viewpoints, architecture frameworks and architecture description languages is specified. Annexes provide the motivation and background for key concepts and terminology and examples of applying ISO/IEC/IEEE 42010:2011.

Like ISO/IEC/IEEE 42010, the next standard treats software "design" as an abstraction, independent of its representation in a document. Accordingly, the standard places provisions on the description of design, rather than on design itself.

IEEE Std. 1016-2009 Standard for Information Technology—Systems Design—Software Design Descriptions

This standard describes software designs and establishes the information content and organization of a software design description (SDD). An SDD is a representation of a software design to be used for recording design information and communicating that design information to key design stakeholders. This standard is intended for use in design situations in which an explicit software design description is to be prepared. These situations include traditional software construction activities (when design leads to code) and reverse engineering situations (when a design description is recovered from an existing implementation). This standard can be applied to commercial, scientific, or military software that runs on digital computers. Applicability is not restricted by the size, complexity, or criticality of the software. This standard can be applied to the description of high-level and detailed designs. This standard does not prescribe specific methodologies for design, configuration management, or quality assurance. This standard does not require the use of any particular design languages, but establishes requirements on the selection of design languages for use in an SDD. This standard can be applied to the preparation of SDDs captured as paper documents, automated databases, software development tools, or other media.

By convention, this appendix treats user documentation as a part of a software system. Therefore, the various aspects of user documentation—its design, its testing, and so forth—are allocated to different KAs. The next standard deals with the design of user documentation.

IEEE Std. 26514-2010 Standard Adoption of ISO/IEC 26514:2008 Systems and Software Engineering—Requirements for Designers and Developers of User Documentation

This standard provides requirements for the design and development of software user documentation as part of the life cycle processes. It defines the documentation process from the viewpoint of the documentation developer and also covers the documentation product. It specifies the structure, content, and format for user documentation and also provides informative guidance for user documentation style. It is independent of the software tools that may be used to produce documentation and applies to both printed documentation and onscreen documentation. Much of this

standard is also applicable to user documentation for systems including hardware.

SOFTWARE CONSTRUCTION

The term "software construction" refers to the detailed creation of working, meaningful software through a combination of coding, verification, unit testing, integration testing, and debugging.

There are few standards on the details of software coding. It has been found through (mostly bad) experience that coding conventions are not appropriate for standardization because, in most cases, the real benefit comes from the consistency of applying an arbitrary convention rather than the convention itself. So, although coding conventions are a good idea, it is generally left to the organization or the project to develop such a standard.

Nevertheless, the subject of secure coding has attracted attention in recent years because some coding idioms are insecure in the face of attack. A Technical Report prepared by ISO/IEC JTC 1/SC 22 (programming languages) describes vulnerabilities in programming languages and how they can be avoided.

ISO/IEC TR 24772:2013 Information Technology—Programming Languages—Guidance to Avoiding Vulnerabilities in Programming Languages through Language Selection and Use

ISO/IEC TR 24772:2013 specifies software programming language vulnerabilities to be avoided in the development of systems where assured behavior is required for security, safety, mission-critical, and business-critical software. In general, this guidance is applicable to the software developed, reviewed, or maintained for any application.

Vulnerabilities are described in a generic manner that is applicable to a broad range of programming languages. Annexes relate the generic guidance to a selection of specific programming languages.

The Technical Report is freely available at http://standards.iso.org/ittf/PubliclyAvailableStandards/index.html.

Two standards are mentioned here because unit testing is often regarded as an activity of software construction. IEEE and ISO/IEC are cooperating in the development of a four-part joint standard, 29119, that will provide a comprehensive treatment of testing and supplant IEEE Std. 1008.

IEEE Std. 1008-1987 Standard for Software Unit Testing
                              See Software Testing KA

ISO/IEC/IEEE 29119 [four parts] (Draft) Software and Systems Engineering—Software Testing
                              See Software Testing KA

The next standard provides for the development of user documentation during an agile development process. It is mentioned here because agile development is sometimes regarded as construction.

ISO/IEC/IEEE 26515:2012 Systems and Software Engineering—Developing User Documentation in an Agile Environment
                              See Software Engineering Models and
                                              Methods KA

Coding is not the only way to create a software product. Often code (as well as requirements and design) is reused from previous projects or engineered for reuse in future projects. IEEE Std. 1517 is mentioned here because it provides a common framework for extending the system and software life cycle processes of IEEE Std. 12207:2008 to include the systematic practice of reuse.

IEEE Std. 1517-2010 Standard for Information Technology—System and Software Life Cycle Processes—Reuse Processes
                              See Software Engineering Process KA

SOFTWARE TESTING

Oddly, there are few standards for testing. IEEE Std. 829 is the most comprehensive.

IEEE Std. 829-2008 Standard for Software and System Test Documentation

Test processes determine whether the development products of a given activity conform to the requirements of that activity and whether the system and/or software satisfies its intended use and user needs. Testing process tasks are specified for different integrity levels. These process tasks determine the appropriate breadth and depth of test documentation. The documentation elements for each type of test documentation can then be selected. The scope of testing encompasses software-based systems, computer software, hardware, and their interfaces. This standard applies to software-based systems being developed, maintained, or reused (legacy, commercial off-the-shelf, nondevelopmental items). The term "software" also includes firmware, microcode, and documentation. Test processes can include inspection, analysis, demonstration, verification, and validation of software and software-based system products.

IEEE Std. 1008 focuses on unit testing.

IEEE Std. 1008-1987 Standard for Software Unit Testing

The primary objective is to specify a standard approach to software unit testing that can be used as a basis for sound software engineering practice. A second objective is to describe the software engineering concepts and testing assumptions on which the standard approach is based. A third objective is to provide guidance and resource information to assist with the implementation and usage of the standard unit testing approach.

IEEE and ISO/IEC JTC 1/SC 7 are cooperating in a project to develop a single comprehensive standard that covers all aspects of testing. One can hope for publication of the four-part standard by 2014. Portions of the content remain controversial. One taxonomical issue is whether "static methods"—such as inspection, review, and static analysis—should fall within the scope of "testing" or should be distinguished as "verification and validation." Although the resolution of the issue is probably of little importance to users of the standard, it assumes great importance to the standards-writers who must manage an integrated suite of interoperating standards.

ISO/IEC/IEEE 29119 [four parts] (Draft) Software and Systems Engineering—Software Testing

The purpose of ISO/IEC 29119 Software Testing is to define an internationally agreed standard for software testing that can be used by any organization when performing any form of software testing.

Testing of user documentation is described in the next standard, providing requirements for the test and review of software user documentation as part of the life cycle processes. It defines the documentation process from the viewpoint of the documentation tester and reviewer. It is relevant to roles involved in testing and development of software and user documentation, including project managers, usability experts, and information developers in addition to testers and reviewers.

IEEE Std. 26513-2010 Standard Adoption of ISO/IEC 26513:2009 Systems and Software Engineering—Requirements for Testers and Reviewers of Documentation

ISO/IEC 26513 provides the minimum requirements for the testing and reviewing of user documentation, including both printed and onscreen documents used in the work environment by the users of systems software. It applies to printed user manuals, online help, tutorials, and user reference documentation.

It specifies processes for use in testing and reviewing of user documentation. It is not limited to the test and review phase of the life cycle, but includes activities throughout the information management and documentation management processes.

Two standards are mentioned here because some sources consider software verification and validation to be taxonomically included in testing.

IEEE Std. 1012-2012 Standard for System and Software Verification and Validation
> See Software Quality KA

IEEE Std. 1044-2009 Standard for Classification for Software Anomalies
> See Software Quality KA

SOFTWARE MAINTENANCE

This standard—the result of harmonizing distinct IEEE and ISO/IEC standards on the subject—describes a single comprehensive process for the management and execution of software maintenance. It expands on the provisions of the software maintenance process provided in ISO/IEC/IEEE 12207.

IEEE Std. 14764-2006 (a.k.a. ISO/IEC 14764:2006) Standard for Software Engineering—Software Life Cycle Processes—Maintenance

ISO/IEC 14764:2006 describes in greater detail management of the maintenance process described in ISO/IEC 12207, including amendments. It also establishes definitions for the various types of maintenance. ISO/IEC 14764:2006 provides guidance that applies to planning, execution and control, review and evaluation, and closure of the maintenance process. The scope of ISO/IEC 14764:2006 includes maintenance for multiple software products with the same maintenance resources. "Maintenance" in ISO/IEC 14764:2006 means software maintenance unless otherwise stated.

ISO/IEC 14764:2006 provides the framework within which generic and specific software maintenance plans may be executed, evaluated, and tailored to the maintenance scope and magnitude of given software products. It provides the framework, precise terminology, and processes to allow the consistent application of technology (tools, techniques, and methods) to software maintenance.

It does not address the operation of software and the operational functions, e.g., backup, recovery, and system administration, which are normally performed by those who operate the software.

ISO/IEC 14764:2006 is written primarily for maintainers of software and additionally for those responsible for development and quality assurance. It may also be used by acquirers and users of systems containing software, who may provide inputs to the maintenance plan.

SOFTWARE CONFIGURATION MANAGEMENT

There is one standard for configuration management.

IEEE Std. 828-2012 Standard for Configuration Management in Systems and Software Engineering

This standard establishes the minimum requirements for processes for configuration management (CM) in systems and software engineering. The application of this standard applies to any form, class, or type of software or system. This revision of the standard expands the previous version to explain CM, including identifying and acquiring configuration items, controlling changes, reporting the status of configuration items, as well as software builds and release engineering. Its predecessor defined only the contents of a software configuration management plan. This standard addresses what CM activities are to be done, when they are to happen in the life cycle, and what planning and resources are required. It also describes the content areas for a CM plan. The standard supports ISO/IEC/IEEE 12207:2008 and ISO/IEC/IEEE 15288:2008 and adheres to the terminology

in ISO/IEC/IEEE Std. 24765 and the information item requirements of IEEE Std. 15939.

ISO/IEC JTC 1/SC 7 has not yet determined what action it should take regarding the new IEEE Std. 828. There are issues concerning the extent of compatibility with ISO/IEC/IEEE 12207 and other standards in the SC 7 suite. It should be noted, though, that SC 7 does not have a competing standard.

SOFTWARE ENGINEERING MANAGEMENT

Most readers will interpret the phrase "software engineering management" to mean the management of a *project* that concerns software. There are at least two possible extensions to this generalization, though. Some software activities are managed according to a service-level agreement (SLA). SLAs do not meet the criteria for "project" according to some definitions. Also, it has become generally agreed that some management of software should occur in the organization at a level above the project, so that all projects can benefit from a common investment. A commonly cited example is the provision of software processes and tooling by the organization.

Software project management can be regarded as a specialization of "project management"—often regarded as a distinct discipline. The Project Management Institute's *Guide to the Project Management Body of Knowledge (PMBOK® Guide)* is often regarded as the authoritative source for this knowledge. From time to time, IEEE adopts the most recent version of the *PMBOK® Guide* as an IEEE standard.

IEEE Std. 1490-2011 Guide—Adoption of the Project Management Institute (PMI®) Standard, A Guide to the Project Management Body of Knowledge (PMBOK® Guide)—Fourth Edition

The *PMBOK® Guide* identifies that subset of the project management body of knowledge generally recognized as good practice. "Generally recognized" means the knowledge and practices described are applicable to most projects most of the time and there is consensus about their value and usefulness. "Good practice" means there is general agreement that the application of these skills, tools, and techniques can enhance the chances of success over a wide range of projects. Good practice does not mean the knowledge described should always be applied uniformly to all projects; the organization and/or project management team is responsible for determining what is appropriate for any given project. The *PMBOK® Guide* also provides and promotes a common vocabulary within the project management profession for discussing, writing, and applying project management concepts. Such a standard vocabulary is an essential element of a professional discipline. The Project Management Institute (PMI) views this standard as a foundational project management reference for its professional development programs and certifications.

The 2008 revisions of ISO/IEC/IEEE 12207 and 15288 provide project management processes for software and systems and relate them to organization-level processes as well as technical processes. The jointly developed 16326 standard, replacing two older standards, expands those provisions with guidance for application.

ISO/IEC/IEEE 16326:2009 Systems and Software Engineering—Life Cycle Processes—Project Management

ISO/IEC/IEEE 16326:2009 provides normative content specifications for project management plans covering software projects and software-intensive system projects. It also provides detailed discussion and advice on applying a set of project processes that are common to both the software and system life cycle as covered by ISO/IEC 12207:2008 (IEEE Std. 12207-2008) and ISO/IEC 15288:2008 (IEEE Std. 15288-2008), respectively. The discussion and advice are intended to aid in the preparation of the normative content of project management plans. ISO/IEC/IEEE 16326:2009 is the result of the harmonization of ISO/IEC TR 16326:1999 and IEEE Std. 1058-1998.

Particularly in high-technology applications and high-consequence projects, the management of risk is an important aspect of the overall project management responsibilities. This standard deals with that subject.

IEEE Std. 16085-2006 (a.k.a. ISO/IEC 16085:2006) Standard for Systems and Software Engineering—Software Life Cycle Processes—Risk Management

ISO/IEC 16085:2006 defines a process for the management of risk in the life cycle. It can be added to the existing set of system and software life cycle processes defined by ISO/IEC 15288 and ISO/IEC 12207, or it can be used independently.

ISO/IEC 16085:2006 can be applied equally to systems and software.

The purpose of risk management is to identify potential managerial and technical problems before they occur so that actions can be taken that reduce or eliminate the probability and/or impact of these problems should they occur. It is a critical tool for continuously determining the feasibility of project plans, for improving the search for and identification of potential problems that can affect life cycle activities and the quality and performance of products, and for improving the active management of projects.

The analysis of risk and risk mitigation depends crucially upon measurement. This international standard provides an elaboration of the measurement process from ISO/IEC/IEEE 15288:2008 and ISO/IEC/IEEE 12207:2008.

IEEE Std. 15939-2008 Standard Adoption of ISO/IEC 15939:2007 Systems and Software Engineering—Measurement Process

ISO/IEC 15939 defines a measurement process applicable to system and software engineering and management disciplines. The process is described through a model that defines the activities of the measurement process that are required to adequately specify what measurement information is required, how the measures and analysis results are to be applied, and how to determine if the analysis results are valid. The measurement process is flexible, tailorable, and adaptable to the needs of different users.

ISO/IEC 15939:2007 identifies a process that supports defining a suitable set of measures that address specific information needs. It identifies the activities and tasks that are necessary to successfully identify, define, select, apply, and improve measurement within an overall project or organizational measurement structure. It also provides definitions for measurement terms commonly used within the system and software industries.

Software projects often require the development of user documentation. Management of the project, therefore, includes management of the documentation effort.

ISO/IEC/IEEE 26511:2012 Systems and Software Engineering—Requirements for Managers of User Documentation

ISO/IEC/IEEE 26511:2012 specifies procedures for managing user documentation throughout the software life cycle. It applies to people or organizations producing suites of documentation, to those undertaking a single documentation project, and to documentation produced internally, as well as to documentation contracted to outside service organizations. It provides an overview of the software documentation and information management processes, and also presents aspects of portfolio planning and content management that user documentation managers apply. It covers management activities in starting a project, including setting up procedures and specifications, establishing infrastructure, and building a team. It includes examples of roles needed on a user documentation team. It addresses measurements and estimates needed for management control, and the use of supporting processes such as change management, schedule and cost control, resource management, and quality management and process improvement. It includes requirements for key documents produced for user documentation management, including documentation plans and documentation management plans. ISO/IEC/IEEE 26511:2012 is independent of the software tools that may be used

to produce or manage documentation, and applies to both printed documentation and onscreen documentation. Much of its guidance is applicable to user documentation for systems including hardware as well as software.

Sometimes software or system components are acquired rather than developed.

IEEE Std. 1062-1998 Recommended Practice for Software Acquisition

A set of useful quality practices that can be selected and applied during one or more steps in a software acquisition process is described. This recommended practice can be applied to software that runs on any computer system regardless of the size, complexity, or criticality of the software, but is more suited for use on modified-off-the-shelf software and fully developed software.

Sometimes user documentation is acquired regardless of whether the software it describes was acquired. The following standard deals with that subject.

ISO/IEC/IEEE 26512:2011 Systems and Software Engineering—Requirements for Acquirers and Suppliers of User Documentation

ISO/IEC/IEEE 26512:2011 was developed to assist users of ISO/IEC/IEEE 15288:2008 or ISO/IEC/IEEE 12207:2008 to acquire or supply software user documentation as part of the software life cycle processes. It defines the documentation process from the acquirer's standpoint and the supplier's standpoint. ISO/IEC/IEEE 26512:2011 covers the requirements for information items used in the acquisition of user documentation products: the acquisition plan, document specification, statement of work, request for proposals, and proposal. It provides an overview of the software user documentation and information management processes which may require acquisition and supply of software user documentation products and services. It addresses the preparation of requirements for software user documentation. These requirements are central to the user documentation specification and statement of work. It includes requirements for primary document outputs of the acquisition and supply process: the request for proposal and the proposal for user documentation products and services. It also discusses the use of a documentation management plan and a document plan as they arise in the acquisition and supply processes. ISO/IEC/IEEE 26512:2011 is independent of the software tools that may be used to produce documentation and applies to both printed documentation and onscreen documentation. Much of its guidance is applicable to user documentation for systems including hardware as well as software.

The next two standards are mentioned here because they supply information used in management decision-making.

IEEE Std. 1028-2008 Standard for Software Reviews and Audits
> See Software Quality KA

IEEE Std. 1061-1998 Standard for Software Quality Metrics Methodology
> See Software Quality KA

The next standard is mentioned because it includes the manager's role in developing user documentation in an agile project.

ISO/IEC/IEEE 26515:2012 Systems and Software Engineering—Developing User Documentation in an Agile Environment
> See Software Engineering Models and
> Methods KA

SOFTWARE ENGINEERING PROCESS

Software and systems engineering processes are central to the standardization of those two disciplines—not just because many are interested in process improvement, but also because processes are effective for the description of improved practices. For example, one might propose an improved practice for software requirements analysis. A naïve treatment might relate the description to an early stage of the life cycle model. A superior approach is to describe the practice in the context of a process that can be applied at any stage of the life cycle. The requirements analysis process, for example, is necessary for the development stage, for maintenance, and often for retirement, so an improved practice described in terms of the requirements analysis process can be applied to any of those stages.

The two key standards are ISO/IEC/IEEE 12207, *Software Life Cycle Processes*, and ISO/IEC/IEEE 15288, *System Life Cycle Processes*. The two standards have distinct histories, but they were both revised in 2008 to align their processes, permitting their interoperable use across a wide spectrum of projects ranging from a standalone software component to a system with negligible software content. Both are being revised again with the intent of containing an identical list of processes, but with provisions specialized for the respective disciplines.

IEEE Std. 12207-2008 (a.k.a. ISO/IEC 12207:2008) Standard for Systems and Software Engineering—Software Life Cycle Processes

ISO/IEC 12207:2008 establishes a common framework for software life cycle processes, with well-defined terminology that can be referenced by the software industry.

ISO/IEC 12207:2008 applies to the acquisition of systems and software products and services and to the supply, development, operation, maintenance, and disposal of software products and the software portion of a system, whether performed internally or externally to an organization. Those aspects of system definition needed to provide the context for software products and services are included.

ISO/IEC 12207:2008 also provides a process that can be employed for defining, controlling, and improving software life cycle processes.

The processes, activities and tasks of ISO/IEC 12207:2008—either alone or in conjunction with ISO/IEC 15288—may also be applied during the acquisition of a system that contains software.

IEEE Std. 15288-2008 (a.k.a. ISO/IEC 15288:2008) Standard for Systems and Software Engineering— System Life Cycle Processes

ISO/IEC 15288:2008 establishes a common framework for describing the life cycle of systems created by humans. It defines a set of processes and associated terminology. These processes can be applied at any level in the hierarchy of a system's structure. Selected sets of these processes can be applied throughout the life cycle for managing and performing the stages of a system's life cycle. This is accomplished through the involvement of all interested parties, with the ultimate goal of achieving customer satisfaction.

ISO/IEC 15288:2008 also provides processes that support the definition, control, and improvement of the life cycle processes used within an organization or a project. Organizations and projects can use these life cycle processes when acquiring and supplying systems.

ISO/IEC 15288:2008 concerns those systems that are man-made and may be configured with one or more of the following: hardware, software, data, humans, processes (e.g., processes for providing service to users), procedures (e.g., operator instructions), facilities, materials, and naturally occurring entities. When a system element is software, the software life cycle processes documented in ISO/IEC 12207:2008 may be used to implement that system element.

ISO/IEC 15288:2008 and ISO/IEC 12207:2008 are harmonized for concurrent use on a single project or in a single organization.

Those two standards specify that processes may produce items of information but do not prescribe their content or format. The next standard provides help with that.

ISO/IEC/IEEE 15289:2011 Systems and Software Engineering—Content of Life-Cycle Information Products (Documentation)

ISO/IEC/IEEE 15289:2011 provides requirements for identifying and planning the specific information items (information products, documentation) to be developed and revised during systems and software life cycles and service management processes. It specifies the purpose and content of all identified systems and software data records and life cycle information items, as well as records and information items for information technology service management. The information item contents are defined according to generic document types (description, plan, policy, procedure, report, request, and specification) and the specific purpose of the document. For simplicity of reference, each information item is described as if it were published as a separate document. However, information items may be unpublished but available in a repository for reference, divided into separate documents or volumes, or combined with other information items into one document. ISO/IEC/IEEE 15289:2011 is based on the life cycle processes specified in ISO/IEC 12207:2008 (IEEE Std. 12207-2008) and ISO/IEC 15288:2008 (IEEE Std. 15288-2008), and the service management processes specified in ISO/IEC 20000-1:2005 and ISO/IEC 20000-2:2005.

The next two guides provide supplementary information helpful in applying 12207 and 15288.

IEEE Std. 24748.2-2012 Guide—Adoption of ISO/IEC TR 24748-2:2011 Systems and Software Engineering—Life Cycle Management—Part 2: Guide to the Application of ISO/IEC 15288 (System Life Cycle Processes)

ISO/IEC TR 24748-2 is a guide for the application of ISO/IEC 15288:2008. It addresses system, life cycle, process, organizational, project, and adaptation concepts, principally through reference to ISO/IEC TR 24748-1 and ISO/IEC 15288:2008. It then gives guidance on applying ISO/IEC 15288:2008 from the aspects of strategy, planning, application in organizations, and application on projects.

IEEE Std. 24748.3-2012 Guide—Adoption of ISO/IEC TR 24748-3:2011 Systems and Software

Engineering—Life Cycle Management—Part 3: Guide to the Application of ISO/IEC 12207 (Software Life Cycle Processes)

ISO/IEC TR 24748-3 is a guide for the application of ISO/IEC 12207:2008. It addresses system, life cycle, process, organizational, project, and adaptation concepts, principally through reference to ISO/IEC TR 24748-1 and ISO/IEC 12207:2008. It gives guidance on applying ISO/IEC 12207:2008 from the aspects of strategy, planning, application in organizations, and application on projects.

The 12207 and 15288 standards provide processes covering the life cycle, but they do not provide a standard life cycle model (waterfall, incremental delivery, prototype-driven, etc). Selecting an appropriate life cycle model for a project is a major concern of ISO/IEC 24748-1.

IEEE Std. 24748.1-2011 Guide—Adoption of ISO/IEC TR 24748-1:2010 Systems and Software Engineering—Life Cycle Management—Part 1: Guide for Life Cycle Management

ISO/IEC TR 24748-1 provides information on life cycle concepts and descriptions of the purposes and outcomes of representative life cycle stages. It also illustrates the use of a life cycle model for systems in the context of ISO/IEC 15288 and provides a corresponding illustration of the use of a life cycle model for software in the context of ISO/IEC 12207. ISO/IEC TR 24748-1 additionally provides detailed discussion and advice on adapting a life cycle model for use in a specific project and organizational environment. It further provides guidance on life cycle model use by domains, disciplines and specialties. ISO/IEC TR 24748-1 gives a detailed comparison between prior and current versions of ISO/IEC 12207 and ISO/IEC 15288 as well as advice on transitioning from prior to current versions and on using their application guides. The discussion and advice are intended to provide a reference model for life cycle models, facilitate use of the updated ISO/IEC 15288 and ISO/IEC 12207, and provide a framework for the development of

updated application guides for those International Standards. ISO/IEC TR 24748-1 is a result of the alignment stage of the harmonization of ISO/IEC 12207 and ISO/IEC 15288.

The next standard extends the provisions of ISO/IEC/IEEE 12207 to deal with systematic software reuse.

IEEE Std. 1517-2010 Standard for Information Technology—System and Software Life Cycle Processes—Reuse Processes

A common framework for extending the system and software life cycle processes of IEEE Std. 12207:2008 to include the systematic practice of reuse is provided. The processes, activities, and tasks to be applied during each life cycle process to enable a system and/or product to be constructed from reusable assets are specified. The processes, activities, and tasks to enable the identification, construction, maintenance, and management of assets supplied are also specified.

IEEE Std. 1220 has been widely applied as a systems engineering process and was adopted by ISO/IEC with the number 26702. Unfortunately, the standard is not completely compatible with ISO/IEC/IEEE 15288 and is being revised to solve that problem. The result will be published as ISO/IEC/IEEE 24748-4.

IEEE Std. 1220-2005 (a.k.a. ISO/IEC 26702:2007) Standard for Application and Management of the Systems Engineering Process

ISO/IEC 26702 defines the interdisciplinary tasks which are required throughout a system's life cycle to transform customer needs, requirements, and constraints into a system solution. In addition, it specifies the requirements for the systems engineering process and its application throughout the product life cycle. ISO/IEC 26702:2007 focuses on engineering activities necessary to guide product development, while ensuring that the product is properly designed to make it affordable to produce, own, operate, maintain, and eventually dispose of without undue risk to health or the environment.

Since SC 7 and IEEE have written so many process standards, one may not be surprised to learn that their model for process description is recorded in a Technical Report.

IEEE Std. 24774-2012 Guide—Adoption of ISO/IEC TR 24474:2010 Systems and Software Engineering—Life Cycle Management—Guidelines for Process Description

An increasing number of international, national, and industry standards describe process models. These models are developed for a range of purposes including process implementation and assessment. The terms and descriptions used in such models vary in format, content, and level of prescription. ISO/IEC TR 24774:2010 presents guidelines for the elements used most frequently in describing a process: the title, purpose, outcomes, activities, task, and information item. Whilst the primary purpose of ISO/IEC TR 24774:2010 is to encourage consistency in standard process reference models, the guidelines it provides can be applied to any process model developed for any purpose.

A very small entity (VSE) is an enterprise, an organization, a department, or a project having up to 25 people. The ISO/IEC 29110 series "profiles" large standards, such as ISO/IEC 12207 for software and ISO/IEC 15288 for systems, into smaller ones for VSEs. ISO 29110 is applicable to VSEs that do not develop critical systems or critical software. Profiles provide a roadmap allowing a start-up to grow a step at a time using the ISO 29110 management and engineering guides.

ISO/IEC 29110 set of standards and technical reports are targeted by audience such as VSEs, customers, or auditors. ISO/IEC 29110 is not intended to preclude the use of different life cycles approaches such as waterfall, iterative, incremental, evolutionary, or agile.

A VSE could obtain an ISO/IEC 29110 Certification. The set of technical reports is available at no cost on the ISO website. Many ISO 29110 documents are available in English, Spanish, Portuguese, Japanese, and French.

ISO/IEC TR 29110-5-1-2:2011 Software Engineering—Lifecycle Profiles for Very Small Entities (VSEs)—Part 5-1-2: Management and Engineering Guide: Generic Profile Group: Basic Profile

ISO/IEC TR 29110-5-1-2:2011 is applicable to very small entities (VSEs). A VSE is defined as an enterprise, organization, department, or project having up to 25 people. A set of standards and guides has been developed according to a set of VSEs' characteristics and needs. The guides are based on subsets of appropriate standards elements, referred to as VSE profiles. The purpose of a VSE profile is to define a subset of ISO/IEC international standards relevant to the VSEs' context.

ISO/IEC TR 29110-5-1-2:2011 provides the management and engineering guide to the basic VSE profile applicable to VSEs that do not develop critical software. The generic profile group does not imply any specific application domain.

The next standard may be viewed as an alternative to 12207 for individual projects. The 1074 standard explains how to define processes for use on a given project. The 12207 and 15288 standards, however, focus on defining processes for organizational adoption and repeated use on many projects. The current 1074 is the update of a standard that was a predecessor of 12207.

IEEE Std. 1074-2006 Standard for Developing a Software Project Life Cycle Process

This standard provides a process for creating a software project life cycle process (SPLCP). It is primarily directed at the process architect for a given software project.

All of the standards described so far in this section provide a basis for *defining* processes. Some users are interested in *assessing* and improving their processes after implementation. The 15504 series provides for process assessment; it is currently being revised and renumbered 330xx.

ISO/IEC 15504 [ten parts] Information Technology—Process Assessment

ISO/IEC 15504-2:2003 defines the requirements for performing process assessment as a basis for use in process improvement and capability determination.

Process assessment is based on a two-dimensional model containing a process dimension and a capability dimension. The process dimension is provided by an external process reference model (such as 12207 or 15288), which defines a set of processes characterized by statements of process purpose and process outcomes. The capability dimension consists of a measurement framework comprising six process capability levels and their associated process attributes.

The assessment output consists of a set of process attribute ratings for each process assessed, termed the process profile, and may also include the capability level achieved by that process.

ISO/IEC 15504-2:2003 identifies the measurement framework for process capability and the requirements for

- performing an assessment;
- process reference models;
- process assessment models;
- verifying conformity of process assessment.

The requirements for process assessment defined in ISO/IEC 15504-2:2003 form a structure that

- facilitates self-assessment;
- provides a basis for use in process improvement and capability determination;
- takes into account the context in which the assessed process is implemented;
- produces a process rating;
- addresses the ability of the process to achieve its purpose;

- is applicable across all application domains and sizes of organization; and
- may provide an objective benchmark between organizations.

The minimum set of requirements defined in ISO/IEC 15504-2:2003 ensures that assessment results are objective, impartial, consistent, repeatable, and representative of the assessed processes. Results of conformant process assessments may be compared when the scopes of the assessments are considered to be similar; for guidance on this matter, refer to ISO/IEC 15504-4.

Several other standards are mentioned here because they are written as elaborations of the processes of 12207 or 15288. They are allocated to other KAs because each one deals with topics described in those other KAs.

IEEE Std. 828-2012 Standard for Configuration Management in Systems and Software Engineering
    See Software Configuration Management KA

IEEE Std. 14764-2006 (a.k.a. ISO/IEC 14764:2006) Standard for Software Engineering—Software Life Cycle Processes—Maintenance
    See Software Maintenance KA

ISO/IEC 15026-4:2012 Systems and Software Engineering—Systems and Software Assurance—Part 4: Assurance in the Life Cycle
    See Software Quality KA

IEEE Std. 15939-2008 Standard Adoption of ISO/IEC 15939:2007 Systems and Software Engineering—Measurement Process
    See Software Engineering Management KA

ISO/IEC 15940:2006 Information Technology—Software Engineering Environment Services
    See Software Engineering Models and Methods KA

IEEE Std. 16085-2006 (a.k.a. ISO/IEC 16085:2006) Standard for Systems and Software Engineering—Software Life Cycle Processes—Risk Management
    See Software Engineering Management KA

ISO/IEC/IEEE 16326:2009 Systems and Software Engineering—Life Cycle Processes—Project Management

See Software Engineering Management KA

ISO/IEC/IEEE 29148:2011 Systems and Software Engineering—Life Cycle Processes—Requirements Engineering

See Software Requirements KA

Some users desire process standards usable for IT operations or IT service management. The ISO/IEC 20000 series describe IT service management. The processes are less rigorously defined than those of the aforementioned engineering standards, but may be preferable for situations where the risks of failure involve money or customer satisfaction rather than public health, safety, and welfare. The ISO/IEC 20000 series now extend to many parts. The foundation of the series, ISO/IEC 20000-1, is briefly described below.

ISO/IEC 20000-1:2011 Information Technology—Service Management—Part 1: Service Management System Requirements

ISO/IEC 20000-1:2011 is a service management system (SMS) standard. It specifies requirements for the service provider to plan, establish, implement, operate, monitor, review, maintain, and improve an SMS. The requirements include the design, transition, delivery and improvement of services to fulfill agreed service requirements.

IEEE has adopted the first two parts of the ISO/IEC 20000 series.

SOFTWARE ENGINEERING MODELS AND METHODS

Some approaches to software engineering use methods that cut across large parts of the life cycle, rather than focusing on specific processes. "Chief Programmer" was one traditional example. "Agile development" (actually an example of traditional incremental delivery) is a current

example. Neither S2ESC nor SC 7 has a standard for agile development, but there is a standard for developing user documentation in an agile project.

ISO/IEC/IEEE 26515:2012 Systems and Software Engineering—Developing User Documentation in an Agile Environment

ISO/IEC/IEEE 26515:2012 specifies the way in which user documentation can be developed in agile development projects. It is intended for use in all organizations that are using agile development or are considering implementing their projects using these techniques. It applies to people or organizations producing suites of documentation, to those undertaking a single documentation project, and to documentation produced internally, as well as to documentation contracted to outside service organizations. ISO/IEC/IEEE 26515:2012 addresses the relationship between the user documentation process and the life cycle documentation process in agile development. It describes how the information developer or project manager may plan and manage the user documentation development in an agile environment. It is intended neither to encourage nor to discourage the use of any particular agile development tools or methods.

Many methodologies are based on semiformal descriptions of the software to be constructed. These range from simple descriptive notations to models that can be manipulated and tested and, in some cases, can generate code. Two relatively old techniques start the list; the first has been widely applied for modeling processes and workflows.

IEEE Std. 1320.1-1998 Standard for Functional Modeling Language—Syntax and Semantics for IDEF0

IDEF0 function modeling is designed to represent the decisions, actions, and activities of an existing or prospective organization or system. IDEF0 graphics and accompanying texts are presented in an organized and systematic way to gain understanding, support analysis, provide logic for potential changes, specify requirements, and support system-level design and integration activities. IDEF0 may be used to model a wide variety of systems, composed of people, machines, materials, computers, and information of all varieties, and structured by the relationships among them, both automated and nonautomated. For new systems, IDEF0 may be used first to define requirements and to specify the functions to be carried out by the future system. As the basis of this architecture, IDEF0 may then be used to design an implementation that meets these requirements and performs these functions. For existing systems, IDEF0 can be used to analyze the functions that the system performs and to record the means by which these are done.

IEEE Std. 1320.2-1998 Standard for Conceptual Modeling Language—Syntax and Semantics for IDEF1X97 (IDEFobject)

IDEF1X 97 consists of two conceptual modeling languages. The key-style language supports data/information modeling and is downward compatible with the US government's 1993 standard, FIPS PUB 184. The identity-style language is based on the object model with declarative rules and constraints. IDEF1X 97 identity style includes constructs for the distinct but related components of object abstraction: interface, requests, and realization; utilizes graphics to state the interface; and defines a declarative, directly executable rule and constraint language for requests and realizations. IDEF1X 97 conceptual modeling supports implementation by relational databases, extended relational databases, object databases, and object programming languages. IDEF1X 97 is formally defined in terms of first order logic. A procedure is given whereby any valid IDEF1X 97 model can be transformed into an equivalent theory in first order logic. That procedure is then applied to a metamodel of IDEF1X 97 to define the valid set of IDEF1X 97 models.

In recent years, the UML notation has become popular for modeling software-intensive systems.

The next two standards provide two versions of the UML language.

ISO/IEC 19501:2005 Information Technology—Open Distributed Processing—Unified Modeling Language (UML) Version 1.4.2

ISO/IEC 19501 describes the Unified Modeling Language (UML), a graphical language for visualizing, specifying, constructing, and documenting the artifacts of a software-intensive system. The UML offers a standard way to write a system's blueprints, including conceptual things such as business processes and system functions as well as concrete things such as programming language statements, database schemas, and reusable software components.

ISO/IEC 19505:2012 [two parts] Information Technology—Object Management Group Unified Modeling Language (OMG UML)

ISO/IEC 19505 defines the Unified Modeling Language (UML), revision 2. The objective of UML is to provide system architects, software engineers, and software developers with tools for analysis, design, and implementation of software-based systems as well as for modeling business and similar processes.

Two more standards build on the base of UML to provide additional modeling capabilities:

ISO/IEC 19506:2012 Information Technology—Object Management Group Architecture-Driven Modernization (ADM)—Knowledge Discovery Meta-Model (KDM)

ISO/IEC 19506:2012 defines a metamodel for representing existing software assets, their associations, and operational environments, referred to as the knowledge discovery metamodel (KDM). This is the first in the series of specifications related to software assurance (SwA) and architecture-driven modernization (ADM) activities. KDM facilitates projects that involve existing software systems by insuring interoperability and exchange of data between tools provided by different vendors.

ISO/IEC 19507:2012 Information Technology—Object Management Group Object Constraint Language (OCL)

ISO/IEC 19507:2012 defines the Object Constraint Language (OCL), version 2.3.1. OCL version 2.3.1 is the version of OCL that is aligned with UML 2.3 and MOF 2.0.

Some organizations invest in software engineering environments (SEE) to assist in the construction of software. An SEE, per se, is not a replacement for sound processes. However, a suitable SEE must support the processes that have been chosen by the organization.

ISO/IEC 15940:2006 Information Technology—Software Engineering Environment Services

ISO/IEC 15940:2006 defines software engineering environment (SEE) services conceptually in a reference model that can be adapted to any SEEs to automate one or more software engineering activities. It describes services that support the process definitions as in ISO/IEC 12207 so that the set of SEE services is compatible with ISO/IEC 12207. ISO/IEC 15940:2006 can be used either as a general reference or to define an automated software process.

The selection of tooling for a software engineering environment is itself a difficult task. Two standards provide some assistance. ISO/IEC 14102:2008 defines both a set of processes and a structured set of computer-aided software engineering (CASE) tool characteristics for use in the technical evaluation and the ultimate selection of a CASE tool.

IEEE Std. 14102-2010 Standard Adoption of ISO/IEC 14102:2008 Information Technology—Guideline for the Evaluation and Selection of CASE Tools

Within systems and software engineering, computer-aided software engineering (CASE) tools represent a major part of the supporting technologies used to develop and maintain information technology systems. Their selection must be carried out with careful consideration of both the technical and management requirements.

ISO/IEC 14102:2008 defines both a set of processes and a structured set of CASE tool characteristics for use in the technical evaluation and the ultimate selection of a CASE tool. It follows the software product evaluation model defined in ISO/IEC 14598-5:1998.

ISO/IEC 14102:2008 adopts the general model of software product quality characteristics and subcharacteristics defined in ISO/IEC 9126-1:2001 and extends these when the software product is a CASE tool; it provides product characteristics unique to CASE tools.

The next document provides guidance on how to adopt CASE tools, once selected.

IEEE Std. 14471-2010 Guide—Adoption of ISO/IEC TR 14471:2007 Information Technology—Software Engineering—Guidelines for the Adoption of CASE Tools

The purpose of ISO/IEC TR 14471:2007 is to provide a recommended practice for CASE adoption. It provides guidance in establishing processes and activities that are to be applied for the successful adoption of CASE technology. The use of ISO/IEC TR 14471:2007 will help to maximize the return and minimize the risk of investing in CASE technology. However, ISO/IEC TR 14471:2007 does not establish compliance criteria.

It is best used in conjunction with ISO/IEC 14102 for CASE tool evaluation and selection. It neither dictates nor advocates particular development standards, software processes, design methods, methodologies, techniques, programming languages, or life cycle paradigms.

Within a software engineering environment, it is important for the various tools to interoperate. The following standards provide a scheme for interconnection.

IEEE Std. 1175.1-2002 Guide for CASE Tool Interconnections—Classification and Description

IEEE Std. 1175.2-2006 Recommended Practice for CASE Tool Interconnection—Characterization of Interconnections

IEEE Std. 1175.3-2004 Standard for CASE Tool Interconnections—Reference Model for Specifying Software Behavior

IEEE Std. 1175.4-2008 Standard for CASE Tool Interconnections—Reference Model for Specifying System Behavior

The purpose of this family of standards is to specify a common set of modeling concepts based on those found in commercial CASE tools for describing the operational behavior of a software system. These standards establish a uniform, integrated model of software concepts related to software functionality. They also provide a textual syntax for expressing the common properties (attributes and relationships) of those concepts as they have been used to model software behavior.

SOFTWARE QUALITY

One viewpoint of software quality starts with ISO 9001, *Quality Management Requirements*, dealing with quality policy throughout an organization. The terminology of that standard may be unfamiliar to software professionals, and quality management auditors may be unfamiliar with software jargon. The following standard describes the relationship between ISO 9001 and ISO/IEC 12207. Unfortunately, the current version refers to obsolete editions of both; a replacement is in progress:

IEEE Std. 90003-2008 Guide—Adoption of ISO/IEC 90003:2004 Software Engineering—Guidelines for the Application of ISO 9001:2000 to Computer Software

ISO/IEC 90003 provides guidance for organizations in the application of ISO 9001:2000 to the acquisition, supply, development, operation, and maintenance of computer software and related support services. ISO/IEC 90003:2004 does not add to or otherwise change the requirements of ISO 9001:2000.

The guidelines provided in ISO/IEC 90003:2004 are not intended to be used as assessment criteria in quality management system registration/certification.

The application of ISO/IEC 90003:2004 is appropriate to software that is

- part of a commercial contract with another organization,
- a product available for a market sector,
- used to support the processes of an organization,
- embedded in a hardware product, or
- related to software services.

Some organizations may be involved in all the above activities; others may specialize in one area. Whatever the situation, the organization's quality management system should cover all aspects (software related and nonsoftware related) of the business.

ISO/IEC 90003:2004 identifies the issues which should be addressed and is independent of the technology, life cycle models, development processes, sequence of activities, and organizational structure used by an organization. Additional guidance and frequent references to the ISO/IEC JTC 1/SC 7 software engineering standards are provided to assist in the application of ISO 9001:2000: in particular, ISO/IEC 12207, ISO/IEC TR 9126, ISO/IEC 14598, ISO/IEC 15939, and ISO/IEC TR 15504.

The ISO 9001 approach posits an organization-level quality management process paired with project-level quality assurance planning to achieve the organizational goals. IEEE 730 describes project-level quality planning. It is currently aligned with an obsolete edition of 12207, but a revision is being prepared.

IEEE Std. 730-2002 Standard for Software Quality Assurance Plans

The standard specifies the format and content of software quality assurance plans.

Another viewpoint of software quality begins with enumerating the desired characteristics of a software product and selecting measures or other evaluations to determine if the desired level of characteristics has been achieved. The so-called SQuaRE (software product quality requirements and evaluation) series of SC 7 standards covers this approach in great detail.

ISO/IEC 25000 through 25099 Software Engineering—Software Product Quality Requirements and Evaluation (SQuaRE)

A few of the SQuaRE standards are selected below for particular attention. The first is the overall guide to the series.

ISO/IEC 25000:2005 Software Engineering—Software Product Quality Requirements and Evaluation (SQuaRE)—Guide to SQuaRE

ISO/IEC 25000:2005 provides guidance for the use of the new series of international standards named Software product Quality Requirements and Evaluation (SQuaRE). The purpose of this guide is to provide a general overview of SQuaRE contents, common reference models, and definitions, as well as the relationship among the documents, allowing users of this guide a good understanding of those international standards. This document contains an explanation of the transition process between the old ISO/IEC 9126 and the 14598 series and SQuaRE, and also presents information on how to use the ISO/IEC 9126 and 14598 series in their previous form.

SQuaRE provides

- terms and definitions,
- reference models,
- guides
- standards for requirements specification, planning and management, measurement, and evaluation purposes.

The next SQuaRE standard provides a taxonomy of software quality characteristics that may be useful in selecting characteristics relevant to a specific project:

ISO/IEC 25010:2011 Systems and Software Engineering—Systems and Software Quality Requirements and Evaluation (SQuaRE)—System and Software Quality Models

ISO/IEC 25010:2011 defines the following:

1. A quality in-use model composed of five characteristics (some of which are further subdivided into subcharacteristics) that relate to the outcome of interaction when a product is used in a particular context of use. This system model is applicable to the complete human-computer system, including both computer systems in use and software products in use.
2. A product quality model composed of eight characteristics (which are further subdivided into subcharacteristics) that relate to static properties of software and dynamic properties of the computer system. The model is applicable to both computer systems and software products.

The characteristics defined by both models are relevant to all software products and computer systems. The characteristics and subcharacteristics provide consistent terminology for specifying, measuring, and evaluating system and software product quality. They also provide a set of quality characteristics against which stated quality requirements can be compared for completeness.

Although the scope of the product quality model is intended to be software and computer systems, many of the characteristics are also relevant to wider systems and services.

ISO/IEC 25012 contains a model for data quality that is complementary to this model.

The scope of the models excludes purely functional properties, but it does include functional suitability.

The scope of application of the quality models includes supporting specification and evaluation of software and software-intensive computer systems from different perspectives by those who are associated with their acquisition, requirements, development, use, evaluation, support, maintenance, quality assurance and control, and audit. The models can, for example, be used by developers, acquirers, quality assurance and control staff, and independent evaluators, particularly those responsible for specifying and evaluating software product quality. Activities during product development that can benefit from the use of the quality models include

- identifying software and system requirements;
- validating the comprehensiveness of a requirements definition;
- identifying software and system design objectives;
- identifying software and system testing objectives;
- identifying quality control criteria as part of quality assurance;
- identifying acceptance criteria for a software product and/or software-intensive computer system;
- establishing measures of quality characteristics in support of these activities.

Some documents in the SQuaRE series deal specifically with the characteristic of usability. The Common Industry Format (CIF) for usability reporting began at the US National Institute for Standards and Technology (NIST) and was moved into ISO/IEC JTC 1/SC 7 for purposes of standardization.

ISO/IEC 25060 through 25064 Software Engineering—Software Product Quality Requirements and

Evaluation (SQuaRE)—Common Industry Format (CIF) for Usability

A family of international standards, named the Common Industry Formats (CIF), documents the specification and evaluation of the usability of interactive systems. It provides a general overview of the CIF framework and contents, definitions, and the relationship of the framework elements. The intended users of the framework are identified, as well as the situations in which the framework may be applied. The assumptions and constraints of the framework are also enumerated.

The framework content includes the following:

- consistent terminology and classification of specification, evaluation, and reporting;
- a definition of the type and scope of formats and the high-level structure to be used for documenting required information and the results of evaluation.

The CIF family of standards is applicable to software and hardware products used for predefined tasks. The information items are intended to be used as part of system-level documentation resulting from development processes such as those in ISO 9241-210 and ISO/IEC JTC 1/SC 7 process standards.

The CIF family focuses on documenting those elements needed for design and development of usable systems, rather than prescribing a specific process. It is intended to be used in conjunction with existing international standards, including ISO 9241, ISO 20282, ISO/IEC 9126, and the SQuaRE series (ISO/IEC 25000 to ISO/IEC 25099).

The CIF family of standards does not prescribe any kind of method, life cycle or process.

Not everyone agrees with the taxonomy of quality characteristics in ISO/IEC 25010. That standard has a quality factor called "reliability" that has subfactors of maturity, availability, fault tolerance, and recoverability. IEC TC 65, which has responsibility for standards on "dependability," defines that term as a nonquantitative composite of reliability, maintainability, and maintenance support. Others use the term "reliability" to denote a measure defined by a mathematical equation. The disagreement over the use of these words means that the standards on the subject are inherently unaligned. A few will be noted below, but the words like those noted above may mean different things in different standards.

IEEE Std. 982.1-2005 Standard for Dictionary of Measures of the Software Aspects of Dependability

A standard dictionary of measures of the software aspects of dependability for assessing and predicting the reliability, maintainability, and availability of any software system; in particular, it applies to mission critical software systems.

IEEE Std. 1633-2008 Recommended Practice for Software Reliability

The methods for assessing and predicting the reliability of software, based on a life cycle approach to software reliability engineering, are prescribed in this recommended practice. It provides information necessary for the application of software reliability (SR) measurement to a project, lays a foundation for building consistent methods, and establishes the basic principle for collecting the data needed to assess and predict the reliability of software. The recommended practice prescribes how any user can participate in SR assessments and predictions.

IEEE has an overall standard for software product quality that has a scope similar to the ISO/IEC 250xx series described previously. Its terminology differs from the ISO/IEC series, but it is substantially more compact.

IEEE Std. 1061-1998 Standard for Software Quality Metrics Methodology

A methodology for establishing quality requirements and identifying, implementing, analyzing, and validating the process and product software quality metrics is defined. The methodology spans the entire software life cycle.

One approach to achieving software quality is to perform an extensive program of verification and validation. IEEE Std. 1012 is probably the world's most widely applied standard on this subject. A revision was recently published.

IEEE Std. 1012-2012 Standard for System and Software Verification and Validation

Verification and validation (V&V) processes are used to determine whether the development products of a given activity conform to the requirements of that activity and whether the product satisfies its intended use and user needs. V&V life cycle process requirements are specified for different integrity levels. The scope of V&V processes encompasses systems, software, and hardware, and it includes their interfaces. This standard applies to systems, software, and hardware being developed, maintained, or reused [legacy, commercial off-the-shelf (COTS), nondevelopmental items]. The term software also includes firmware and microcode, and each of the terms system, software, and hardware includes documentation. V&V processes include the analysis, evaluation, review, inspection, assessment, and testing of products.

There are other standards that support the verification and validation processes. One describes techniques for performing reviews and audits during a software project.

IEEE Std. 1028-2008 Standard for Software Reviews and Audits

Five types of software reviews and audits, together with procedures required for the execution of each type, are defined in this standard. This standard is concerned only with the reviews and audits; procedures for determining the necessity of a review or audit are not defined, and the disposition of the results of the review or audit is not specified. Types included are management reviews, technical reviews, inspections, walkthroughs, and audits.

In many cases, a database of software anomalies is used to support verification and validation activities. The following standard suggests how anomalies should be classified.

IEEE Std. 1044-2009 Standard for Classification for Software Anomalies

This standard provides a uniform approach to the classification of software anomalies, regardless of when they originate or when they are encountered within the project, product, or system life cycle. Classification data can be used for a variety of purposes, including defect causal analysis, project management, and software process improvement (e.g., to reduce the likelihood of defect insertion and/or increase the likelihood of early defect detection).

In some systems, one particular property of the software is so important that it requires special treatment beyond that provided by a conventional verification and validation program. The emerging term for this sort of treatment is "systems and software assurance." Examples include safety, privacy, high security, and ultrareliability. The 15026 standard is under development to deal with such situations. The first part of the four-part standard provides terminology and concepts used in the remaining parts. It was first written before the other parts and is now being revised for complete agreement with the others.

IEEE Std. 15026.1-2011 Trial-Use Standard Adoption of ISO/IEC TR 15026-1:2010 Systems and Software Engineering—Systems and Software Assurance—Part 1: Concepts and Vocabulary

This trial-use standard adopts ISO/IEC TR 15026-1:2010, which defines terms and establishes an extensive and organized set of concepts and their relationships for software and systems assurance, thereby establishing a basis for shared understanding of the concepts and principles central to ISO/IEC 15026 across its user communities. It provides information to users of the subsequent parts of ISO/IEC 15026, including the use of each part and the combined use of multiple parts. Coverage of assurance for a service being operated and managed on an ongoing basis is not covered in ISO/IEC 15026.

The second part of the standard describes the structure of an "assurance case," which is intended as a structured argument that the critical property has been achieved. It is a generalization of various domain-specific constructs like "safety cases."

IEEE Std. 15026.2-2011 Standard Adoption of ISO/IEC 15026-2:2011 Systems and Software Engineering—Systems and Software Assurance—Part 2: Assurance Case

ISO/IEC 15026-2:2011 is adopted by this standard. ISO/IEC 15026-2:2011 specifies minimum requirements for the structure and contents of an assurance case to improve the consistency and comparability of assurance cases and to facilitate stakeholder communications, engineering decisions, and other uses of assurance cases. An assurance case includes a top-level claim for a property of a system or product (or set of claims), systematic argumentation regarding this claim, and the evidence and explicit assumptions that underlie this argumentation. Arguing through multiple levels of subordinate claims, this structured argumentation connects the top-level claim to the evidence and assumptions. Assurance cases are generally developed to support claims in areas such as safety, reliability, maintainability, human factors, operability, and security, although these assurance cases are often called by more specific names, e.g., safety case or reliability and maintainability (R&M) case. ISO/IEC 15026-2:2011 does not place requirements on the quality of the contents of an assurance case and does not require the use of a particular terminology or graphical representation. Likewise, it places no requirements on the means of physical implementation of the data, including no requirements for redundancy or colocation.

In many systems, some portions are critical to achieving the desired property while others are only incidental. For example, the flight control system of an airliner is critical to safety, but the microwave oven is not. Conventionally, the various portions are assigned "criticality levels" to indicate their significance to the overall achievement of the property. The third part of ISO/IEC 15026 describes how that is done. This part will be revised for better fit with the remainder of the 15026 standard.

ISO/IEC 15026-3:2011 Systems and Software Engineering—Systems and Software Assurance—Part 3: System Integrity Levels

ISO/IEC 15026-3:2011 specifies the concept of integrity levels with corresponding integrity level requirements that are required to be met in order to show the achievement of the integrity level. It places requirements on and recommends methods for defining and using integrity levels and their integrity level requirements, including the assignment of integrity levels to systems, software products, their elements, and relevant external dependences.

ISO/IEC 15026-3:2011 is applicable to systems and software and is intended for use by:

* definers of integrity levels such as industry and professional organizations, standards organizations, and government agencies;
* users of integrity levels such as developers and maintainers, suppliers and acquirers, users, and assessors of systems or software, and for the administrative and technical support of systems and/or software products.

One important use of integrity levels is by suppliers and acquirers in agreements; for example, to aid in assuring safety, economic, or security characteristics of a delivered system or product.

ISO/IEC 15026-3:2011 does not prescribe a specific set of integrity levels or their integrity level requirements. In addition, it does not prescribe the way in which integrity level use is integrated with the overall system or software engineering life cycle processes.

ISO/IEC 15026-3:2011 can be used alone or with other parts of ISO/IEC 15026. It can be used with a variety of technical and specialized risk analysis and development approaches. ISO/IEC

TR 15026-1 provides additional information and references to aid users of ISO/IEC 15026-3:2011.

ISO/IEC 15026-3:2011 does not require the use of the assurance cases described by ISO/IEC 15026-2 but describes how integrity levels and assurance cases can work together, especially in the definition of specifications for integrity levels or by using integrity levels within a portion of an assurance case.

The final part of 15026 provides additional guidance for executing the life cycle processes of 12207 and 15288 when a system or software is required to achieve an important property.

ISO/IEC 15026-4:2012 Systems and Software Engineering—Systems and Software Assurance—Part 4: Assurance in the Life Cycle

This part of ISO/IEC 15026 gives guidance and recommendations for conducting selected processes, activities and tasks for systems and software products requiring assurance claims for properties selected for special attention, called critical properties. This part of ISO/IEC 15026 specifies a property-independent list of processes, activities, and tasks to achieve the claim and show the achievement of the claim. This part of ISO/IEC 15026 establishes the processes, activities, tasks, guidance, and recommendations in the context of a defined life cycle model and set of life cycle processes for system and/or software life cycle management.

The next standard deals with a property—safety—that is often identified as critical. It was originally developed in cooperation with the US nuclear power industry.

IEEE Std. 1228-1994 Standard for Software Safety Plans

The minimum acceptable requirements for the content of a software safety plan are established. This standard applies to the software safety plan used for the development, procurement, maintenance, and retirement of safety-critical software.

This standard requires that the plan be prepared within the context of the system safety program. Only the safety aspects of the software are included. This standard does not contain special provisions required for software used in distributed systems or in parallel processors.

Classical treatments suggest that "verification" deals with static evaluation methods and that "testing" deals with dynamic evaluation methods. Recent treatments, including ISO/IEC draft 29119, are blurring this distinction, though, so testing standards are mentioned here.

IEEE Std. 829-2008 Standard for Software and System Test Documentation
See Software Testing KA

IEEE Std. 1008-1987 Standard for Software Unit Testing
See Software Testing KA

IEEE Std. 26513-2010 Standard Adoption of ISO/IEC 26513:2009 Systems and Software Engineering—Requirements for Testers and Reviewers of Documentation
See Software Testing KA

ISO/IEC/IEEE 29119 [four parts] (Draft) Software and Systems Engineering—Software Testing
See Software Testing KA

SOFTWARE ENGINEERING PROFESSIONAL PRACTICE

IEEE is a provider of products related to the certification of professional practitioners of software engineering. The first has already been described, the *Guide to the Software Engineering Body of Knowledge*. The *SWEBOK Guide* has been adopted by ISO/IEC as an outline of the knowledge that professional software engineers should have.

ISO/IEC TR 19759:2005 Software Engineering—Guide to the Software Engineering Body of Knowledge (SWEBOK)
See General

An SC 7 standard provides a framework for comparisons among certifications of software engineering professionals. That standard states that the areas considered in certification must be mapped to the *SWEBOK Guide*.

ISO/IEC 24773:2008 Software Engineering—Certification of Software Engineering Professionals

ISO/IEC 24773:2008 establishes a framework for comparison of schemes for certifying software engineering professionals. A certification scheme is a set of certification requirements for software engineering professionals. ISO/IEC 24773:2008 specifies the items that a scheme is required to contain and indicates what should be defined for each item.

ISO/IEC 24773:2008 will facilitate the portability of software engineering professional certifications between different countries or organizations. At present, different countries and organizations have adopted different approaches on the topic, which are implemented by means of regulations and bylaws. The intention of ISO/IEC 24773:2008 is to be open to these individual approaches by providing a framework for expressing them in a common scheme that can lead to understanding.

SC 7 is currently drafting a guide that will supplement 24773.

SOFTWARE ENGINEERING ECONOMICS

No standards are allocated to this KA.

COMPUTING FOUNDATIONS

No standards are allocated to this KA.

MATHEMATICAL FOUNDATIONS

No standards are allocated to this KA.

ENGINEERING FOUNDATIONS

No standards are allocated to this KA.

STAYING CURRENT

This article was obsolescent the moment it was drafted. Some readers will need to know how to get current designations and descriptions of standards. This section describes some helpful resources.

WHERE TO FIND STANDARDS

The list of standards published for ISO/IEC JTC 1/SC 7 can be found at www.iso.org/iso/iso_catalogue/catalogue_tc/catalogue_tc_browse.htm?commid=45086.

Because the URL might change, readers might have to navigate to the list. Begin at www.iso.org/iso/store.htm, then click on "browse standards catalogue," then "browse by TC," then "JTC 1," then "SC 7."

Finding the current list of standards for S2ESC is a bit more difficult. Begin at http://standards.ieee.org/. In the search box under "Find Standards," type "S2ESC." This should produce a list of published standards for which S2ESC is responsible.

Keep in mind that the searchable databases are compilations. Like any such database, they can contain errors that lead to incomplete search results.

WHERE TO OBTAIN THE STANDARDS

Some readers will want to obtain standards described in this article. The first thing to know is that some international standards are available free for individual use. The current list of ISO/IEC standards available under these terms is located at http://standards.iso.org/ittf/PubliclyAvailableStandards/index.html.

One of the publicly available standards is the ISO/IEC adoption of the *SWEBOK Guide*, ISO/IEC 19759.

The definitions contained in ISO/IEC/IEEE 24765, *System and Software Vocabulary*, are freely available at www.computer.org/sevocab.

However, the vast majority of standards are not free. ISO/IEC standards are generally purchased from the national standards organization of the country in which one lives. For example, in the US, international standards can be purchased from the American National Standards Institute at http://webstore.ansi.org/. Alternatively, standards can be purchased directly from ISO/IEC at www.iso.org/iso/store.htm. It should be noted that each individual nation is free to set its own prices, so it may be helpful to check both sources.

IEEE standards may be available to you for free if your employer or library has a subscription to IEEE Xplore: http://ieeexplore.ieee.org/. Some subscriptions to Xplore provide access only to the abstracts of standards; the full text may then be purchased via Xplore. Alternatively, standards may be purchased via the IEEE standards store at www.techstreet.com/ieeegate.html. It should be noted that IEEE-SA sometimes bundles standards into groups available at a substantial discount.

Finally, the reader should note that standards that IEEE has adopted from ISO/IEC, standards that ISO/IEC has "fast-tracked" from IEEE, and standards that were jointly developed or revised are available from both sources. For all standards described in this article, the IEEE version and the ISO/IEC version are substantively identical. The respective versions may have different front and back matter but the bodies are identical.

WHERE TO SEE THE SWEBOK GUIDE

The *SWEBOK Guide* is published under an IEEE copyright. The current version of the *SWEBOK Guide* is available free to the public at www.swebok.org/. The ISO/IEC adoption of the *SWEBOK Guide*, ISO/IEC TR 19759, is one of the freely available standards.

SUMMARY LIST OF THE STANDARDS

Number and Title (listed in order of number)	Most Relevant KA
IEEE Std. 730-2002 Standard for Software Quality Assurance Plans	SW Quality
IEEE Std. 828-2012 Standard for Configuration Management in Systems and Software Engineering	SW Configuration Management
IEEE Std. 829-2008 Standard for Software and System Test Documentation	SW Testing
IEEE Std. 982.1-2005 Standard for Dictionary of Measures of the Software Aspects of Dependability	SW Quality
IEEE Std. 1008-1987 Standard for Software Unit Testing	SW Testing
IEEE Std. 1012-2012 Standard for System and Software Verification and Validation	SW Quality
IEEE Std. 1016-2009 Standard for Information Technology—Systems Design—Software Design Descriptions	SW Design
IEEE Std. 1028-2008 Standard for Software Reviews and Audits	SW Quality
IEEE Std. 1044-2009 Standard for Classification for Software Anomalies	SW Quality
IEEE Std. 1061-1998 Standard for Software Quality Metrics Methodology	SW Quality
IEEE Std. 1062-1998 Recommended Practice for Software Acquisition	SW Engineering Management
IEEE Std. 1074-2006 Standard for Developing a Software Project Life Cycle Process	SW Engineering Process
IEEE Std. 1175.1-2002 Guide for CASE Tool Interconnections—Classification and Description	SW Engineering Models and Methods
IEEE Std. 1175.2-2006 Recommended Practice for CASE Tool Interconnection—Characterization of Interconnections	SW Engineering Models and Methods
IEEE Std. 1175.3-2004 Standard for CASE Tool Interconnections—Reference Model for Specifying Software Behavior	SW Engineering Models and Methods
IEEE Std. 1175.4-2008 Standard for CASE Tool Interconnections—Reference Model for Specifying System Behavior	SW Engineering Models and Methods
IEEE Std. 1220-2005 (a.k.a. ISO/IEC 26702:2007) Standard for Application and Management of the Systems Engineering Process	SW Engineering Process
IEEE Std. 1228-1994 Standard for Software Safety Plans	SW Quality
IEEE Std. 1320.1-1998 Standard for Functional Modeling Language—Syntax and Semantics for IDEF0	SW Engineering Models and Methods
IEEE Std. 1320.2-1998 Standard for Conceptual Modeling Language—Syntax and Semantics for IDEF1X97 (IDEFobject)	SW Engineering Models and Methods
IEEE Std. 1490-2011 Guide—Adoption of the Project Management Institute (PMI®) Standard, A Guide to the Project Management Body of Knowledge (PMBOK® Guide)—Fourth Edition	SW Engineering Management
IEEE Std. 1517-2010 Standard for Information Technology—System and Software Life Cycle Processes—Reuse Processes	SW Engineering Process

Number and Title (listed in order of number)	Most Relevant KA
IEEE Std. 1633-2008 Recommended Practice for Software Reliability	SW Quality
IEEE Std. 12207-2008 (a.k.a. ISO/IEC 12207:2008) Standard for Systems and Software Engineering—Software Life Cycle Processes	SW Engineering Process
IEEE Std. 14102-2010 Standard Adoption of ISO/IEC 14102:2008 Information Technology—Guideline for the Evaluation and Selection of CASE Tools	SW Engineering Models and Methods
ISO/IEC 14143 [six parts] Information Technology—Software Measurement—Functional Size Measurement	SW Requirements
IEEE Std. 14471-2010 Guide—Adoption of ISO/IEC TR 14471:2007 Information Technology—Software Engineering—Guidelines for the Adoption of CASE Tools	SW Engineering Models and Methods
IEEE Std. 14764-2006 (a.k.a. ISO/IEC 14764:2006) Standard for Software Engineering—Software Life Cycle Processes—Maintenance	SW Maintenance
IEEE Std. 15026.1-2011 Trial-Use Standard Adoption of ISO/IEC TR 15026-1:2010 Systems and Software Engineering—Systems and Software Assurance—Part 1: Concepts and Vocabulary	SW Quality
IEEE Std. 15026.2-2011 Standard Adoption of ISO/IEC 15026-2:2011 Systems and Software Engineering—Systems and Software Assurance—Part 2: Assurance Case	SW Quality
ISO/IEC 15026-3 Systems and Software Engineering—Systems and Software Assurance—Part 3: System Integrity Levels	SW Quality
ISO/IEC 15026-4:2012 Systems and Software Engineering—Systems and Software Assurance—Part 4: Assurance in the Life Cycle	SW Quality
IEEE Std. 15288-2008 (a.k.a. ISO/IEC 15288:2008) Standard for Systems and Software Engineering—System Life Cycle Processes	SW Engineering Process
ISO/IEC/IEEE 15289:2011 Systems and Software Engineering—Content of Life-Cycle Information Products (Documentation)	SW Engineering Process
ISO/IEC 15504 [ten parts] Information Technology—Process Assessment	SW Engineering Process
IEEE Std. 15939-2008 Standard Adoption of ISO/IEC 15939:2007 Systems and Software Engineering—Measurement Process	SW Engineering Management
ISO/IEC 15940:2006 Information Technology—Software Engineering Environment Services	SW Engineering Models and Methods
IEEE Std. 16085-2006 (a.k.a. ISO/IEC 16085:2006) Standard for Systems and Software Engineering—Software Life Cycle Processes—Risk Management	SW Engineering Management
ISO/IEC/IEEE 16326:2009 Systems and Software Engineering—Life Cycle Processes—Project Management	SW Engineering Management
ISO/IEC 19501:2005 Information Technology—Open Distributed Processing—Unified Modeling Language (UML) Version 1.4.2	SW Engineering Models and Methods

Number and Title (listed in order of number)	Most Relevant KA
ISO/IEC 19505:2012 [two parts] Information Technology—Object Management Group Unified Modeling Language (OMG UML)	SW Engineering Models and Methods
ISO/IEC 19506:2012 Information Technology—Object Management Group Architecture-Driven Modernization (ADM)—Knowledge Discovery Meta-Model (KDM)	SW Engineering Models and Methods
ISO/IEC 19507:2012 Information Technology—Object Management Group Object Constraint Language (OCL)	SW Engineering Models and Methods
ISO/IEC TR 19759:2005 Software Engineering—Guide to the Software Engineering Body of Knowledge (SWEBOK)	[General]
ISO/IEC 19761:2011 Software Engineering—COSMIC: A Functional Size Measurement Method	SW Requirements
ISO/IEC 20000-1:2011 Information Technology—Service Management—Part 1: Service management system requirements	SW Engineering Process
ISO/IEC 20926:2009 Software and Systems Engineering—Software Measurement—IFPUG Functional Size Measurement Method	SW Requirements
ISO/IEC 20968:2002 Software Engineering—Mk II Function Point Analysis—Counting Practices Manual	SW Requirements
ISO/IEC 24570:2005 Software Engineering—NESMA Functional Size Measurement Method Version 2.1—Definitions and Counting Guidelines for the Application of Function Point Analysis	SW Requirements
IEEE Std. 24748.1-2011 Guide—Adoption of ISO/IEC TR 24748-1:2010 Systems and Software Engineering—Life Cycle Management—Part 1: Guide for Life Cycle Management	SW Engineering Process
IEEE Std. 24748.2-2012 Guide—Adoption of ISO/IEC TR 24748-2:2011 Systems and Software Engineering—Life Cycle Management—Part 2: Guide to the Application of ISO/IEC 15288 (System Life Cycle Processes)	SW Engineering Process
IEEE Std. 24748-3:2012 Guide—Adoption of ISO/IEC TR 24748-3:2011 Systems and Software Engineering—Life Cycle Management—Part 3: Guide to the Application of ISO/IEC 12207 (Software Life Cycle Processes)	SW Engineering Process
ISO/IEC/IEEE 24765:2010 Systems and Software Engineering—Vocabulary	[General]
ISO/IEC TR 24772:2013 Information technology—Programming Languages — Guidance to Avoiding Vulnerabilities in Programming Languages through Language Selection and Use	SW Construction
ISO/IEC 24773:2008 Software Engineering—Certification of Software Engineering Professionals	SW Engineering Professional Practice
IEEE Std. 24774:2012 Guide—Adoption of ISO/IEC TR 24474:2010 Systems and Software Engineering—Life Cycle Management—Guidelines for Process Description	SW Engineering Process
ISO/IEC 25000:2005 Software Engineering—Software Product Quality Requirements and Evaluation (SQuaRE)—Guide to SQuaRE	SW Quality

Number and Title (listed in order of number)	Most Relevant KA
ISO/IEC 25000 through 25099 Software Engineering—Software Product Quality Requirements and Evaluation (SQuaRE)	SW Quality
ISO/IEC 25010:2011 Systems and Software Engineering—Systems and Software Quality Requirements and Evaluation (SQuaRE)—System and Software Quality Models	SW Quality
ISO/IEC 25060 through 25064 Software Engineering—Software Product Quality Requirements and Evaluation (SQuaRE)—Common Industry Format (CIF) for Usability	SW Quality
ISO/IEC/IEEE 26511:2012 Systems and Software Engineering—Requirements for Managers of User Documentation	SW Engineering Management
ISO/IEC/IEEE 26512:2011 Systems and Software Engineering—Requirements for Acquirers and Suppliers of User Documentation	SW Engineering Management
IEEE Std. 26513-2010 Standard Adoption of ISO/IEC 26513:2009 Systems and Software Engineering—Requirements for Testers and Reviewers of Documentation	SW Testing
IEEE Std. 26514-2010 Standard Adoption of ISO/IEC 26514:2008 Systems and Software Engineering—Requirements for Designers and Developers of User Documentation	SW Design
ISO/IEC/IEEE 26515:2012 Systems and Software Engineering—Developing User Documentation in an Agile Environment	SW Engineering Models and Methods
ISO/IEC 29110 [several parts] Software Engineering—Lifecycle Profiles for Very Small Entities (VSE)	SW Engineering Process
ISO/IEC/IEEE 29119 [four parts] (Draft) Software and Systems Engineering—Software Testing	SW Testing
ISO/IEC/IEEE 29148:2011 Systems and Software Engineering—Life Cycle Processes—Requirements Engineering	SW Requirements
ISO/IEC/IEEE 42010:2011 Systems and Software Engineering—Architecture Description	SW Design
IEEE Std. 90003:2008 Guide—Adoption of ISO/IEC 90003:2004 Software Engineering—Guidelines for the Application of ISO 9001:2000 to Computer Software	SW Quality

APPENDIX C

CONSOLIDATED REFERENCE LIST

The Consolidated Reference List identifies all recommended reference materials (to the level of section number) that accompany the breakdown of topics within each knowledge area (KA). This Consolidated Reference List is adopted by the software engineering certification and associated professional development products offered by the IEEE Computer Society. KA Editors used the references allocated to their KA by the Consolidated Reference List as their Recommended References. Collectively this Consolidated Reference List is

- Complete: Covering the entire scope of the *SWEBOK Guide*.
- Sufficient: Providing enough information to describe "generally accepted" knowledge.
- Consistent: Not providing contradictory knowledge nor conflicting practices.
- Credible: Recognized as providing expert treatment.
- Current: Treating the subject in a manner that is commensurate with currently generally accepted knowledge.
- Succinct: As short as possible (both in number of reference items and in total page count) without failing other objectives.

[1*] J.H. Allen et al., *Software Security Engineering: A Guide for Project Managers*, Addison-Wesley, 2008.

[2*] M. Bishop, *Computer Security: Art and Science*, Addison-Wesley, 2002.

[3*] B. Boehm and R. Turner, *Balancing Agility and Discipline: A Guide for the Perplexed*, Addison-Wesley, 2003.

[4*] F. Bott et al., *Professional Issues in Software Engineering*, 3rd ed., Taylor & Francis, 2000.

[5*] J.G. Brookshear, *Computer Science: An Overview*, 10th ed., Addison-Wesley, 2008.

[6*] D. Budgen, *Software Design*, 2nd ed., Addison-Wesley, 2003.

[7*] E.W. Cheney and D.R. Kincaid, *Numerical Mathematics and Computing*, 6th ed., Brooks/Cole, 2007.

[8*] P. Clements et al., *Documenting Software Architectures: Views and Beyond*, 2nd ed., Pearson Education, 2010.

[9*] R.E. Fairley, *Managing and Leading Software Projects*, Wiley-IEEE Computer Society Press, 2009.

[10*] D. Galin, *Software Quality Assurance: From Theory to Implementation*, Pearson Education Limited, 2004.

[11*] E. Gamma et al., *Design Patterns: Elements of Reusable Object-Oriented Software*, 1st ed., Addison-Wesley Professional, 1994.

[12*] P. Grubb and A.A. Takang, *Software Maintenance: Concepts and Practice*, 2nd ed., World Scientific Publishing, 2003.

[13*] A.M.J. Hass, *Configuration Management Principles and Practices*, 1st ed., Addison-Wesley, 2003.

[14*] E. Horowitz et al., *Computer Algorithms*, 2nd ed., Silicon Press, 2007.

[15*] IEEE CS/ACM Joint Task Force on Software Engineering Ethics and Professional Practices, "Software Engineering Code of Ethics and Professional Practice (Version 5.2)," 1999; www.acm.org/serving/se/code.htm.

[16*] *IEEE Std. 828-2012, Standard for Configuration Management in Systems and Software Engineering*, IEEE, 2012.

[17*] *IEEE Std. 1028-2008, Software Reviews and Audits*, IEEE, 2008.

[18*] *ISO/IEC 14764 IEEE Std. 14764-2006, Software Engineering—Software Life Cycle Processes—Maintenance*, IEEE, 2006.

[19*] S.H. Kan, *Metrics and Models in Software Quality Engineering*, 2nd ed., Addison-Wesley, 2002.

[20*] S. McConnell, *Code Complete*, 2nd ed., Microsoft Press, 2004.

[21*] J. McGarry et al., *Practical Software Measurement: Objective Information for Decision Makers*, Addison-Wesley Professional, 2001.

[22*] S.J. Mellor and M.J. Balcer, *Executable UML: A Foundation for Model-Driven Architecture*, 1st ed., Addison-Wesley, 2002.

[23*] D.C. Montgomery and G.C. Runger, *Applied Statistics and Probability for Engineers*, 4th ed., Wiley, 2007.

[24*] J.W. Moore, *The Road Map to Software Engineering: A Standards-Based Guide*, 1st ed., Wiley-IEEE Computer Society Press, 2006.

[25*] S. Naik and P. Tripathy, *Software Testing and Quality Assurance: Theory and Practice*, Wiley-Spektrum, 2008.

[26*] J. Nielsen, Usability Engineering, 1st ed., Morgan Kaufmann, 1993.

[27*] L. Null and J. Lobur, *The Essentials of Computer Organization and Architecture*, 2nd ed., Jones and Bartlett Publishers, 2006.

[28*] M. Page-Jones, *Fundamentals of Object-Oriented Design in UML*, 1st ed., Addison-Wesley, 1999.

[29*] K. Rosen, Discrete Mathematics and Its Applications, 7th ed., McGraw-Hill, 2011.

[30*] A. Silberschatz, P.B. Galvin, and G. Gagne, *Operating System Concepts*, 8th ed., Wiley, 2008.

[31*] H.M. Sneed, "Offering Software Maintenance as an Offshore Service," *Proc. IEEE Int'l Conf. Software Maintenance* (ICSM 08), IEEE, 2008, pp. 1–5.

[32*] I. Sommerville, *Software Engineering*, 9th ed., Addison-Wesley, 2011.

[33*] S. Tockey, *Return on Software: Maximizing the Return on Your Software Investment*, 1st ed., Addison-Wesley, 2004.

[34*] G. Voland, *Engineering by Design*, 2nd ed., Prentice Hall, 2003.

[35*] K.E. Wiegers, *Software Requirements*, 2nd ed., Microsoft Press, 2003.

[36*] J.M. Wing, "A Specifier's Introduction to Formal Methods," *Computer*, vol. 23, no. 9, 1990, pp. 8, 10–23.

Made in United States
Troutdale, OR
07/13/2023

11234013R00193